Dominican Migration

New World Diasporas Series

Florida A&M University, Tallahassee
Florida Atlantic University, Boca Raton
Florida Gulf Coast University, Ft. Myers
Florida International University, Miami
Florida State University, Tallahassee
University of Central Florida, Orlando
University of Florida, Gainesville
University of North Florida, Jacksonville
University of South Florida, Tampa
University of West Florida, Pensacola

New World Diasporas
Edited by Kevin A. Yelvington

This series seeks to stimulate critical perspectives on diaspora processes in the New World. Representations of "race" and ethnicity, the origins and consequences of nationalism, migratory streams and the advent of transnationalism, the dialectics of "homelands" and diasporas, trade networks, gender relations in immigrant communities, the politics of displacement and exile, and the utilization of the past to serve the present are among the phenomena addressed by original, provocative research in disciplines such as anthropology, history, political science, and sociology.

More Than Black: Afro-Cubans in Tampa, by Susan D. Greenbaum (2002)
Carnival and the Formation of a Caribbean Transnation, by Philip W. Scher (2003)
Dominican Migration: Transnational Perspectives, edited by Ernesto Sagás and Sintia E. Molina (2004)

Dominican Migration

Transnational Perspectives

Edited by Ernesto Sagás and Sintia E. Molina

University Press of Florida
Gainesville · Tallahassee · Tampa · Boca Raton
Pensacola · Orlando · Miami · Jacksonville · Ft. Myers

09 08 07 06 05 04 6 5 4 3 2 1

Library of Congress Cataloging-in-Publication Data
Dominican migration: transnational perspectives /
edited by Ernesto Sagás and Sintia E. Molina.
p. cm.—(New World diaspora series)
Includes bibliographical references and index.
ISBN 0-8130-2712-8 (cloth: alk. paper)
1. Dominican Republic—Emigration and immigration.
2. Transnationalism. I. Sagás, Ernesto. II. Molina, Sintia.
III. New World diasporas series.
JV7395.D58 2004
304.8'097293—dc22 2004042564

The University Press of Florida is the scholarly publishing agency
for the State University System of Florida, comprising Florida A&M
University, Florida Atlantic University, Florida Gulf Coast University,
Florida International University, Florida State University, University
of Central Florida, University of Florida, University of North Florida,
University of South Florida, and University of West Florida.

University Press of Florida
15 Northwest 15th Street
Gainesville, FL 32611-2079
http://www.upf.com

To migrants everywhere

Not bound to swear allegiance to any master,
wherever the wind takes me I travel as a visitor.

Horace (20 B.C.)

Contents

Figures

Tables

Series Editor's Foreword

The appearance of a multidisciplinary examination of diasporic processes as is contained in *Dominican Migration: Transnational Perspectives* suggests a (re)visiting of the academic production of knowledge on this topic. As Ernesto Sagás and Sintia E. Molina make clear in their introduction, the academic division of labor as heretofore constituted has construed diasporic social and cultural fields in overly narrow ways. The methodologies and ways of seeing distinctive of disciplines like economics, geography, political science, anthropology, sociology, and literature studies—when taken singly—have in themselves developed necessary but arguably not sufficient protocols to capture on paper diasporic spaces and places, both on the ground and in the heart and mind. The question, then, might be phrased: How is the study of diasporic processes related to disciplinary traditions? Or, more tortuously but perhaps more succinctly: How does diaspora-ing emerge from disciplining? And there are numerous spin-offs: What is the role of diasporic intellectuals—intellectual workers as well as community leaders—in promulgating particular frames of reference? Who benefits politically from the promulgation of a certain theoretical perspective? How are traditional disciplines transformed when inserted into rubrics of area studies or, by contrast, diaspora studies? What is it about the postcolonial, postmodern moment of the present that produces *diaspora* as an urgent category of study? And the consideration of how such a subject has been framed and by whom leads to the questions How can it be reframed? and Why should we do so at this time?

As scholars such as Brian Keith Axel (in "Time and Threat: Questioning the Production of the Diaspora as an Object of Study," *History and Anthropology* 9(4) [1996]: 415–43), Dipesh Chakrabarty (in "Reconstructing Liberalism?: Notes Toward a Conversation between Area Studies and Diasporic Studies," *Public Culture* 10(3) [1998]: 457–81), and Khachig Tölölyan (in "Rethinking Diaspora(s): Stateless Power in the Transnational Moment," *Diaspora* 5(1) [1996]: 3–36) have suggested, the axis of differentiation in the study of (a) diaspora is area studies, on the one hand, and the diffuse academic practices that Axel refers to as cultural studies, on the other. Area studies scholars, he continues, emphasize the relation between a displaced population and its point of origin while those working in the cultural studies tradition (inspired as it is by Marxian and Foucaultian models) emphasize the relation between a displaced population and the nation-state(s) in which it is located. And he identifies as the central problem "that most research on diasporas situated within area studies has been unable to include sophisticated analyses of the nation-state, and research situated within cultural studies has not produced discussions of a 'homeland'—and because of their radically different approaches, the conclusions of one cannot be superimposed upon the other" (416). Ironically, the institutionalization of Caribbean Studies as area studies in the United States and Europe might be traced to the effects of the settlement of Caribbean migrants on the various metropolises—and it was given impetus with the Cuban Revolution in the Cold War context. The Caribbean was conceived of as a "sending area," and a foreign area at that, and the study of Caribbean migrant communities was largely regarded as an offshoot of Caribbean (area) Studies. This was often reflected in the biographies of individual scholars who started their research careers in a particular island society and followed "their" transmigrants into diaspora. In my discipline, anthropology, the highly respected work of Nancy Foner comes to mind. Her earlier fieldwork in Jamaica (*Status and Power in Rural Jamaica: A Study of Educational and Political Change*, 1973) was followed by studies of Jamaicans in London (*Jamaica Farewell: Jamaican Migrants in London*, 1978), and on West Indians in New York (*Islands in the City: West Indian Migration to New York*, 2001), placing such migration in comparative perspective (*From Ellis Island to JFK: New York's Two Great Waves of Immigration*, 2000). And yet should we share Axel's pessimism about the noncompatibility and noncombinability of approaches that search for push and pull factors in connection to a homeland *as well as* the generation of immigrant/racial/ethnic subjectivities in the hostland? There are, after all, some scholars of Caribbean dispersions who take diaspora, broadly conceived, as a condition and set of practices that call for a dynamic and dialectic formulation from the beginning. We can look for examples no further than the careers of two members of editorial board of this series, Jorge Duany and Sherri Grasmuck.

While not necessarily addressing these issues directly, the contributors to this volume, led by the example set by Sagás and Molina, develop comfortably catholic approaches to such controversial issues as, for example, whether either *diaspora* or *transnationalism* as concept metaphors correctly characterizes the Dominican experience of migration, the establishment of overseas communities, return, rereturn, remittances, what the second and succeeding generations understand as their legacy, the way the whole thing gets inscribed bodily and imaginatively, and so on. The contributors are quite naturally motivated to engage in theoretical discussions and they do so comprehensively and eloquently, challenging any presumption of relegation to a secondary status in academic distinction. But to their credit they do not tarry and become preoccupied—and paralyzed—here but instead take as their point of departure what might be called "structural facts" of the Dominican diaspora that underlie and can be construed as causative of Durkheimian "social facts"—consisting of ways of acting, thinking, and feeling, external to the individual, and the public conscience—of the transnational spaces Dominicans inhabit and the communities they constitute. As Duany states in his chapter, these include the following: The Dominican Republic became in the 1990s one of the top five migrant-sending countries to the United States, after much larger countries like Mexico, the Philippines, Vietnam, and China, and only Mexico, Puerto Rico, Cuba, and El Salvador were larger sources of the U.S. Latino population; nearly 10 percent of the Dominican Republic's population resides in the United States; and more than half of the more than three-quarters of a million Dominicans in the United States live in New York. Migrants' remittances totaled $1.5 billion in 1999, and represented the largest source of foreign exchange earnings in the Dominican Republic after tourism; nearly 20 percent of all families there receive remittances. Dominicans can now maintain dual citizenship and have become a force in New York as well as Dominican politics. With these as the starting points, though each is in its own way not unproblematic, the contributors take up the traditional claims of area and cultural studies and, much like the Dominicans they study, carve out spaces in between established regimes (in this case, of knowledge) where innovation often originates. So when taken as a whole, this book, in morphing from multidisciplinary to interdisciplinary, keeps one eye on academic knowledge and another on the production of politics and culture in studying the practices of diaspora—and this is just one way in which it is exemplary.

Kevin A. Yelvington
Series Editor

Acknowledgments

We would like to thank the many individuals who—in one way or another—contributed to the successful completion of this volume. First, our deepest appreciation must go to the anonymous reviewers who freely gave of their usually overcommitted time and their expertise to evaluate critically the chapters that make up this book. Peer review is the basis of academic excellence and our colleagues never faltered when the call came. Second, we would like to thank the contributors to this volume for bearing with our demands, reminders, and shifting deadlines. Coordinating all these contributors was a lengthy and complicated process that required us to juggle schedules, deadlines, and our personal and academic commitments. Our contributors responded in kind with a deep sense of professionalism. Certainly, without their support, there would have been no book. Third, we must thank those colleagues who contributed in indirect—but often equally important—ways to this volume. Forrest D. Colburn read and improved on the book's prospectus when it was only a vague idea. Jorge Duany and Carmen Whalen read and provided valuable comments on the introduction. Xavier Totti, Pedro Cabán, and Luis Martínez-Fernández offered guidance on publication options. Finally, we would like to thank the series editor, Kevin Yelvington, and the staff at University Press of Florida, in particular Meredith Morris-Babb and John Byram, for their help in seeing this book to its successful completion. It has been a pleasure to work with them.

On a more personal note, we would like to thank our relatives, friends, and colleagues who wholeheartedly offered us that priceless and intangible commodity that we call "moral support," either through their loyal friendship or just by being there at the right time. Ernesto Sagás wants to thank his colleagues at Rutgers, The State University of New Jersey for their support, intellectual stimulation, and enjoyable friendship: Luis Martínez-Fernández, Frank Argote-Freyre, Larry LaFountain-Stokes, Carmen Whalen, Pedro Cabán, Ana Y. Ramos-Zayas, Yanet Baldares, Asela Rodríguez de Laguna, and Humberto García Muñiz. Also his children, Antonio Ernesto and Anaís, second-generation Dominican-Americans who, in spite of receiving an English-only education in school, play, argue, and express their feelings in Spanish.

Sintia Molina would like to thank her colleague and friend Tricia Lin for reading her chapter and making valuable comments. Also, Francis Greene, chairperson of the Department of International Cultural Studies, Fine Arts, and Foreign Languages of St. Francis College, for his support and encouragement, as well as her other colleagues. Finally, she would also like to thank her husband, Pete, her daughters, Liz and Cristie, and her parents for their ongoing babysitting and attention. Thanks to all of them.

Last but not least, the editors would also like to thank St. Francis College for its generous support through a Faculty Research Grant.

1

Introduction

Dominican Transnational Migration

Ernesto Sagás and Sintia E. Molina

On May 30, 1961, the nightmare was over. General Rafael L. Trujillo, the despot who had ruled the Dominican Republic with an iron fist for almost thirty-one years, was assassinated by a group of conspirators. Trujillo's death brought about the collapse of his bloody dictatorship and ushered in a period of rapid and intense changes in the Dominican Republic. Up to then, Dominican migration had been relatively small and sporadic, but the end of the Trujillo regime unleashed social, political, and economic pressures that had been accumulating for decades. First by the hundreds, and then by the thousands, Dominicans started migrating: from country to town, from the interior to the capital, and from the Dominican Republic to the United States (see table 1.1) and other countries. The political and economic upheaval of the ensuing four decades further accelerated these trends. Hundreds of thousands of Dominicans now reside outside their country of origin. It is a massive migration of diasporic proportions.[1]

Starting in the late 1970s, several book-length works began examining different aspects of Dominican migration.[2] So far, its study has produced excellent case study monographs by distinguished sociologists and anthropologists. However, these tend to be single-author works that concentrate on a specific aspect of the Dominican migratory experience, and mostly on New York City's Dominican population (e.g., Hendricks 1974; Georges 1990; Grasmuck and Pessar 1991; Torres-Saillant and Hernández 1998). There are still no multi-author edited works published in the United States on the interdisciplinary study of Dominican migration that unite the different perspectives on the Dominican migratory experience. This book fills that void by examining the large-scale flow of Dominicans across international borders, and studying how they are becoming more transnational and transcultural. If transmigration is understood as the process of crossing over diverse social

Table 1.1. Dominicans Admitted into the United States, 1931–2000

Period	Number
1931–1940	1,150
1941–1950	5,627
1951–1960	9,897
1961–1970	93,292
1971–1980	148,135
1981–1990	252,035
1991–2000	335,251

Source: U.S. Immigration and Naturalization Service 2003.
Note: These figures represent individuals admitted as permanent residents.

and cultural boundaries, and tying together the values of local, national, and global traditions (García Canclini 1990; Portes and Zhou 1991), then Dominicans are transnationals. Moreover, their transcultural nature has allowed them to develop a broader cultural identity that rearticulates their *dominicanidad* (Dominicanness).

This book also contributes to the study of the Dominican migratory experience in two more ways. First, while still emphasizing the New York Dominican experience, this work moves beyond New York City-centered studies by including multi-disciplinary perspectives on other Dominican overseas communities (Spain, Providence, and South Florida). Though Dominicans in New York City (and environs) still represent the bulk of the overseas population, the presence of Dominicans in other parts of the United States and overseas has increased considerably (see table 1.2). Within the United States, large—and growing—Dominican communities now exist in Puerto Rico, Miami, Providence, and Boston.[3] By the same token, besides the large Dominican community in Spain, Dominicans have a growing presence in Venezuela, St. Maarten, Antigua, Curaçao, St. Thomas, Italy, Switzerland, and other countries in Europe. Obviously, New York City remains vital to the understanding of Dominican transmigratory processes (and that is reflected in this work in the number of contributions that deal with New York's Dominicans), but in order to fully understand the transnationalization of the Dominican people we must go beyond the New York City case and examine the transmigratory experiences of other Dominican overseas communities. Transnational practices among Dominicans in Miami, Providence, and Madrid seem to differ in scope and size from those among New York City's large Dominican community and may even force us to reconsider previously held notions about transnationalism.

Table 1.2. Dominicans in the United States, by States of Greatest Concentration (1990 and 2000)

State	1990 Census	Percentage	2000 Census	Percentage	Percentage growth	2000 est.[a]	Percentage	Percentage growth[b]
New York	357,868	68.80	455,061	59.49	27.16	652,347	58.18	82.29
New Jersey	52,807	10.15	102,630	13.42	94.35	143,317	12.78	171.40
Puerto Rico	41,193	7.92	56,146	7.34	36.30	n/a	n/a	n/a
Florida	34,268	6.59	70,968	9.28	107.10	107,009	9.54	212.27
Massachusetts	30,177	5.80	49,913	6.53	65.40	73,646	6.57	144.05
Rhode Island	9,374	1.80	17,894	2.34	90.89	25,187	2.25	168.69
Connecticut	3,946	0.76	9,546	1.25	141.92	13,326	1.19	237.71
U.S. Total	520,151		764,945		47.06	1,121,257		115.56

Sources: Logan 2001; U.S. Bureau of the Census, 1990 and 2000 Censuses of Population and Housing.

a. Estimate from Lewis Mumford Center for Comparative Urban and Regional Research, University at Albany, N.Y. (www.albany.edu/mumford).

b. Compared to 1990 U.S. Census data.

Second, this book is also a multidisciplinary study of the Dominican transmigrant experience that combines the different insights of the social sciences and the humanities. Topically and spatially, we employ a diversity of perspectives and approaches by including scholars from different academic and geographical locations. Therefore, to the traditional socioeconomic interpretations of the Dominican experience in New York City, we add contributions on identity, education, literature, and music, providing a fuller view of the rich human tapestry of Dominican migration. Transnationalism has traditionally been the realm of anthropologists and sociologists who specialize in migration. As such, their definition of what is—or is not—transnational is often limited by disciplinary boundaries. Often, certain themes and transnational practices are overlooked, ignored, or rejected simply because they do not fit into traditional disciplinary theoretical schemes. This book goes beyond those traditional disciplinary boundaries by employing approaches from various social sciences and humanities disciplines, and by broadly extending the concept of transnationalism to other practices common to transmigrants, such as long-distance political participation, hybrid musical expressions, literary production, and the reorganization of family structures and values.

The Case of the Dominican Republic in a Transnational Perspective

The Dominican Republic provides a textbook example of a transnational migration; one that has served as a theoretical basis for the development and refinement of transnationalism as a theoretical construct (see Georges 1990; Guarnizo 1994, 1997). The concept of transnationalism has revolutionized the way one looks at migration. Though transnationalism has been around for some decades now, it was not until the 1990s that it became an object of sustained academic inquiry. In the past, migration was considered a major and definitive step in an individual's life—often with no expectation of ever returning to his or her native homeland. Nowadays, modern transportation provides easy and cheap travel back and forth between host and receiving societies. New communications technology allows migrants to stay in touch with relatives and developments back home. Thus, migration is now visualized (under the optic of transnationalism) as a multilevel, multinational phenomenon that encompasses a complex web of interconnected locations. Moreover, the traditional concepts of "host" and "sending" societies have practically lost their meaning in light of globalizing trends in which economic exchange, political sovereignties, social structures, and even cultural practices transcend national boundaries.

According to Nina Glick Schiller, Linda Basch, and Cristina Blanc-

Szanton, transnationalism refers to "the processes by which immigrants build social fields that link together their country of origin and their country of settlement" (1992, 1). Moreover, "immigrants who build such social fields are designated 'transmigrants.' Transmigrants develop and maintain multiple relations—familial, economic, social, organizational, religious, and political—that span borders. Transmigrants take actions, make decisions, and feel concerns, and develop identities within social networks that connect them to two or more societies simultaneously" (1992, 1–2). More recently, Nina Glick Schiller has refined the concept of "transnationalism" by reserving its use to "the collective outcome of multiple forms of transnational processes," thus it would be more appropriate to speak simply of "transnational migration" or "transmigration" (1999, 117n. 2). In this work, we will employ the term "transnationalism" to refer to the body of theory developed throughout the 1990s to examine the processes of transnational migration—largely a result of the trendsetting work of Nina Glick Schiller, Linda Basch, and Cristina Blanc-Szanton.

Transmigration goes far beyond the conventional movements of the past to a degree that was impossible decades ago. Up to the mid–twentieth century (around World War II), migration was still considered a mostly one-way road—though it is now recognized that many migrants returned home and managed to maintain regular contacts with their relatives in the "old country." The literature on migration was then based on—and mostly reflected—the particular experiences of the millions of European migrants who arrived on the shores of the United States. These migratory trends changed rapidly after World War II. As such, transmigration is a relatively recent phenomenon. It is the result of profound transformations, such as "the globalization of capitalism with its destabilizing effects on less industrialized countries; the technological revolution in the means of transportation and communication; global political transformations such as decolonization and the universalization of human rights; and the expansion of social networks that facilitate the reproduction of transnational migration, economic organization, and politics" (Guarnizo and Smith 1998, 4).

The first of these transformations—the globalization of capitalism—lends novelty to transmigration, while its impact on less industrialized countries further explains its emergence. Global capitalism, now reaching practically every corner of the world, has disrupted traditional economies, making them more dependent on the external sector. Increased foreign investment in tourism, agribusiness, and assembly industries has reshaped peripheral countries by moving them from their traditional economic activities into new, export-oriented activities (Glick Schiller, Basch, and Blanc-Szanton 1992, 9). This shift has not only been economic, but has also impelled the physical movement of people from rural areas to urban centers. Bloated primary cities—with extensive industrial areas—now dot the developing world as a result of these economic trends. Unfortunately, global capitalism has not solved the economic problems of less industrialized countries. Rather, it has displaced millions of individuals who now look unsuccessfully for work in the new economic sectors. The huge gap between the supply and demand for jobs, and the new consumer values created by global capitalism have forced the surplus labor force of these peripheral countries to migrate to core countries in order to try to improve their economic situations (Basch, Glick Schiller, and Szanton Blanc 1994, 11–12, 23–27). Thus, transmigration is primarily an economic phenomenon, though it also has political and social ramifications.

Transmigration is different, not only for its causing factors, but also for the myriad ways in which it develops. For example, early twentieth-century migrants who arrived in the United States were motivated by the ideal of political freedom and economic opportunity in the United States, the country that they came to adopt as their own. Coming to the United States usually involved a long journey by ship, sometimes with no expectation of return. Nowadays, transmigrants arrive mostly attracted by the ideal of economic opportunity, but not with a clear objective of establishing an "American" identity or a permanent home in the United States. Also, their trip usually takes just hours, which adds a touch of temporal relativity to their journey.

Recent advances in transportation and communications technology have not only facilitated the relocation of peoples from peripheral to core countries, but also the maintenance of close contacts with their countries of origin. While the jet plane now puts any global destination within a few hours' reach, technological innovations such as the telephone, fax, wire transfers, the Internet, videos, cable TV, cassettes, and previously recorded foreign TV programing help transmigrants maintain very close economic and emotional bonds with their relatives living overseas. As a result, there is a greater interplay between "host" and "sending" societies than was possible half a century ago. Transmigrants create social networks that link them to their countries and often to the multiple destinations (involving two or more countries or regions within them) that have become part of their migratory journey (Basch, Glick Schiller, and Szanton Blanc 1994, 7). These new migrants move within a web that connects several locales. For example, it is not rare to find a Dominican migrant in New York City who is part of social networks that include Providence, Miami, or Puerto Rico, maybe even Spain or Venezuela, and certainly more than one town in the Dominican Republic.

These spatially extended, web-like networks help further migration by providing prospective migrants with the contacts and information that will facilitate their arrival and survival in the host society. Social networks also provide access to "role models" that prospective immigrants may emulate. Furthermore, transnational social networks act as transmitters of cultural practices among several locales. They bring "foreign" culture into the sending society, supply "home" culture to transmigrants overseas, and in the process mediate the creation of new, hybrid cultural forms.[4] In the economic arena, social networks help sustain formal and informal transnational economic activities ranging from individual-level petty trading to large-scale foreign investment. Finally, social networks are also transnational political networks. Transmigrants operate within several sovereignties and jurisdictions. They may be undocumented immigrants or they may hold more than one citizenship. They may co-participate in several political systems or refrain from political action. Such is the case of Dominicans, who since 1994 may become citizens of a foreign nation without losing their Dominican citizenship or their political rights. In any case, transmigration has radically altered our conception of "local" and "national" politics.

Cultural theorists argue that transmigration unites people by exchanging space, language, and cultural elements (García Canclini 1990, 1995). The exchange is facilitated by the rapid movement of people who concentrate in communities in large industrialized cities. Metropolitan centers such as New York, Madrid, Caracas, and San Juan have suffered a rapid transformation owing to the constant flow of people from different backgrounds, ideologies, and social strata. This transformation has affected the ethnic structures, languages, and cultural patterns of many urban populations. Thus, the migrants' need to stay in touch with those left behind, coupled with advances in communications technology, have given them the accessibility to contact the latter, and to maintain bonds with their native culture—while blending it with their newly acquired one. It is a way of coping with the sense of displacement so common among immigrants. It is also a process of building cultural bonds among multicultural and multiethnic individuals and communities in a given society. In the case of Dominicans, the exchange occurs, mainly, among themselves—between those nationals in and outside the homeland who exchange experiences, norms, and attitudes. Different factors contribute to this constant exchange between Dominican nationals on and off the island. There is a sentiment, a longing to return, a desire to be home that pushes Dominicans to visit the country constantly. Moreover, as shown above, there are also economic, political, and social factors that contribute to the constant movement of overseas' Dominicans to the island—especially from New York—and to their habitual communication.

Traditionally, many Dominican migrants "retain strong cultural and economic links with their homeland even when they live in distant places over long periods of time" (Duany 1997, 198). These links still exist, but nowadays, Dominicans, both *aquí* (here) and *allá* (there) are more receptive to cultural exchanges and to "border crossings." For Dominicans to cross borders is to find a solution to their own social, political, and cultural reality. It is a pathway to retain their identity and to express it among the different ethnic groups with which they come into contact (Molina 1998a, 79).

Transmigration also creates a system for exchanging names, space, practices, and even ways of thinking and of living. It tends to juxtapose two very diverse worlds: the modern and the traditional. Typically, it is the migrant's world in the host country that overlaps the traditional world left behind. The crossover of norms and values between countries or societies permits migrants to expand and integrate, without reservation, other people's reality and culture into their native one. For Dominicans, the exchange has influenced their understanding and acceptance of the "other" world. It is a means to alleviate the burden of strong, absolutist, oppressive cultural patterns and ideologies imposed on them. Transmigration has transformed Dominican culture into a vast global phenomenon that makes individuals receptive to changes from abroad. For example, traditional Dominican names—such as Juan, María, and Altagracia—representative of a local, peasant culture mainly sustained by religious images, are being affected by the cultural exchange. These names are now often replaced by Michelle, Sean, and Dianne, which are not representative of the Dominican Hispanic-Catholic tradition. This name-changing represents the acceptance of the linguistic identity crossover Dominican culture and society have experienced for the last thirty years—as it is particularly observed among the second generation of Dominican immigrants or the latest arrivals.

Urban experiences are constantly being transported by Dominicans from a more developed world, such as New York City, to the Dominican Republic. For Walter Benjamin, the city "is a place of disintegration of experience" (Gilloch 1996, 23). That disintegration leads to the transportation of experiences from one place to another. Patricia Pessar argues that Dominicans have experienced the back and forth or "swinging" migration that modern technology makes possible (1995, 69). The rapid displacement of Dominicans all over the world and their constant return to the homeland create a variety of norms and patterns unknown to traditional Dominican culture. Thus, the "swinging process," as we call the constant traveling of Dominicans to the island and back to other destinations, also prepares transmigrants to take risks and face challenges. Even though many Dominican migrants work in menial jobs, they endure risks and challenge "the system" by opening small shops, *bodegas* (grocery stores), beauty salons, and other small businesses often without knowing English, without a clear understanding of the city's business bureaucracy, and with small amounts of capital that, on many occasions, they borrow from family members and friends. Dominican migrants also participate as recipients and as providers in the educational system. Nowadays, Dominicans constitute a large percentage of the student population in New York City's elementary, secondary, and post-secondary public education system. Likewise, many Dominican and Dominican-American educators have become a part of that system. In other places, such as San Juan, Providence, and Boston, Dominicans are a growing part of the student population.

As a new, growing immigrant group in the United States, Dominicans are becoming increasingly visible within the small business sector—by now probably the largest group in New York City's Hispanic small business community. As participants in a more stable economy, Dominicans are able to share with their counterparts back in the island their U.S.-acquired wealth and "American" ideas. The sharing does not happen exclusively when the migrant returns to the island laden with gifts and stories to tell; it also occurs through a constant informal exchange via personal telephone conversations and the oral testimony of family members.

The transposition of language forms, life-styles, ways of thinking, and goods is responsible for the ambivalence many first-generation Dominican migrants experience when they return home. However, many never feel displaced from home because either "there" or "here" they have found a place similar to home with the language, music, consumer goods, and people with which they identify. This phenomenon is tangible in New York City and in Puerto Rico, where there are large concentrations of Dominicans and the exchanges with home, and with other Dominican nationals, occur on a daily basis.

Young second-generation Dominican migrants (also popularly known as Dominican-Yorks) have adjusted to the transnational-global life that the outside (or "other") world—New York, generally—has opened for them. Undoubtedly, Dominicans have been successful in creating a transnational life, in maneuvering within their limited opportunities and resources (Pessar 1995, 71). Understanding that this geographical space that society and culture map onto does not necessarily constitute a nation (Gupta and Ferguson 1997, 34), Dominicans have created a borderless nation outside the national territory from which they do not feel disconnected. The fact that they have easy contact with relatives back in the island, their frequent use of the Spanish language, the daily news they receive from the Dominican Republic, and an array of cultural patterns and norms they find in the host country inflict in them a sense of belonging. The longing to return is no longer affecting the young generation of Dominicans who reside overseas. For example, for young Dominican migrants, New York City has been transformed into an extension of the island—with the exception of the dominant language and the weather (Molina 1998b). They seem to find no hindrance in adapting. English is not an obstacle for Dominicans to succeed and to adapt to the new nation; many build transnational lives without the use of the English language. In New York City's Dominican neighborhoods, such as Washington Heights, the English language is foreign; Spanish dominates. However, the Dominican modality of the Spanish language suffers a natural transformation once it comes into contact with English. That transformation is part of the transnational, swinging process that linguistic cultural patterns have followed. That process also occurs simultaneously from "here" to "there" and within the Dominican enclaves, where the Spanish spoken by Dominicans adopts not only those modalities created by previous immigrants from other countries, but by Dominicans themselves. The end result could be a linguistic modality some are already calling Dominicanish (as in Spanglish), which still needs to be studied.

The essays in this book seek to contribute not only to a better understanding of the Dominican case in particular but also of transmigration in general. First, the Dominican case clearly and convincingly shows how a transmigrant population can construct transnational networks that span several countries and continents. So far, most studies of transnational migration have examined a particular transmigrant group in the United States (e.g., Mexicans, Ecuadorans, Haitians, Filipinos). This volume will go beyond those confines to examine the broad spatial spectrum of Dominican migration that includes North and South America, the Caribbean, and Europe. Without any doubt, Dominicans are one of the most transnational people in Latin America.

Second, the essays in this volume contribute to explaining how transmigration has evolved in the Dominican case. Though Dominican transnational practices have been extensively described, few studies have analyzed how and when Dominicans—as a group or individually—"became" transnational. Given the very broad definition of transnationalism and the inherent complexities of the Dominican migratory experience, this is a complex task. Though economically Dominican migrants have been "transnational" since the 1970s (e.g., by continuously sending remittances), cultural and political transnationalization are phenomena of the 1980s and 1990s. What determines this progression? Is it time and numbers? Or are there other factors involved? Since not all Dominican migrants become "transnational" at the same time or at the same speed, is there a certain threshold, or it is a matter of degrees of transnationalization?[5]

Third—and in line with the previous argument—the essays in this volume show that there is much more to transmigration than long-distance economic exchanges. Although transnational economic practices seem to be the main foundation of a transnational community, in the case of Dominicans cultural transnationalization is a strong element of cohesion among their overseas communities. The transnational culture of the Dominican people fosters migration, facilitates the insertion and adaptation of the transmigrant, keeps him or her in contact with the developments in the Dominican Republic and elsewhere, and influences the country's "native" culture.

Finally, though the essays in this book analyze at length the pervasiveness of transnational institutions and practices, they also acknowledge their limitations. Transnationalization is not the same everywhere, nor does it operate with the same intensity beyond the developed countries. Certainly, while Dominican transnationalization seems to have thrived in the permissive environment of New York City and its surrounding areas (where political correctness and the sheer magnitude of the Dominican community preclude major ethnic backlashes), the same cannot be said of other Dominican communities overseas.[6] For example, Dominicans in Spain are considerably less politically active, while Dominicans in Puerto Rico (particularly undocumented ones) often resort to concealing their real national origin and trying to "pass" as Puerto Ricans, a survival strategy facilitated by cultural commonalities and dictated by a xenophobic anti-Dominican bias that has recently surfaced in the island. Are the latter Dominican migrants then, less "transnational"?

A combination of political instability and uneven capitalist penetration, coupled with new transportation and communication technologies, have turned more than one million Dominicans into transnational migrants. Moreover, the need to escape an oppressing national reality, the desire to establish an identity abroad, and the curiosity that is part of Dominican idiosyncrasy have created a pathway to the transnationalization of Dominicans in and out of the Dominican Republic. The following section examines the recent past of the Dominican Republic in light of the arguments advanced by the transnationalism literature, and looks at how the Dominican people—like so many others in the developing world—have become transnational.

Historical Origins of Dominican Transmigration

Like most former colonies of Spain in Latin America, the Dominican Republic inherited a legacy of centralized authoritarian rule. After achieving independence from Haiti in 1844 (after twenty-two years of occupation), and from Spain in 1865 (after four years of colonial reannexation), the country came to be ruled by a succession of military *caudillos* who reinforced the authoritarian, anti-democratic tradition. Between 1916–1924, the Dominican Republic was occupied by U.S. military forces. The United States, as part of an imperial strategy, resorted to military intervention in the circum-Caribbean region to protect and defend its national interests, especially the Caribbean access routes to the Panama Canal, and to enforce the payment of external debts among the region's insolvent countries. The deep changes brought about by the U.S. military occupations also set the stage for a new breed of *caudillos,* who through their control over modern armed forces monopolized, centralized, and personalized power to an extent never seen before.

The strongman that emerged from the U.S. military occupation of the Dominican Republic was General Rafael L. Trujillo. He had been a cadet during the occupation who later rose to military prominence. In 1930, after ousting president Horacio Vásquez, he was "elected" into office. He did not relinquish power until his assassination in 1961. Trujillo's rule had most of the characteristics of a sultanistic regime: the use of coercive violence, deep-seated corruption, centralization of power in the figure of the leader, and ideological appeals to justify the regime's authoritarian tactics (Hartlyn 1998).

Migration—and even occasional travel—were jealously curtailed by the Trujillo dictatorship. Travel provided the opportunity for disaffected individuals to join the political exile community, and it was feared that travel would expose Dominicans to "dangerous" democratic ideas. Thus overseas travel was strictly restricted and the travelers' activities were monitored by the regime. As a result, very few Dominicans migrated abroad during the Trujillo era. Only 16,674 Dominicans legally migrated to the United States from 1931 to 1960 (see table 1.1). A small Dominican community developed in New York City during the first decades of the twentieth century, but it did not grow much between 1930–1961. Small communities of anti-Trujillo political exiles also developed in New York, Puerto Rico, Cuba, and Venezuela. Things took a drastic turn after the dictator's assassination.

The period from Trujillo's death in 1961 to the U.S. military intervention of April 28, 1965, was characterized by political instability and—as a result—economic uncertainty. In rapid succession, the remnants of the dictatorship were dismantled and the Trujillo family left the country (November 1961); a transitional government led by a council of state restored a sense of normalcy and scheduled the first free elections in decades (December 1962); Juan Bosch of the Partido Revolucionario Dominicano (Dominican Revolutionary Party, or PRD) assumed the presidency, only to be overthrown by a right-wing military coup (September 1963); a supposedly civilian triumvirate ruled the country while favoring military interests (1964–1965); and a "constitutional" faction of the military tried to return Bosch to power, which led to the early stages of a civil war and the intervention of U.S. military forces "to prevent a second Cuba" (April 1965). These rapid developments and extralegal changes of government had a powerful impact on the Dominican economy, which stagnated during this period. The combination of political repression and economic uncertainty, plus the lifting of the restrictions on traveling abroad, led to the first upsurge in Dominican migration in decades.

The U.S. military intervention imposed political stability on the country, which was later guaranteed by the election of conservative Joaquín Balaguer in 1966. Balaguer, Trujillo's former puppet president, had been living in exile in the United States, and he was the candidate favored by the Lyndon B. Johnson administration. He ran against a beleaguered Bosch, who had to face the opposition of entrenched military interests and of a people fearful of renewed violence. Balaguer held on to power for two more terms (1966–1978) by obtaining his reelection in questionable elections where—amid a climate of political repression from the military and death squads—most of the opposition abstained from participating. It was not until 1978, when the political opposition coalesced around the figure of PRD candidate S. Antonio Guzmán, that Balaguer was finally voted out of office.

Balaguer also led the Dominican Republic through a process of thorough economic restructuring, based on opening the country to foreign investment while protecting state-owned industries and certain private interests.[7] This distorted, dependent development model produced uneven results. For most of Balaguer's first nine years in office the country experienced high growth rates (e.g., an average GDP growth rate of 9.4 percent between 1970–1975), to the extent that people talked about the "Dominican miracle." Foreign—mostly U.S.—investment, as well as foreign aid, flowed into the country (Lozano 1985, 123, 193–215). Sugar (then the Dominican Republic's main export product) also enjoyed good prices in the international market. However, this excellent macroeconomic performance was not accompanied by an equitable distribution of wealth. While a group of new millionaires flourished during Balaguer's administrations, the poor simply became poorer. Moreover, the poor were commonly the target of state repression, and their socioeconomic claims were labeled "communist" and dealt with appropriately by the state security apparatus (Cassá 1991, chap. 3). Global capitalism, with all of its dire connotations for the poor, now firmly gripped the Dominican Republic.

The twelve-year administration of Balaguer certainly induced the migration of thousands of Dominicans abroad. Political repression and economic woes were its two main catalysts or "push" factors. But conditions in the United States also favored the migration of Dominicans to this destination. In

1965, Congress passed the Immigration and Nationality Act, which greatly facilitated legal migration to the United States for individuals who had relatives living in this country. Moreover, the industrial centers of the northeastern United States sought cheap, unskilled labor, and that helped Dominicans—and other immigrants—find employment in this sector. Finally, another contributing factor was the tacit agreement between the U.S. government and the Balaguer administration to send "troublemakers" from the 1965 civil war to the United States, thus helping defuse the highly polarized political situation in the Dominican Republic (Mitchell 1992, 102). In the 1960s, 93,292 Dominicans were admitted as legal immigrants to the United States, primarily to New York, where an estimated 70 percent of them resided (see table 1.1; Hendricks 1978, 292). Another 636,058 were admitted with temporary visas—often overstaying in the United States—while others entered the country illegally (Georges 1990, 38). Regardless of the mode of entry or the legal status of these immigrants, one thing was certain: by the 1970s Dominican migration was reaching diasporic proportions in its magnitude, with 148,135 individuals legally admitted during that decade (see table 1.1). If the death of Trujillo was the spark that ignited Dominican migration, Balaguer's social and economic policies were the fuel that propagated it.

Dominicans expected better times with the transition to the new PRD administration in 1978. Though the military staged a self-coup to try to keep Balaguer in power, its effort collapsed in less than forty-eight hours. A new political climate brought renewed hopes to the Dominican people. However, the PRD administrations' economic performance crushed them. Both Guzmán (1978–1982) and his successor, Salvador Jorge Blanco (1982–1986), failed to revitalize the Dominican economy. On the contrary, their economic blunders plunged the country into a deeper crisis and almost brought it to the brink of bankruptcy (Espinal 1987). They resorted to extensive foreign borrowing and then failed to meet the International Monetary Fund's conditions. Inflation went out of control and the Dominican currency devalued steadily during this period. For example, inflation rates went from 3.6 percent in 1978 to 37.6 percent in 1985, while the Dominican peso went (officially) from 1.00 peso per U.S. dollar in 1984 to 3.11 pesos per U.S. dollar in 1985 (Economist Intelligence Unit 1987, 8; 1990, 9, 12). Meanwhile, poor and middle-class Dominicans saw their purchasing power dwindle, and there were major food riots in 1984, with an estimated one hundred people killed by the government's troops.

The economic crisis did not abate with the election of Balaguer to a new term in 1986. By taking advantage of the PRD's dismal administrative record, Balaguer was able to convince the Dominican electorate that at least he was an able administrator. He inherited a crippled economy, which his policies sank deeper into misery. By 1989, inflation had reached a shocking 59.5 percent, while the exchange rate had climbed to 8.53 pesos per U.S. dollar (Economist Intelligence Unit 1993, 10, 13). A gaping trade deficit curtailed the importation of vital inputs, and for the first time in recent memory gasoline was rationed, amid prolonged and economically crippling electric service blackouts. Once again, suffering Dominicans—including a growing proportion of the middle class—opted for migration as a solution to their plight.

The 1980s were boom years for Dominican migration. More than a quarter million Dominicans were legally admitted into the United States during that decade (see table 1.1), plus countless others entered through other means. For example, while in 1981 some 78,000 Dominicans entered the United States with nonimmigrant visas, by 1990 that figure had more than doubled to about 189,000 (U.S. Immigration and Naturalization Service 1999, 113). Several thousand more left for destinations in the Caribbean, Latin America, and Europe. The new, freer political climate in the Dominican Republic also meant that migrants during the 1980s were mostly of economic origin. The economic crisis of the "lost decade" (as the 1980s were known in Latin America) certainly propelled Dominican migration to an unprecedented scale. By the 1980s, Dominican migration had become a truly transnational phenomenon. As the chapters in this book will show, Dominicans developed migratory webs that transcended state boundaries, economic systems, national cultures, and traditional social strata.

Though inflation was put under control during the 1990s, Dominican migration continued unchecked. The Dominican Republic's macroeconomic picture certainly looks better now than during the chaotic 1980s, but an underlying state of permanent economic crisis persists. Unemployment and underemployment are still high in an economy that has divested from agriculture and into tourism, free trade zones (dominated by assembly industries), and other service sector activities, but where major challenges, contradictions, and inconsistencies still persist. Fiscal frailty, high interest rates, a high external deficit, low monetary reserves, fluctuating oil prices, low tax collection rates, an inefficient and unfair tax system, burdensome and restrictive banking laws, confusing investment laws, lack of well-established rules for the protection of foreign investments, an expensive and inefficient bureaucracy, and low levels of investment in education and health are among some of the many complex factors behind the persistence of low levels of socioeconomic development in the Dominican Republic (International Monetary Fund 1999; Héctor Cordero-Guzmán, personal communication)

Politically, the system is still characterized by corruption, personalism, authoritarianism, and the reluctance of electoral *caudillos* to leave their positions of preeminence in party politics. Even when a new generation of political leaders have replaced the old *caudillos,* their political style does not differ much from their predecessors. Dominican electoral politics is still based on charisma, a populist discourse, and a bitter struggle for the system's scarce spoils. The Dominican political system also suffers from an acute lack of meaningful participation among its citizenry, lack of respect for the rule of law, and a constitution that does not respond to the people's needs. For the majority of the population, political participation simply consists of going to the polls every few years to elect a president.

Recent presidential elections have also been questionable, thus making the system lose legitimacy in the eyes of the people. Balaguer was again reelected in 1990, by a small margin, in an election denounced as fraudulent by the opposition's Partido de la Liberación Dominicana (Dominican Liberation Party, or PLD). In 1994, Balaguer won again, this time amid documented charges from the PRD that as many as two hundred thousand of its sympathizers had been disfranchised and prevented from voting. A post-electoral crisis lasted for close to three months, until the three major parties agreed to let Balaguer serve a reduced two-year term and then scheduled new presidential elections in 1996.[8] With Balaguer prevented from running, the 1996 presidential election was won by Leonel Fernández of the PLD. Ironically, his victory was made possible by Balaguer's endorsement during the run-off election. In 1998, the electoral pendulum swung back with a major victory for the PRD in the congressional and municipal elections of that year; in 2000, the PRD's Hipólito Mejía easily won the presidential election; and in the 2002 elections, the PRD retained overwhelming control of Congress. From spending years in the opposition, the PRD has quickly become the hegemonic party in Dominican politics.

For the past three and one-half decades, Dominican politicians from all persuasions have promised in vain the abatement of the country's economic woes, with few visible results. Their failure, coupled with a succession of questionable elections and an exclusionary political system, have contributed to the persistence—and growth—of Dominican transnational migration. Moreover, the development of social networks stretching from the Dominican Republic to overseas communities has sustained Dominican migration during the last decade. From 1991 to 2000, Dominican migration to the United States surpassed the figure for the previous decade: 335,251 Dominicans legally migrated during this period, while additionally there are an estimated 75,000 Dominicans residing illegally in the United States (U.S. Immigration and Naturalization Service 1999, 2003). Moreover, Dominicans are migrating to even more destinations now, including several European countries (for example, Italy, Germany, the Netherlands, and Switzerland) and Caribbean islands (for example, St. Thomas, Antigua, and St. Maarten).

Recently released figures from the U.S. Census Bureau indicate that there were 764,945 Dominicans residing in the United States at the time of the 2000 census (Guzmán 2001). However, these figures—as well as those for other Hispanic groups—have been questioned on the basis of poor question design. Question 5 of the 2000 census questionnaire asked individuals if they were Spanish/Hispanic/Latino. While Mexicans/Mexican-Americans/Chicanos, Puerto Ricans, and Cubans had their own separate box to check, other Hispanic groups were asked to check a different box and then write in their group's name. More than six million individuals who checked the "other" box did not indicate a particular group, but instead wrote "Hispanic," "Latino," or left it blank. That could point to a severe undercount among these "other" Hispanic groups who did not have a box with their national origin already indicated, including Dominicans. Table 1.2 provides a set of revised figures for the number of Dominicans in the United States based on growth rates from Current Population Survey data and prepared by the University at Albany's Lewis Mumford Center for Comparative Urban and Regional Research.[9]

As the table indicates, though New York still has the largest concentration of Dominicans in the United States, its percentage of the total Dominican population on U.S. soil has dropped. Dominicans are spreading out into other states, mainly New Jersey, Florida, Rhode Island, Massachusetts, and Connecticut, as indicated by growth rates over the past decade. This dispersion of Dominicans into other states and away from New York follows similar patterns by previous Hispanic immigrant groups, most notably Puerto Ricans, who decades earlier centered around New York City and are now dispersed over other states.

The Dominican experience has also mirrored that of other Hispanic groups, such as Mexicans and Puerto Ricans, in the fact that most come from—or currently belong to—lower-income brackets. As recent studies have indicated, poverty rates for Dominicans are high and their income levels are among the lowest for Hispanics (Hernández and Rivera-Batiz 1997; Castro and Boswell 2002). These are related to below average educational skills for Dominican immigrants and high rates of employment in declining economic sectors, such as manufacturing. Fortunately, there is hope in the second generation, which seems to be benefiting from access to better educational opportunities in the United States, as reflected by their higher incomes and employment in professional or skilled occupations (Castro and Boswell 2002).

Certainly, Dominican transnational migration has acquired a life of its own. In spite of a stable—though not improved—economic situation in the Dominican Republic, a languishing industrial sector in the U.S. Northeast, and a rising wave of anti-immigrant discourses and policies in the United States and Europe, tens of thousands of Dominicans still leave their homeland every year. Thousands more travel back and forth between the Dominican Republic and foreign countries, often staying at any one location for a few weeks or months, while others visit the country briefly to see their relatives but maintain strong affective and economic links with their country of origin. Throughout time, Dominican transmigrants have established a web of social networks that now spans most of the Atlantic world—and it keeps growing. The following section details how the contributors to this volume explain this complex transnational migratory phenomenon.

Multidisciplinary Perspectives on Dominican Migration

The second chapter, by Jorge Duany, sets the tone for the study of transnational Dominican migration. Duany examines the origins and development of Dominican migration starting in the 1960s. Dominicans have quickly become a major migrant group, particularly in the New York City metropolitan area (where 70 percent of Dominicans within the United States live), while at the same time reshaping the Dominican Republic's economic, political, and cultural affairs. This substantial human flow has taken place within the last four decades, making Dominican migration a relatively new phenomenon. These trends have led to the development of strong transnational practices among Dominicans, such as the reproduction of businesses, traditions, and daily habits (e.g., food, dress, music, beliefs) in their ethnic enclaves overseas. They, in turn, have led to the establishment of a transnational identity, by which Dominican migrants retain cultural and emotional attachments to the homeland, an invaluable "emotional safety net" in a foreign country. Duany then goes on to examine the profound economic influence of transmigrants on the Dominican Republic. Remittances from overseas Dominicans have become a major source of foreign income for their country, helping palliate the economic crisis and fostering economic activities. The economic power of overseas Dominicans has still not provided them with their fair share of political power back in the Dominican Republic but—as Duany notes—"absent" Dominicans have exacted important concessions from the Dominican state in recent years (e.g., dual citizenship). Finally, Duany looks at the issue of shifting racial identities among Dominican transmigrants. He argues that Dominicans—like many other Hispanics—shun the bipolar racial model prevalent in U.S. society and instead place themselves in a third "racial" category, neither Anglo-American nor African-American.

Chapter 3, by Ernesto Sagás, looks at Dominican domestic politics from the perspective of overseas Dominicans, analyzing how transmigrants are recognized politically vis-à-vis the Dominican state. Sagás traces the political development of Dominican transmigrants from the 1960s, when overseas Dominicans were considered "absent" citizens, to the 1990s, when they rose to the status of dual nationals. He begins by framing Dominican overseas politics within the context of transnationalism, with its overlapping, contending, and sometimes simultaneous multiple jurisdictions. Sagás then examines the features of the Dominican overseas community that facilitated its political development: its rapidly increasing size, its economic influence back home, its ties to U.S. domestic politics, and the changing political climate in the Dominican Republic. The momentous alignment of these factors led to the extension of dual citizenship to Dominican transnationals and—ostensibly—the right to vote from overseas. However, Sagás argues that the extension of voting rights to Dominican transmigrants will not necessarily lead to the actual implementation of overseas voting, as huge logistical obstacles will have to be overcome first. Several hundred thousand Dominicans qualify to vote overseas, and the Dominican state does not seem to have the resources—or inclination—to carry out the process. Finally, Sagás analyzes the short- and long-term implications of a politically powerful Dominican transmigrant community. Besides its potential political power that may threaten traditional, well-entrenched political interests, the Dominican overseas community also has the weight to influence the country's economy (something that it already does) and even conventional, elite-defined conceptions of national identity.

Chapter 4 deals with another "invisible," yet rapidly growing Dominican overseas community: Providence, Rhode Island. Within the past decade, Providence has witnessed an upsurge in its transmigrant Dominican population. José Itzigsohn examines why this secondary city has attracted—and continues to attract—a large flow of Dominicans. Moreover, he describes the nature of Providence's Dominican community by looking at census data, which he combines with fieldwork. Dominicans in Providence, as in other overseas locations, have developed a number of community and business organizations that cater to the transnational needs of their compatriots. Itzigsohn analyzes the development of these organizations and their role as facilitators of transnational exchanges by examining the transnational practices of a sample of Providence's Dominican transmigrants. He then classifies their different transnational practices into "narrow" and "broad" transnational practices. The former refers to very active, recurrent transnational practices, while the latter points to sporadic, intermittent transnational contacts, often with little physical involvement. Itzigsohn concludes by looking at the formation—and transformation—of identity among Dominican transmigrants in Providence. He argues that it is still too early to tell if the effects of transnationalism will go beyond the first generation of transmigrants, particularly if they no longer have family ties in the country of origin that would require them to engage in transnational practices.

Chapter 5 is the first scholarly study published about Miami's Dominican community. Carol Hoffman-Guzmán examines how this out-of-the-way Dominican transmigrant community has emerged on its own from two different, yet related, sources: international migration from the Dominican Republic and domestic migration from other parts of the United States, mostly New York City and environs. According to her research, Dominicans in South Florida tend to be, on the average, better educated, upwardly mobile, and geographically dispersed than those in New York City. In other words, they are more middle and upper class. Except for the small, and lower-class, Dominican enclave of Allapattah in Miami, most of them are spread throughout Miami-Dade and Broward counties. Moreover, their education and resources allow them to undergo a process of transnationalization that is often very different from other, lower-class transmigrants. Middle-class Dominicans in South Florida, owing to their greater resources and education, have the capability to become more transnational than lower-class Dominicans. However, it is precisely their good standard of living in the United States that discourages them from doing so. Having "made it" in American society, middle-class Dominicans have few incentives to maintain strong political or economic contacts with the Dominican Republic, though the first generation may still maintain strong cultural and emotional bonds. As Hoffman-Guzmán argues, at some point in their lives the complications of transnational behavior outweigh its benefits. Another important difference has to do with the setting. Miami is a city that prides itself on its multiculturalism. Thus, for upwardly mobile middle-class Dominicans the retention of their cultural traits, such as the ability to speak Spanish, is considered an asset, rather than an obstacle to finding employment or assimilating. While discrimination against Spanish-speaking lower-class workers is very common throughout the United States, it is less common in Miami, and very rare in middle- and upper-class job settings that thrive on the multilingual capabilities of their employees.

Chapter 6 gives a refreshing European perspective on Dominican migration. Domingo Lilón and Juleyka Lantigua study the major Dominican community in Europe: Spain's. Lilón and Lantigua begin by analyzing Dominican migration to Spain in the context of major political, demographic, and socioeconomic changes. In a few decades, Spain has gone from being one of Europe's major exporters of migrants to becoming a country with a labor shortage. Moreover, Spain's admission to the European Union, and its linguistic and historical ties to Latin America, made it an even more attractive destination for Dominican migrants. Lilón and Lantigua then tackle the difficult task of "guesstimating" the number of Dominicans residing in Spain. In spite of the difficulty of establishing demographic parameters, one trend seems clear: the overwhelming majority of Dominican migrants in Spain are female. Lilón and Lantigua also provide a panoramic view of Dominican migrants in Spain: their regions of origin, means of travel, skills, main economic activities, organizations, and idiosyncrasies. This portrait suggests that Dominican migration to Spain follows a different track than Dominican migration to the United States. Dominican migrants to Spain are typically those that do not have the resources or family connections to migrate to the United States—usually the most desired destination. An undercurrent cuts through their analysis: Spain (Madrid in particular) is no paradise for Dominican migrants, particularly undocumented ones. Long work hours, fear of deportation, and racial discrimination are their constant companions. The latter issue merits a detailed analysis through the examination of the case of Lucrecia Pérez, a Dominican woman murdered by four young Spaniards imbued with anti-immigrant ideas. Pérez's murder brought the plight of migrants to the forefront of Spanish public opinion, and forced a reexamination of Spanish social values in light of an increasingly multiracial society. The authors conclude that the future of the Dominican community in Spain depends in large measure on the ability of Spanish society to develop a sense of tolerance toward the migrant "other."

Chapter 7, by Karin Weyland, examines the gender and cultural dimensions of Dominican transnational migration. Weyland, using ethnographic data collected in interviews with (mostly) Dominican female migrants, introduces the reader to the concept of "border cultures." That is, Dominican transnational migrants, particularly females, operate within the interstices of two or more cultures. An exploitative capitalist system and a patriarchal culture force Dominican women into socially submissive roles and make them subject to economic exploitation in the labor market. In order to better themselves socially and economically, Dominican women thus resort to migration. In destinations like New York City, gender discrimination still exists, mostly centered around a gender-based division of labor. However, the new income level achieved by Dominican women in New York City allows them some comforts that they did not have back home, plus it helps them support their relatives, particularly children left in the care of others, and even start small businesses. According to Weyland, such trends, in spite of their intrinsic load of discrimination and accompanying feelings of displacement, are also empowering to Dominican women. Thus, Dominican transnational migrants, by becoming part of a "border culture" are making a big social and emotional investment that eventually pays off by opening to them new avenues of social mobility. In addition, by contesting existing cultural paradigms, Dominican females are forcing a reexamination of gender-based social roles and are also redefining the interplay between power and culture in global as well as local manifestations. Finally, Weyland, an amateur photographer, illustrates her arguments with a collection of photographs of Dominican women taken during her fieldwork in New York City and Santo Domingo. Each one tells a story of migration, work, and sacrifice, but also of triumph and achievement. They are a testament to the resilience, devotion to family, and spirit of sacrifice of Dominican women.

Chapter 8 examines a transcendental theme for any recent immigrant group: education. The achievement of the American dream has presumably been based on the opportunities that education provides for migrants seeking vertical social mobility. In her essay, Nancy López employs ethnographic data to examine the relationships between gender and education among second-generation Dominicans in New York City. López begins by framing her study in a question that educators in Latino/a communities often ask themselves: Where are the men? (That is, why is there such a noticeable gender gap in educational attainment?) López finds a big part of the answer, at least for Dominicans, in gender roles. Among Dominicans, she contends, females and males are raised under different standards and with different expectations. Females, for example, acquire adult responsibilities at an early age. While their mothers work, young Dominican females have to take care of the house, cook, clean, and baby-sit. Moreover, young Dominican females have their mothers as role models of how tough life can be for uneducated immigrant females. In a society dominated by machismo, their mothers usually work two shifts: one in the workplace and one at home. In spite of how much admiration they may deserve, their mothers are often examples of what they do not want to become. For young Dominican females, the only way out of this potential fate is education. Dominican males, in contrast, are not subjected to these household responsibilities. They are usually given free rein and simply expected to behave well in general. With more leisure time on their hands, and often with little privacy in their cramped apartments, Dominican boys end up spending much of their time in the streets. There, the value scales are much different. Asserting their maleness and earning the respect of others take precedence over achieving success through education. Thus, according to López, young Dominican males place little value on education. While for Dominican females, who have stronger family bonds and values, education is the (often only) key to success and a new life, for Dominican males education is usually inconsequential.

In chapter 9 Janira Bonilla examines two recent, major literary figures on the Dominican experience in the United States: Julia Alvarez (author of *How the García Girls Lost Their Accents*) and Junot Díaz (author of *Drown*). Alvarez and Díaz are currently the two most celebrated Dominican-American authors in the United States. Contrary to other accounts of the Dominican experience in the United States, they do not long to return to their "homeland." Rather, they are caught between two worlds—the United States and the Dominican Republic—feeling both at home and alien in the two countries. Another distinctive feature is their use of the English language as their main medium of expression. Until recently, the Dominican experience in the United States had been narrated by adult Dominican immigrants, writing in Spanish, and mostly for a Dominican audience (see Molina 1998a). Alvarez and Díaz, who arrived as young children to the United States, write in English, and for the U.S. general public. Bonilla delves deeply into their work to identify some topics that are specific to their writings and to the immigrant experience in general: political persecution, machismo and gender roles, class and racial cleavages, assimilation and the definition of a new hybrid identity, oppressive poverty, and more recently, transmigration. These are issues faced by practically most Latin American—and in this particular case, Dominican—migrants. In addition, Bonilla highlights an undercurrent that flows through both authors' work: the migratory experience as a concomitantly traumatic and liberating process. As Bonilla herself recounts from her own family experience, being a Dominican-American means living in two worlds at the same time while not belonging to any one in particular, but it also means being able to draw strength from two rich, complex cultures. Therein lies the uniqueness of the Dominican-American hybrid.

In chapter 10, Sintia Molina examines how Dominican transmigrants have portrayed New York City in their literature. For immigrants and natives alike, New York City is a unique place. The "World's Capital" is certainly an impressive metropolis. Every single immigrant group has described the city and the group's experiences living, working, and loving in it. Molina describes how Dominicans compare and contrast to other immigrant groups in their portrayal of New York City as a city of hopes and dreams, but also as a city of suffering and deprivation. New York City is the place for immigrants to realize their cherished dreams of improving their socioeconomic status, but it usually comes at a personal cost. Families are separated, marriages are broken, long work hours are the norm, and there is the always present danger of violent crime. As a result, the lives of Dominican migrants are portrayed in less than rosy terms in their literature. Molina also examines the differences between two groups of Dominican-American writers: those who write in Spanish, mostly for a narrow Hispanic/Dominican public; and those who write in English, for the large English-speaking American market and English-dominant Latinos. These two groups represent the generational duality of the Dominican transmigrant experience: those from "here" (the English speakers) and those from "there" (even though they too live and write here). Finally, Molina analyzes the connections between Dominican literature in the United States and the idiosyncrasies of the Dominican transnational experience. According to her, transmigration lies at the heart of this literature and its depiction of New York City. It is a transnational literature, with transnational themes and subjects, and for an increasingly transnational public.

In chapter 11, Thomas van Buren and Leonardo Iván Domínguez trace the development of Dominican music in New York City within the context of transnationalism. If there is one thing the Dominican people are universally characterized by, it is their music, particularly the contagious popular rhythm of *merengue*. Van Buren and Domínguez detail the emergence and establishment of Dominican music in the metropolis, from the first recordings made in the late 1920s to the current worldwide popularity of New York-based *merengue* and *bachata*. Dominican music in New York City has been more than the simple transplantation of rhythms from the Dominican Republic. Music among Dominican transmigrants has evolved with migration itself: changing and adapting to new environments, blending with others' rhythms, and ultimately growing into a unique, hybrid musical category. For example, van Buren and Domínguez examine how *merengue* has traveled with Dominican transmigrants as an instrument of cultural reaffirmation, and how it has evolved into new rhythms, such as *meren-house, meren-rap, bachata-rengue,* and *perico rapeao*. But *merengue* is not the only musical rhythm associated with overseas Dominicans. The authors also examine the transnational movement, development, and transformation of other Dominican rhythms like the folkloric *merengue típico* and *mangulina,* the religious-based *palos* drumming and *gagá,* and the recently-popularized *bachata*. Finally, van Buren and Domínguez analyze the lyrics of New York-produced songs to identify some of the major themes that run through them. While themes related to the transmigratory experience appear in some of the songs (e.g., urban hardship, crime, economic struggle), the majority of Dominican songs produced in New York City are not very different in content from their counterparts in the Dominican Republic; they are celebrations of love and life to be danced to and enjoyed socially. The main objective of composers and musicians is to sell records. As such, New York's Dominican rhythms are designed to appeal to a broad transnational market: Dominicans in the island

and overseas (the main target audience), and non-Dominican Hispanics in the United States, Latin America, and increasingly, Europe (particularly Spain).

The essays included in this book seek to place into context the transnational theoretical perspectives and the historical narrative presented above. This detailed examination of the multifaceted Dominican case should not only help shed some light on a transmigratory phenomenon that in many ways is still in a process of flux, being constantly reshaped, but it should also help us understand transmigration in a clearer way.

Notes

1. The use of the term "diaspora" to describe the Dominican migratory experience has generated an intense, and sometimes acrimonious, academic debate. For opposing views, see Torres-Saillant 1999, 2000 (speaking in favor of the term), and Levitt 1998 and Glick Schiller 1999 (both against its use).

2. See Ricourt 1998 (11–14) for a good review of the literature on Dominican migration.

3. See Duany's 1990 classic about Dominicans in Puerto Rico, and Levitt 2001 for an excellent study about Boston's Dominicans.

4. For example, see Peggy Levitt's (1998) article on social remittances, and José Itzigsohn et al.'s (1999) article on "narrow" and "broad" transnational practices.

5. This debate has been going on for years now and it is nowhere near its conclusion. For example, see Glick Schiller 1999; and Guarnizo and Smith 1998.

6. Alex Dupuy has made this argument in the case of Haitian transmigration. While the Haitian-American community is well known for its political activism, Haitians in the Dominican Republic have been traditionally marginalized and silenced, even though they number in the hundreds of thousands (personal conversation with author).

7. Months after Trujillo's assassination and the departure of his family, their holdings (which included several industries and sugar plantations) were nationalized, thus leaving the Dominican Republic with one of the largest state economic sectors in Latin America.

8. Besides the gentlemen's agreement made by the top Dominican political leadership, it was also accorded to modify the constitution to introduce electoral changes such as separate congressional and presidential elections, a ban on consecutive presidential terms, and the use of run-off elections if no candidate obtains at least 50 percent of the votes.

9. For more detailed information, visit the center's web page at www.albany.edu/mumford.

References

Basch, Linda, Nina Glick Schiller, and Cristina Szanton Blanc. 1994. *Nations Unbound: Transnational Projects, Postcolonial Predicaments, and Deterritorialized Nation-States.* Langhorne, Pa.: Gordon and Breach.

Cassá, Roberto. 1991. *Los doce años: Contrarevolución y desarrollismo.* 2d ed. Santo Domingo: Editora Búho.

Castro, Max J., and Thomas D. Boswell. 2002. "The Dominican Diaspora Revisited: Dominicans and Dominican-Americans in a New Century." *The North-South Agenda,* Paper No. 53. Miami, Fla.: The Dante B. Fascell North-South Center, University of Miami.

Duany, Jorge, ed. 1990. *Los dominicanos en Puerto Rico: Migración en la semi-periferia.* Río Piedras, P.R.: Ediciones Huracán.

———. 1997. "The Creation of a Transnational Caribbean Society: Dominican Immigrants in San Juan and New York City." In *Ethnicity, Race, and Nationality in the Caribbean,* ed. Juan Manuel Carrión. San Juan, P.R.: Institute of Caribbean Studies, University of Puerto Rico.

Economist Intelligence Unit. 1987. *EIU Country Profile 1986/87: Dominican Republic, Haiti, Puerto Rico.* London: The Economist.

———. 1990. *EIU Country Profile 1990/91: Dominican Republic, Haiti, Puerto Rico.* London: The Economist.

———. 1993. *EIU Country Profile 1992/93: Dominican Republic, Haiti, Puerto Rico.* London: The Economist.

Espinal, Rosario. 1987. "Pactos y participación, élites y pueblos: El PRD en el poder o el episodio de una democracia maltratada." *Ciencia y Sociedad* 12(2): 285–316.

García Canclini, Néstor. 1990. *Culturas híbridas: Estrategias para entrar y salir de la modernidad.* Mexico City: Grijalbo.

———. 1995. *Consumidores y ciudadanos: Conflictos multiculturales de la globalización.* Mexico City: Grijalbo.

Georges, Eugenia. 1990. *The Making of a Transnational Community: Migration, Development, and Cultural Change in the Dominican Republic.* New York: Columbia University Press.

Gilloch, Graeme. 1996. *Myth and Metropolis: Walter Benjamin and the City.* Cambridge: Blackwell Publishers.

Glick Schiller, Nina. 1999. "Transmigrants and Nation-States: Something Old and Something New in the U.S. Immigrant Experience." In *The Handbook of International Migration: The American Experience,* ed. Charles Hirschman, Philip Kasinitz, and Josh DeWind. New York: Russell Sage Foundation.

Glick Schiller, Nina, Linda Basch, and Cristina Blanc-Szanton. 1992. "Transnationalism: A New Analytic Framework for Understanding Migration." In *Towards a Transnational Perspective on Migration: Race, Class, Ethnicity, and Nationalism Reconsidered,* ed. Nina Glick Schiller, Linda Basch, and Cristina Blanc-Szanton. New York: New York Academy of Sciences.

Grasmuck, Sherri, and Patricia R. Pessar. 1991. *Between Two Islands: Dominican International Migration.* Berkeley: University of California Press.

Guarnizo, Luis E. 1994. "Los *Dominicanyorks:* The Making of a Binational Society." *Annals of the American Academy of Political and Social Science* 533: 70–86.

———. 1997. "The Emergence of a Transnational Social Formation and the Mirage of Return Migration among Dominican Transmigrants." *Identities* 4(2): 281–322.

Guarnizo, Luis Eduardo, and Michael Peter Smith. 1998. "The Locations of Transnationalism." In *Transnationalism from Below,* ed. Michael Peter Smith and Luis Eduardo Guarnizo. New Brunswick, N.J.: Transaction Publishers.

Gupta, Akhil, and James Ferguson. 1997. "Beyond 'Culture': Space, Identity, and the Politics of Difference." In *Culture, Power, Place: Explorations in Critical Anthropology,* ed. Akhil Gupta and James Ferguson. Durham, N.C.: Duke University Press.

Guzmán, Betsy. 2001. "The Hispanic Population." Census 2000 Brief. Washington, D.C.: U.S. Census Bureau.

Hartlyn, Jonathan. 1998. "The Trujillo Regime in the Dominican Republic." In *Sultanistic Regimes,* ed. H. E. Chehabi and Juan J. Linz. Baltimore: Johns Hopkins University Press.

Hendricks, Glenn. 1974. *The Dominican Diaspora: From the Dominican Republic to New York City—Villagers in Transition.* New York: Teachers College Press.

———. 1978. *Los dominicanos ausentes: Un pueblo en transición.* Trans. Eduardo Villanueva. Santo Domingo: Alfa y Omega.

Hernández, Ramona, and Francisco Rivera-Batiz. 1997. *Dominican New Yorkers: A Socioeconomic Profile, 1997.* New York: CUNY Dominican Studies Institute.

International Monetary Fund. 1999. "Dominican Republic: Selected Issues." IMF Staff Report No. 99/117. Washington, D.C.: IMF Publication Services.

Itzigsohn, José, Carlos Dore Cabral, Esther Hernández Medina, and Obed Vázquez. 1999. "Mapping Dominican Transnationalism: Narrow and Broad Transnational Practices." *Ethnic and Racial Studies* 22(2): 316–39.

Levitt, Peggy. 1998. "Social Remittances: Migration Driven Local-Level Forms of Cultural Diffusion." *International Migration Review* 32(4): 926–48.

———. 2001. *The Transnational Villagers.* Berkeley: University of California Press.

Logan, John R. 2001. "The New Latinos: Who They Are, Where They Are." Report for Lewis Mumford Center for Comparative Urban and Regional Research, University at Albany, N.Y.

Lozano, Wilfredo. 1985. *El reformismo dependiente: Estado, clases sociales, y acumulación de capital en República Dominicana, 1966–78.* Santo Domingo: Taller.

Mitchell, Christopher. 1992. "U.S. Foreign Policy and Dominican Migration to the United States." In *Western Hemisphere Immigration and United States Foreign Policy,* ed. Christopher Mitchell. University Park, Pa.: Pennsylvania State University Press.

Molina, Sintia E. 1998a. "Duality and Displacement in the Dominican Literature in the United States." *Latino Studies Journal* 9(3): 65–84.

———. 1998b. "La mujer dominicana y la educación superior en los Estados Unidos." *Estudios Sociales* 31(113): 81–99.

Pessar, Patricia R. 1995. *A Visa for a Dream: Dominicans in the United States*. Boston: Allyn and Bacon.

Portes, Alejandro, and Min Zhou. 1991. "The Second Generation: Segmented Assimilation and Its Variants among Post-1965 Immigrant Youth." Working Paper 34. New York: Russell Sage Foundation.

Ricourt, Milagros. 1998. "Patterns of Dominican Demography and Community Development in New York City." *Latino Studies Journal* 9(3): 11–38.

Torres-Saillant, Silvio. 1999. *El retorno de las yolas: Ensayos sobre diáspora, democracia, y dominicanidad*. Santo Domingo: Librería La Trinitaria.

———. 2000. "Diasporic Disquisitions: Dominicanists, Transnationalism, and the Community." Dominican Studies Working Paper Series 1. New York: CUNY Dominican Studies Institute.

Torres-Saillant, Silvio, and Ramona Hernández. 1998. *The Dominican Americans*. Westport, Conn.: Greenwood Press.

U.S. Immigration and Naturalization Service. 1999. *1997 Statistical Yearbook of the Immigration and Naturalization Service*. Washington, D.C.: U.S. Government Printing Office.

———. 2003. *2002 Statistical Yearbook of the Immigration and Naturalization Service*. Washington D.C.: U.S. Government Printing Office.

2

Los Países

Transnational Migration from the Dominican Republic to the United States

Jorge Duany

In the 1990s, the Dominican Republic became one of the top five migrant-sending countries to the United States, after the much larger countries of Mexico, the Philippines, Vietnam, and China. Only Mexico, Puerto Rico, Cuba, and El Salvador were larger sources of the Hispanic population. The 2000 census found 764,945 persons of Dominican origin in the United States (Guzmán 2001). This figure represents nearly 9 percent of the population of the Dominican Republic (8.6 million). More than half of all Dominicans in the United States have settled in New York City, where they constitute distinctive and growing communities, especially in Washington Heights, on the northwestern tip of Manhattan. The Dominican diaspora has reshaped practically every aspect of daily life in the homeland, from family structure and business enterprises to political ideology and religious affiliation. Since the 1960s, migration has thoroughly transnationalized the Dominican Republic, metaphorically blurring its frontier with the United States. It has also transformed the physical and cultural landscape of several American neighborhoods, cities, and states.

This chapter traces the main contours of contemporary migration from the Dominican Republic to the United States. First, I outline the field of transnationalism as the term has been applied to recent population movements. This theoretical framework helps to conceptualize the massive flow of people between the Dominican Republic and the United States as a process embedded in the globalization of the world economy. Second, I describe the basic characteristics of the Dominican diaspora in the United States, particularly its volume, history, and settlement patterns. I give special attention to the development of spatial practices and cultural identities across geopolitical borders. In particular, I show that transnational migrants have become key actors in the Dominican economy and politics, at the same time that they have incorporated into the U.S. economy and politics. Finally, I suggest that migration has reconfigured the national, ethnic, and racial identities of Dominicans in the United States and the Dominican Republic. The large number of U.S. Dominicans who classify themselves as neither black nor white, but rather as "other" has profound repercussions for racial and ethnic relations in the United States and in their country of origin. In states like New York and Florida, Dominicans and other Latinos already constitute a "third force" in racial discourses, business enterprises, community organizations, interethnic contacts, and cultural politics.

Rethinking Transnationalism

One of the most promising theoretical frameworks in current research on migration emerged during the 1990s under the code word "transnationalism." The earliest and most influential statement of this paradigm was the volume edited by Nina Glick Schiller, Linda Basch, and Cristina Blanc-Szanton (1992). This book was followed shortly by the coauthored work *Nations Unbound* (Basch, Glick Schiller, and Szanton Blanc, 1994), which spelled out more systematically the conceptual and methodological implications of the new model. Many scholars are currently working with a transnational approach to migration (see Cordero-Guzmán, Smith, and Grosfoguel 2001; Goldring 1996; Levitt 2001; Olwig 1997; Portes 1998; Rouse 1995; Smith and Guarnizo 1998; Sørensen 1997). Although several writers have developed their own version of transnationalism, they all agree that the contemporary phase of the world economy, which has accelerated the volume and speed of international population flows, requires a new approach to migration. Many are actively engaged in rethinking traditional categories for social analysis, such as nation, state, citizenship, race, ethnicity, class, gender, and identity, in light of current trends. A key intellectual puzzle for contemporary migration scholars is how people reconstruct their cultural identities and imagine their communities across geopolitical borders. Instead of assimilation, some authors favor the terms transnationalization, hybridization, or creolization to refer to the cultural dimensions of diasporic movements (Appadurai 1996; Hannerz 1996).

In the 1990s, social scientists began to widen the use of the concept "transnational" to include individuals and groups who move across national boundaries yet remain tied to their home communities. Originally, the term referred to multinational corporations and other organizations simultaneously operating in several countries. Political economists have long preferred to write about "transnational" instead of "multinational" or "international" companies, because these conglomerates are often controlled by capital from various cores, which are usually located in the more industrialized world—in North America, western Europe, and Japan (Glick Schiller, Basch, and Blanc-Szanton 1995). When applied to migrants rather than corporations, "transnationalism" suggests that people may transgress national borders and inhabit the interstitial social spaces between them; hence such migrants have been called borderless or stateless people (Kearney 1991; Smith 1994).

Despite some romanticization, the territorial extension of migrant households, social networks, economic resources, political activities, and cultural practices across borders often sustains transnational communities and identities such as those from the Hispanic Caribbean in the United States. In particular, women are responsible for much of the emotional and ritual work required to maintain kinship ties between home and diaspora communities. Through constant visiting, writing, and talking on the phone, migrant women often keep transnational households in touch with each other across wide distances and over long periods of time. More so than men, women frequently travel back and forth to take care of relatives, raise children, and participate in their family's rites of passage, such as baptisms, birthdays, weddings, and funerals (Alicea 1997).

Glick Schiller and her colleagues (1992) have provided a basic definition of transnationalism as the process whereby people establish and maintain sociocultural connections across geopolitical borders. For instance, Dominican migrants may simultaneously participate in several political systems, retain dual citizenship, send large amounts of money back home, and define their identities in culturally hybrid terms, such as Dominican-American. Ulf Hannerz (1996) prefers a minimal definition of transnationalism as any phenomenon that does not take place within the confines of a state. The utility of this approach is that it allows one to compare transnational actors and practices with variable scales and distributions, but it runs the risk of diluting the precise character of the "transnational."

In contrast, Alejandro Portes (1998) has proposed that transnationalism involves only occupations and activities that require *regular* and intense contact between two or more nations. Thus, for Portes, certain kinds of economic activities, such as the growing trade in ethnic goods and services between the Dominican Republic and the United States, are genuinely transnational, while others, such as occasional shopping trips to Miami or New York, are not. This definition is too limited for my purposes here, because it leaves out many symbolic and material practices that tie together Dominicans in the United States and the Dominican Republic, such as consuming American clothes, music, and food. In this chapter, I use the term transnational as a middle-ground concept between Hannerz's minimal definition and Portes's restricted approach. By transnationalism, I mean the construction of dense social fields across national borders as a result of the circulation of people, ideas, practices, money, goods, and information (see Goldring 1996).

More recently, José Itzigsohn and his colleagues (1999), following up on Luis Guarnizo's and Sarah Mahler's suggestions (see Guarnizo and Smith 1998), have elaborated a useful distinction between "narrow" and "broad" transnational practices. Narrowly defined, transnationalism refers to highly institutionalized activities and constant population flows between two countries, such as membership in Dominican political parties in the United States. Broadly defined, transnationalism involves a low level of institutionalization and sporadic physical displacement between two countries, such as carrying bags full of merchandise on infrequent trips from the United States back to the Dominican Republic. Although this typology helps to classify various kinds of transnational practices, it does not provide an adequate explanation for their origins and development.

Regardless of how one defines it, transnationalism is often accompanied by an incessant back and forth movement of people, facilitated by rapid transportation and communication systems. The jet airplane, the telephone, video, fax, e-mail, and the Internet have greatly reduced the time and cost of moving people, images, and ideas between the Caribbean, the United States, and other parts of the world. Most scholars agree that the increasing globalization of capitalism, which has stimulated such technological advances, is the primary cause of transnationalism. In this context, the transnational movement of people is only one aspect, albeit a crucial one, in the worldwide exchange of capital, commodities, technology, information, ideology, and culture (see Appadurai 1996; Basch, Glick Schiller, and Szanton Blanc 1994; Guarnizo and Smith 1998; Hannerz 1996; R. Ortiz 1996, 1997).

Transnationalism is as much a political as an economic phenomenon. For instance, many states (including Colombia, Mexico, and the Dominican Republic) have recently extended citizen rights, such as voting privileges, to their growing diasporic populations. Furthermore, social institutions linking several nations (such as confederations of political parties, churches, grassroots movements, and other nongovernmental organizations) have proliferated in the past few decades. Nation-states have surrendered much of their sovereignty to global and regional forces by establishing common markets, free trade, and other international agreements. In many countries, public policies have moved toward "de facto transnationalism," accepting the limitations of strictly national approaches to such issues as the movement of capital, labor, and even controlled substances (Sassen 1998). Such globalizing tendencies do not contradict but complement local trends; for example, Dominican immigrants expanded their political participation in New York City as well as in the Dominican Republic during the 1990s (Graham 1998, 2001). In other words, the forces of deterritorialization vie with those of reterritorialization. I will develop this point in my discussion of the migrants' spatial practices.

Although the scholarly understanding of transnationalism has advanced swiftly since the early 1990s, several issues merit further research and reflection. Much of the available literature takes for granted that transnational migration occurs between nation-*states,* that is, sovereign or postcolonial countries. However, contemporary movements of people include the massive flow of Puerto Ricans to the United States and other Caribbean migrants to their European metropolises, such as Great Britain, France, and the Netherlands. Clara Rodríguez (1989) and Ramón Grosfoguel (1994–1995) have argued that the participants in the Puerto Rican diaspora have more in common with other colonial migrants than with citizens of independent countries such as the Dominican Republic. For instance, colonial migrants do not have to apply for a visa or change their legal status to vote in the metropolitan countries. Thus, the differences and similarities among various transnational migrants should be spelled out, depending on whether and how they actually cross state frontiers.

Unfortunately, scholars (such as Roger Rouse [1995] and Michael Kearney [1991]) sometimes portray transnationalism as an undifferentiated global phenomenon linking sending and receiving societies into "one world." But each group of migrants develops a distinctive brand of transnationalism, based on its own historical legacy, cultural practices, settlement patterns, mode of incorporation into the host society, state policies of sending and receiving countries, and other factors. For example, the Dominican diaspora may be classified as "transnational" along with the Puerto Rican and Cuban diasporas, but the three differ greatly in their citizenship status, relationship to the homeland, possibility of return, timing of the flows, length of stay, and so on. As Silvia Pedraza (letter to the author, October 21, 1998) has argued, Cuban émigrés have not created a truly transnational community in the United States because contact with Cuba is much more limited and irregular than with Puerto Rico and the Dominican Republic. Since 1959, U.S. and Cuban policies toward migration—as well as the politics of exile—have severely curtailed the flow of people, goods, and ideas between Cuba and the United States. To invert the title of a chapter by Basch, Glick Schiller, and Szanton Blanc (1994), similar settings may produce different outcomes for transnationalism.

Another problem with the transnational approach is that it tends to be ahistorical. Many writers imply that contemporary transnational migration represents a radical rupture with previous population movements. A growing body of scholarship shows that past migrants built and maintained transnational connections over long periods of time, including returning and sending remittances to their homelands en masse (see Foner 2001; Pedraza and Rumbaut 1996; Portes and Rumbaut 1996). Thus, a longitudinal perspective that highlights both temporal changes and continuities should temper analyses of current transnational flows. It would be revealing to compare current transnational practices among Dominicans with those of Polish, Italian, or Irish immigrants in the United States at the beginning of the twentieth century. Although not entirely new, transnational migration has assumed a greater scale, intensity, diffusion, and speed at the turn of the twenty-first century, partly as a result of new transportation and communications technologies. Again, this trend is strongly correlated with the growth of the global economy.

Finally, the counter-hegemonic potential of transnational migrants should not be overstated. Although the large-scale mobility of the population may herald the breakdown of national identities "from the bottom up," crossing a border does not erase it. On the contrary, state policies in the advanced industrial world (such as the United States, France, Germany, and Japan) are increasingly hostile to migrant workers. While migrant-sending governments may be formulating more transnational policies, most laws and regulations in the major receiving countries remain driven by domestic agendas that seek to reassert, control, and protect the borders of individual nation-states (Sassen 1998). Although migrants often transgress such borders, these borders continue to structure much of their daily lives. Furthermore, rather than represent a subversive form of popular resistance to existing structures of domination (whether between states, classes, ethnic groups, or genders), transnationalism may in the long run reinforce social inequality on a global scale (Guarnizo and Smith 1998). Power asymmetries are often relocated and reproduced in the diaspora.

With these caveats in mind, I will apply the transnational approach to contemporary migration from the Dominican Republic to the United States. To begin, the residential locations of the Dominican population are increasingly transnational. That is to say, an ever growing proportion of Dominicans is living outside their homeland, while retaining strong ties to it. Second, the migrants have thoroughly transformed local spaces in cities such as New York and San Juan, Puerto Rico, where they have relocated in large numbers. To what extent this is a new phenomenon or simply a reproduction of previous "ethnic neighborhoods" remains an open empirical question. Third, the diaspora is playing a prominent role in the economic, political, and cultural affairs of the Dominican Republic. Never before have overseas Dominicans been so well poised to influence, and thereby transform, their nation of origin. Last, Dominican migrants are helping to redefine ethnic and racial identities in both sending and receiving societies. The emergence of a "Latino" or "Hispanic" pan-ethnicity in the United States is due in no small measure to the growing presence of Dominicans and other Latin American and Caribbean immigrants who avoid classifying themselves along a bipolar racial model, often choosing the label "other." The ideological impact of this "othering" process should be carefully examined in the Dominican Republic as well as in the United States.

The Rise of Transnational Communities

Since the 1960s, hundreds of thousands of Dominicans have moved abroad. In 1997, nearly one out of ten persons of Dominican origin was living in the U.S. mainland. Of these, 24 percent were born in the United States, a figure that speaks of a growing second generation of Dominican immigrants (U.S. Census Bureau 1998). In addition, substantial Dominican communities have emerged in Puerto Rico, Venezuela, Curaçao, Spain, and the U.S. Virgin Islands over the past few decades (Duany, Hernández Angueira, and Rey 1995; Sørensen 1996). Thus, the Dominican population has become increasingly deterritorialized, with regard to nativity and residence. The massive displacement of Dominicans to the United States and elsewhere is popularly known in the Dominican Republic as *irse a los países* (literally, "moving to the countries"). As I will argue later, the plural and generic way that Dominicans refer to their current migration patterns suggests the development of a translocal, diasporic, or transnational identity.

A second feature of the Dominican diaspora is its extraordinary growth. The number of Dominican migrants was so small until the mid-1960s that the U.S. Immigration and Naturalization Service (INS) did not collect separate data for them before 1930. In 1950, the Census Bureau found only 4,200 persons of Dominican birth in the United States (Graham 1998, 45). Large-scale population movements from the Dominican Republic began with the end of Rafael Trujillo's dictatorship in 1961 and especially after the civil war and U.S. military occupation in 1965. In turn, changes in the U.S. economy and immigration policy fostered the Dominican exodus, such as increasing demand for cheap labor in northeastern cities as well as the abolition of immigration quotas by national origin in 1965. As a result, Dominican migration to the United States jumped from 9,897 persons in the 1950s to 93,292 in the 1960s. The outflow continued to increase in the 1970s, when 148,135 Dominicans were legally admitted to the United States. During the

1980s, the INS counted 252,035 Dominican immigrants, a figure quickly surpassed by the 300,065 persons admitted between 1991 and 1998 (U.S. Immigration and Naturalization Service 1999).

Compared to other Latino groups such as Mexicans or Puerto Ricans, Dominican population movements are relatively new. More than 98 percent of the 810,201 Dominicans legally admitted to the United States between 1931 and 1998 arrived after 1961. The statistics suggest a sudden and steadily increasing tide of immigrants from the Dominican Republic in the past four decades. By the 1980s, Dominicans had become one of the fastest growing segments of the foreign-born population in the United States. In the 1990s, the Dominican exodus continued unabated and diversified its regional destinations to new places in Europe, Latin America, and the Caribbean, as well as North America. Sizeable Dominican communities now exist in Italy, Switzerland, Canada, Panama, Aruba, Martinique, and St. Thomas. Again, the folk term *los países* seems particularly apt to capture the wide dispersal of the Dominican diaspora.

A third significant pattern is the geographic concentration of Dominicans within the United States. In 2000, more than 59 percent of the immigrants (or 455,061 persons) lived in the state of New York. Dominicans had secondary concentrations in New Jersey (102,630 persons), which can be considered a byproduct of Dominican migration to New York, and in Puerto Rico (56,146), which has served as a springboard for many Dominicans moving to New York (U.S. Census Bureau 2001). Smaller Dominican communities have mushroomed in Florida, Massachusetts, and Rhode Island. The extreme clustering of Dominicans in New York means that, for many of them, moving abroad (to *los países*) is practically synonymous with relocating in that state. Hence, a recent popular movie and its sequel, focusing on Dominican migration to the United States, were simply titled *Nueba Yol* (New York).

Within their primary places of destination, Dominican migrants have carved out distinctive niches, especially in New York, New Jersey, and Puerto Rico. In 2000, the top metropolitan areas of settlement for Dominicans were New York City (406,806), San Juan (44,444), Miami-Ft. Lauderdale (36,454), Bergen-Passaic (36,360), and Boston (25,057) (U.S. Census Bureau 2001). Some of these metropolitan areas, especially New York and San Juan, have more people of Dominican origin than many places in the Dominican Republic. For some time now, New York City has had more Dominican residents than Santiago de los Caballeros, the second largest city of the Dominican Republic. As one informant told Ninna Nyberg Sørensen (1996), "New York is just another Dominican capital."

What do these demographic, historical, and geographic patterns mean for Dominican transnationalism? Above all, they document the magnitude of physical and cultural displacement among Dominicans. The vast number of Dominicans living overseas points to the need to rethink the island's traditional geopolitical boundaries. For many Dominicans, New York City (and to a lesser extent San Juan) is a symbolic extension of their homeland. Furthermore, an increasing number of Dominicans in the United States are second-generation immigrants. The cultural implications of this shift from the first to the second generation need to be better documented. Lastly, most Dominicans and their descendants have relocated in New York, New Jersey, Puerto Rico, and Florida, and in certain urban centers, such as Manhattan, Santurce, Puerto Rico, Dade County, Florida, and Providence, Rhode Island. Their impact has been felt most profoundly in inner-city neighborhoods such as Washington Heights and the Lower East Side of Manhattan, or Barrio Gandul and Barrio Capetillo in San Juan, where immigrants have thoroughly reshaped the physical and cultural landscape. Such places display the local effects of increasing globalization.

Transnational Spatial and Cultural Practices

Dominican communities in the diaspora remain connected to the homeland through specific spatial practices, such as renaming streets and schools, establishing businesses with the same names as in the home country, redecorating inner and outer spaces, establishing hometown associations, and organizing parades and festivals based on Dominican folk traditions. In Washington Heights, the immigrants have rechristened several schools with Dominican names like Salomé Ureña de Henríquez and Juan Pablo Duarte. In Santurce, Puerto Rico, they have established a chain of popular cafeterias with names like El Mangú (a typical Dominican staple made with boiled plantain and pork) and El Padrino (The Godfather). In Madrid, the Plaza of Aravaca is commonly associated with the name of Lucrecia Pérez, the Dominican domestic who was murdered there in 1992. Initially deterritorialized identities have taken hold across national boundaries through such settlement patterns. Transnational connections are especially evident in the Dominican neighborhoods and homes of Washington Heights, the main focus of this section.

In New York City, Dominican residents tend be segregated from non-Hispanic whites, blacks, and other Latinos such as Puerto Ricans and Colombians. Even where they share the same neighborhoods with other ethnic and racial groups, such as African-Americans or Ecuadorians, Dominicans tend to remain socially encapsulated in their own communities. In Washington Heights, 79 percent of the residents of one block I studied intensively were Dominican (Duany 1994a). Although residential segregation has many pernicious effects, it allows for the consolidation of compact *barrios* and the transformation of the urban landscape along transnational lines. It also makes possible some degree of political representation through concentration in certain electoral districts (Graham 1998).

In 2000, 53.2 percent of all Dominicans in the United States lived in New York City. Washington Heights houses the largest concentration of Dominicans outside of the Dominican Republic—about a third of the city's Dominicans. Grocery stores *(bodegas),* restaurants, bakeries, travel agencies, gypsy cabs, remittance agencies, and retail stores, along with dozens of voluntary associations, create the unmistakable Dominican atmosphere of "Quisqueya Heights," as many Dominican residents now call their neighborhood (Sørensen 1994; Weyland 1998).[1] A recent community festival has been dubbed "Quisqueya on the Hudson," the title of my own monograph on Dominican migration to the United States (Duany 1994a). New York City, especially Washington Heights, is so closely associated with the Dominican diaspora that scholars tend to focus on this urban area as a microcosm of the immigrants' experience (see Pessar 1995; Ricourt 1998; Torres-Saillant and Hernández 1998). It is here that the transnational identity of Dominicans abroad has taken shape most completely.

I spent part of the summer of 1993 studying the Dominican community of Washington Heights (Duany 1994a). In a typical block, itinerant traders sold oranges, corn, flowers, music cassettes, and ice cones *(frío-fríos).* On a hot summer day, dozens of small carts selling *frío-fríos* were stationed on main traffic intersections. Children opened fire hydrants and played with water in the streets. Men usually spoke Spanish, listened to *merengue* music, complimented young women walking by, played dominoes, drank Presidente beer, and read Dominican newspapers like *El Nacional, El Siglo,* and *Listín Diario.* Women pushed their baby strollers, shopped in neighborhood *bodegas,* and chatted with friends in front of their buildings. Teenagers walked to the nearby George Washington public school, swam in neighborhood pools, or listened to rap and house music from enormous cassette players. Some passers-by seemed to be Mexican or Central American because of their accent, indigenous features, and small stature. But the vast majority of the area's residents were Dominican immigrants.

In the mornings, many people took the subway to work in downtown Manhattan and returned home in the afternoons. Others took the bus to work in the factories of New Jersey, across the Hudson River. Near the subway station, several businesses specialized in sending remittances to the Dominican Republic, such as Banco Dominicano. Gypsy cabs from the Dominican-owned Riverside Company, usually large dark American cars, constantly crossed the streets searching for potential customers. A newspaper stand on the corner of 181st Street and Saint Nicholas Avenue offered ten Dominican newspapers, which arrived daily from the island.

Many cafeterias and restaurants sold typical Dominican food. *Comida criolla* included main entrées such as *mangú, carne guisada, sancocho, moros, tostones, mondongo, locrio cocido,* and *cabeza de cerdo;* drinks such as *jugo de caña, morir soñando,* and *batida de fruta;* and various delicacies such as *empanada de yuca, pastelillos de guayaba, yaniqueque, habichuelas con dulce, dulce de coco,* and *pan dulce relleno.* Local grocery stores imported all kinds of tropical fruits and vegetables, ranging from plantains to *mamey.* A beauty parlor sold a large variety of "Dominican products," such as Lafier and Capilo. Small businesses specializing in telephone calls to the Dominican Republic have proliferated. Many store owners displayed their national origin by playing loud music in front of their stores, usually *merengue* and salsa, and occasionally *bachata* and bolero. Some businesses were local subsidiaries of enterprises established in the Dominican Republic, such as Nitín Bakery. Others sold Dominican drinks such as Cola Quisqueya, Refrescos Nacionales, and Presidente beer.

Commercial signs confirmed the strong presence of immigrants from the Cibao region, such as Acogedor Cibao Supermarket, Cibao Vision Center, Cibao Meat Products, and Hielo Cibao. A Dominican immigrant who longed to have his own "small Cibao" in New York planted corn and black beans on the corner of Broadway and 153rd Street. During my fieldwork, a young man paraded down the sidewalk with two fighting roosters, a common sight in the Dominican countryside. Dozens of hometown associations carried the names of Cibao places such as Moca and Tamboril. Some Dominicans even referred to Washington Heights as "El Cibao."

Most immigrants maintained their cultural traditions at home. Some tenants placed Spanish signs on their apartment doors, as if to announce their national origin, especially religious messages such as "Jesus is our only hope," "Christ will change your life," and "Let's build peace with Christ." Within their households, many Dominicans hung religious images on the walls, such as the Sacred Heart of Jesus and the Last Supper.

Some families had Spanish-language calendars with an image of the Virgin Mary, acquired in a local *bodega.* Others placed a flag or emblem of the Dominican Republic in a visible corner of the living room. Many displayed the faceless ceramic dolls that have become typical of the Dominican Republic, as well as colorful painted plates with their country's folk themes, usually a rural landscape, a peasant scene, the Santo Domingo Cathedral, or a tropical beach. Such objects recreated the visual iconography of the Dominican Republic in Washington Heights.

Many Dominican households and businesses had small niches with images of the Catholic saints and the Virgin Mary in a corner of the main room or private area. These humble shrines were usually surrounded with flowers, candles, food, and glasses of water, wine, and other drinks. Although the most popular figures were the Virgin of Altagracia, the patron of the Dominican Republic, and Saint Lazarus, the altars represented a wide variety of religious images: Saint Claire, Saint Anthony of Padua, Saint Barbara, the Holy Child of Atocha, the Sacred Heart, the Sacred Family, the Virgin of Fatima, and the Virgin of Mercedes, among others. Like other devout Catholics, many Dominicans believe that the saints protect them from evil and help them to progress economically. A woman who carried a medallion of the Virgin of Altagracia told me, "When you're away from your country, you need protection. And your country too." In sum, the traditional Dominican devotion to the saints and the Virgin has been transplanted to Washington Heights, in a new transnational space.

Establishing Transnational Economic Ties

Despite their relative socioeconomic disadvantage in the United States, Dominican migrants are playing an increasing role in their home country, especially as a result of the prolonged crisis that plagued the Dominican economy in the 1980s. This role can be documented most clearly in the large volume of remittances that migrants send to their relatives back home. Most of these funds are used to cover basic household needs such as shelter, food, clothing, health care, and education. Secondarily, remittances have financed small businesses and other productive activities in the recipient countries (Meyers 1998; M. Ortiz 1997; Portes and Guarnizo 1991). Scholars currently disagree as to whether remittances tend to increase or reduce further emigration.

As table 2.1 shows, the value of monetary transfers sent home from workers living outside of the Dominican Republic expanded quickly between 1970 and 1999. In 1999, the International Monetary Fund estimated that Dominicans abroad sent U.S.$1.519 billion to the Dominican Republic. This figure exceeds the value of all merchandise exports and represents the second source of foreign currency in the country after tourism. A recent survey found that 19.4 percent of all Dominican households received remittances from abroad (Lizardo 2001).

How, then, can one characterize the economic impact of transnational migration on the Dominican Republic? Increased emigration since the mid-1960s has had the primary effect of reducing local unemployment rates and, above all, providing additional income for those remaining at home. Most Caribbean governments have long encouraged emigration to decrease popu-

Table 2.1. Migrant Remittances from the United States to the Dominican Republic, 1970–1999

Year	Amount (in millions of US$)
1970	25
1971	14
1972	24
1973	24
1974	27
1975	28
1976	112
1977	124
1978	132
1979	161
1980	183
1981	183
1982	190
1983	195
1984	205
1985	242
1986	225
1987	273
1988	289
1989	301
1990	315
1991	330
1992	347
1993	721
1994	757
1995	795
1996	914
1997	1,089
1998	1,326
1999	1,519

Source: *Migration News* 2001.
Note: Net transfer payments, including private remittances and donations.

lation growth and the size of the labor force (Duany 1994a). Like other countries, the Dominican Republic has recently attempted to capitalize on remittances as an untapped economic resource. Although remittances have mixed effects on economic development (see Meyers 1998), Dominicans increasingly depend on this cash inflow to square their balance of payments and generate new economic ventures. Remittances—along with other transactions related to migration, such as periodic visits to and direct investment in the homeland—have created a dense transnational economic field between the United States and the Dominican Republic. Whether such linkages are ultimately beneficial or detrimental to self-sustained economic growth remains in dispute.

According to José Itzigsohn and his colleagues (1999), migrant remittances became central to the Dominican economy during the 1980s, just as local political leaders acknowledged the growing political clout of the Dominican diaspora. The conjunction of these two factors fostered a profound reevaluation of the role of *dominicanos ausentes* (literally, "absent Dominicans"), who are now usually called *dominicanos en el exterior* ("Dominicans abroad"). Like other countries with large overseas populations, the Dominican government began to revise its major constitutional premises and public policies toward citizenship and identity in the 1990s (see Graham 1998; Sagás, this volume). Hence, as Itzigsohn, Hernández Medina, and Vázquez (1999) point out, the official as well as the popular discourse of Dominicanness became increasingly transnational and deterritorialized.

Politics Beyond the Nation-State

Like other transnational migrants, Dominicans often maintain political ties to their home country, as well as establish new links to the host society. The public behavior of Dominican politicians in both the United States and the Dominican Republic suggests that their constituencies are located in the Caribbean as well as in North America. Transnational ties have been key to the election of Dominican leaders in New York, such as Guillermo Linares and Adriano Espaillat (Graham 1998). Conversely, fund-raising trips to New York and San Juan have become standard features of presidential campaigns in the Dominican Republic. The diaspora plays an increasing role in the domestic politics of the home country, as recent discussions of dual citizenship and voting abroad suggest (Sagás, this volume). To a lesser extent, immigrant communities have also sought to influence U.S. foreign policy toward the Dominican Republic.

Still, Dominican immigrants have a long way to go in the process of political empowerment. In 1997, less than one-third (195,000) of all foreign-born Dominicans in the United States were naturalized citizens (U.S. Census Bureau 1998). Dominicans have one of the lowest naturalization rates among recent migrants, such as Cubans and Chinese. In 1999, only 13 percent of all Dominicans admitted to the United States since 1961 had become U.S. citizens (U.S. Immigration and Naturalization Service 1999). In addition, an unknown number of Dominicans (as many as 51,000 according to 1996 INS estimates) are undocumented immigrants in the United States. Consequently, Dominicans have not achieved a proportionate degree of political representation at federal and state levels. The U.S. House of Representatives does not yet have a Dominican member, although the N.Y. State Assembly and N.Y. City Council do (Espaillat and Linares, respectively). The electoral participation of Dominicans in the United States may improve as a result of the 1994 approval of dual citizenship by the Dominican legislature, which makes it easier for migrants to become U.S. citizens without relinquishing their Dominican nationality. Dual citizenship offers many practical advantages for those who move back and forth between the mainland and the island, just as Puerto Ricans have done for decades.

Since the 1960s, Dominican politicians have favored migration to the United States as a safety valve for demographic and economic pressures. After World War II, most Caribbean states openly or covertly stimulated the relocation of surplus labor abroad. In the Dominican Republic, Joaquín Balaguer's first administration (1966–1978) also used emigration as a way to export political dissidents and excess workers (Torres-Saillant and Hernández 1998). Overall, public planners and decision makers have viewed emigration as a short-term solution for rising unemployment. However, government officials have usually perceived Haitian immigration to the Dominican Republic as a national security problem as well as a threat to the country's cultural identity. Since the 1980s, Dominican authorities have been increasingly concerned with an increase in return migration from the United States, blaming it for many of the Dominican Republic's social problems.

The Discourses of Transnationalism

Public opinion toward migration is surprisingly similar throughout the Hispanic Caribbean. In the Dominican Republic, nonmigrants often view transnational migrants with a mixture of fright and admiration, envy and resentment, familiarity and suspicion. For many orthodox nationalists, leaving the country represents a betrayal to the homeland. For working-class families, migration is often a survival strategy under harsh economic conditions. For the middle classes, it might be a way to maintain or improve their social status. Like Puerto Rico and Cuba, the Dominican Republic has developed an ambivalent folklore surrounding migration to the United States.

During the past few decades, Dominicans coined the pejorative term Dominican-York (as well as *cadenú* and *Joe*) to refer to the massive movement of people back home (Guarnizo 1997; Pessar 1995). On the island, the term is commonly used to describe both Dominican-born migrants and their offspring raised abroad. As in Puerto Rico and Mexico, return migrants to the

Dominican Republic are frequently represented as alien to national culture and used as scapegoats for numerous social problems. Since the 1980s, the stereotype of the tasteless, Americanized, and pushy Dominican-York has become widespread in the home country. Especially popular is the idea that the returnees have made their fortunes in the drug traffic business abroad (hence the epithet *cadenú,* alluding to their avowed inclination to sport gold necklaces). It is now difficult for Dominican-Yorks to enter certain neighborhoods, schools, and clubs, which discriminate against them. Most recently, journalists have frequently associated deported and returning Dominican-Yorks with an increasing crime rate in the Dominican Republic. The Dominican experience follows closely an earlier pattern of Puerto Rican migration, with its intense stigmatization of those who go back home, often with money but seldom with more prestige.

The migrants themselves have often rejected negative stereotypes and sought alternative ways of asserting their identity. For years, Dominican migrants considered themselves *dominicanos ausentes,* which had a nostalgic nationalistic ring to it, but their descendants are slowly embracing the Dominican-American label (Torres-Saillant and Hernández 1998). In my 1993 fieldwork in Washington Heights, I found that most Dominican immigrants, and even second-generation youth, disliked the category "Dominican-American" and favored calling themselves simply "Dominican" (Duany 1994b). Similarly, the term Dominican-York is seldom heard within New York's Dominican community, except among some artists, writers, intellectuals, and activists, who have appropriated it for their own political purposes. Moreover, like other migrants from the Hispanic Caribbean, Dominicans continue to assert their national origin rather than claim a pan-ethnic category such as "Hispanic" or "Latino," much less American (see de la Garza et al. 1992).

The dominant image of Dominicans in the United States has been uncharitable from the start. In the 1980s and 1990s, Dominicans joined Puerto Ricans as one of the most stigmatized ethnic minorities in the United States. The American public can easily associate both groups with poverty, urban blight, and violence, as witnessed by a host of Hollywood films and TV series. Journalistic reports consistently identify Dominicans as one of the main culprits of drug trafficking and money laundering in the east coast of the United States, and Washington Heights is commonly known as the "crack capital" of New York City (see Rohter and Krauss 1998a, 1998b). During my fieldwork in Washington Heights, several violent confrontations pitted young Dominicans against the police and firefighters in the area. Invariably, the mainstream media portrayed New York's Dominican community as strange, disorderly, and dangerous. Like other "colored" groups from the

Caribbean and Latin America, Dominicans have been intensely criminalized and racialized in the popular imaginary of the United States, Puerto Rico, and other countries.

Transnationalizing Identities

A final issue is the transformation of collective identities as a result of transnational migration from the Dominican Republic to the United States. I would like to approach this topic from two complementary angles: first, how moving abroad sharpens the migrants' awareness of their race and ethnicity; and, second, how their prolonged residence in the United States alters prevailing views of those two constructs. On the one hand, transnational migration can erode hegemonic discourses on race and ethnicity in both sending and receiving countries. On the other, the racialization of Dominicans in the United States—as well as Haitians in the Dominican Republic or Dominicans in Puerto Rico—can harden fundamentalist concepts of cultural difference. This section will concentrate on the immigrants' clash with the dominant system of racial classification in the United States.

Since 1980, the Census Bureau has asked U.S. residents to classify their race separately from their Hispanic origin. In 1990, 29.2 percent of Dominicans responded that they were white, while 30 percent considered themselves black. The most striking finding in this regard was the high proportion of Dominicans choosing the "other" category—39.8 percent of the total (Rodríguez 2000, 9). These figures parallel a general trend among U.S. Hispanics—42.2 percent in 2000—who prefer the intermediary label "other" to describe their racial identity. (At the time of this writing, 2000 census figures on the racial breakdown of specific Latino groups were unavailable.) In the Dominican case, the prevalence of the "other race" category probably reflects the large number of people with mixed African and European ancestry, usually grouped under the folk term *indio* in the Dominican Republic.

These statistics suggest three main patterns in the social construction of race and ethnicity among Dominican migrants. First, many avoid the bipolar model of racial classification into white or black, the so-called one-drop rule, which still dominates in the United States. Rather, they continue to use a tripartite system that recognizes a mulatto or mixed race location along the color continuum. Elsewhere I have explored in more detail the profound ideological transformation produced by the confrontation of the Dominican model of race relations with the American classification system (Duany 1998). Other scholars have also noted the strong reluctance among Dominicans to label themselves as "black" in the United States. Most consider themselves to be neither black nor white, but other, such as Hispanic, Latino,

Dominican, or Dominican-American (see Bailey 1999; Itzigsohn and Dore Cabral 2000).

Second, the census figures, even though they avowedly distinguish between race and ethnicity, tend to collapse the two categories, insofar as government publications routinely compare Hispanics to "racial" groups such as non-Hispanic whites and blacks, Native Americans, and Asians. (Note that Dominicans are usually classified in the "other Hispanic" category, which makes their national origin even more invisible.) In practice, the official treatment of Dominicans as neither black nor white places them squarely in the category of "people of color." Again, such treatment contrasts sharply with the usual disclaimer that "Hispanics can be of any race."

Third, many Hispanics (and others as well) employ the term "other" (or an equivalent one like Latino) as a racial label similar to "brown" or "colored." To this extent, Dominicans and other Latinos have become a "middle race" between whites and blacks in the United States (Domínguez 1973). They have also been artificially separated from Afro-Caribbean migrants, such as Jamaicans and Haitians, with whom they share much culture and history. In any case, most Dominican migrants do not align themselves with the African-American nor with the European-American population when describing themselves. Instead, they tend to make common cause with other Hispanics, such as Puerto Ricans, Colombians, and Ecuadorians in New York.

In sum, the racialization of Dominicans in the United States has pushed them toward a third "racial" category, such as Latino, Hispanic, Spanish, or Spanish-American. This cognitive shift is transnational insofar as it draws on ideological elements from both sending and receiving societies. On the one hand, the migrants tend to resist the rigid white/black dichotomy prevalent in the United States. Hence they recur to Caribbean models of race based on phenotypic gradation of skin color from white to brown to black. On the other hand, they increasingly define their racial identity in ethnic terms—that is, based on their national origin—or in pan-ethnic terms, such as Hispanics or Latinos. Thus, Dominican migrants contest the U.S. hegemonic discourse on race by expanding the number of possible racial categories (white, black, other) and pressing for the public recognition of racially mixed persons (mulattos, mestizos). It remains unclear whether the growing presence of nonwhite minorities will transform how Americans think about race and ethnicity, or whether such minorities will be absorbed into the dominant racial imaginary, based on a rigid color line between black and white. At any rate, the current system of racial classification in the United States does not capture well the multiracial Hispanic experience, as recent research suggests (U.S. Census Bureau 1996).

Conclusion

Since World War II, the transnational flow of people, money, goods, and ideas has intensified greatly. Although not entirely new, transnationalism now links migrant-sending countries with their diaspora communities in stronger ways than in the past. The migrants' kinship and friendship networks, extended households, remittances, spatial practices, political activities, and cultural identities increasingly cut across national boundaries. Dominicans based in the United States are questioning such boundaries as effective and exclusive markers of their cultural citizenship, subjective affiliations, and collective projects. Contemporary transnational migration has profoundly restructured Dominican society and is having a growing effect on the United States and Puerto Rico, especially in New York, New Jersey, Florida, Massachusetts, and Rhode Island.

The transnational framework helps to raise important issues regarding the socioeconomic impacts of migration on both the United States and the Dominican Republic. First, it serves to blur the artificial boundaries between sending and receiving communities, which have been bridged through longstanding networks of social, economic, political, and cultural exchange. Second, the concept of transnationalism calls attention to how migrants lead their daily lives in two or more separate but connected spaces, markets, polities, and often languages. Third, a transnational framework allows one to locate migration in the broader context of the worldwide movement of capital, labor, commodities, and technology. Fourth, the study of transnational migration encourages the interrogation of traditional discourses on statehood, nationality, citizenship, ethnicity, race, class, gender, and other master narratives in the social sciences.

The evidence presented in this essay has helped to substantiate the four points mentioned before. Massive migration has strengthened and broadened the transnational linkages between the Dominican Republic and the United States. In particular, the migrants' far-flung kinship and friendship networks span the two countries, despite their geopolitical boundaries. Since the 1960s, Dominicans have moved abroad en masse in response to recent changes in the global political economy and their local repercussions. However, the Dominican exodus has not improved the relative position of the Dominican Republic vis-à-vis the United States, but has accentuated the former's dependency on outside sources of support. As other scholars have argued, transnational migration can reproduce and intensify, rather than diminish, existing inequalities between countries, regions, classes, ethnic groups, and genders (Guarnizo 1997). Documenting the internal rifts *within* the Dominican diaspora (such as those produced by regional, racial, generational, or gender differences) remains an important research priority.

At the same time, the case study of Dominican migration can help us to rethink transnationalism. On the one hand, extensive transnational linkages between the sending and receiving countries were established *prior* to large-scale migration, as a consequence of U.S. hegemony in the Caribbean region since 1898. On the other hand, the uprooting of the population from the Dominican Republic, as well as from Cuba and Puerto Rico, was initiated well before the current phase of globalization accelerated in the 1970s. Today, the Dominican Republic has developed a unique form of transnationalism as a result of its close political, economic, and cultural ties with the United States. As relatively recent immigrants from a neocolonial country, Dominicans are increasingly retaining their nationality while becoming U.S. citizens in larger numbers. Massive population movements have contributed to blurring—without eliminating—the frontiers between the Dominican Republic and the United States. During the 1990s, stricter U.S. immigration policies have made it painfully clear that the border matters. Many Dominicans have responded by shifting their travel routes and migration destinies, such as to Europe or other countries of the Caribbean.

Finally, transnational migration has had a lasting impact on national, ethnic, and racial identities in the Dominican Republic. Throughout the twentieth century, Dominican nationalism evolved largely in opposition to U.S. hegemony: to be a nationalist almost automatically meant to be anti-American as well as anti-Haitian. But the emergence of a large transnational community in "the belly of the monster," in José Martí's inevitable phrase, has enormously complicated matters. Dominican migrants participate simultaneously in two distinct political systems that define them as members of a separate nation, an ethnic minority, or a pan-ethnic and quasi-racial group called Hispanic or Latino. The émigrés may accept, contest, or negotiate such definitions of their identity, as they have on countless occasions. But at least one thing is certain: transnational migration has expanded the territorial boundaries of the Dominican nation and undermined conventional assumptions about who is a Dominican. In the last hundred years, the Dominican Republic has been thoroughly Americanized, just as parts of New York and San Juan have been Dominicanized (and Latinized) by the diaspora. As increasing globalization has stimulated both local and translocal notions of cultural identity, Dominican migrants constantly negotiate the two competing claims in their daily lives, thereby blurring the frontiers between home and host societies.

Acknowledgments

The first draft of this chapter was originally prepared for the conference entitled "The Caribbean and the United States Since 1898: 100 Years of Transformation," which was sponsored by Lehman College, City University of New York, Bronx, N.Y., October 13–15, 1998. A revised version was presented at the workshop entitled "Migration and Transnational Theory Reexamined: Place, Generation, and Identity," which was organized by the Center for Development Research, Copenhagen, Denmark, and held in Santo Domingo, Dominican Republic, April 22–24, 1999. I appreciate the encouraging comments and useful suggestions on earlier drafts of this chapter by Silvia Pedraza, Edgardo Meléndez, Ninna Nyberg Sørensen, Ernesto Sagás, Yolanda Martínez-San Miguel, Marifeli Pérez-Stable, Vicky Muñiz, Karen Fog Olwig, Lisa Maya Knauer, and two anonymous reviewers.

Note

1. Quisqueya is believed to have been one of the original names of the island of Hispaniola, in the language of the Taíno Indians.

References

Alicea, Marisa. 1997. "'A Chambered Nautilus': The Contradictory Nature of Puerto Rican Women's Role in the Social Construction of a Transnational Community." *Gender & Society* 11(5): 597–626.

Appadurai, Arjun. 1996. *Modernity at Large: Cultural Dimensions of Globalization.* Minneapolis: University of Minnesota Press.

Bailey, Benjamin. 1999. "Language and Ethnic/Racial Identity of Dominican American High School Students in Providence, Rhode Island." Ph.D. diss., University of California, Los Angeles.

Basch, Linda, Nina Glick Schiller, and Cristina Szanton Blanc. 1994. *Nations Unbound: Transnational Projects, Postcolonial Predicaments, and Deterritorialized Nation-States.* Basel, Switzerland: Gordon and Breach.

Cordero-Guzmán, Héctor R., Robert C. Smith, and Ramón Grosfoguel, eds. 2001. *Migration, Transnationalization, and Race in a Changing New York.* Philadelphia: Temple University Press.

de la Garza, Rodolfo O., Louis DeSipio, F. Chris García, John García, and Angelo Falcón. 1992. *Latino Voices: Mexican, Puerto Rican, and Cuban Perspectives on American Politics.* Boulder, Colo.: Westview.

Domínguez, Virginia. 1973. "Spanish-speaking Caribbeans in New York: 'The Middle Race.'" *Revista/Review Interamericana* 3(2): 135–42.

Duany, Jorge. 1994a. "Beyond the Safety Valve: Recent Trends in Caribbean Migration." *Social and Economic Studies* 43(1): 95–122.

———. 1994b. *Quisqueya on the Hudson: The Transnational Identity of Dominicans in Washington Heights*. New York: Dominican Studies Institute, City University of New York.

———. 1998. "Reconstructing Racial Identity: Ethnicity, Color, and Class among Dominicans in the United States and Puerto Rico." *Latin American Perspectives* 25(3): 147–72.

Duany, Jorge, Luisa Hernández Angueira, and César A. Rey. 1995. *El Barrio Gandul: Economía subterránea y migración indocumentada en Puerto Rico*. Caracas: Nueva Sociedad.

Foner, Nancy. 2001. "Transnationalism Then and Now: New York Immigrants Today and at the Turn of the Twentieth Century." In *Migration, Transnationalization, and Race in a Changing New York*, ed. Héctor R. Cordero-Guzmán, Robert C. Smith, and Ramón Grosfoguel. Philadelphia: Temple University Press.

Glick Schiller, Nina, Linda Basch, and Cristina Blanc-Szanton. 1995. "From Immigrant to Transmigrant: Theorizing Transnational Migration." *Anthropological Quarterly* 68(1): 48–63.

———, eds. 1992. *Towards a Transnational Perspective on Migration: Race, Class, Ethnicity, and Nationalism Reconsidered*. New York: New York Academy of Sciences.

Goldring, Luin. 1996. "Blurring Borders: Constructing Transnational Community in the Process of Mexico-U.S. Migration." *Research in Community Sociology* 6: 69–104.

Graham, Pamela M. 1998. "The Politics of Incorporation: Dominicans in New York City." *Latino Studies Journal* 9(3): 39–64.

———. 2001. "Political Incorporation and Re-incorporation: Simultaneity in the Dominican Migrant Experience." In *Migration, Transnationalization, and Race in a Changing New York*, ed. Héctor R. Cordero-Guzmán, Robert C. Smith, and Ramón Grosfoguel. Philadelphia: Temple University Press.

Grasmuck, Sherri, and Patricia R. Pessar. 1991. *Between Two Islands: Dominican International Migration*. Berkeley: University of California Press.

Grosfoguel, Ramón. 1994–1995. "Caribbean Colonial Immigrants in the Metropoles: A Research Agenda." *Centro* 7(1): 82–95.

Guarnizo, Luis E. 1994. "*Los Dominicanyorks:* The Making of a Binational Society." *Annals of the American Academy of Political and Social Sciences* 533: 70–86.

———. 1997. "The Emergence of a Transnational Social Formation and the Mirage of Return Migration among Dominican Transmigrants." *Identities* 4(2): 281–322.

Guarnizo, Luis E., and Michael P. Smith. 1998. "The Locations of Transnationalism." In *Transnationalism from Below*, ed. Michael Peter Smith and Luis E. Guarnizo. New Brunswick, N.J.: Transaction.

Guzmán, Betsy. 2001. "The Hispanic Population: Census 2000 Brief." Electronic document. http://www.census.gov/population/www/cen2000/briefs.html.

Hannerz, Ulf. 1996. *Transnational Connections: Culture, People, Places*. London: Routledge.

Itzigsohn, José, and Carlos Dore Cabral. 2000. "Competing Identities? Race,

Ethnicity, and Panethnicity among Dominicans in the United States." *Sociological Forum* 15(2): 225–47.

Itzigsohn, José, Carlos Dore Cabral, Esther Hernández Medina, and Obed Vázquez. 1999. "Mapping Dominican Transnationalism: Narrow and Broad Transnational Practices." *Ethnic and Racial Studies* 22(2): 316–39.

Kearney, Michael. 1991. "Borders and Boundaries of State and Self at the End of Empire." *Journal of Historical Sociology* 4(1): 52–74.

———. 1995. "The Local and the Global: The Anthropology of Globalization and Transnationalism." *Annual Review of Anthropology* 24: 547–66.

Levitt, Peggy. 2001. *The Transnational Villagers.* Berkeley: University of California Press.

Lizardo, Freddy. 2001. "Altas remesas en los últimos años. . . ." Electronic document. http://www.intec.edu.do/~indes.

Meyers, Deborah Waller. 1998. *Migrant Remittances to Latin America: Reviewing the Literature.* Washington, D.C.: Inter-American Dialogue.

Migration News. 2001. "Remittances: Dominican Republic." Electronic document. http://www.migration.ucdavis.edu/Data.remit.on.www./remittances.html.

Olwig, Karen Fog. 1997. "Hacia una reconceptualización de la migración y transnacionalización." *Estudios Sociales* 30(109): 53–75.

Ortiz, Marina. 1997. *Microempresas, migración, y remesas en la República Dominicana, 1996–1997.* Santo Domingo: Fondomicro.

Ortiz, Renato. 1996. *Otro territorio: Ensayos sobre el mundo contemporáneo.* Buenos Aires: Universidad Nacional de Quilmes.

———. 1997. *Mundialización y cultura.* Madrid: Alianza.

Pedraza, Silvia, and Rubén G. Rumbaut, eds. 1996. *Origins and Destinies: Immigration, Race, and Ethnicity in America.* Belmont, Calif.: Wadsworth.

Pessar, Patricia R. 1995. *A Visa for a Dream: Dominicans in the United States.* Boston: Allyn and Bacon.

Portes, Alejandro. 1998. "Latin Americans in the U.S. and the Rise of Transnational Communities." Paper presented at the 21st International Congress of the Latin American Studies Association, Chicago, Ill., September 24–26.

Portes, Alejandro, and Luis E. Guarnizo. 1991. *Capitalistas del trópico: La inmigración en los Estados Unidos y el desarrollo de la pequeña empresa en la República Dominicana.* Santo Domingo: FLACSO.

Portes, Alejandro, and Rubén G. Rumbaut. 1996. *Immigrant America: A Portrait.* 2d ed. Berkeley: University of California Press.

Ricourt, Milagros. 1998. "Patterns of Dominican Demography and Community Development in New York City." *Latino Studies Journal* 9(3): 11–38.

Rodríguez, Clara E. 1989. *Puerto Ricans: Born in the U.S.A.* Boston: Unwin Hyman.

———. 2000. *Changing Race: Latinos, the Census, and the History of Ethnicity in the United States.* New York: New York University Press.

Rohter, Larry, and Clifford Krauss. 1998a. "Dominican Drug Traffickers Tighten Grip on the Northeast." *New York Times,* May 11.

———. 1998b. "Dominicans Allow Drugs Easy Sale." *New York Times,* May 10.

Rouse, Roger. 1995. "Thinking through Transnationalism: Notes on the Cultural Politics of Class Relations in the Contemporary U.S." *Public Culture* 7: 353–402.

Sassen, Saskia. 1998. *Globalization and Its Discontents: Essays on the New Mobility of People and Money.* New York: The New Press.

Smith, Michael Peter. 1994. "Can You Imagine? Transnational Migration and the Globalization of Grassroots Politics." *Social Text* 39: 15–34.

Smith, Michael Peter, and Luis E. Guarnizo, eds. 1998. *Transnationalism from Below.* New Brunswick, N.J.: Transaction.

Sørensen, Ninna Nyberg. 1994. "Telling Migrants Apart: The Experience of Migrancy among Dominican Locals and Transnationals." Unpublished manuscript, Institute of Anthropology, University of Copenhagen, Denmark.

———. 1996. "Nueva York es sólo otra capital dominicana—Madrid es otro mundo: Prácticas espaciales y culturales de desplazamiento entre migrantes dominicanos en Nueva York y Madrid." *Género y Sociedad* 4(1): 160–220.

———. 1997. "Spatial Practices and Cultures of Displacement among Dominicans: Transnationalism Reconsidered." Paper presented at the 20th International Congress of the Latin American Studies Association, Guadalajara, Mexico, April 17–19.

Torres-Saillant, Silvio, and Ramona Hernández. 1998. *The Dominican Americans.* Westport, Conn.: Greenwood.

U.S. Census Bureau. 1996. "Findings on Questions on Race and Hispanic Origin Tested in the 1996 National Content Survey." Population Division Paper No. 16. Electronic document. http://www.census.gov/population/socdemo/96natcontent survey.

———. 1998. "Current Population Survey, March 1997." Electronic document. http://www.census.gov/population/socdemo/hispanic/cps97.

———. 2001. "American Factfinder: Census 2000 Data." Electronic document. http://www.census.gov/main/www/cen2000.html.

U.S. Immigration and Naturalization Service. 1999. "1998 Statistical Yearbook of the Immigration and Naturalization Service." Electronic document. http://www.ins.usdoj.gov/stats/annual.

Weyland, Karin. 1998. "Dominican Women 'Con un pie aquí y otro allá': International Migration, Class, Gender, and Cultural Change." Ph.D. diss., New School for Social Research.

3

From *Ausentes* to Dual Nationals

The Incorporation of Transmigrants into Dominican Politics

Ernesto Sagás

In December 1997, the National Congress of the Dominican Republic took the unprecedented step of approving a new electoral code that allowed Dominicans permanently residing overseas to vote in the country's presidential elections (Congreso Nacional de la República Dominicana 1997, 41–42). There were even calls to implement overseas voting in time for the 2000 presidential elections.[1] In this fashion, the Dominican Republic joined Bolivia, Colombia, Venezuela, and Peru, the other Latin American nations that also allow overseas voting for their nationals. Moreover, Ecuador and Mexico already allow their nationals to acquire a second citizenship without losing their original one. Their leaders are also discussing the possibility of implementing overseas voting. In the case of Haiti (the Dominican Republic's island neighbor), its constitution declares the intention of allowing for a greater participation of its diaspora[2] in its internal affairs, an effort reflected in the creation of the Ministry of Diasporic Affairs (Ministère des Haïtiens Vivant à l'Etranger) (Laguerre 1997, 175).

At first glance, these events do not appear to be different from previous electoral practices. Many countries routinely allow their diplomats, students in foreign universities, and even businessmen who spend a long time overseas, to cast absentee ballots by mail, or at their countries' embassies and consulates. The emerging trend, however, is for the incorporation of large populations that permanently reside overseas into the national political mainstream. This new trend accounts for a quantitative and qualitative difference from previous electoral practices. Instead of the typical handful of students and diplomats, overseas voting calls for the incorporation of hundreds of thousands of citizens who reside in foreign countries into their national electoral systems (as would be the case of the Dominican Republic). These are no longer absentee ballots, votes from nationals who, for particular reasons, are living outside their countries at election time. These are votes from nationals who have migrated and established permanent (or semi-permanent) residence in foreign nations, mostly in search of economic opportunities. Thus, their political recognition is an acknowledgment of both their important role in their nations' destiny and of the redefinition of the nation-state in the face of globalizing trends.

This chapter examines the incorporation of a large, overseas-residing community into its sending country's political system. In a little over three decades, but particularly within the last few years, Dominicans residing overseas (mainly in the United States and Puerto Rico, but also in other countries such as Spain and Venezuela) have improved their political status from *dominicanos ausentes* (absentee Dominicans) to full-fledged members of their nation. I argue that globalization and the transnationalization of Dominican overseas communities, plus their vital contribution to the Dominican economy, have forced the Dominican state to reconsider its posture regarding those who emigrated. From being practically invisible beings in the national mainstream, the members of the Dominican overseas communities have developed into a critical mass that the Dominican state can no longer ignore. This chapter also examines the often unintended problems and complications arising from the political incorporation of a large overseas population. Finally, this chapter reflects on the different possible outcomes of this process, which seems to straggle the road between regional integration and globalization, and still powerful feelings of nationalism and *patriachiquismo*.

Transmigration and Political Participation

In a relative sense, Caribbean politics has always been transnational. Since the nineteenth century, after the independence of the mainland, the inhabitants of Cuba, Santo Domingo (the Dominican Republic after 1844), and Puerto Rico established overseas communities of political exiles. These exiles fought for the independence of their countries from imperial powers, or for the overthrow of the then-current dictatorship. In spite of the lack of adequate communications technology, these exiles kept in touch with developments back home and plotted for their eventual return. New York City, and in the Caribbean, St. Thomas and Curaçao, became hotbeds of exile activity. In the second half of the twentieth century, two developments modified the life of these small exile communities and made them truly transnational: the rapid advances in communications technology (e.g., jet planes, television, and expanded telephone services), and the massive migration of their countrymen overseas. Both developments took place within the context of the globalization of capitalism around the same period. The technological advances brought about by the expansion of capitalism provided new, improved means of communications, while the disruptions of the economies of peripheral—or developing—countries, induced by capitalism's onslaught, created hundreds of thousands of migrants.

According to Glick Schiller, Basch, and Blanc-Szanton, "Within the complex web of social relations, transmigrants draw upon and create fluid and multiple identities grounded both in their society of origin and in the host societies. While some migrants identify more with one society than the other, the majority seem to maintain several identities that link them simultaneously to more than one nation" (1992, 11). These multiple, transnational allegiances are an important qualitative difference between the political exiles of yesterday and the transmigrants of today. While their forefathers were political exiles who spent years overseas, organizing, plotting, and yearning to return home eventually, without really fully integrating into their host societies, today's transnational migrants live—and politically participate—in several worlds. Even the term immigrant no longer aptly describes the complex web of social, cultural, economic, and political interactions in which these transmigrants participate. They may choose to participate—or not—in two or more political systems. Moreover, their perceptions are shaped by the often conflicting hegemonic claims of several nation-states, at the same time that they also play a role in (re)shaping the traditional perceptions of nation, state, and sociopolitical boundaries of their sending and host societies.[3]

Such is the case of overseas-residing Dominicans, a growing transmigrant group that in about four decades has gone from being primarily a small community of political exiles to becoming a truly massive transnational community.[4] Dominican transmigrants, first ignored, then used (and abused), are now part of two (or more) sociopolitical systems separated by hundreds of miles of ocean, but encapsulated within each Dominican transmigrant. Moreover, the Dominican state is being "deterritorialized" by transmigration and the globalization of capitalism: "This new conception of nation-state includes as citizens those who live physically dispersed within the boundaries of many other states, but who remain socially, politically, culturally, and often economically part of the nation-state of their ancestors" (Basch, Glick Schiller, and Blanc-Szanton 1994, 8).

Beginning with periodic waves of migration to the United States since the 1960s, expanding to new destinations such as Spain since the 1980s, and now including such "far away" destinations as western Europe and South America, Dominican transmigrant communities have indeed dispersed across thousands of miles. And while they have become one of its economic pillars, they still remain a largely undefined part of the Dominican nation-state. This process of transnational dispersion, economic ascendancy, and political (re)integration took place in a relatively short period of time, as a result of the semi-permanent economic crisis of the Dominican Republic since the late 1970s.

From Political Exiles to *Dominicanos Ausentes*

There were few Dominicans living outside their country for most of the first half of the twentieth century.[5] With the exception of the occasional traveler or the student sent abroad, most Dominicans residing overseas were political exiles (Rodríguez de León 1998). Their number increased considerably with the advent of the Trujillo dictatorship (1930–1961). Since the dictatorship imposed heavy restrictions on travel, most of these exiles left the country in the early 1930s or were defectors who seized the opportunity to travel abroad to join the exile community. Dominican political exile communities soon developed in New York, Havana, Caracas, and San Juan. For example, the Partido Revolucionario Dominicano (Dominican Revolutionary Party, or PRD), the main anti-*Trujillista* exile organization, was founded in Havana in 1939, and soon had chapters in several cities with concentrations of Dominicans.

The assassination of Rafael L. Trujillo on May 30, 1961 and the collapse of his dictatorial regime opened the floodgates of migration for the Dominican people, who up to then had been kept in partial isolation from the rest of the world. Political instability up to 1966 (including an aborted democratic transition in 1963, a civil war, and U.S. military intervention), coupled with economic woes, motivated Dominicans to leave their country, particularly for the United States. Even former presidents Juan Bosch and Joaquín Balaguer spent some time in exile in the United States in the 1960s. Moreover, changes in U.S. immigration laws and a receptive economic climate attracted Dominicans to urban centers such as New York City.

For decades thereafter, state policies in the Dominican Republic and the United States facilitated migration. After Trujillo's death, the Dominican government did not impose any serious restrictions on emigration, a process that actually benefited the country by alleviating economic pressures. Likewise, new immigration policies in the United States (such as the 1965 law that facilitated family reunification) induced large-scale Dominican migration. This receptive climate lasted until the 1980s when an anti-immigrant political movement developed in the United States, which began enacting tougher legal barriers for Third World immigrants. Finally, social networks, that is, the myriad of kinship, friendship, and acquaintanceship links that Dominicans slowly erected also determined the direction of the flow to specific neighborhoods in these global cities. While in the 1960s many Dominicans were "political" exiles who fled persecution or just the prevailing climate of insecurity, by the 1970s Dominican migration was a mostly "economic" phenomenon.[6]

Dominican mass migration is also a fairly recent event. As such, Dominican transmigration grew aided by easy transportation and communications. Jet planes, telephones, and more recently, fax machines, portable video cameras, VCRS, wire transfers, video conferencing, and the Internet have allowed Dominicans overseas to stay in close touch with their nation of origin and its political life. Dominican political exiles, particularly in New York City, maintained a regular agenda of political activism, a trend related to the reasons behind their migration and to their longing for the country that they left behind. Economic migrants, again owing to their recent arrival, also retained strong links to their homeland.

The most important political link was the establishment of overseas sections or chapters by the main Dominican political parties. Initially, they were the result of the long-standing practice of Dominican political activism overseas (e.g., the PRD's activism versus Trujillo, and later, versus Balaguer), but eventually, as the size of the overseas community increased, they became fund-raising organizations. Other Dominican political parties, particularly of the radical left, also organized sections among New York's Dominican community, such as the Partido Comunista Dominicano (Dominican Communist Party, or PCD), the Movimiento Popular Dominicano (Dominican Popular Movement, or MPD), and the Partido de los Trabajadores Dominicanos (Dominican Workers' Party, or PTD) (Rodríguez de León 1998, chap. 10).

For years, the transmigrants, or *dominicanos ausentes* (as they were popularly known back in the Dominican Republic), had a symbiotic, but unequal, relationship with Dominican political parties. Dominican migrants felt the bond of participating, albeit indirectly, in their country's political life, sharing a social space with their fellow citizens, and reproducing some of the activities (such as meetings, parades, and celebrations) that they remembered fondly. In exchange, the Dominican political parties raised thousands of dollars in personal donations, raffles, and social activities (such as dinners with prominent Dominican politicians).

By the mid-1980s, the economic power of overseas Dominicans was well recognized and periodically wooed by Dominican political candidates. In 1978, watershed elections brought the PRD to power and signaled the beginning of a democratic opening in the Dominican Republic. High hopes were placed on the *dominicanos ausentes* returning home with their capital and skills. Unfortunately, and in spite of an improved human rights climate, economic conditions consistently deteriorated during the 1980s and early 1990s, sparking a deluge of migrants, even to nontraditional destinations such as Spain, Italy, the U.S. Virgin Islands, St. Maarten, and Canada. Increasingly, and in the midst of severe foreign exchange problems, the Dominican economy came to depend on foreign remittances from its transmigrants. Families torn apart by migration in particular, and the Dominican economy in general, came to rely on the steady foreign influx of dollars and other foreign currencies. In 1999 alone, remittances were estimated at around U.S.$1.689 billion, surpassing all national economic activities, except tourism, in the earning of foreign exchange (Banco Central de la República Dominicana 2001, 70).

Dominican politicians increasingly came to depend on the economic support of overseas Dominicans. By the early 1990s, it was common for Dominican presidential hopefuls to visit New York City and other Dominican overseas communities in well-publicized fund-raising trips. For the heavily contested 1994 elections, for example, José F. Peña Gómez of the PRD visited New York seven times in a thirteen month period, raising hundreds of thousands of dollars. Peña Gómez's followers in New York City also organized campaign committees that collected personal donations from wealthy overseas entrepreneurs. Joaquín Balaguer was the only presidential candidate who did not visit New York City during the electoral campaign. And he did not need to. As president, he had access to the funds remitted by Dominican consulates around the world, which were estimated at U.S.$20 million per year (Redacción Listín USA 1994). Within a matter of years, *dominicanos ausentes,* though politically "invisible," had become a powerful economic force.

From *Dominicanos Ausentes* to Dual Nationals

The big challenge for overseas Dominicans was how to transform their obvious economic power into political leverage. Several elements contributed to this process. First, the transmigrants rapidly increased in numbers. While during the 1960s only 93,292 Dominicans were legally admitted into the United States, their numbers rose to 148,135 individuals legally admitted during the 1970s, 252,035 during the 1980s, and 335,251 during the 1990s (U.S. Immigration and Naturalization Service 2003). These official figures do not take into consideration the large number of undocumented Dominican migrants, which has been estimated at about 75,000 more immigrants (U.S. Immigration and Naturalization Service 2003), or those that entered by other legal means (e.g., a tourist or student visa) and stayed in the United

States. This critical mass of Dominicans residing overseas could not be ignored forever by Dominican politicians.

Second, as the number of Dominican transmigrants increased, so did their economic influence over Dominican society. While in 1970 Dominicans overseas sent a paltry U.S.$25 million back home, by the mid-1990s remittances had surpassed the U.S.$1 billion mark (*Migration News* 1998). These are figures that do not include undocumented monetary flows or money personally carried back home. According to a recent poll, 28 percent of Dominicans (or about 2.4 million people out of a population of 8.5 million) receive money from abroad (*El Siglo* 1999a). *Dominicanos ausentes* also spent considerable amounts of money on vacation trips, to the extent that the U.S. dollar exchange rate typically stabilizes during the Christmas season. Moreover, Dominican transmigrants not only sustained their relatives in the Dominican Republic, they also brought consumer goods into the country, bought homes and land, invested in businesses, and stimulated the growth of certain economic sectors, such as construction.

Third, Dominican transmigrants have also grown roots in U.S. domestic politics. By the late 1980s, Dominican-American politicians were poised to compete for local elective positions within their ethnic enclaves. In 1991, as a result of the redistricting of New York City's councilmanic districts, Guillermo Linares became the first Dominican elected to New York City's City Council. In 1996, his long-time rival, Adriano Espaillat, became the first New York state assemblyman of Dominican origin (Graham 1998, 50–55). Both have since been reelected,[7] and after term limits were implemented for members of the New York City Council, Miguel Martínez, another candidate of Dominican origins, replaced Linares.

The local political empowerment of Dominican transmigrants had to be acknowledged by Dominican politicians who, in their frequent fund-raising trips, now met with Dominican-American politicians and sought their endorsement. In exchange, Dominican-American leaders reiterated the transmigrants' long-standing requests of improved consular services, economic concessions for Dominicans investing in their home country, facilities for returnees to settle back in the Dominican Republic, and particularly, incorporation into the Dominican Republic's political system. Given the need of Dominican politicians for the support of (mainly) New York City's Dominican community, and the increasingly prominent standing in U.S. politics of Dominican-American politicians,[8] it was becoming more difficult for them to resist these pressures. By the early 1990s, Dominican politicians began promising the incorporation of the overseas Dominicans into Dominican politics.

Finally, junctural events helped Dominican transmigrants. The 1994 post-electoral crisis in the Dominican Republic, which lingered for more than two months, led to a hurried constitutional reform that included a long-standing claim from overseas Dominicans: dual citizenship. Among electoral changes such as the introduction of runoff elections, the prohibition on consecutive presidential reelection, and the separation of presidential elections from congressional and municipal elections, the 1994 Dominican Constitution also allowed Dominicans to acquire a second citizenship without losing their original one (República Dominicana 1994, 15–16). That constitutional modification allayed the traditional fears that many Dominicans held of becoming U.S. citizens, a status that complicated their potential return and resettlement back home. Overseas Dominicans now could freely choose to participate in any of two political systems, or in both.

In general, the Partido de la Liberación Dominicana (Dominican Liberation Party, or PLD)[9] and the PRD have been more receptive to the transmigrants' concerns than the administrations of Balaguer. Balaguer really never expressed a serious interest in overseas Dominicans. Quite the opposite, and particularly during *los doce años,* those who left the country were seen as the disaffected ones, a potential political opposition that was best left unincorporated from the national mainstream (they were, of course, occasionally publicly recognized for their economic contributions). As opposition and minority parties for decades, the PLD and the PRD needed the transmigrants more than Balaguer did. Funds provided by overseas communities, as well as the meager votes that they could contribute, were much more valuable to the opposition's parties than to Balaguer, who could always count on well-stocked campaign coffers. Their dependency on transmigrants certainly made the PLD and the PRD more pliant to political (and economic) pressures from Dominican overseas communities. Thus it was the political opposition that pushed through the constitutional modifications establishing dual citizenship, so as to ingratiate themselves with Dominicans living overseas.

In 1996, the election of Leonel Fernández marked another chapter in the political incorporation of overseas Dominicans. Fernández, born in Santo Domingo, but reared in New York, returned to the Dominican Republic as an adolescent to complete his education. He joined the PLD in the early 1970s, and became its presidential hopeful after Juan Bosch retired from politics in 1994. Young and dynamic, he speaks English well and has often labeled himself as a product of New York City's public education system. Regardless of personal political affiliations, the members of the Dominican overseas communities finally had a political role model with whom they could identify. Fernández had personally endured and had direct knowledge of the myriad of problems that faced Dominicans in the United States.

Fernández, in turn, also seemed to identify himself with overseas Dominicans. He visited New York City often, and just weeks after his inauguration—in an unprecedented event—addressed overseas Dominicans on American television. Fernández's speech was in response to recent changes in the U.S. social welfare system, which now excluded thousands of legal residents (Fisher 1996). Recognizing the importance of U.S. welfare programs for poor Dominican immigrants, and in turn the importance of the remittances of these migrants for the Dominican Republic, Fernández called on Dominicans to become naturalized U.S. citizens so as not to lose their welfare benefits. He reminded them that the 1994 constitutional provisions allowed them to maintain their Dominican citizenship, even if they chose to become U.S. citizens. Fernández's discourse is a powerful example of the transnationalization of Dominican politics (and policies): a Dominican president addressing Dominican nationals in a foreign country, urging them to become U.S. citizens to protect themselves from changes in U.S. laws, and guaranteeing that they would not be less Dominican for doing so.

Fernández also appointed local overseas leaders to consular positions, ending the traditional practice of appointing consuls to communities in which they were practically unknown. For example, in New York City, Miami, San Juan, and other important Dominican overseas communities, local PLD leaders were appointed as consul generals. (This practice has been continued by the new PRD administration of Hipólito Mejía.) In addition, the Fernández administration promised to streamline bureaucratic consular procedures in order to make services easier and less expensive to Dominicans residing overseas. In mid-1999, a special civil service bureau was opened in Santo Domingo, which provides services only to Dominicans who reside abroad. This office allows them to acquire the new voting card in an expeditious manner (supposedly in just one day), thus saving them from making numerous trips spread over several weeks in order to get their documents.

Still, and in spite of his rhetoric, Fernández did not act as the "transmigrants' president." Though greater political participation for the Dominican overseas communities was promised, no members of these communities were appointed to high-level government positions, nor was a government office in charge of transmigrants' affairs created. The only minor political "concession" to overseas Dominicans was the nomination of Dominican political leaders residing overseas to elective positions during the 1998 congressional and municipal elections in the Dominican Republic. That practice, however, was solely party-related, and it was carried out by both the PLD and the PRD.

The PRD's Hipólito Mejía (elected in 2000) has not fared much better. Although the creation of an Overseas Secretaryship (Secretaría de Estado de Ultramar) was promised by the PRD administration, and a legal project was submitted to Congress on May 8, 2001, it languishes in the Senate. The project has faced the stiff opposition of the Secretaryship of Foreign Affairs and its secretary, Hugo Tolentino Dipp, who are concerned about potential overlaps in roles and jurisdictions (Reyes 2001).

Electoral Participation

The final test of the transmigrants' political incorporation, and of the transnationalization of Dominican politics, will be their participation in Dominican elections. Traditionally, Dominicans who wished to vote had to maintain de jure—though not de facto—residence in the Dominican Republic. They also had to travel to the Dominican Republic to keep their voting documents in order and to register for upcoming elections. Finally, they had to be physically present in the Dominican Republic on election day (May 16). These time-consuming and expensive procedures (since they involved traveling to the Dominican Republic) meant that only a small percentage of Dominican transmigrants could actually vote in Dominican elections. Periodically, some of the local chapters of Dominican political parties organized "voting trips" to the Dominican Republic, but these were mostly attended by a handful of the committed party faithful and their relatives.

In December 1997, after months of national discussions and several open hearings in Dominican overseas communities, new electoral legislation (Electoral Law 275–97) allowed Dominicans residing overseas to vote in the country's presidential elections (Congreso Nacional de la República Dominicana 1997, 41–42). The law did not detail the manner in which Dominicans living overseas were to vote; it only stipulated that, if possible, overseas voting would begin with the 2000 presidential elections.

In spite of the altruistic efforts of this legislation, the logistics of organizing overseas elections for a small country with limited resources, but with a huge transmigrant population, seems like an insurmountable obstacle for their successful implementation. Typically, nations that allow for overseas voting ask their citizens to register and vote at their nearest embassy or consulate. In the case of overseas Dominicans, it would be practically impossible. For example, assuming that if only ten thousand Dominicans in the New York City metropolitan area (of an estimated half a million) showed up to vote, the consulate would not be able to handle such a large number of people in a single day. Other methods would have to be devised.

One possibility under consideration would be to set up registration centers and voting booths in neighborhoods where Dominicans concentrate (e.g., Washington Heights in northern Manhattan). Carrying out elections in a foreign country, however, implies potential legal questions that have yet to be resolved. Since up to now absentee and overseas voting in the United States has taken place within the confines of foreign embassies and consulates (which are legally considered foreign soil), the U.S. Department of State and the U.S. Department of Justice do not have an official position regarding large-scale foreign elections in U.S. territory. It is still up to the U.S. government to decide on the legality of these plans. Furthermore, U.S. law does not recognize dual citizenship for immigrants who become naturalized U.S. citizens. Candidates for naturalization are required to renounce their former citizenship in order to become U.S. citizens. The U.S. courts would still have to decide on the legality of the status of Dominican-Americans and other dual citizens who claim and employ two citizenships at the same time, based on the constitutions of their original countries. Finally, the current U.S. anti-immigrant wave may have deleterious consequences for the future of overseas voting, as it will be seriously questioned by U.S. conservatives seeking to assert the sovereignty of the United States vis-à-vis the potential threat perceived in an extensively deterritorialized Third World state.

Setting up voting centers for the use of Dominican transmigrants implies considerable expense in foreign currencies. Particularly in areas of heavy Dominican presence, such as New York City and environs, dozens of voting centers would have to be set up by the Dominican authorities. These places would need to be rented, personnel would have to be trained, and voting supplies would have to be provided. In addition, a voters' registration drive would need to be carried out months before the elections in order to create a roster of registered overseas voters. Moreover, a public educational campaign would be necessary to inform Dominicans about the registration and voting process, plus details about election day procedures and the location of voting centers.

Another, and more practical, possibility would be voting through the mail, that is, mailing completed ballots to the nearest Dominican embassy or consulate. By using mail ballots, the Dominican government would save precious resources that otherwise would have to be spent in renting and preparing voting centers. Bulk mailing voting forms or blank ballots would be cheap, plus they would even reach Dominicans living far away from Dominican embassies or consulates. Moreover, by using mail ballots, Dominicans could vote from home. Many Dominicans who otherwise could not leave their workplaces on May 16, which is not a holiday outside the Dominican Republic, to go and vote could easily participate in this fashion. Mail ballots can also maintain the secrecy of the vote, as ballots can be placed inside blank envelopes (enclosed within pre-addressed envelopes) that would be deposited into a box; all of the ballots would then be opened at the end of election day. The only reasonable requirement would be for mail ballots to be postmarked by a certain date (presumably before May 16) in order for them to be valid.

To date, the Dominican government and the JCE, the Junta Central Electoral, have proceeded at a snail's pace regarding the registration of Dominicans overseas and the creation of voters' lists. Voter registration centers have been opened in some Dominican consular offices, but few Dominicans have showed up to register. For example, only thirty Dominicans registered during the first three months of operation of Miami's JCE registration center (Peña Brito 2002). According to the JCE, as of January 2004, only about thirty-four thousand Dominicans residing overseas had registered to vote, half of them in New York City. It is very likely that the drive to register will pick up as the 2004 presidential election nears, but so far Dominicans living overseas have not responded as expected, particularly considering that voting rights have been a long-standing demand by overseas political leaders.

A Pandora's Box?

The massive political participation of transmigrants in Dominican politics may have uncertain and unexpected consequences for the Dominican political system and for the (re)definition of the nation-state as a result of transnationalization. At the least, it will open a new world of previously unthought of possibilities.

The Dominican overseas community, if seen as a single demographic unit, could become the second largest Dominican province, after the National District (Santo Domingo and environs). With a population of more than one million people, the Dominican overseas community could represent ±12 percent of the current Dominican population of more than eight million inhabitants. This demographic mass would give overseas Dominicans considerable political leverage in presidential elections, and the power to veto or get candidates elected. As a result, Dominican politicians would have to take Dominican overseas communities very seriously, to lobby intensively their huge mass of voters, to listen to their claims, and to reward them with political patronage. The transmigrant community, a formerly ignored group, could instantaneously become a large, important political entity that Dominicans politicians would be forced to court.

The overseas "province" could become a powerful demographic, political, and, above all, economic force in its own right, no longer as an appendage of Dominican society. So far, Dominican politicians have not conceived of overseas communities as a single entity. But that could be a matter of time. For example, in the case of Haiti, its overseas population was initially ignored for years. For some years now, however, the Haitian diaspora has been known as the "tenth *département*" (political subdivision equivalent to a province), and is considered by the Haitian Constitution as an integral part of the Haitian nation. President Jean-Bertrand Aristide incorporated it into his speeches and the Haitian diaspora played a vital role in financing his electoral campaign, and in supporting his return to Haiti in 1994 (Laguerre 1997; Richman 1992). Dominican politicians have been following a similar path by increasingly incorporating references to the "overseas community" or the *ausentes* in their speeches and highlighting their importance for the nation's welfare. Both ex-president Leonel Fernández and, more recently, president Hipólito Mejía have repeatedly done so.

Conceivably, Dominican overseas communities could become a sort of huge overseas province, with tremendous political leverage and economic power. There are already pleas for extending the voting rights of overseas Dominicans beyond presidential elections to include the election of overseas representatives to the Dominican Congress. The Comité Permanente de los Partidos Políticos Dominicanos en el Exterior (Permanent Committee of Dominican Political Parties Overseas) has requested the election of one senator per every 150,000 Dominicans residing in an urban center overseas, and a *diputado* (deputy or representative) for every 50,000 (Mateo 2002). There are some precedents in the region to this claim. For example, Peru allows its citizens residing overseas to participate in presidential and congressional elections, in which candidates are selected from national lists. Colombia has a global extraterritorial electoral district that represents overseas Colombians in the Colombian National Congress. More recently, overseas Colombians were given the right to vote for congressional candidates representing their native regions (Guarnizo 2001, 235). In the case of Dominican transmigrants, the claims include both the right to elect overseas representatives and the right to participate in congressional elections.

The consequences of this potential development would open a political Pandora's box for the Dominican political system. First, giving overseas Dominicans the right to participate in congressional elections would be a logistical and legal nightmare. The current Dominican electoral law stipulates that citizens have the right to elect representatives based on their place of residence. But what about voters who reside in New York City, San Juan, or Madrid? Are they going to vote by declaring a place of residence in the Dominican Republic? Are they going to vote instead based on their last place of residence in the Dominican Republic? Or, are they going to vote based on their place of birth (as in the Colombian case)? Thus, how are votes to be allocated? Obviously, the complications are enormous.

Second, giving overseas Dominicans the right to elect their own representatives is also problematic and potentially troubling for the Dominican political system. The Dominican electoral law calls for one senator to be elected from each province, and one *diputado* for every 50,000 inhabitants or fraction over 25,000. In this case, how many senators would Dominican overseas communities get? Only one for the whole overseas population, or several for the largest concentrations of Dominicans (as is being currently demanded)? Also, how are electoral districts for the election of deputies going to be drawn, particularly in foreign countries? Even if these complications are resolved, the political power of the "Dominican overseas province" would be enormous, second only to the National District and maybe Santiago. It could conceivably have one or more senators, and more than fifteen deputies. It is unlikely that Dominican politicians would accept such a new, powerful, and "foreign" competitor over which they have questionable leverage. Finally, there is the question of whether or not the Dominican people would accept it. Is it fair and politically convenient for a community residing overseas to yield so much power over a territory that is, in most cases, thousands of miles away? Many overseas Dominicans left their country years ago, while others, who were taken out as children, do not even remember "their" country. They do not pay taxes or endure the daily struggle of survival of the majority of the Dominican people. (However, it can be counter-argued that they contribute a disproportionate amount of resources to the nation.)

Transmigrants and Dominican Identity

Finally, the existence and massive growth of a transnational Dominican community has, and will likely continue to, influence a redefinition of Dominican identity. So far, the definition of identity (or identities) in the Dominican Republic has taken the form of the traditional contest between popular forms or definitions of identity and elite-created representations of Dominican identity. The existence of a large Dominican overseas population adds a new and influential player to this configuration. As a result of the transmigrants' influence—and the penetration of global capitalism in the Dominican Republic—Dominican culture is now more "Americanized" and "globalized" than ever. Dominican transmigrants have acted as a conduit for American products and cultural norms, which have been mediated by the individuals' own experiences and by those receiving them back in the Dominican Republic.

For example, Dominican Spanish (as is also the case throughout the Hispanic Caribbean) contains an inordinate amount of English words and Anglicisms, a result of American cultural penetration, which is facilitated by the returnees. The Dominican marketplace is controlled by American consumer products. American brand names are common in Dominican households. Hitherto unknown American traditions such as Halloween and Thanksgiving—and their commercialization by businesses—are increasingly popular among the Dominican youth. Even traditional racial perceptions of Dominican "whiteness" are being challenged by a transnational population that has suffered in its own flesh the sting of racism in the United States (see Duany 1998). Different social expectations regarding the role of government, accountability, efficiency, and competitiveness are also being brought back by economically successful transmigrants. Finally, globalization has become the "catchword" of Dominican politicians when talking about the country's future. Some are now actively promoting their own brand of globalization by signing free trade accords with neighboring countries to remove trade barriers.

These are rather recent developments that force us to reexamine Dominican identity in the light of an increasingly transnational nation-state. Moreover, the long-standing concept of citizenship has lost some of its original meaning as a result of transmigration. According to Laguerre, "Citizenship was once defined to meet the needs of the residents of Athens, then to meet the needs of the nationals in the era of the bound nation-state; now it needs to be redefined to take stock of globalization, transnational processes, and the porous nature of the modern nation-state" (1998, 7). Dominican citizenship is no longer the legal straitjacket that the dictator Trujillo used to control his subjects. Nowadays it has become one of the many tools that Dominican transnationals use to negotiate different, and sometimes overlapping, jurisdictions among several nation-states. If Dominican migrants are now "transnationals," then traditional Dominican citizenship has now become "diasporic citizenship."[10]

Still, there remains the issue of recalcitrant, reactionary nationalism. Dominican identity has traditionally been shaped by its elites in ultranationalist terms, usually in the face of undue external influences. Thus, Dominican nationality is typically expressed in anti-Haitian, and sometimes, even in anti-American terms. Already, some right-wing Dominican intellectuals are questioning the foreign values and norms being brought home by returnees, and the influence of U.S. popular culture spreading into the country in the form of movies, cable TV programs, and music (Núñez 1990). The Dominican overseas population is also often portrayed as rude, ostentatious, and prone to criminal activities. Crude stereotypes of Americanized Dominican-Yorks are common in the Dominican Republic, such as the *cadenú* (for their bold display of many gold chains) and the *yo* (for their hip-hop dress styles). The recently rising crime wave in the Dominican Republic is also being attributed to the massive repatriation of Dominicans convicted of serious crimes in the United States.[11] Thus, the increasing political power of overseas Dominicans might well lead to a counter-reaction by "establishment" politicians, with the support or indifference of large sectors of the Dominican people. The potential political clout of Dominican transmigrants looms as a menacing shadow over the traditional power bases of Dominican politicians, and the preservation of their interests and privileges.

Another important obstacle is the relative power of the overseas communities vis-à-vis the Dominican state. The overseas population is by no means a monolithic entity with a single, common agenda. It is rather a large mass with a few voices, divided by ideological, class, gender, and geographical cleavages. Political activists overseas—just like in Dominican society—are few, and usually belong to (or sympathize with) one of the three major Dominican political parties. Moreover, political participation involves certain costs, which most poor migrants cannot afford in their daily struggle to make ends meet. Thus, political activism is usually the realm of the educated and the well-to-do migrants. In the case of Dominican transmigrants, professionals (e.g., lawyers, doctors, community organizations' staff) and businessmen (e.g., supermarket owners) are its two most visible components. Dominican professional and business associations in overseas communities are the major contributors to Dominican political campaigns and many of their members are also active in U.S. local politics.[12] Also, just like in the Dominican Republic, political participation among transnational Dominicans is a predominantly male activity, with females playing mostly marginal roles. Finally, though most overseas Dominicans reside in the New York City metropolitan area, there are dozens of Dominican leaders elsewhere, representing thousands of Dominican transmigrants.

In contrast, the Dominican state is a powerful, unified force. Given the centrality of the president as the axis of the state, the Dominican state usually acts with a single voice regarding policymaking and its overseas population. In spite of the transmigrants' political leverage and economic resources, change has come slowly and only when the Dominican political elites have allowed it, such as the case of the 1994 constitutional modifications. While most of the pressure for change has come from the bottom of the political system, change has only been possible with the rare acquiescence of the Dominican elites at the top. It seems very unlikely that the Dominican overseas communities will ever match their power, so change, whenever it takes place, will most likely come from the top down, or "transnationalization from above," as Guarnizo (2001, 214) calls it.

Conclusion

The transnationalization of Dominican politics has important implications for transnationalism theory and other transmigratory experiences. First, as Pamela Graham (1996) has suggested, there is a clear economic basis to the incorporation of Dominican transmigrants into the politics of their nation of origin. Neither ideological nor nationalist appeals proved to be effective tools in influencing the Dominican political elites to concede extraterritorial political rights to Dominican transmigrants. Obviously it was the transmigrants' economic leverage, plus their connections to local U.S. politics, that ultimately forced Dominican politicians to deliver on their long-standing promises. Second, the apparent deterritorialization of Dominican politics should make us reconsider traditional conceptions of the nation-state as a bound territory (particularly when dealing with insular states where the national territory is clearly defined). Nowadays, boundaries seem to have blurred and national jurisdictions overlap. States make extraterritorial claims on their subjects and have even expanded the definition of whom may be considered a citizen. Still, we must not forget that most states are still immersed in traditional conceptions of sovereignty and nationalistic pride, and what may seem a concession to transmigrants could be just an acknowledgment of an economic reality. Finally, the Dominican case shows how selective, and paradoxical, the application of these new concepts of "diasporic citizenship" could be. For example, while the Dominican state expands its concept of citizenship to include its overseas transmigrant communities, the recognition of the Dominican citizenship of children of Haitian ancestry still raises major objections among the Dominican political elites (Cedeño 1992). This selective, and exclusionary, application of jus soli contradicts and calls into question its otherwise new, inclusionary transnational nature.[13]

The Dominican nation-state now finds itself at a crossroads: in the face of globalizing trends, and with a vulnerable, dependent economy penetrated by U.S. capitalism, its political class still clings fiercely to traditional conceptions of nationalism, sovereignty, and political autonomy. The Dominican economy has undergone deep transformations since the 1960s, and it is on an seemingly irreversible path toward more openness and integration with the external world. These rapid transformations have caused acute internal economic dislocations, propelling thousands of Dominicans to seek a better life elsewhere. In spite of these rapid and profound economic changes, and the progressive political stewardship that they demand, political change has been slow to come.

The Dominican political system is still deeply mired in the politics of caudilloism, authoritarianism, and clientelism. It is still to be seen if this upcoming generation of political leaders will update and liberalize the system, making it more responsive to meet the demands of the global economy. This contradiction has permitted, though also retarded, the political incorporation of overseas Dominicans. The recurrent economic crisis in the Dominican Republic, coupled with the transmigrants' relative economic success overseas, allowed the latter to play a larger role in their sending society and to demand (re)incorporation. The traditional political classes have tried to resist these pressures, but see their position weakened by the country's increasing dependency on remittances. The transmigrants' political space looks like the proverbial crack in the dam, which the Dominican political elites have tried to contain.

It is at this critical juncture that overseas Dominicans can force a de jure deterritorialization of the Dominican nation-state (since it is being de facto deterritorialized). The Dominican elites' nationalism, with its traditional definition of the nation-state, which excludes overseas populations, is still a very powerful force, but with a weak foundation. In the face of a continuing economic crisis with no simple solution in sight, increasing emigration, and a political system that has run out of options and is no longer responsive to—and representative of—the needs of the people, a well-organized overseas population can achieve significant gains in the Dominican political space. As in other Latin American countries, the Dominican political system seems to be deadlocked. Baffled by the neoliberal structural adjustment policies, Dominican politicians have few practical options to offer to their constituencies. With decreasing credibility for traditional politicians and policies, the Dominican political system is ripe for deep transformations, thus offering overseas Dominicans an opening to further their own political agendas.

Eventually, if these deterritorializing trends continue, the Dominican nation-state will undergo a major redefinition. The role that its transnational population will play in this process will depend on the transmigrants' level of political organization, its leverage vis-à-vis the Dominican ruling elites, and its continuing role in helping bail out the ailing Dominican economy.

Notes

1. In June 1999, the Dominican Republic's Junta Central Electoral (Central Electoral Board, or JCE) determined that—for logistical reasons and lack of time—overseas voting could not be implemented in time for the 2000 presidential elections.

2. In spite of the fact that Haitian migration does not represent a veritable historical diaspora (as in the case of the Jewish people), the term "diaspora" is widely used by Haitian leaders to refer to Haiti's overseas population. Some scholars and overseas Dominican political leaders, as well as the general public, are already starting to use it to refer to the Dominican case (see note 1 in chapter 1).

3. For a recent reassessment of transnationalism theory, see Glick Schiller 1999.

4. This process has not been so even, though. There were economic immigrants from the Dominican Republic in the past, just like there are political exiles today, though more infrequently (e.g., former Customs director Anisia Rissi, who was barred by the Balaguer administration from reentering the country). By the same token, not all Dominican migrants can be characterized as transnational.

5. Only 1,150 Dominicans were legally admitted into the United States during the 1930s, 5,627 during the 1940s, and 9,987 during the 1950s. In contrast, 93,292 Dominicans were admitted into the United States during the 1960s (U.S. Immigration and Naturalization Service 1997, 27).

6. When dealing with semi-authoritarian regimes, such as Balaguer's twelve-year rule (1966–1978), it is often difficult to distinguish between purely "political" and purely "economic" reasons for explaining migration, as they often overlap. Political repression during *los doce años* (Balaguer's twelve years), and an exclusionary, dependent economic model, were both powerful incentives for Dominican migrants.

7. See Graham 1996 for an in-depth study of the insertion of Dominicans into U.S. politics.

8. For example, the U.S. Democratic Party now has a representative in the Dominican Republic. The designee, Leo Pérez Minaya, was appointed to register and organize U.S. citizens living in the Dominican Republic (who presumably include a large number of Dominican-Americans), so they could vote during the 2000 U.S. elections and beyond (*El Siglo* 1999b). This is the first time that a U.S. political party has appointed a representative in a foreign country, and is a good example of the transnational nature of contemporary politics, which now operates within several national jurisdictions.

9. The PLD was founded in 1973 after Juan Bosch left the PRD with a group of disgruntled followers.

10. Laguerre (1998, 12–13) defines it as "the situation of the individual who lives outside the boundaries of the nation-state to which he or she had formerly held primary allegiance and who experiences through transnational migration (or the redesigning of the homeland boundaries) the subjective reality of belonging to two or more nation-states."

11. Though the Fernández administration was careful in not blaming the rising crime wave on the deportees, police chief General Pedro de Jesús Candelier publicly affirmed that deportees were involved in most major crimes.

12. There is also the perennial debate over whether the overseas population is withering its power by concentrating on Dominican issues and elections, instead of focusing solely on the politics of the country where these transmigrants reside.

13. Jus soli is the right of individuals to the citizenship of the nation in whose territory they are born, and is the citizenship principle used by the Dominican Constitution (República Dominicana 1994, 15)

References

Banco Central de la República Dominicana. 2001. *Balanza de pagos de la República Dominicana, 1995–2000*. Santo Domingo: Banco Central.

Basch, Linda, Nina Glick Schiller, and Cristina Szanton Blanc. 1994. *Nations Unbound: Transnational Projects, Postcolonial Predicaments, and Deterritorialized Nation-States*. Langhorne, Pa.: Gordon and Breach.

Cedeño, Carmen. 1992. "La nacionalidad de los descendientes de haitianos nacidos en la República Dominicana." In *La cuestión haitiana en Santo Domingo: Migración internacional, desarrollo, y relaciones inter-estatales entre Haití y República Dominicana,* ed. Wilfredo Lozano. Santo Domingo: FLACSO.

Congreso Nacional de la República Dominicana. 1997. "Ley Electoral, No. 275–97." *Gaceta Oficial* 9970: 3–79.

Duany, Jorge. 1998. "Reconstructing Racial Identity: Ethnicity, Color, and Class among Dominicans in the United States and Puerto Rico." *Latin American Perspectives* 25(3): 147–72.

Fisher, Ian. 1996. "A Dominican Leader Receives an Official Embrace." *New York Times,* October 5, 27.

Glick Schiller, Nina. 1999. "Transmigrants and Nation-States: Something Old and Something New in the U.S. Immigrant Experience." In *The Handbook of International Migration: The American Experience,* ed. Charles Hirschman, Philip Kasinitz, and Josh DeWind. New York: Russell Sage Foundation.

Glick Schiller, Nina, Linda Basch, and Cristina Blanc-Szanton. 1992. "Transnationalism: A New Analytic Framework for Understanding Migration." In *Towards a Transnational Perspective on Migration: Race, Class, Ethnicity, and Nationalism Reconsidered,* ed. Nina Glick Schiller, Linda Basch, and Cristina Blanc-Szanton. New York: New York Academy of Sciences.

Graham, Pamela M. 1996. "Defining the District and Re-imagining the Nation: Transnational Political Practices among Dominican Migrants." Ph.D. diss., University of North Carolina, Chapel Hill.

———. 1998. "The Politics of Incorporation: Dominicans in New York City." *Latino Studies Journal* 9(3): 39–64.

Guarnizo, Luis E. 2001. "On the Political Participation of Transnational Migrants: Old Practices and New Trends." In *E Pluribus Unum?: Contemporary and Historical Perspectives on Immigrant Political Incorporation,* ed. Gary Gerstle and John Mollenkopf. New York: Russell Sage Foundation.

Laguerre, Michel S. 1997. "The Role of the Diaspora in Haitian Politics." In *Haiti Renewed: Political and Economic Perspectives,* ed. Robert I. Rotberg. Washington, D.C.: Brookings Institution Press.

———. 1998. *Diasporic Citizenship: Haitian Americans in Transnational America.* New York: St. Martin's Press.

Mateo, Nicolás. 2002. "Dominicanos del exterior quieren representación en Congreso Nacional." *El Nacional,* March 24.

Migration News. 1998. "Remittances: Dominican Republic." Electronic document. http://migration.ucdavis.edu/Data/remit.on.www.DomRep.html

Núñez, Manuel. 1990. *El ocaso de la nación dominicana.* Santo Domingo: Alfa y Omega.

Peña Brito, Arelis. 2002. "En Miami sólo se registran 30 dominicanos en oficina JCE." *Última Hora,* April 9.

Redacción Listín U.S.A. 1994. "Nueva York: Importante plaza para partidos." *Listín U.S.A.*, March 2–8, 16.

República Dominicana. Asamblea Nacional. 1994. *Constitución de la República Dominicana.* Santo Domingo: Editora El Estudiante.

Reyes, Leo. 2001. "Cancillería bloquea proyecto crea secretaría." *El Siglo,* August 15.

Richman, Karen. 1992. "A *Lavalas* at Home/A *Lavalas* for Home: Inflections of Transnationalism in the Discourse of Haitian President Aristide." In *Towards a Transnational Perspective on Migration: Race, Class, Ethnicity, and Nationalism Reconsidered,* ed. Nina Glick Schiller, Linda Basch, and Cristina Blanc-Szanton. New York: New York Academy of Sciences.

Rodríguez de León, Francisco. 1998. *El furioso merengue del norte: Una historia de la comunidad dominicana en los Estados Unidos.* New York: n.p.

Rohter, Larry. 1996. "New York Dominicans Strongly Back Candidates on Island." *New York Times,* June 29, 21, 24.

El Siglo. 1999a. "Casi 2.4 millones de dominicanos reciben remesas desde EU y otros países." November 17.

———. 1999b. "Dominicano organizará aquí ciudadanos de EEUU." December 2.

U.S. Immigration and Naturalization Service. 2003. *2002 Statistical Yearbook of the Immigration and Naturalization Service.* Washington, D.C.: U.S. Government Printing Office.

4

Dominicans in Providence

The Formation of a Transnational Community in a Secondary City

José Itzigsohn

Providence is an old New England city. Part of the region that was the cradle of the American Industrial Revolution, Providence was transformed in the twentieth century into a secondary city in the shadow of the major cities of the Northeast, particularly Boston, its close neighbor to the north. Providence is not a place that comes to mind when thinking of contemporary immigration and emerging transnational communities. Its image is either that of an old "Yankee" city or one formed by Italian and Irish migration.[1] Yet, in the last thirty years, Providence has undergone rapid change owing to the influx of immigrants from the Caribbean, Latin America, East Asia, and West Africa. Today, the city is a mirror of the multiethnic and multicultural trends that are changing the face of this nation. The influx of Dominicans has inserted Providence in circuits of movements of people, information, and goods that involve the Dominican Republic, New York, and other cities such as Miami. These circuits have something to do with the position of the city in the local economy, but mostly they are the result of the creation of these migration-related transnational networks.

In the last two decades, Dominicans have been one of the largest immigrant groups in the United States. While most Dominican immigration is concentrated in New York, there is an increasingly larger Dominican presence in numerous other U.S. states and cities (Torres-Saillant and Hernández 1998). Providence is one of those places. Dominican immigrants are changing the face of Providence. From Spanish language radio, through political campaigns for city and statewide offices, to an annual festival that congregates more than thirty thousand people, Dominicans are leaving a profound imprint on the everyday life of the city.

The study of migration is undergoing change. Previously, scholars studying immigration concentrated on the process of acculturation/assimilation. Today, scholars know that this process is not unidirectional. Immigrants do no completely sever their ties to their country of origin. On the contrary, they create complex webs of institutions and practices that link the country of origin with the country of reception; in other words, they create transnational communities (Foner 1997; Glick Schiller 2000; Portes, Guarnizo, and Landolt 1999). More precisely, transnational communities link particular places in the countries of origin and reception (Kyle 1999; Levitt 1998; Popkin 1999; Smith 1998). Transnational communities, however, exist through a number of concrete practices, institutions, and discourses (Itzigsohn and Giorguli Saucedo 2002; Itzigsohn et al. 1999). In order to understand the structure and dynamics of transnational communities we need to focus our research attention on the social practices and institutions that sustain and renew them.

This chapter describes and analyzes the formation of the Dominican community in Providence, Rhode Island. This is a community that is putting down roots in the city while simultaneously maintaining tight linkages with the Dominican Republic. The chapter has three parts; the first part focuses on the process of Dominicans' incorporation into Providence's social and economic life. It presents a brief review of the history of Dominicans in Providence, and it looks at their insertion in the local economy and at the way they experience this process of incorporation. The second part focuses on the social practices and linkages that sustain the transnational community. It analyzes a number of social practices that link Dominicans in Providence to the Dominican Republic. The third part focuses on the formation of local and transnational cultural discourses and practices of identity. This part focuses on the cultural and political activities of a particular Dominican organization through which we can glance at the local and transnational character of the identity building process.

The data for this analysis come from three main sources: first, the data provided by the 1990 census and other reports on population and the economy in Providence; second, a survey of Dominican immigrants conducted in the south side of town, the area with the largest concentration of Dominicans, in the winter and spring of 1997–1998;[2] finally, ethnographic interviews that I conducted and my own participation in community activities and community life. This chapter, then, portrays the complexity of the process of transnational community building. It looks at how this process unfolds in a secondary city, one that is generally not thought of in contemporary analyses of migration, but that has become immersed in dense transnational spaces created by the numerous immigrant groups that live in it.

History and Incorporation of Dominicans in Providence

Dominicans began to arrive to Providence in the late 1960s and early 1970s. The first Dominican immigrants to Providence recount that they found a quiet place, with affordable housing and plenty of jobs in manufacturing. As families began arriving in the city, networking mechanisms kicked in and the city became a viable destination for Dominicans. There were not many Latinos then in Providence and Dominicans tell of efforts to convince family, friends, and acquaintances to come to live in this town. These early migrants tell how they were received and helped by the families that were already in Providence. These families hosted them until they could afford housing and helped them find jobs in local factories. At that time, Providence afforded newcomers plenty of opportunity for employment in manufacturing. Employers asked workers to bring their acquaintances to work for them and it was relatively easy to obtain immigration papers.[3] Still, during the 1970s there was only a very small Dominican presence in Providence. The 1980 census recorded Dominicans only as foreign born. In Rhode Island, there were then 1,905 Dominicans born in the Dominican Republic, two-thirds of whom arrived between 1970 and 1980.

Dominican immigrants began to arrive in large numbers in Providence only in the mid-1980s and the 1990s. The 1980s saw the emergence of the first Dominican social and cultural clubs. It was during this decade that the Broad Street area, although a multiethnic area, came to be associated with Dominican immigration. Dominican small businesses began to open up on the main streets of that area, particularly Broad Street itself, transforming a part of town that had been abandoned by mainstream businesses. Also those years saw the emergence of Spanish radio in Providence and, in 1987, the first Dominican festival took place. This event has been conducted every year since and currently attracts more than thirty thousand people to a day of celebration of Dominican identity and pride. During that decade, numerous churches in town began to offer services in Spanish and became an important center of sociability for the community.

The 1980s were indeed years of community consolidation. The 1990 census recorded the presence of 7,973 Dominicans in Providence and 9,374 in Rhode Island. Most Dominicans in the city, 70.4 percent, were foreign born, 15.6 percent were born in Rhode Island, and 11.6 percent were born in a different U.S. state (presumably New York). These numbers, which are considered to be an underestimation of the real presence of Dominicans in the city, constituted about 5 percent of the population of the city and close to 1 percent of the population of the state. The 1990s saw further growth and strengthening of the Dominican institutions in Providence. Cultural, social,

Table 4.1. 1990 Selected Income, Labor Market, and Poverty Data by Race/Ethnicity for Providence

	Median household income ($)	Labor force participation (percentage)	Unemployment (percentage)	Manufacturing (percentage)	Families below poverty line (percentage)
All Providence	22,147	60.5	9.2	24.1	18.3
Dominicans	17,538	68.4	17.4	57.4	38.5
Latinos	16,848	67.3	15.0	53.9	29.3
Whites (non-Hispanic)	24,828	64.5	14.2	26.7	29.1
Blacks (non-Hispanic)	17,813	59.3	6.8	24.1	12.0

Source: 1990 U.S. Census.

and sporting organizations now have a visible presence in the everyday life of the community. The economic upswing of the last part of the 1990s brought the emergence of numerous Dominican small businesses mainly in the Broad Street area, but also all around town. The last decade also saw the rise of the first attempts at Dominican and Latino political organization in the American political system.

The 2000 census shows that 90,820 Latinos live in Rhode Island, out of which 52,146 live in Providence, constituting 30 percent of the population of the city. The population of the city and the state has remained stable for the last ten years. Yet the stability in numbers conceals a process of change in the ethnic composition: white ethnics have moved out of the city to the suburbs or out of the state and have been replaced mainly by immigrants, in particular Latino and East Asian immigrants. The 2000 census indicates that Providence is currently a minority-majority city. The number of Dominicans living in the city is 14,638, and it is estimated that they are the largest group among Latino immigrants in the state. Community activists estimate that the current Dominican population in the state is more than twice that of ten years ago.

In spite of this constant growth of the presence and strength of community institutions, the incorporation of Dominicans in the Providence socioeconomic system follows the old pattern in which a new immigrant group finds a niche at the bottom of the labor market queues. Table 4.1 portrays the socioeconomic position of Dominicans in Providence and Rhode Island in 1990. The table shows that Dominicans, as well as Latinos, were then concentrated in the manufacturing sector. Dominicans have the highest rate of labor force participation[4] among the different groups in Providence. They had twice as many families below the poverty line and double the unemployment rate of the general population of the city.

Many things have changed in the last ten years and we will not know the shape of the city's socioeconomic structure until the complete publication of the detailed results of the 2000 census. We have, however, partial information on employment from a survey of Dominican immigrants conducted in the city in the winter and spring of 1997–1998. The survey was conducted in the southern neighborhoods of the city, which are those that are most heavily populated by Dominicans. The goal of the survey was to investigate transnational practices and institutions among Dominicans. The survey encompassed 159 respondents. Slightly more than half of the respondents (86 cases or 54.1 percent) were chosen randomly while the rest were chosen through "snowball" chains designed to locate people involved in transnational activities in the economic, political, or social field. The survey, then, is not representative, yet it provides a glimpse of the lives of Dominicans in the city.

Table 4.2 provides a look at the occupational trajectories of Dominicans in the United States. The table presents the occupation of the respondents before migration, the first occupation they had in the United States, and the current occupation. The latter is presented for the sample as a whole and for the randomly drawn sub-sample. This is so because the purposive part of the sample deliberately oversampled self-employed people and small business owners. Concerning the occupation before migration, the table shows a wide dispersion. The modal category is those that did not work abroad, or at least did not work formally. Three quarters of this group are women. The table shows that the main form of incorporation in the American labor market is as a laborer. Indeed, this was the first occupation for 99 respondents, almost two-thirds of the sample. Laborer was the first occupation for 60.4 percent of the men in the sample and 64.7 percent of the women.

Laborer is still the largest occupation for the respondents in the sample. Its proportion goes down to 35.2 percent for the whole sample, but this is due to the biases introduced by the snowball segment of the survey. When we look at the random sample segment, 55.8 percent of the respondents are laborers and 15.1 percent are out of work. These numbers are very similar to those of the 1990 census, suggesting that the overall position of Dominicans in the socioeconomic structure of the city may not have changed that much in the period between the 1990 census and the survey.

Moreover, immigrants who arrived in the 1970s report that in the earlier period they could expect to have occupational stability and mobility within the factories where they were working. In the 1990s, however, the remaining manufacturing jobs,[5] as well as many of the emerging services jobs, were mediated by employment agencies, meaning that workers that incorporate to the labor market cannot expect job stability or career mobility. Many of the "old timers" who lost their jobs were forced to go back to work for much lower salaries and no benefits.

Table 4.2. Occupation Abroad, First Occupation in the United States, and Current Occupation of Dominicans in Providence

	Occupation abroad	First occupation in the U.S.	Current occupation (total sample)	Current occupation (random sample)
Not working	43 (27.0)	10 (6.3)	14 (8.8)	13 (15.1)
Laborer	23 (14.5)	99 (62.3)	56 (35.2)	48 (55.8)
Sales or office worker	4 (2.5)	2 (1.3)	2 (1.3)	1 (1.1)
Foreman or supervisor	3 (1.9)	—	—	—
Administrator of a business or farm	3 (1.9)	3 (1.9)	8 (5.0)	—
Technician	11 (6.9)	6 (3.8)	6 (3.8)	3 (3.4)
Salaried professional	35 (22.0)	10 (6.3)	22 (13.8)	10 (11.6)
Independent professional	9 (5.7)	4 (2.5)	12 (7.5)	2 (2.3)
Owner of a business, firm or farm	4 (2.5)	3 (1.9)	31 (19.5)	7 (8.1)
Self-employed	5 (3.1)	1 (0.6)	8 (5.0)	2 (2.3)
No data	19 (11.9)	21 (13.2)	—	—
Total	159 (100.0)	159 (100.0)	159 (100.0)	86 (100.0)

This, however, is not the whole story. In the sample we see a rise in business ownership and in salaried professionals vis-à-vis the first occupation column. This suggests the presence of a process of social mobility for at least part of the Dominican community. If our data reflect the actual trends, what we are witnessing then is a process of internal stratification within the community, where the majority is locked in declining manufacturing jobs or low-wage service jobs, but there is an important segment that experiences upward mobility, a process of mobility that takes place through entrepreneurship or education. The process of internal stratification is also seen very clearly in educational attainment: on the one hand, there is an increasing number of local Dominican students in the state universities and colleges, and, on the other hand, a persistent number of high school dropouts.

The rising Dominican middle class is composed of professionals such as lawyers and medical doctors, and people who find employment in the public sector as teachers, social workers, and public workers in general. Increasing internal stratification has not led, or at least has not yet led, to social polarization and the creation of separate class-oriented social and spatial niches. Some middle-class Dominicans move away from areas densely populated by Dominicans, but many professionals and small business people still reside in parts of town that have large numbers of Dominicans. The small businesses that exist cater mostly to the community. This helps create an ethnic economy of sorts, providing some jobs to new arrivals and guaranteeing that some of the money spent in those businesses returns to the community. Many of the young professionals keep in touch with the community through their work in the public sector—mostly schools, social services, and nonprofit community agencies—and an important number are involved in community cultural, social, and political organizations.

There is no way to tell which form the process of internal class differentiation will take in the future. Perhaps once the Dominican-American middle class feels secure in its economic position and confident enough in its class identity it will create its own separate social niches. For the time being, however, increasing internal stratification has led to an increase in the resources available to the community and hence to its strengthening.

The survey also presents a complex picture concerning the way in which Dominican immigrants experience this process of incorporation. A majority of those interviewed, 59.7 percent, believes that they have received enough opportunities in the United States and 57.2 percent responded that their occupation fits their education and aptitude. These results suggest that Dominican immigrants are content with the evolution of their incorporation to this country. Nevertheless, only 40.9 percent affirm that their current occupation fits their initial aspirations and only one-third expressed satisfaction with their current income. Moreover, almost two-thirds of the sample believe that there is discrimination in economic opportunities in the United States: 37.7 percent report having experienced discrimination and 57.7 percent believe that Dominicans are discriminated against in the United States. So the survey data present a picture of mixed attitudes concerning the position of Dominicans in American society. On the one hand, respondents indicate recognition of the opportunities offered by this country, on the other, they express frustration with truncated upward mobility and perceptions of discrimination against the group.

The survey also provides two other pieces of information relevant for our discussion. First, for half of our sample, Providence was their first place of destination in the United States, suggesting that migration to secondary cities is no longer dependent on the movement of people out of New York. Moreover, ethnographic observation suggests the beginning of a migration movement from Providence to South Florida, in search of better climate and/or better employment opportunities. We do not know yet the size of this movement, but it also suggests a community geography in which New York still maintains a central place, but through which not all the population flows. Second, the survey indicates that one-third of the respondents have children in the Dominican Republic. This shows that for a large number of immigrants, family relations straddle both countries, pointing to the transnational character of the Dominican community in Providence.

Finally, an important aspect of the process of incorporation of immigrants is political participation and Dominicans are beginning to establish their presence on the Rhode Island political map. After many years of relative apathy toward the American political process, the first Dominican elected official, León Tejada, was voted in as state representative in the 2000 elections. He ran on a platform of promotion of youth activities, education, and economic development in the southern part of the city. This is a part of the city that in the last decade has been revitalized through the efforts of immigrant entrepreneurs but that still suffers from social problems that are the result of the low incomes earned by most of the population of the area. Tejada was elected because Latinos sensed the need to achieve political representation. In both the primaries and the general elections of 2000 Latinos had a higher participation rate than the general population, becoming an important political force in the city and the state.

In the Democratic primaries of that year another two Dominicans competed for elected positions. One of them, Juan Pichardo, was a candidate for the state senate and lost the election owing only to the results of the mail-in ballots. The other one, Angel Taveras, ran in the primary for a congressional position and although he arrived only third, he performed much better than expected, gathering about 12 percent of the vote, a result that transformed him into an important political actor in the state. The three Dominican candidates that ran in the 2000 Democratic primaries presented themselves as Latino candidates as well as Dominican and the three of them asserted that they ran to represent their whole constituencies rather than just the Latino or the Dominican population. Nevertheless, the three received most of their votes from the Latino population. Moreover, the Latino population in the area in which they ran is majority Dominican.

The Dominican Transnational Community

Currently there is increasing consensus among scholars that immigration is not a unidirectional process. Immigrants indeed acculturate and create new lives and identities in their host countries, but they also maintain multifaceted ties with their countries of origin. They establish webs of social relations that cut across national borders, creating in this way transnational spaces of social interaction (Basch, Glick Schiller, and Szanton Blanc 1994; Laguerre 1999; Levitt 1998). These ties vary in the degree of commitment that they demand from people and in their degree of institutionalization, but they affect the daily life of large segments of immigrant communities. The structure and institutional shape of these transnational linkages, however, has not been sufficiently studied. Transnational communities are created and sustained by the practices of immigrants in conducting their everyday lives. We do not know, however, what sort of transnational practices are more common, nor how involved is the community in the different transnational practices and institutions (Itzigsohn and Giorguli Saucedo 2002; Itzigsohn et al., 1999; Mahler 1995). This section attempts to map a series of social practices that form the transnational aspect of Dominican community building in Providence. The sources for this analysis are the 1997–1998 survey and my own participant observation in many of these activities.

Before reaching the core of the analysis, however, I need to specify my approach to the study of the immigrant transnational fields. For the purposes of the present work, it is useful to distinguish between two opposing views of transnational communities and practices. On the one hand, some scholars have focused on those immigrants who are intensely involved in businesses or political activities both in the country of origin and the country of reception (Portes 1996). On the other hand, other scholars have focused on a broad array of everyday social practices and identity formations that have symbolic references that transcend national boundaries (Basch, Glick Schiller, and Szanton Blanc 1994). In a previous paper, my colleagues and I suggested that these two approaches are complementary rather than contradictory, and proposed to bridge the gap between them through a differentiation between narrow and broad transnational practices (Itzigsohn et al. 1999). Broad and narrow transnational practices were conceptualized as

> two poles of a continuum defined by the degree of institutionalization, degree of movement within the transnational field, or the degree of involvement in transnational activities. Transnationality in a "narrow" sense refers to those people involved in economic, political, social, or cultural practices that involve a regular movement within the geographic transnational field, a high level of institutionalization, or constant personal involvement. Transnationality in a "broad" sense refers to a series of material and symbolic practices in which people engage that involve only sporadic physical movement between the two countries, a low level of institutionalization, or just occasional personal involvement, but nevertheless includes both countries as reference points. (Itzigsohn et al. 1999, 323)

The purpose of this differentiation was to maintain an inclusive definition of the transnational communities while proposing a conceptual framework to distinguish different degrees of involvement in the transnational social field. The 1997–1998 survey conducted among Dominican immigrants in

Providence included several questions about transnational practices in different areas of social life and also questioned the degree of involvement of people in these practices. Hence, it allows us to describe and analyze the prevalence of these transnational practices among Dominican immigrants in Providence. We saw above, for example, that about one-third of the sample has children living in the Dominican Republic, meaning that for an important segment of the community family life is split between the two countries. For analytical purposes, this section differentiates between the economic, political, and sociocultural transnational practices that tie Dominicans in Providence to the Dominican Republic.

Economic Transnational Practices

The transnational entrepreneur—that is, the person involved in business activities in both the home and receiving country—was the social actor that was at the center of Portes's initial reflections on transnationalism (1996).[6] These transnational economic activities are those that correspond to our view of narrow transnationalism: they demand regular movement between the two places and constant participation, yet their degree of institutionalization can be low. Table 4.3 looks at this type of narrow economic transnationalism. The table focuses on people who have taken goods from the United States to sell in the Dominican Republic or who bring goods from the Dominican Republic to sell in the United States. Table 4.3 shows that only a small fraction of the community engage in "full time" transnational entrepreneurship. This result is even stronger given the fact that we biased the sampling procedure to include this type of entrepreneurial activity. A somehow larger percentage engage in these practices in a sporadic way—that is, in a broader form of transnationalism—but most of the community does not engage in this form of narrow transnational entrepreneurship.

The picture changes when we look at practices that demand less movement or participation from people, that is, at broader transnational practices.

Table 4.3. Indicators of Narrow Economic Transnational Practices

Type of Activity	Degree of Involvement		
	Never	Once in a while	Regularly
Taken goods from the U.S. to sell in the Dominican Republic	132 (83.0)	19 (12.2)	5 (3.1)
Brought goods from the Dominican Republic	139 (87.4)	15 (9.4)	3 (1.9)

Table 4.4. Indicators of Broad Economic Transnational Practices

	Yes	No
Send remittances to the Dominican Republic	119 (74.8)	38 (23.9)
Own real estate in the Dominican Republic	60 (37.7)	90 (56.6)

Table 4.4 looks at people who send remittances to or own property in the Dominican Republic. Almost three-quarters of the sample send money back to the Dominican Republic and 40.3 percent of the sample send money once a month or more. Indeed, remittances have become one of the most important sources of livelihood for the people in the Dominican Republic and many families depend on the money sent by their relatives abroad (Itzigsohn 1995). As we saw previously, about one-third of the sample has children there and probably a larger percentage has parents or siblings there. The amounts sent vary considerably, 23.3 percent of the sample report sending between U.S.$100 and U.S.$500 a year, 11.3 percent send between U.S.$500 and U.S.$1,000, 18.9 percent send between U.S.$1,000 and U.S.$3,000, and 8.1 percent send more than U.S.$3,000 a year per person.

Sending remittances is probably the most widespread transnational activity. Although it demands the commitment of the immigrant toward his or her family abroad, it does not demand the mobility of the immigrant between the two countries or a high degree of institutionalization. Most remittances are sent through formal certified agencies. Some remittance-sending agencies are Dominican owned, and in that sense they are part of the narrow transnational economic practices described above; other agencies are local business that work with large international money-wiring companies (such as Western Union).

Table 4.4 also indicates that close to 40 percent of the sample own property in the Dominican Republic. Qualitative interviews suggest that this property is in most cases purchased by immigrants thinking about returning at retirement time. In the meantime, the property is sometimes rented out or occupied by family members. The dreamed-of return happens occasionally, but in many cases the returning immigrants find it hard to adapt to the life they left behind years ago and sometimes they return to the United States (Guarnizo 1997). In some cases, dreams of return are frustrated because immigrants' sons and daughters prefer to stay in the United States and parents do not want to split the family. The dream of return, however, is very powerful in guiding the social behavior of immigrants in the country of reception. Regardless of whether they return to the Dominican Republic or not, many immigrants adjust their savings and investment strategies to correspond with this dream.

Political Transnational Practices

Dominicans are passionate about politics, whether in the Dominican Republic, New York, Providence, or anywhere else. Political discussions are always a topic of conversation and at election time the political parties organize meetings and caravans in the streets of the cities and towns of the Dominican Republic as well as in most cities in the United States in which there is a sizable Dominican presence. The Dominican political parties devote considerable effort to gather electoral and financial support among the immigrant community. Presidential candidates, government officials, and party leaders make a point of visiting the principal communities abroad to establish networks with party members and sympathizers. The financial contributions of the immigrant community are without a doubt important to the political parties (Graham 1997).[7] Political leaders in the Dominican Republic also seem to hold the belief that immigrants can influence the vote of their relatives back home.

Immigrant organizations, in turn, have demanded recognition for their role as part of the Dominican nation. Their pressure was instrumental in obtaining the recognition of dual citizenship and the passage of legislation that gives immigrants the right to vote abroad. This legislation, however, has not yet been implemented. It is currently expected that Dominicans living abroad will be able to vote in the 2004 presidential elections. In other words, the Dominican government recognizes the right to dual citizenship for Dominican immigrants, but has not yet created the institutional mechanism to allow them to exercise their right to vote abroad. The need for remittances, the practices of the political parties, and the pressure of immigrant organizations have led to the creation of a transnational political space in which the nation and its political rights do not coincide with the boundaries of the state (Itzigsohn 2000).

Table 4.5 addresses two forms of political transnational practices: financial contributions to Dominican campaigns and participation in campaigns in support of candidates in Dominican elections. These are activities that arise regularly (i.e., every election cycle), and that, in general, are highly institutionalized since the people that participate in them are members of or linked to Dominican political parties. Hence I consider them closer to the narrow end of the continuum of transnational practices. The table indicates that about a quarter of the sample participates occasionally or regularly in these type of activities. These results are biased, however, by the fact that the

Table 4.5. Indicators of Political Transnational Practices

Type of Activity	Degree of Involvement		
	Never	Once in a while	Regularly
Financial contributions to electoral campaigns in the Dominican Republic	114 (71.7)	24 (15.1)	18 (11.3)
Help organize campaigns in support of candidates in Dominican elections	118 (74.2)	19 (11.9)	21 (13.2)

non-random sub-sample included several political leaders. A look at the randomly drawn sample shows that the proportion that engages regularly or occasionally in these activities is slightly higher than 10 percent of the respondents. The table shows that narrow political transnationalism is slightly more prevalent than narrow economic transnationalism.

Do these numbers indicate a high or a low degree of transnational political participation? It would be interesting to compare these numbers with the percentage of people that engage in these practices in the Dominican Republic. The author, however, does not have these data. Nevertheless, I think that a 10 percent rate of active participation in Dominican politics by people who do not live in the country can be considered a high rate of political participation. There are also a large number of people who do not participate actively in political campaigns in the Dominican Republic, but who do take a strong interest in Dominican politics. Again, as with economic transnationalism, the distinction between broad and narrow transnational political practices proves useful to understand the structure of the transnational community.

We have an interesting example of transnational politics in the person of León Tejada, the recently elected Dominican state representative mentioned in the previous section. A successful local small businessman and now successful local politician, he epitomizes the successful immigration story. Moreover, he is deeply involved in the local political scene and his legislative agenda is oriented toward addressing the problems of his local constituency. Yet, he is also a member of the currently governing party in the Dominican Republic (the Partido Revolucionario Dominicano [Dominican Revolutionary Party], or PRD) and was involved in the party campaign that led to the electoral victory in the presidential elections in 2000. Moreover, upon his election to the Rhode Island state house, he traveled to the Dominican Republic, where he was received by government officials as a Dominican elected official in the United States. This case illustrates the complexity and interwoven character of the processes of immigrant incorporation and transnational community formation.

Sociocultural Transnational Practices

Sociocultural transnationalism refers to those transnational linkages that involve the recreation of a sense of community that encompasses migrants and people in the place of origin. Sociocultural transnationalism concerns the emergence of practices of sociability, mutual help, and public rituals rooted in the cultural understandings that pertain to the sense of belonging and social obligations of immigrants. These practices constitute the backbone of emergent communities without propinquity.

Table 4.6 presents the survey results concerning participation in organizations that support the community of origin, financial contributions to projects in these communities of origin, visits home for local celebrations, membership in sport clubs with links to the Dominican Republic, and involvement with charity organizations with links to the Dominican Republic. These are widespread activities among Dominican immigrants. It is indeed very common among many immigrant groups to find associations of immigrants from a certain town or region that gather to support their place of origin (Landolt 2000; Landolt, Autler, and Baires 1999). In Providence there have been some examples of this type of association, but they have not lasted long (as opposed to New York, for example, where there are stable associations from many Dominicans' towns). The table shows that about a quarter of the sample are involved regularly or occasionally in activities that support their hometowns, while the lower part of the table depicts participation in sport clubs with links to the Dominican Republic or relationships with organizations that engage in charity in the Dominican Republic.

The transnational activities in the upper part of the table demand a certain degree of institutionalization, such as membership in a hometown association, or a certain level of personal mobility to be able to attend the town

Table 4.6. Indicators of Sociocultural Transnational Practices

Type of Activity	Degree of Involvement		
	Never	Once in a while	Regularly
Participate in organizations that support hometown	117 (73.6)	27 (17.0)	14 (8.8)
Send money for projects in hometown	116 (73.0)	29 (18.2)	12 (7.5)
Visit hometown for local celebrations	117 (73.6)	32 (20.1)	7 (4.4)
Member of sports clubs with links to the Dominican Republic	109 (68.6)	28 (17.6)	20 (12.6)
Work with charity organization with links in the Dominican Republic	105 (66.0)	33 (20.8)	19 (11.9)

festivities. In contrast, participation in sport clubs is something that many people (particularly Dominican males) do in their everyday lives. The sport clubs often involve occasional trips to the Dominican Republic to play against other sport clubs with which the members are acquainted. Very rarely do these contacts translate into regular institutional relations. Regarding charity, in most cases it arises in times of natural disasters. An example is the massive relief efforts organized in response to Hurricane Georges in 1998. In these cases, the community organizations mobilize as a group to give a helping hand and there is usually an enormous response. As expected, table 4.6 shows that this is the form of transnational practice that has the widest participation, about 30 percent of the sample.

The previous analysis describes a series of social practices that structure the everyday life of the community, giving to it its transnational character. Overall, between 10 and 30 percent of the sample participates in each of these different transnational practices. This may give the impression of a limited involvement of the community in transnational practices. The survey shows, however, that close to 60 percent of the sample—close to 50 percent if we look only at the random sample—are involved in some form in one or other of these transnational activities. Economic transnationalism in the form of people who conduct regular businesses in both countries is the most limited form of transnational practice, perhaps because this is a practice that demands a high amount of resources. Sociocultural transnationalism is the most widespread form of transnational practice. The tables above portray a community in which there is a wide participation in broad forms of transnationalism, those that do not involve a large personal commitment, a high degree of mobility between places, or a high degree of institutionalization. As we look at more specific and narrow forms of transnationalism, participation in transnational activities declines.

Local and Transnational Identities

This section focuses on the creation of local and transnational cultural discourses and practices that are relevant in the formation of collective and individual identities. These discourses are produced at many sites, including the bureaucratic agencies of the receiving society, the media, and the education system. The Dominican state is involved in the discursive field, appealing to the sentiments of the migrants toward their country of origin. Community organizations and community activists are also engaged in the production of discourses and practices of identity. At any point in time, these different discourses compete with each other to define the identity of the group and gain its allegiance toward that definition and the social practices attached to it.

One of the key sites of production of discourses and practices of identity are the institutions of the ethnic community. The latter are important because they are sites of cultural agency by the immigrant group. That is, immigrant/ethnic organizations are the place in which immigrants are actively involved in the shaping of their culture and identity within the cultural and symbolic order of the receiving country.[8] In this section I focus on the discourses of identity and cultural practices of one community organization. The organization on which I focus in this section is a social and cultural organization called Quisqueya en Acción (Quisqueya in Action).[9] The focus on this organization by no means exhausts the discursive field in which Dominican immigrants find themselves. Moreover, the discourses and practices of this organization interact with a number of other discourses that influence its own identity definitions. Yet, the analysis of the cultural discourses and practices of this organization provides us with a view—albeit partial—at the efforts of sectors of the community to re-create a Dominican identity in the United States.

Quisqueya in Action is not the only Dominican organization in town.[10] This organization, however, is important because it organizes the annual Dominican festival, which is the main Dominican event in town and brings together more than thirty thousand participants for a day of celebration of Dominicanness. Through the actions of Quisqueya in Action we can see the formation of local and transnational discourses and practices that are formative of the group identity. The goal of the organization is to work with youth to transmit Dominican culture. This being said, what is the content of a Dominican identity in the American context? A look at the actions of this cultural organization shows us the emergence of a particular discourse of identity, an identity that is at the same time local and transnational. Quisqueya in Action was founded by a group of Dominican youth, of what is known as generation "one and a half" (that is, people who were born abroad but who grew up in the United States). This group of people, who attended Providence public schools, which provided few opportunities for them to study and express their culture, wanted to create an organizational space to transmit and celebrate Dominican culture. Later on, additional people joined Quisqueya in Action, some of them from the second generation, some of them from the first generation, and even some non-Dominicans. The organization, then, has within its boundaries representatives of all the generations in the community and people of different orientations toward the relationship between American and Dominican culture and identity.

The annual Dominican festival in Providence is an example of the many ethnic festivals that take place routinely in American cities. In that sense, it reinforces the Dominican identity in America. A cursory look at the celebration shows the importance of Dominican symbols in this process of identity formation. A spontaneous procession and display of symbolic elements of Dominican nationality accompany the festival. The Dominican flag is the most conspicuous, yet not the only symbol displayed. Cars are painted indicating regional origin, hats and t-shirts with the flag's colors are worn by the audience, and *merengue* blares from sound systems.

During the festival the dance group of Quisqueya in Action performs traditional dances or scenes from the Dominican carnival. The culminating act of the festival is always performances by popular Dominican artists (the last three years saw the presentation of Fernando Villalona, Mily Quezada, and Kinito Méndez).[11] The festival, however, also gives space to other forms of cultural expression. For example, many groups of young people perform hip-hop or rap music in Spanish and in English. So while the festival emphasizes the traditional Dominican elements of the Dominican-American cultural definition, it also allows space for newer, "hybrid" Dominican-American cultural forms that incorporate more elements of American popular culture.

Quisqueya in Action also has a theater group and a folkloric dance group, which work on Dominican dances and theater pieces. The person who has organized these groups is a first-generation immigrant. In these groups, however, many young and second-generation people participate. The dance group, in particular, is a vehicle for the development of the creativity of the younger members of the organization. So while the themes of the dances are Dominican, the choreographies are often the result of the creativity of local second-generation youth. In addition, Quisqueya in Action organizes talks on Dominican cultural issues, to make Dominican culture available to the younger Dominican-Americans who were born or grew up in the United States. Yet, sometimes, as in the case of the talk on Dominican racial identity, the discourse is also informed by Dominicans' experiences in America. For example, in that event, the mainstream Dominican view of racial identity, which negates the African components in the formation and present of the Dominican people and culture, was heavily criticized.

A look at the political activities of Quisqueya in Action shows the same pattern of both local and transnational orientation. On the one hand, the organization participates in all the local Latino struggles. In Providence these struggles have been related to the questions of amnesty for undocumented immigrants, and access to health care, social security, and education. Thus, the organization participates in the formation of a local discourse of Latino identity and rights. On the other hand, Quisqueya in Action has been involved in the formation of a national agenda of Dominican-Americans in the United States. The organization coordinated and hosted the second annual conference of the Dominican American Round Table, an initiative to develop a lobbying organization for Dominican issues in Washington, D.C. This initiative is clearly focused on the process of increasing Dominican participation in the American political system and in establishing a Dominican-American political agenda that is oriented toward the needs and aspirations of the Dominican population in the United States. In that sense, this initiative is an example of well-established patterns of immigrant incorporation through participation in the political process. Yet, the Dominican embassy and the Dominican government support this initiative. The reason for this support is that Dominican-American issues are defined in ways that also concern the Dominican Republic. In addition to local demands such as education, health, and community development, the initiative also addresses issues that concern the Dominican Republic directly, such as deportations, immigrant rights, and parity in trade. These issues involve immigrants, second-generation people, and their families, but they are also issues that closely concern the Dominican Republic. Hence there is a convergence between the Dominican-American agenda and the Dominican agenda.[12]

Quisqueya in Action is also involved in the type of civil-societal transnationalism described in the previous section. The organization maintains close ties with the neighborhood development association of one of the neighborhoods in the northern part of Santo Domingo and has helped organize fund-raising events on behalf of this organization. However, here we see the sporadic character of this form of transnationalism to which I alluded before. This relationship, although close, is based on personal links, not institutional networks. The fund-raising events are not organized regularly but arise out of the initiative of individuals. Similarly, Quisqueya in Action filled a key role in organizing the solidarity efforts to help the victims of Hurricane Georges. The organization sent money and goods to the Dominican Republic and even a delegation of the organization traveled there to express solidarity and bring information to the local community concerning the relief efforts.

This brief and incomplete account of the cultural practices of Quisqueya in Action shows the multidimensional character of the identities being forged among Dominicans in Providence. On the one hand, Quisqueya in Action is involved in defining Dominican culture and identity in the United States. On the other hand, Quisqueya in Action is also involved in the formation of a local Latino agenda and in an effort to develop a Dominican-American agenda with emphasis on incorporation into the American political system. This complex picture shows the local and transnational character of cultural production and identity formation.

Conclusion

This chapter has portrayed the building of a transnational community in a small city. Providence is not in the financial circles that define contemporary global cities. Yet it has become a small mirror of the process of social and cultural change in urban centers in the United States. The initial drive for this change was the demand for immigrant labor that originated in a declining yet still strong manufacturing sector. That, together with relatively cheap housing, relative security—at least in comparison to other urban centers—and relatively good health services, accounts for the arrival of new immigrants. Yet, for established groups such as Dominicans, the presence of a community and the networks it generates are the principal force in encouraging the continuous arrival of immigrants.

This chapter portrays different aspects of the community-building process, a process that has local and transnational components. On the one hand, immigrants try to build their new lives in the United States. They try to progress in their jobs and as they become more involved with American life they follow the common immigrant path of trying to acquire political power. They recreate a Dominican culture that has strong Dominican components, that maintains symbolic and affective ties with the country of origin, but is mainly Dominican-American. On the other hand, this indisputable process of incorporation and acculturation, of becoming American, is intertwined with the maintenance of ties of sociability and solidarity with the country of origin, that is, with the constitution of a transnational social field.

Some Dominican immigrants live economic or political lives closely linked to the country of origin. Some of the people involved in these narrow forms of transnationalism will eventually return to the Dominican Republic, but many will remain here. A large part of the community is involved in broader forms of transnational linkages. These range from regular forms of transnational solidarity, such as sending remittances to the family in the country of origin, to moments of massive solidarity, such as in the relief efforts in response to natural disasters. The community maintains deep personal and institutional relations with the country of origin, transferring resources from here to there—in the forms of remittances, solidarity aid, political contributions, and investments—yet the main effort of the individuals and the community as a whole are toward carving a space in the United States.

If so, what is the future of transnational communities? Will they last beyond the first generation? My answer to that question is that as long as the migration movement continues, the transnational ties will continue. The continuous arrival of immigrants will renew the transnational institutions and practices. Moreover, we can expect that as long as some members of the second generation and beyond maintain family ties with the Dominican Republic they will keep some form of involvement in transnational practices. Yet, at the same time, the community will keep getting increasingly involved in American life and developing a Dominican culture and identity oriented toward American culture, society, and politics. For the time being, the two processes are concurrent, not contradictory.

Notes

1. In the popular TV series *Providence,* which put the city on the map of popular culture, the viewer could sometimes see the presence of white ethnics—mostly Italians—and there was an African-American doctor or nurse in the clinic run by the main character, but the viewer was hard pressed to find any Latinos or Asian-Americans in the city imagined by the series script writers.

2. The survey data were gathered in the framework of the Comparative Immigrant Enterprise Project (CIEP), a collaborative study that involved a survey of immigrant households among three immigrant communities—Dominicans, Salvadorans, and Colombians—in four cities of the United States—New York City, Los Angeles, Washington, D.C., and Providence, R.I. Part of the sample was reached through a random survey and part through snowball chains. The random sample respondents were selected using a three-stage sampling strategy. In the first stage, key areas of residential concentration of Dominicans were identified. In the second stage, a random sample of blocks was selected in those areas. These city blocks served as primary sample units (PSUs). In the third stage, a systematic random sample of households was conducted within each block using a fixed sampling fraction, thus ensuring identical probabilities of selection for eligible households. The reason for the purposive selection of one-third of the sample was that the primary focus of the survey was to study transnational practices. The referral section of the sample attempted to reach people who engage in transnational practices to insure that there were enough cases of transnational migrants in the sample. The random sample was conducted to avoid the problem of sampling on the dependent variable.

3. At the same time that this process was taking place among Dominicans, there were organized efforts by the textile and jewelry factories in the neighboring towns of Central Falls and Pawtucket to recruit workers from Colombia.

4. The rate of labor force participation is the percentage of people sixteen and older who are either working or looking for a job.

5. In the 1990s manufacturing was not offering jobs to all the newcomers as in the 1970s. In fact, as in much of the post-industrial Northeast, employment in manufacturing has declined from 38.4 percent of the labor force in 1975 to 23.8 percent in 1995.

6. In his recent work (Portes, Guarnizo, and Landolt 1999; Portes 1996), Portes takes a broader view of transnational communities, recognizing different transnational practices according to their level of institutionalization.

7. Graham (1997) estimated that parties raise about 15 percent of their campaign funds in the United States.

8. Obviously, ethnic institutions are not the only site of the production of discourses of cultural identity, nor do all ethnic organizations share the same discourse. Yet, these are important sites of cultural creation and identity formation from the point of view of the experience of the immigrant community.

9. Quisqueya (supposedly) was the native name of the island and it is still used by Dominicans to refer to it.

10. In Providence there are different sport leagues, with baseball, softball, basketball, and bowling being the more prominent among Dominicans. There is a social and cultural club that hosts many of the sport leagues, the Juan Pablo Duarte Club. There are representations of the main Dominican political parties, there is a Dominican Political Action Committee (as well as a Latino Political Action Committee to which most of the members of the former belong). There are several churches whose parishes are composed mainly of Latinos. Those in the southern part of Providence are composed of and work with mostly Dominicans.

11. These are three of the most popular contemporary *merengue* singers in the Dominican Republic.

12. The Dominican government, as are other Latin American governments, is interested in the rights of immigrants in the United States because the immigrants' remittances are one of the main sources of foreign currency and the Dominican government is interested in their continuous flow.

References

Basch, Linda G., Nina Glick Schiller, and Cristina Szanton Blanc. 1994. *Nations Unbound: Transnational Projects, Postcolonial Predicaments, and Deterritorialized Nation-States*. Langhorne, Pa.: Gordon and Breach.

Foner, Nancy. 1997. "What's New about Transnationalism?: New York Immigrants Today and at the Turn of the Century." *Diaspora* 6: 355–75.

Glick Schiller, Nina. 2000. "Transmigrants and Nation-States: Something Old and Something New in the U.S. Immigrant Experience." In *The Handbook of International Migration: The American Experience,* ed. Charles Hirschman, Philip Kasinitz, and Josh DeWind. New York: Russell Sage Foundation.

Graham, Pamela. 1997. "Reimagining the Nation and Defining the District: Dominican Migration and Transnational Politics." In *Caribbean Circuits: New Directions in the Study of Caribbean Migration,* ed. Patricia Pessar. New York: Center for Migration Studies.

Guarnizo, Luis E. 1997. "The Emergence of a Transnational Social Formation and the Mirage of Return Migration among Dominican Transmigrants." *Identities* 4(2): 281–322.

Itzigsohn, José. 1995. "Migrant Remittances, Labor Markets, and Household Strategies: A Comparative Analysis of Low-Income Household Strategies in the Caribbean Basin." *Social Forces* 74(2): 633–57.

———. 2000. "Immigration and the Boundaries of Citizenship: The Institutions of Immigrants' Political Transnationalism." *International Migration Review* 34(4): 1126–54.

Itzigsohn, José, Carlos Dore Cabral, Esther Hernández Medina, and Obed Vázquez. 1999. "Mapping Dominican Transnationalism: Narrow and Broad Transnational Practices." *Ethnic and Racial Studies* 22: 316–39.

Itzigsohn, José, and Silvia Giorguli Saucedo. 2002. "Immigrant Incorporation and Sociocultural Transnationalism." *International Migration Review,* 36(3): 766–98.

Kyle, David. 1999. "The Otavalo Trade Diaspora: Social Capital and Transnational Entrepreneurship." *Ethnic and Racial Studies* 22: 422–46.

Laguerre, Michel S. 1998. *Diasporic Citizenship: Haitian Americans in Transnational America.* New York: St. Martin's Press.

———. 1999. "State, Diaspora, and Transnational Politics: Haiti Reconceptualized." *Millennium: Journal of International Studies* 28(3): 633–51.

Landolt, Patricia. 2000. "Exploring the Spaces of Political Transnationalism: Insights from Salvadoran Transnational Migration." Paper presented at the Latin American Studies Association conference, Miami, March 2000.

Landolt, Patricia, Lilian Autler, and Sonia Baires. 1999. "From Hermano Lejano to Hermano Mayor: The Dialectics of Salvadoran Transnationalism." *Ethnic and Racial Studies* 22: 290–315.

Levitt, Peggy J. 1997. "Transnationalizing Community Development: The Case of Migration Between Boston and the Dominican Republic." *Nonprofit and Voluntary Sector Quarterly* 26(4): 509–26.

———. 1998. "Social Remittances: Migration Driven Local-Level Forms of Cultural Diffusion." *International Migration Review* 32(4): 926–48.

Mahler, Sara J. 1995. *American Dreaming: Immigrant Life on the Margin.* Princeton, N.J.: Princeton University Press.

———. 1998. "Theoretical and Empirical Contributions toward a Research Agenda for Transnationalism." *Comparative Urban and Community Research* 6: 64–102.

Popkin, Erik. 1999. "Guatemalan Mayan Migration to Los Angeles: Constructing Transnational Linkages in the Context of the Settlement Process." *Ethnic and Racial Studies* 22: 267–89.

Portes, Alejandro. 1996. "Transnational Communities: Their Emergence and Significance in the Contemporary World System." In *Latin America in the World Economy,* ed. Roberto Patricio Korzeniewicz and William C. Smith. Westport, Conn.: Greenwood Press.

Portes, Alejandro, Luis E. Guarnizo, and Patricia Landolt. 1999. "Introduction: Pitfalls and Promise of an Emergent Research Field." *Ethnic and Racial Studies* 22(2): 217–37.

Roberts, Bryan, Reanne Frank, and Fernando Lozano-Ascencio. 1999. "Transnational Migrant Communities and Mexican Migration." *Ethnic and Racial Studies* 22(2): 238–66.

Smith, Robert C. 1998. "Transnational Localities: Community, Technology, and the Politics of Membership within the Context of Mexico and U.S. Migration." *Contemporary Urban and Community Research* 6: 196–238.

Torres-Saillant, Silvio, and Ramona Hernández. 1998. *The Dominican Americans.* Westport, Conn.: Greenwood Press.

5

Transnationalism and Middle-Class Dominican Immigrants in South Florida

Carol Hoffman-Guzmán

Guido: The Dominican Republic is not just geography.
The nation is everywhere. I love being around Dominicans.
Gabriela, Guido's wife: I miss the whole island. We go every year.
I get so emotional when we land.
Guido: I have a sense of belonging there that I don't have anywhere else.

Guido and Gabriela Estrella are typical middle-class Dominicans living in South Florida.[1] They have resided in the United States for more than thirty-five years, ever since their families left the Dominican Republic because of the 1965 civil war. They first settled in the New York City area, then moved south and have lived for nearly twenty years in a suburban Miami-Dade neighborhood that is middle class with a 69.9 percent home ownership and a median age of 35–44 (2000 census). Guido has college degrees in two different fields; he now works in middle management with an international industrial corporation. Gabriela has a medical staff position. The couple has several adult children; numerous relatives from their extended family also live in South Florida. Some family members still live in the Dominican Republic.

Both Guido and Gabriela claim a staunch Dominican identity and belonging. Guido keeps up with news from the Dominican Republic, he goes to selected local Dominican events, and he helps support a local Dominican organization with his involvement and money. He is disappointed and hurt by the negative image given to Dominicans, both in the American and Hispanic media. He communicates with other Dominicans, both locally and in the Dominican Republic through the Internet; the family visits frequently from Santo Domingo. For Guido, Miami is almost a suburb of the Dominican Republic: "You see, what you have here is a lot of Dominicans, who think they are residents in Miami, but they also have residences in Santo Domingo. If you go to Publix around the El Doral Country Club, you see so-and-so from the government, or some guy who was an official in Balaguer's government. I see faces in the Dominican newspaper, and then I see their faces here. You wouldn't believe the number of Dominicans who live in Santo Domingo and have apartments here."

However, the Estrellas live at least forty-five to sixty minutes from the locations where many Dominican events are held. Their neighborhood is very mixed ethnically, and their closest friends, outside of family, are the people they meet at church, which has members from twenty-one different nations, both Spanish- and English-speaking. According to the 2000 census, their community is 36.7 percent Hispanic, of which 86.6 percent are non-Cuban and only 4.5 percent are Dominican. Guido is comfortable with this diversity of his community and his multiple frames of reference: "I am Dominican, but I love this country very much. The freedom of expression, of speech, to say whatever you want. I love the lifestyle. In the Dominican Republic everybody watches you, the neighbors, they watch what others do. I like the privacy here. I like the fact that my children were born here."

Should Guido and Gabriela be considered examples of transnational migrants, as discussed by scholars such as Glick Schiller (2000), José Itzigsohn et al. (1999), Alejandro Portes, Luis Guarnizo, and Patricia Landolt (1999), or Sarah Mahler (1998)? Although the Estrellas visit the Dominican Republic yearly, they doubt that they would move back. Gabriela says they used to visit the Dominican Republic more when they lived in New York. "Return?" comments Guido, "No, I don't think so. I want to be here close to the kids. I would see a day when we could go back, for two or three months. . . . I think for the majority of us, unless our retirement fund is depleted, the majority will stay here and just go back for a few months." Their children? "They feel, especially the oldest son and daughter, they feel very Dominican—and the youngest too. They feel proud of Sammy Sosa and things like that. But they are Americans too."

Transnational Dominican Immigrants in South Florida

Miami and South Florida[2] appear to be fertile sites for the nurturing and maintenance of Dominican transnational networks and bi-national activity. Many Dominicans have the affluence that permits easy transnational activity. Dominican professionals are represented in most occupational fields in South Florida, including banking, the law, education, business, public administration, and medicine. The 1990 U.S. census hinted at an upscale assimilation, with nearly 40 percent of all Dominicans in Miami having a college or graduate school education, 45.5 percent owning their own homes (Miami-Dade County PUMS 1990 Census[3]), and more than 90 percent living in neighborhoods that would be considered middle class or higher. The 2000 census figures indicate that, across the board, Hispanics have spread throughout South Florida, with 40 and 50 percent[4] of the total Dominican population in Miami-Dade being concentrated in the western suburban neighborhoods and the northeastern Miami-Dade gated communities, which are festooned with names like "The Hammocks," "Kendall West," and "Fontainbleau" (a strong Dominican presence). Home ownership in these areas ranges from about 50 percent to 75 percent. Similarly in Broward County, nearly 65 percent of the Dominicans are in the western or central western suburbs.

South Florida's Dominican immigrants, in addition to possessing the resources for transnational activity, have an easy accessibility to and communication with the Dominican Republic. Two-hour direct flights connect Miami at least twice daily with Santo Domingo, varying from a cheap U.S.$175 to a pricey U.S.$500. Most Dominican newspapers are available weekly and often daily at numerous news outlets or online. Dominican food supplies are available not only in the Dominican neighborhood of Allapattah, but also in other Hispanic and American supermarkets. Many middle-class Dominicans are connected via the Internet with Dominican news and family, both in the United States and abroad.

Among sixty-six middle-class Dominicans interviewed in 1998–2000 for my doctoral dissertation, however, transnational activity does not seem as intense as might be expected, especially considering their middle-class resources and close proximity to the Dominican homeland. As will be detailed below, only one-third of the sixty-six interviewed individuals actively participates in continuing transnational activities (and I suspect that this percentage will decrease over time). The remaining two-thirds participate only in less active transnational behavior, such as occasional travel, local group identification, and/or symbolic behavior. Moreover, nearly one-third exhibits merely personal or familial identification with Dominican culture. This lack of intense transnational behavior is coupled with a dispersed, unconnected Dominican community, comprised of 47,043 individuals (Miami-Dade and Broward counties), many of whom are often unaware of local Dominican events, conferences, cultural happenings, or publications.

Transnationalists theorize that there are numerous types and degrees of transnational immigrant behavior, ranging from intensive mobility and economic exchange to infrequent, more symbolic expressions of transnationalism and biculturalism. Some scholars, such as Alejandro Portes, prefer to delimit the transnationalist concept to "occupations and activities that require regular and sustained social contacts over time across national borders" (Portes, Guarnizo, and Landolt 1999, 219). Writers such as José Itzigsohn (Itzigsohn et al. 1999) and Sarah Mahler (1998) address a broader range of transnational activities, including remittances, travel "home" with gifts and merchandise, communication of all types, local charitable and cultural meetings, and ethnic self-identification. In response to debates about the role of mobility in transmigrant conceptualization, Mahler states that there appear to be multiple ways that migrants can participate in transnational activities, ranging from the physical to the informational.[5] For the purposes of this study, I utilize the broadest definition of transnationalism, which includes people who travel frequently between two countries and perhaps maintain two homes, to those who primarily have bifocal or bi-national attachments and frames of reference.

My study identifies and maps a portion of South Florida's Dominican community: sixty-six managers, entrepreneurs, social service workers, educators, and other professionals. Who exactly *are* these middle-class immigrants who have migrated directly from the Dominican Republic and indirectly through second migration from other areas in the United States? How and when did they arrive, and why? I present statistics and personal stories that describe their transnational behavior, related economic activities, social affiliations, attachments of "home," and personal identity reconfigurations. Also presented in the following pages are seeming incongruities within the Dominican community in South Florida, including selective multiple identifications, conflicting attachments and loyalties, and a gradual shift from more active to more passive transnational behavior. Finally, I will discuss whether these middle-class Dominicans, as they become increasingly embedded in their local neighborhoods and into American culture and social life, can still be viewed as "transnational" migrants.

I will argue that immigrant transnational behavior, including the less mobile and more symbolic forms of behavior, should be viewed as a fluid continuum of activities that transpire over time, from emigration to transnational migration to localized cosmopolitanism. I argue that this continuum, which is both spatial and temporal, terminates not in total assimilation, but in negotiated compromise and hybridization. The term "localized transnationalism" (or a multi cultural cosmopolitanism) is borrowed from authors such as Pheng Cheah and Bruce Robbins (1998) and Ulf Hannerz (1990) to describe migrants and immigrants who become increasingly tied to local places and people, while still retaining strong connections with their homeland, both symbolically and through active communication and interchange, thanks to today's advanced technology.

Moreover, I believe that the dispersion, anonymity, and lack of solidarity observed among South Florida's Dominicans do not represent a diminishing biculturalism; instead, many avenues of communication are now available that keep Dominicans interconnected both locally and between the two nations. A Dominican friend of mine in Miami recently became an *abuelito* (grandfather) when his daughter gave birth in Santo Domingo, and just two days later he saw e-mailed photos taken of the mother and baby in the hospital. Then they "talked" each day via e-mail and chat lines; he sent her clippings from the Internet on postpartum depression while he monitored Travelocity.com for cheap plane flights back home. These cosmopolitan, binational connections seem, for many Dominicans, to have replaced "traditional" connections such as continuing travel abroad or ties to a local ethnic community.

The South Florida Dominican "community" is not unique in its middle-class cosmopolitanism and its expressions of transnational behavior. Similar situations are found among Jamaicans, Haitians, Colombians, Nicaraguans, Puerto Ricans, Venezuelans, and other ethnic groups from the Americas. Until the 2000 census, researchers had documented immigrant expansion into South Florida suburbs through secondary statistics such as profiles of students in public schools, Immigration and Naturalization figures, real estate sales, retail and banking statistics, and anecdotal information. Finally, the recent census validated many people's suspicions about population shifts. The white non-Hispanic population in Miami-Dade has decreased 20 percent, and populations in African-American neighborhoods, many lower income, have flat-lined or are decreasing in number. And while the Cuban population grew only 15 percent, other groups from throughout the Americas have increased substantially: Colombians, 31 percent; Mexicans, 65 percent; Dominicans, 55 percent; Hondurans, 48 percent; Argentineans, 55 percent; Venezuelans, 119 percent; and West Indians, 117 percent (Driscoll and Henderson 2001; Elliott 2001). Except for several lower-income Mexican and Central American neighborhoods, this Latin immigrant explosion seems to be occurring primarily in middle- or higher-income neighborhoods. More than eighty census tracts were added in the 2000 census to western suburbs in Miami-Dade.

Research Methodology and the Characteristics of Dominicans in the South Florida Study

My interviews and participant observation with middle-class Dominicans began in 1998 and continued through 2000. These informants or respondents were selected by "snowball" sampling, whereby I interviewed several key Dominican leaders and then used their referrals to obtain further interviewees, who in turn mentioned other possible candidates. The research consisted of qualitative interviews and observation with sixty-six individuals, accompanied by continued communication and interaction with many of the informants. The sampling gave a surprisingly balanced gender selection of 50/50 male and female, with a decent bell curve of age (ranging from nineteen to sixty-five years) and a variety of marital status (forty-five married, eighteen divorced/single, and three homosexual). Skin color ranged from white/light (twenty persons) to brown (thirty) to dark/black (sixteen). Of the sixty-six interviewees, sixty-four were born in the Dominican Republic; two were born in the United States, but lived a significant time in the Dominican Republic. I utilized the "grounded theory" approach of Strauss and Corbin (1990) for qualitative data collection, coding, categorization, and analysis. Based on results of open-ended interviews, I constructed many tables of quantified results, which were used primarily as indicators of trends and for developing hypotheses.

Sixty-four Dominicans in the South Florida study group were employed in middle-class positions that ranged from professional and managerial to clerical and technological. One individual was on the high end of the professional scale in his position as the C.E.O. of a major Dominican corporation. At the other end was a service worker, who had formerly been in the upper middle class in the Dominican Republic, both by profession and political appointment. Determination of class, both abroad and in the United States, was somewhat complicated because of variations of class definitions in the two countries. Class in the Dominican Republic is not defined just by income and profession, but also by family, color, and sociopolitical connections. As one interviewee commented, "Upper class is determined by who your father was—either you were or were not born in it." Initially the respondents were asked to "self-identify" their class in both countries; then factors such as neighborhood, education, profession, and political and family connections were also considered to make class determinations. Among the recently arrived immigrants the numbers were greater in the lower- and upper-class categories (by Dominican classification), but after resettlement in the United States there was a drift toward the middle class (by American classification) (see table 5.1). The inverted bell had flipped into a standard bell curve.

The History of Dominican Immigration to Miami and South Florida

Although the Dominican presence in South Florida has been rather unnoticed by scholars and the media, small numbers of elite, lighter-skinned Dominicans have continually visited Miami or claimed it as home or a second home since the 1950s. George Velez, who has lived in Miami since the early 1970s, comments, "Miami was one of Trujillo's favorite places to visit. He had a residency in Coral Gables. Dominicans came on a regular basis. After his death, his family came here and established a home." According to César

Table 5.1. Occupation and Class of Dominican Migrants (in South Florida study)

Occupation in South Florida	Number	Percentage
Public administration, social services	11	16.7
Professional, clergy	11	16.7
Entrepreneurial, the arts	10	15.2
Management	9	13.6
Sales, real estate	6	9.1
Secretarial/clerical, office support	4	6.3
Journalism	4	6.3
Education	4	6.3
Dominican government	3	4.6
Technology	2	3.0
Owner-manager of large corporation	1	1.5
Service worker	1	1.5
Total	66	

Class	Dominican Republic	Percentage	U.S.	Percentage
Upper	10	15.2	2	3.0
Upper-middle	14	21.2	15	22.7
Middle-middle	9	13.6	42	63.6
Lower-middle	9	13.6	7	10.6
Lower	24	36.4	0	0
Total	66		66	

Lima, whose affluent father was active in the Dominican military, "My first visit to Miami was a long time ago in 1963 [at the age of twelve]. I used to come with my parents a lot of times. During 1965 and 1966, my father sent my family to Puerto Rico, during the war of the Dominican Republic [the 1965 civil war]."

Many current Dominican residents in South Florida, however, officially immigrated to the United States through other ports of entry. Based on my research, I believe that the current Dominican population in South Florida primarily consists of two distinct influxes: upper-middle-class and elite Dominicans who had immigrated directly to Miami and then moved somewhat downward into the U.S. middle class; and a variety of other Dominicans, mostly lower-middle and lower class, who initially came to the northeast United States, worked their way up into the middle class, and now have resettled in the more culturally and climatically friendly area of South Florida. There seems to be a slight color distinction between the two groups, with

Table 5.2. Initial Port of Entry into the United States for Dominicans (South Florida Study)

Port of entry	Number	Percentage
Miami, South Florida	14	21.2
New York City	38	57.6
Other east coast cities	4	6.1
Other U.S. cities	4	6.1
Puerto Rico	4	6.1
Born in United States	2	3.0
Total	66	

the Miami-entry group being more white/light, while the northeast-entry group is more brown and/or black. Among the sixty-six Dominicans interviewed, only 21.2 percent migrated directly through Miami (table 5.2). A comparison of entry dates into the United States versus arrival dates into South Florida shows that while 65.2 percent of the Dominicans in the South Florida study (57 percent in the 1990 Miami-Dade PUMS Census) had emigrated to the United States before the 1980s, only 24.2 percent of the interviewees had actually come into Florida by this time (table 5.3), indicating that South Florida has often been a site of secondary migration.

Further information about later or secondary settlement by Dominicans into the South Florida area can be learned through comparative urban statistics from the 1990 census. Table 5.4 contrasts Dominican movement into six

Table 5.3. Date of Dominican Emigration to the United States versus Arrival in South Florida (PUMS and South Florida study)

Decade	Miami-Dade PUMS arrival in the U.S.		Date of entry to U.S. (South Florida Study)		Date of arrival in So. Florida (South Florida Study)	
	Number	Percentage	Number	Percentage	Number	Percentage
<1950	7	1.8	0	0	0	0
1950s	17	4.3	4	6.1	0	0
1960s	98	24.6	25	37.9	1	1.5
1970s	105	26.3	14	21.2	15	22.7
1980s	141	35.3	13	19.7	18	27.3
1990s	N/A	—	8	12.1	32	48.5
Born in the United States	31	7.8	2	3.0	0	0
Total	399		66		66	

Table 5.4. Dominican Mobility into Different States: Most Recent Place from Which an Individual Relocated (in the Five Years Prior to the Census)

Most recent migration	City, Area or State											
	South Florida study group		Miami PUMS[a]		Rhode Island[b]		Providence[b]		New York City[b]		Manhattan[b]	
	Number	Percentage	Number	Percentage	Number	Percentage	Number	Percentage	Number	Percentage	Number	Percentage
Different state	37	56.1	101	62.4	1,715	44.5	1,324	39.9	3,356	6.0	1,067	5.2
Abroad	29	43.9	61	37.7	1,861	48.3	1,906	57.4	52,799	94.2	19,422	94.8
Total	66		162[b]		3,576		3,320		56,155		20,489	

Note: 119 of the 399 Dominicans in the PUMS report did not answer, or answered "inappropriate."

a. PUMS is a sample of 1.7 percent of the total population of 23,475 Dominicans.

b. Figures adapted from a census table constructed by Itzigsohn (1999, 322).

states or cities, from either abroad or another state. While in Manhattan and greater New York City, 94–95 percent of all Dominicans entering the state/city came from abroad (from the Dominican Republic, presumably), both Rhode Island/Providence and South Florida/Miami show figures respectively of only 48–57 percent and 38–44 percent relocating from abroad. These figures suggest that a large percentage of the Dominican residents settled there through secondary migration.

A comparison of Dominican "immigrant" versus "non-immigrant" status visas in three states also reveals the nature of "entry" into Miami/South Florida versus other areas of the United States (table 5.5). Using two recent years when such figures were available (1996 and 1998), one learns that the ratio of non-immigrants to immigrants in Florida greatly exceeds the national average and that of other states. While the ratio elsewhere ranged from 2.3 percent to 10.8 percent, in Florida the ratio ranges from 33.9 percent to 54.7 percent; that is, in Florida in 1996 the ratio was nearly seven times greater than the national ratio; and in 1998, more than five times greater.

Table 5.5. Comparison of Dominican Immigrant and Nonimmigrant Visas in Key Ports of Entry, 1996 and 1998 (INS Annual Statistics for 1996 and 1998)

	1996		1998	
	Immigrants	Non-immigrant entries	Immigrants	Non-immigrant entries
Florida	2,050	69,543	1,483	81,140
Percentage of national total	5.3	36.2	7.3	39.8
Ratio of Nonimmigrant to Immigrant	33.9		54.7	
New York City	20,579	53,577	10,719	55,566
Percentage of national total	52.0	27.9	52.6	27.3
Ratio of Nonimmigrant to Immigrant	2.7		5.2	
New Jersey	5,006	7,373	2,478	5,779
Percentage of national total	12.6	3.8	12.2	2.8
Ratio of Nonimmigrant to Immigrant	1.5		2.3	
Other (including Puerto Rico)	11,969	61,470	5,707	61,324
Percentage of national total	30.2	32.0	28.0	30.1
Ratio of Nonimmigrant to Immigrant	5.2		10.8	
National total	39,604	191,963	20,387	203,712
Ratio of Nonimmigrant to Immigrant	4.9		10.0	

One might conclude that these figures merely reflect the close proximity of Miami to the island, a fact that would make the area more logical for vacations and occasional trips. Indeed, Max Castro, sociologist and *Miami Herald* columnist writing frequently on immigrant communities, calls Miami the "shopping border" of the Caribbean (personal communication 1998). These low percentages of regular immigrants into Florida also probably reflect the lack of opportunities in Miami for unskilled or under-skilled labor. According to Antonio Gil, an entrepreneur in the technology field, "It pays more to clean a bathroom in New York than in Miami. It pays more to work in a factory in New York. Here [in South Florida] most of the Dominicans are educated. Here I have a lot of friends [who] are doctors, lawyers." Many Dominican relocations into South Florida have been made after the primary wage earners gained an education, job experience, and good English skills; once they have obtained a certain socioeconomic level, they are willing to sacrifice some economic benefits for proximity. At the same time, however, for Dominicans relocating directly from the island, Miami appears to hold the strongest attraction for people in the higher income levels. Long-time resident Bernardo Ricart, a C.E.O., comments: "Miami is a second city for Dominican businessmen. They mix shopping and business. It's very versatile and 'very status.' Middle class to high end. Eighty thousand to ninety thousand dollar apartment in Kendall. They come often and need an apartment. Also, there are two million dollar apartments in Brickell."

The motives for relocating or immigrating specifically to Miami and South Florida, versus the motives for immigrating to the United States, are also interesting indicators of the uniqueness of this segment of Dominican immigration to the United States (table 5.6). For Dominicans immigrating to the United States and/or directly into Miami, the primary motive has usually been anticipated economic benefits (81.8 percent). Since many respondents came with or followed family members, familial influence was the second most mentioned factor for migrating (78.7 percent).

However, when Dominicans relocate from another U.S. city or state to South Florida, the reasons are not so purely economic (only 38.5 percent mentioned economic factors). The reasons for relocation are instead based on issues of climate, proximity to the Dominican Republic (both physically and culturally), and/or the presence of other family members. Manuel Báez, who works in middle management, says, "I had always heard nice things about Miami. There was always orange on the weather map in Florida, when other areas were blue." Another factor influencing relocation was a dislike of the area where these Dominicans had initially settled (e.g., issues of crime, harsh winters, drugs, and other negative influences). According to Griselda Díaz, a banker, "Last summer we went back to New York. It was extremely

Table 5.6. Comparisons of Motives for Relocating to Miami/South Florida versus Migrating to the United States (South Florida Study Group)[a]

Reason	Climate like DR, proximity	To benefit the children	Dislike of prior U.S. location	Family network in Miami	Escape family/social situation	Repeat migration[c]	Political reasons	Economic benefits
To Miami from other states	30	7	13	23	10	20	0	20
N=52	57.7%	13.5%	25.0%	44.2%	19.2%	38.5%	0	38.5%
Direct from Dominican Republic	9	5	N/A	4	7	N/A	0	12
N=14	64.3%	35.7%	28.6%	50.0%	na	0	0	85.7%
To United States								
All Dom. in South Florida study	N/A	5[b]	N/A	52	19	N/A	23	54
	N/A	7.6%	N/A	78.7%	28.8%	N/A	34.8%	81.8%

a. Many of the study respondents had two or more interconnected motives for immigrating to the United States and/or relocating to Miami; thus the following table is used simply to indicate possible trends.

b. Most Dominican immigrants in the study did not immigrate as parents, but as children or youth. Only five came as parents with children and they came recently and directly from the Dominican Republic.

c. Twenty people came or returned to Miami when they were not successful in returning to live in the Dominican Republic; Miami was the most agreeable alternative.

loud, all the honking. My mother said, 'They just killed someone on the corner.' I said, 'Oh my God.' The hours weren't short enough to get back here." This escape from unpleasant areas is sometimes coupled with the desire for a better environment to raise children.

Characteristics of the Dominican Population in South Florida

The Dominican "communities" of Miami-Dade and Broward Counties are more upscale than the Dominican communities of Washington Heights or Corona in New York City (as is also mentioned by Guarnizo 1997, Kerner 1992, and Duany 1997). The most specific demographics information on Dominican income in South Florida comes from the 1990 census; these figures, however, predate the considerable Dominican influx to South Florida occurring in the 1990s, when an economic crisis in the Dominican Republic forced the emigration of many middle-class Dominican families and also discouraged the return migration of middle-class Dominicans already living in the United States. Delia Fernández, a counselor, comments, "In 1990 there occurred a *fuga de cerebros* [brain drain]. Economically, we were in a good status. But we saw what was coming, in a social, moral and economic way." Results from my South Florida study group mirror a proportionally similar influx; of the sixty-six Dominicans interviewed, nearly half (thirty-two) came in the 1990s. Of these thirty-two Dominicans, only eight (25 percent) immigrated directly through the port of Miami.

The 2000 census shows a current Dominican population of 36,454 in Miami-Dade, a 55.3 percent increase over 1990; Broward County shows 10,498, or a 201 percent increase; and Florida, a 107 percent increase (Driscoll and Henderson 2001). Previous estimates of the increase had been slightly higher. Dionis Pérez (real name), a former Dominican vice consul in Miami, estimated that the South Florida population might be 50,000–80,000 (1999 interview), and Rhadamés Peguero (real name), the director of the Dominican American National Foundation in Miami, gave a figure of 80,000 to 100,000 (2001 interview). Sociologist John R. Logan, of the State University of New York at Albany, estimates that the number of Dominicans in Miami-Dade and Broward Counties has been undercounted, respectively, by 18,500 and 5,000, which he extrapolated from the over-inflated 664 percent increase of "other Hispanic" figures in Miami-Dade (Driscoll and Henderson 2001). The Lewis Mumford Center at the State University of New York at Albany shows similar undercounts for Dominicans, which would increase the Miami-Dade population to 53,940; Broward County to 15,633; and the state of Florida from 70,968 to 107,009 (http://www.albany.edu/mumford/census/ - Dec. 27, 2001). These sets of figures indicate that census figures should be 66–67 percent greater than stated.

Local Dominican leadership believes that the recent population increase has occurred primarily in the middle classes: "Miami is basically a place of middle-class Dominicans—professionals who come not only from the Dominican Republic, but also from New York, Boston, New England. They get a little bit of progress, then they come here" says Pablo Rodríguez (real name), a community leader. The 1990 census in South Florida hinted at this Dominican shift to the middle class. Miami-Dade County Dominicans appear to be better educated than Dominicans in New York City. Of the Dominicans in Miami, only 3 percent have less than a high school education, while in New York City the rate is 54.5 percent.[6] In Miami 39.1 percent had some college education; while in New York City, only 20.3 percent did. Miami Dominicans also have good English skills, with 68.3 percent claiming that they speak English well or very well versus 31.6 percent in New York City. Miami's Dominicans had a 48.5 percent rate of home ownership (no New York City figures are available). However, the 1990 figures on occupation and salary/wages do not corroborate this claim of emerging middle-class Dominicans, with only 13.3 percent in professional or managerial positions (compared to New York City's 8.9 percent) and a mean salary/wage income of only $17,210 (this low figure needs further investigation).

According to both the 1990 and 2000 census figures, Dominicans in Miami-Dade County were spread over more than a forty-mile stretch of land (sandwiched between the Everglades and the Atlantic), with larger concentrations in the new single-family homes and gated communities in the western areas. Of the 266 census tracts in 1990, Dominicans resided in 225 of them; in 2000 Dominicans resided in 378 of the 380 census tracts. In both 1990 and 2000 only 5 tracts had more than five hundred Dominican residents. The 1990 figure of 12.9 percent of Miami's Dominicans in the Allapattah/Wynwood area decreased from 12.9 percent to 9 percent. Among the middle-class Dominicans in my South Florida study, none lived in Allapattah, and less than 10 percent lived in neighborhoods that might be considered generally lower-middle or lower income. These sixty-six interviewees were dispersed throughout Miami-Dade and Broward Counties, with no more than five persons in one zip code.

This dispersion and dilution of the Dominican population has effectively camouflaged its presence. Few South Florida residents would identify Dominicans as a key ethnic component in this new global community. In 1998, Oliver Kerr of the Miami-Dade Department of Planning and Zoning commented to me that the Dominican population was not considered numerically significant enough to warrant special study, even though Dominicans constituted the fifth largest Hispanic group in 1990 and the sixth largest in 2000—after Cubans, Puerto Ricans, Colombians, Mexicans, and Nicaraguans. Some Dominicans lament this lack of image: "There is no image.

People only think about Cubans," according to Wanda Epson, a small business owner. Other Dominicans consider this rather good news, particularly in contrast to the negative publicity often given to Dominicans in New York City. Says Delia Fernández, "Dominicans? People think Dominicans are black people. Dealing drugs. Loud people, always dancing the *merengue*. Chewing 'chicle.' With lots of make-up, tight pants, and jewelry." Other South Florida Dominicans, however, feel that they have a recognizable image in Miami: "I think that the image is positive. . . . The reason is that many of the Dominicans who are here are professionals. They give us a good name," says Millie Muñoz, who works in education.

Currently around twenty civic, professional, and political organizations, including three Chambers of Commerce (each representing a political party), are somewhat active in Miami-Dade. One community leader estimated, however, that only a couple of hundred Dominicans are involved in these organizations, some of which have active memberships of less than ten people. Such ethnic affiliations do not seem to offer the primary source of camaraderie or congregation for South Florida's Dominicans. Instead, these Dominican interviewees had a wide range of informal friendships. More than seventy percent (71.2 percent) had Dominican friends and nearly 50 percent chose family as their most important friends (45.5 percent); some of the interviewees also had professional friends (32.8 percent), friends in organizations (28.8 percent), friends in churches and synagogues (13.7 percent), friends who were other Hispanics (15.2 percent), or just a mixed batch of friends (36.4 percent). Ginetta Lara, a journalist, gathers friends from many different communities: "My friends are a combination of everything. Peruvian, Cuban, Venezuelan—like a mixture. Some friends are even in New York." Friendship and professional networks span neighborhoods and even cities.

Several people mentioned that they had Dominican and other friends in distant neighborhoods in both Miami-Dade and Broward counties. These far-flung networks could be viewed as either the cause or a reflection of Dominican dispersion in South Florida. Conversely, few Dominicans claimed to have good friends directly in their own neighborhoods, and some complained about the lack of neighborliness in South Florida; Millie Muñoz says that in her area it is just "hi and good-bye." Although this friendship pattern differs from the typical ethnic enclave or from neighborhoods in the Dominican Republic, it not unlike many other middle-class neighborhoods in the United States.

Transnational Activities of Dominicans Living in South Florida

Portes (Portes, Guarnizo, and Landolt 1999, 221) has proposed a three-pronged typology for categorizing transnational immigrant activity: economic initiatives, political activities, and sociocultural enterprises, each of which he subdivides into low and high levels (that is, activities "from above" and "from below"). Itzigsohn et al. (1999) has developed a similar but expanded mapping scheme for Dominican (and other) transnational practices, including occasional transnational behavior. He proposes four basic types of behaviors: economic, political, civil-societal, and cultural, which he subdivides into "narrow" and "broad" practices (1999, 323–25). Mahler suggests additional considerations that help distinguish between the activities of the majority and of smaller groups: gender, class, age/generation, mobility, and regionalism. Mahler also emphasizes the importance of "power" in transnationalism; that is, one must ask who benefits from the activity and how power/privilege is accordingly reaffirmed and/or configured (1998, 81–92).

The typologies and categories suggested by Portes, Mahler, and Itzigsohn were incorporated into the following table (table 5.7), which first divides transnational activities into two categories: frequent, physical, and mobile activities; and occasional, symbolic, and mnemonic behavior. Economic, political, and civic/charitable activities fall into the first category, as does a limited amount of social interaction (this activity often accompanies other frequent behavior and may dissipate as situations change). The second category includes occasional visits, the sending/transporting of money and gifts, local group cultural activities, family activities, and individual sentiments of identification and belonging. (Individuals' transnational activities were categorized according to their 1999 interviews. Since then, people have moved and/or changed jobs, a new Dominican government was elected, and family interactions have changed.)

Of the sixty-six respondents, approximately one-third participated in active transnational behavior; the other two-thirds merely in occasional and passive activities. Many individuals participated in two or more practices; therefore, the above percentages of activities do not total 100 percent. However, it was possible to place each individual in one of the two broad categories, as shown in the table's final row. As can be seen in the table, only nine Dominican immigrants had strong economic ties in the Dominican Republic. Three people retained their commitment to their country through sizable charitable activities. Seven had some type of political connection, either with the ruling party or with the opposition. These people would fit Portes's definition of transnationalism. The remaining two-thirds of the interviewees, though falling into the occasional and symbolic category, were by no means apathetic nationalists or converted Americans, as can be seen below where

Table 5.7. Transnational Activity and Behavior (South Florida Study)

Type of Activity	Number	Percentage
Frequent, Intense; Physical Mobility, Business and Social Interaction		
Economic exchanges		
Firms, corporate management	2	3.0
Entrepreneurs, journalists, and artists	7	10.6
Organizations, civil, charity	3	4.6
Political	7	10.6
Social/cultural interaction and mobility	16	24.2
Some type of strong, frequent transnational involvement, plus symbolic and/or local involvement	22	33.3
Occasional, Symbol, Mnemonic		
Occasional mobility and travel		
Transnational attachment retirement plans	25	37.9
Symbolic group identification—local group	34	51.5
Individual familial cultural identification only		
Individual, family only	20	30.3
Only symbolic, occasional, local cultural behavior	44	66.7

nearly 90 percent identified themselves as "Dominican!" Yet for a great variety of reasons, they found their time and energy consumed primarily by more local events, networks, and obligations. Most of them were comfortable with their decision of local adaptation; I would estimate that only three were saddened and remorseful about their diminishing Dominican nationalism.

One of the initial attractions for living in South Florida was the closeness to the Dominican Republic. Thus, travel should represent a substantial subcategory for transnational behavior in South Florida. Among the sixty-six interviewees, the median frequency for travel to the Dominican Republic was every two to four years. As the Estrellas discovered, proximity does not always guarantee frequent visits; their visits actually declined after moving to Miami. Nor did the length of stay in the United States seem to be a major determinant in travel frequency. Instead, the primary determinant of frequent travel was consistent, institutionalized transnational obligations, usually of an economic nature. One person who arrived in New York City in the mid-1960s has never returned for a visit. On the other extreme is Bernardo, who came in the mid-1970s and returns at least four times a year for business purposes. Comments Bernardo, "Circumstances have kept me close to the Dominican Republic. So I don't miss it. Dominicans are always longing for the Dominican Republic. I never did that. . . . I call the Dominican Republic on a daily basis."

Most of these interviewed Dominicans, whether or not they visited frequently, had some type of on-going communication with family, friends, or professional associates in the Dominican Republic. Some felt that today's technology made connections and relationships "closer" than was possible in the past. Flora, who works in media, stated, "Now on the Internet, you develop a community of friends." Over a period of three years, I watched local Dominicans slowly coming "on-line" as they realized that they could send letters and photos, communicate on a talk line, or even have live conversations via the Internet. Websites were developed; individuals created interactive e-mail lists that emphasized specific topics of interest. Old friendships are being rediscovered and revived; new communities of interest and friends are evolving. Older Dominicans who never touched a keyboard are suddenly on-line.

Many Dominicans initially emigrate to the United States with the intention of returning—when the Dominican economy improves, when the political situation changes, or when the migrants have gained experience, education, and sufficient money. However, as the years lengthen, this anticipated return to the Dominican Republic no longer is a realistic option because of diminishing possibilities in the Dominican Republic and increasing social, economic, and personal ties in the United States. Notwithstanding, some people do attempt a return. Among the Dominicans interviewed, nineteen of the sixty-six interviewees (28.8 percent) tried to return home to live and work. Fourteen (73.7 percent) of the returnees moved back because they believed they could earn enough money to maintain a tolerable lifestyle. Three returned for high school or college education; and two left because they were simply disillusioned with life in the United States. Stays ranged from several months to ten years.

All sixteen of the adult returnees eventually discovered that it is not easy to return "home," and they moved back to the United States. Reasons for not remaining in the Dominican Republic ranged from social to personal. As is noted by other researchers, returnees often discovered that the Dominican Republic is not overly receptive to newly affluent returnees. Additionally, the country itself has not improved enough politically and economically to satisfy some returnees. More strategic to their U.S. return, however, was the discovery that the immigrants themselves had changed and become accustomed to American lifestyles and values. Some returnees had underestimated the importance of their ties to the United States and had misjudged the remaining connections in the Dominican Republic. Others found that their memories and expectations of their homeland surpassed reality.

Transnationalism as Related to Class of Origin and Port of Entry

As mentioned above, there appear to be two broad classifications of Dominicans living in South Florida: people from the upper middle and elite classes, many of whom had immigrated directly to Miami, and people from the lower and lower middle classes, who often immigrated initially to another area of the country. Of the fourteen Dominicans who entered South Florida directly, nine come from the upper middle or upper classes. Conversely, of the forty-four who came into the northeastern United States, the greatest number, twenty, were in the lowest class. However, about 13 percent of the New York entries were in each of the other categories of class. Notwithstanding the port of entry, one's ascribed class in the Dominican Republic often seems to govern, to some extent, friendships, networks, and social classification among Dominican immigrants living in South Florida. Dominican events and music festivals in Dominican Allapattah or at outdoor arenas attract few middle-class Dominicans, who instead might attend a smaller professional event or picnic. The traditional upper class is aware of who has transcended old class barriers; associations may occur for business purposes, but as one woman said, "You don't have to invite them into your kitchen."

One's familial class also seems to have a predictable correlation with the transnational behavior of these Dominican immigrants (keep in mind that this survey was small). The two interviewees who now travel abroad extensively with large international firms came from the upper class in the Dominican Republic. The upper-middle-class interviewees have the highest percentage of transnational occupations, such as journalism, art, and politics/government (42 percent). The middle and lower middle classes have less physical forms of transnational activities (economic, social, and political) than do the upper or upper middle classes. The lower class has the least physical, either economic or political, transnational involvement (4 percent to 13 percent in various categories).

Those born into the Dominican upper class also had the highest percentage of more-than-annual travel to the Dominican Republic (50 percent); the lower class exhibited much less frequency, with 33.3 percent going about once every ten plus years and 20.8 percent going once every two to four years. Visits by the upper middle, middle, and lower middle classes fell between the two extremes, with the lower middle having slightly more frequent travel. Dominicans who were born into the lower class had the lowest percentage of attempts to return and live in the Dominican Republic (13 percent). All other classes had relatively similar rates of attempted returns (30–43 percent). The elite class had a relatively high attachment to the homeland (50 percent), but so did the lower middle with 67 percent. Conversely, the upper and upper middle classes had lower percentages of symbolic group-identification behavior (40 percent and 43 percent), while the middle and lower middle classes had increased symbolic group identification (67 percent–77 percent). For the lower class, among all the types of nonphysical transnationalism, the most significant was symbolic group identification (50 percent).

Some correlation was demonstrated between Dominican-based class and one's choices of friends and associations. The upper class placed its greatest emphasis on family (80 percent), then on mixed social contacts (50 percent), professional relationships (40 percent), and casual Dominican relationships (40 percent). The upper class mentioned American and mixed cultural friends more than other classes and had fewer relationships in church or with people of shared interests. Members of the upper middle class placed their greatest emphasis on casual Dominican friendships (78.6 percent), then on Dominican associations (42.9 percent), family (35.7 percent), and work (28.6 percent). The middle class had relatively equal emphases on family, casual Dominicans, profession, church, Dominican organizations, and mixed friendships. The lower middle class also had a large emphasis on casual Dominican friendships (88.9 percent), then on family (44.4 percent) and Dominican organizations (44.4 percent). Dominican associations and politics rated highest among the lower classes and least among the upper class. Casual Dominican friendships rated high among all, but least among the upper classes; in turn, family and professional contacts rated higher among the upper class. Shared interests seemed to rate highest among the lower middle classes. The upper middle class had the highest percentage of relationships with other Hispanics. Only people in the upper middle class mentioned "class" as a reason for choosing friends—possibly characteristic of the upwardly mobile nouveau riche.

Regarding transnationalism and ports of entry, those who entered through Miami had greater continuing involvement, in general, in the physical forms of transnationalism, plus the greatest sense of attachment to the homeland (66.7 percent). However, they had the least percentage of people who have attempted to return to live in the Dominican Republic (6.7 percent); possibly this is related to their proximity and the ease of short-term return. Both groups have similar percentages of symbolic group attachment (50–60 percent). The primary difference between people who entered through South Florida and those who entered through the eastern seaboard is that the latter group includes individuals who very infrequently visit the Dominican Republic, that is, never or once every ten years or less. However, both groups have similar percentages of people who visit more frequently. Regarding associations and friendships, those Dominicans who entered through South Florida place their emphasis, in order of descending frequency, on informal Dominican relationships, other Hispanics, Dominican organizations, and family. Those who entered the eastern seaboard place their emphasis in the following order: informal Dominican relationships and Dominican organizations (tied at 60 percent) and family at 40 percent.

Identity, Place Attachment, and Transnationalism

In addition to more obvious indicators of transnational behavior, interviewees were also questioned about identification, attachment, and belonging. I hypothesized that transnational sentiments can sometimes be revealed in statements about identity, "home," and what they liked and disliked (projections) about both the Dominican Republic and the United States. When asked directly about "identity," nearly 90 percent of the respondents answered "Dominican," and more than 25 percent used the term "Dominican-American" (table 5.8). This result is no surprise to anyone who has studied the persistence of national identification.

However, it was interesting to note that nearly 50 percent of the interviewees responded with two or more identities. A few respondents really felt that they did not belong to or identify with any one particular place or culture. Delia Fernández commented, "I am the daughter of the light and a citizen of the world. I can't say I'm just Dominican. I can't even say I am just Hispanic. I see the good in both. I'm just a person." Ofelia Cabral, an artist, shares a similar feeling: "I am like an international thing. I don't know. . . ." Says Bernal Linares, "I see myself as a man of the earth, global." One-third of the sixty-six interviewees stated that their identity was bicultural or multicultural, international, flexible, and/or subject to change upon need. Several interviewees specifically detailed their ability to create or mold their identity: "After a while, we accept the fact that we are bicultural. We can turn it on or off. We've been in both places," says Mercedes Báez. In fact, many were proud of their flexible identity; they felt that this was what made it possible for Dominicans to prosper and to survive the difficulties of migration: "I am bicultural. I don't have to eat Dominican or Latin food, but I love it. I don't have to watch Dominican TV or Channel 37. I watch Leno," says Bernardo. These comments on strategic shifts in identity reinforce Smith and Guarnizo's argument that people can selectively accentuate or downplay their ethnicity and solidarity according to local dictates and needs (1998, 14). Mary C. Waters, in her study of Caribbean migrants, comments that they can code-switch in speech and body language when appropriate and have a portfolio

Table 5.8. Individual Identification by Dominicans in South Florida

How one identifies oneself	Number	Percentage
Dominican	59	89.4
Dominican-American, Americanized Dominican	17	25.8
Latin, Hispanic	9	13.6
Bicultural, multicultural	9	13.6
Flexible, adapt or change per situation	7	10.6
Human, international, of the world, etc.	6	9.1
American	4	6.1
Spanish, other European origin	3	4.6
Afro-Caribbean, Haitian, black roots	3	4.6
Taíno	1	1.5
Don't know, confused	1	1.5
Two or more answers	32	48.5

Note: Percentages do not add up to 100 percent because some people gave two or more answers.

of identities, including skin colors, national identities, regional identities, and immigrant identities. She also notes that the complexities of these identity decisions are usually economic (1999, 77, 91, 331). Miguel Montalvo, a dark-skinned Dominican who is well respected in the social service field, talks about his self-construction of identity: "For Hispanics, I am not Hispanic. For African-Americans, I am not African-American. I had to make my own identity, my own world. I had to find and fight for my rights. . . . I created my own space too." Susan B. Stafford's study of upscale Haitian immigrants in New York City similarly shows them manipulating language and history to enhance an elite identity (1987, 143).

Sidney Mintz argues that the long history of colonization and intervention in the Caribbean has encouraged a certain adaptability among all classes. According to Mintz, in the oppressive plantation communities, a "forced-draft Westernization" and multicultural exposure demanded an adaptable style of life (Mintz and Price 1985; Mintz 1974). In her study of Dominicans, Ninna Sørensen agrees with Mintz and states that the presence of local and global images in Dominican identity is the outcome of Dominican mobility (Sørensen 1997). In other words, through travel and multicultural experiences, a wide variety of differing cultural elements have been incorporated into *dominicanidad,* which makes Dominican identity construction a collaboration of identities, not a linear process toward one common national identity. Barbara Martínez, a medical administrator, gives her personal interpretation of versatile *dominicanidad:* "We Dominicans come from an island which was the first colony in the New World. We have received different migrations from different countries. Our people mixed with others since the beginning, and we have maintained the custom of getting information, fashion, music, art from almost every part of the world."

Class and port of entry seems to have some correlation with identity. The upper class had more emphasis than other classes on a flexible identity. The upper middle class placed its greatest emphasis on Dominican identity. The middle and lower middle classes had the greatest assortment of identification and seem more willing to accept identities ascribed by others. The lower class was the most likely of all the classes to accept the bicultural identification of Dominican-American. Regarding port of entry, those who came directly into South Florida asserted a Dominican identity slightly less than those who came in through the eastern seaboard (78.6 percent versus 90.7 percent). The direct-Miami group had no sense of being Hispanic or Latin, versus those who came in from the eastern seaboard (16.3 percent); however, this non-Hispanic identification is characteristic of all Hispanics in South Miami. The Miami-entry group was also more likely to adopt an American identity (11.6 percent) or Dominican-American, bicultural, and flexible (16.3 percent–23.3 percent). I suggest that these differences relate primarily to the situations and communities into which the two respective groups entered and settled in the United States. For instance, in the Northeast, where for years Dominicans were relegated to the underclass and had little power, it is not surprising that they would identify with a larger Hispanic or Latino identity as a point of solidarity and as is done elsewhere in the United States. I would suggest also that enjoying flexible and multiple identities is characteristic of more upscale, cosmopolitan populations who do not have to accept or react to an imposed identity. Miami-Dade is a place where diversity is expected and even prized. Not only does Miami-Dade have the greatest percentage of Hispanics nationally (57 percent), but it has a high diversity index of 73 (Driscoll 2001a).

The interviewees also expressed their sense of belonging and identity in statements about "home" (responses could select multiple "homes"). Of the sixty-six interviewees, forty-two (67.2 percent) called Miami "home"; thirty-one called the Dominican Republic "home." Some selected other U.S. locations or no location. But nearly 25 percent of the respondents (nineteen) gave a very transnational response; that is, these Dominicans claimed at least two homes, both here in the United States and in the Dominican Republic, as demonstrated in the following somewhat ambiguous comment by Francisco Alvarez, a physician: "I don't think that I'm 'out' [of the Dominican Republic]. And 'back' doesn't mean that you are physically there. I don't feel that I left. For a while I 'left' so that I could put my feet here, to be stable emotionally and economically. But I feel that I have not left . . . . My girls are being raised here, so I don't see them going back. So I won't go back there physically. So I won't leave here, but I will be 'there' too."

Smith and Guarnizo state that, in transnational migrant communities, there is a continual struggle as people produce narratives of belonging, resistance, or escape (1998, 22). In an article on Dominican return migration, Guarnizo reflects that migrants build a web of cultural, social, economic, and political relationships, practices, and identities across national borders (1997, 287–88). He also comments (282) that contemporary Dominican transnational migration seems more like the mobility of people within national borders than across international ones, and Dominican society seems as closely connected to transmigrants abroad as it is to any other group residing in the national territory. Even for Dominicans who left the country decades ago, there is a sense of traveling and moving between two real homes.

Four questions in the interview questionnaire targeted more elusive indications of identification and attachment by asking what Dominican immigrants liked and disliked about the Dominican Republic and the United States. I theorized that individual preferences and dissatisfactions about the two nations could also reflect how individuals are selectively re-identifying themselves in the midst of transnationalism. For instance, the respondents' "likes" about the United States centered around issues of lifestyle, economy/business, and a democratic government; the appreciation of organization and order in American life was a recurrent theme. In contrast, the "likes" about the Dominican Republic centered around social characteristics and national/cultural pride. I would suggest that many Dominican-Americans see themselves as selectively integrating the best of both cultures: someone who is successful in business, likes a fair government, and enjoys a comfortable lifestyle, but someone who also appreciates family, friends, fun, and the Dominican culture and homeland. These characteristics are reemphasized in the "dislikes" answers. The transnational Dominican has left behind shortages, disorganization, corruption, the abuses of power, and various types of favoritism that have been historically characteristic of Dominican government, business, and social structure. But while enjoying the American style, this cosmopolitan Dominican has tried to avoid becoming too Americanized, that is, overworked, overstressed, nonsocial, nonfamilial, and driven by money and materialism alone (see tables 5.9, 5.10, 5.11, and 5.12 for likes and dislikes about the United States and the Dominican Republic). Carmen Darío comments, "You are not torn between two cultures. You don't lose one country, you can have both." In a *Miami Herald* interview, novelist/poet Julia Alvarez commented that people are always asking her which part is Spanish and which is English. She replied, "I believe that the new identity is a mix that is produced and is converted to another thing. . . . It is something fluid, and this excites me."

Table 5.9. Likes about the United States

Likes	Number	Percentage
Life-style	68	36.8
Quality of life, consumer goods	26	
Family benefits from life-style	21	
Freedom of expression	12	
Privacy, social freedom	9	
Economic, business	54	29.2
Opportunities	35	
Style of business	12	
Educational preparation	7	
Government	37	20.0
Equal rights	16	
Civic responsibility	8	
Organization and stability	7	
Laws, order, process	6	
Style of organization (general)	21	11.4
Morals, ethics	5	2.2
Total answers	185	

Table 5.10. Likes about the Dominican Republic

Likes	Number	Percentage
Social Characteristics	88	63.3
Warmth, friendship	34	24.5
Easy-going, innocent, fun-loving, free	27	19.4
Family strength	15	10.8
Security; protection by family, friends	7	5.0
Amenities of higher classes	5	3.6
Cultural, national pride	51	36.7
Culture, tradition, and roots	27	19.4
Climate, geography	6	4.3
Sophistication, resourcefulness, global nature	6	4.3
Small country, one can be "somebody"	5	3.6
Values more important than materialism	4	2.9
Schools and education	3	2.2
Total	139	

Table 5.11. Dislikes about the United States

Dislikes	Number	Percentage
American social characteristics	32	50.0
Isolation, nonsocial, cold, too mobile	13	
Over-stressed, don't relax or enjoy life	6	
American family (lacking values and strength, youth problems, disrespect of elderly)	5	
Lack of upper-class benefits	3	
Discrimination, color/ethnicity[a]	5	
Economic, job aspects	20	31.3
Money emphasis, materialistic	4	
Work too hard, pressure	6	
Corporate power, individual is number	3	
Ethnocentric, nonglobal	1	
Education not available to all	6	
Taxes, rules, regulations	7	10.9
Crime, violence, homelessness	5	7.8
Total	64	

a. Some Dominicans had experienced discrimination in the United States, but did not view it as a negative aspect of the United States, but rather as a trait of humans, certain ethnic groups, or uneducated people.

Table 5.12. Dislikes about the Dominican Republic

Dislikes	Number	Percentage
Business	52	35.1
Few opportunities	19	
Favoritism, not merit	15	
Unprofessional, unstable	16	
Lack of resources, supplies	2	
Politics	40	27.0
Abuse of power	10	
Power of parties, cronyism	11	
Corruption and lack of rights	19	
Social characteristics	39	26.4
Classism, favoritism	19	
Unorganized, time management problems	11	
Machismo	7	
Social codes, gossip, unaccepting of differences	2	
Lacks, shortages, crises (general)	17	11.5
Total	148	

Conclusions

Based on my research on middle-class immigrants in South Florida, I want to suggest some possible conclusions and topics for further consideration and study. As the following conclusions unfolded, I realized I was constructing a certain paradoxical behavior for middle-class immigrants. These incongruities included the following: increased resources for transnational activities, but a decrease in such behavior; diminishing ethnic ties balanced by a professionally sanctioned retention of culture; a selective flexibility of identity versus a fixity of place; and a localized transnationalism (or bounded cosmopolitanism). I suggest that these contradictions reflect the tension that is inherent in the transitional process of transnational migration.

Diminishing Returns of Transnational Activity

Although middle-class status, affluency, and proficiencies allow transnational migrants to develop and maintain transnational activities more easily, conversely these attributes can also weaken the very rationale for transnationalism. Wealth, education, technological tools, and class connections facilitate activities such as transnational commerce, political involvement, travel, and communication. Affluent, educated immigrants can, with relative ease, travel more frequently between nations, develop commercial ventures that transcend borders, and interact and identify with a more globalized class.

These attributes of professional-class immigrants, however, also facilitate their integration into the dominant culture of their host community, as has been recognized by numerous scholars. Nancy Foner, in her study of Jamaicans in New York City, comments that higher class immigrants "make it" in their new home because of their entrepreneurial background, a history of solid economic institutions, loftier goals, and the confidence to achieve these goals (1987, 113–16). Mary C. Waters notes similar advantages of middle-class Caribbean migrants, who are aided by their world view, work ethics, English skills, networks, and ambitions (1994, 330; 1999, 6–7). Delia Fernández, who has migrated between the United States, Puerto Rico, and the Dominican Republic, shares her personal experience on the benefits of her class background: "The middle class are more clear on what they are coming to do. They know the culture is different. We will have to do this, this, and this. They are willing to go through that." Sharon Zukin, giving a more spatial interpretation to this mobility of global professionals, comments that this group develops a multi-spatial identity and interacts with the landscape from multiple perspectives, in direct contrast to lower-class immigrants who are more place-bound (1992, 225).

Lower-class immigrants, in contrast, frequently have more difficulty adapting in the basic areas of immigrant life because they do not have the acquired skills that could cushion them against localized situations and allow them to be flexible within various frames of reference (Peters 1997, 91). Such inabilities in the host country, argue some writers, encourage transnational behavior. In a study of Mexican immigrants, Luin Goldring discovered that when less affluent immigrants fail to achieve upward mobility in their host country, transnational social spaces can offer a context for re-valorization (1998, 167, 173–75; see also Smith and Guarnizo 1998, 22–23). Jorge Duany states that among lower-class Dominican immigrants their symbolic extension of households, networks, and communities across national borders fosters a sense of cultural affirmation and resistance (1997, 196–200).

Lower-class immigrants, however, are limited in their transnational activities by a lack of capital and other resources. The middle and higher classes, however, have the resources for transnationalism, but not necessarily the need or motivation. Excluding certain situations of obvious economic profit, political involvement, and sanctioned cultural exchange, middle-class immigrants often find that the difficulties of transnational activity outweigh the benefits. Some of the Dominicans in the South Florida study talked specifically about the diminishing opportunities for transnational behavior in their lives. Francisco Alvarez, a physician in Miami, has a good position locally, is well respected in his field, and travels frequently to the Dominican Republic to lecture and bring supplies for Dominican children. He loves his homeland and worries about the inadequate medical treatment available to the majority of the population. But his home is "here" because his girls call it "home." The girls are growing, independent. "They will go to Duke or the University of Miami. They will study here, marry here, live here. So they will live here." In addition, Francisco's career is more lucrative than it ever was in Santo Domingo.

Other South Florida Dominicans expressed similar feelings about the flourishing of local (but not neighborhood) ties. According to Patria Almonte, who works in sales, "Your children are going to be here. Your grandchildren. All the people you knew there have moved. You already have a life." I argue that although immigrants of every class may initially be connected on many levels to their homeland, among the lower classes these connections and dreams are sometimes the only way of sustaining themselves against the hardships of worker-class existence abroad. Higher-class immigrants, however, whether their class is ascribed prior to migration or subsequently acquired, usually discover that new positive realities in their adopted country have replaced less probable hopes back home. At some point chronologically the middle-class immigrant finds that the complications of transnational activities and dual frames of reference outweigh the benefits and valorization. Localized economic, social, and political involvement eventually supplant transnational activities, and the only remaining transnational activities are of a more symbolic or occasional nature, such as periodic travel, communication, and ethnic identification.

Benefits from Non-binding, Multi-ethnic Ties

The complications of bi-nationalism have been noted by theorists who detail the tension produced by transnational ties, bifocality, and dual frames of reference (Duany 1997; Mahler 1998). Among the more affluent classes, such ties can bring unwanted obligations and complications, both locally and abroad. Portes and Guarnizo comment that economically successful immigrants are often embedded or "enmeshed in a dense grid of social expectations and reciprocal obligations" that can constrain individual profit seeking (1990, 3; see also Smart and Smart 1998, 107). In South Florida's Dominican communities, such connections can also entangle individuals in a web of political divisiveness and social favoritism—the very things that many Dominicans sought to escape. Patricio Rufino, who works in the human service field, has judiciously avoided Dominican political affiliations: "I don't get involved in politics, I keep my opinion to myself. . . . We Dominicans are fanatics of political parties. If you're not in my party, you're not my friend. If you are in my party, you are my friend."

Mark Granovetter uses the phrase "the strength of weak ties" to describe the less obligating, non-ethnic connections that global entrepreneurs strategically develop as they take their business beyond their own community (1973). In other words, it is easier to obtain economic success when one's business is not built on ethnic connections, but rather on less obligating, distant ties. Smart and Smart discovered that, among Chinese businessmen with economic ties in both China and Hong Kong, entrepreneurial effectiveness was often related to their deniability of ethnic networks, which were often ambiguous or even contentious (1998, 107–8).

Among South Florida's Dominicans, numerous people spoke about how their formal networks and professional connections extended beyond their own ethnic community. Doctors, for example, join professional associations with physicians from all backgrounds. However, informal Dominican friendships remained important, but they were not organizationally structured. Churches become a good source of friendship and support on a community level; most of the interviewees who attend religious services selected ones where the congregation was ethnically diverse, often English speaking. Although some Dominicans said they might enjoy Dominican groups, it was not a major concern; several stated specifically that they avoided Dominican-only groups, primarily because of politics or a desire to have a broader friendship base.

Retention of Cultural Identity

Having argued for the diminishing returns of transnational activity and ethnic ties, I would argue, conversely, that certain characteristics of the middle-class professional communities in South Florida reduce the necessity for complete assimilation and encourage, instead, the retention of some cultural characteristics and distinctiveness. This occurrence is linked to the uniqueness of Miami and also to what I feel are class-specific differences in assimilation, identification, and transnationalism. Nonaffluent immigrants are often forced into one of three forms of assimilation: complete assimilation into the dominant culture, retreat into an ethnic enclave, or identification with an underclass group.[7] Middle- and higher-class immigrants, however, can often obtain economic success without total assimilation and have choices about cultural retention. Portes and Stepick documented this inversion of assimilation among Miami's Cuban community, where economic success often precedes acculturation (1993, 216). Waters similarly comments that among West Indians their middle-class institutions allow for the maintenance of a distinct West Indian identity and provide for sharper cultural boundaries around the group (1994, 329–30).

When middle- or higher-class immigrants live in an upscale, culturally diverse neighborhood (as seen in South Florida), work in a business community that rewards multilinguistic ability and biculturalism, and "wear" the symbols of economic success (clothing, cars, education, English proficiency), such individuals are more easily tolerated/forgiven for slipping into their native language, admitting their ethnic heritage, and professing a desire for comforting cultural habits. The upscale neighborhood of Brickell, which is adjacent to the financial and banking center of Miami-Dade, has a diversity index of 81 (Driscoll 2001a). Ethnic characteristics, which might erect barriers for laborers working in an Anglo-dominated industrial or service field, are often viewed in more upscale, multicultural environments as colorful attributes of individual difference. Because middle-class immigrants in South Florida are not forced to assimilate completely in order to gain employment and social acceptance, they can more confidently retain this symbolic identification with their culture and nationality. That is not to say that discrimination against Dominicans is nonexistent in Miami; however, the group most commonly mentioned in acts of discrimination against Dominicans were the Cubans, not the Anglo community. The complaints were based more on inclusion versus exclusion; in other words, Cubans hired their "own" first, then other Hispanics.

"Strategic" Flexibility of Identity and Loyalty

As mentioned above in the section on identity, numerous interviewees prided themselves on their flexible identification and attributed their economic success to their adaptability and strategic utilization of different identities. Some felt it was a personal ability for selective acculturation. Paola Tavárez, who relocated directly to Miami for its freedom of lifestyle, comments, "Let's say that I am the one who adapts easy. I studied the culture, the laws. I read the paper, watch TV. I know my rights." Amelia Degás, who worked her way up into telecommunications management, was careful to avoid classifications ascribed by others: "I never put myself in one category, I never pigeonholed myself."

Other Dominicans felt that their ascendancy into the U.S. middle class was related to education and social capital. Delia comments, "When one has education and social status, one can adapt." Others say adaptability is a unique Dominican attribute. "We blend," comments Antonio, who propelled himself from the "lowest of low" to a well-financed entrepreneurial and suburban life in Pembroke Pines. "We can be many people and play many roles," states Katia Rojas, who champions the rights of poor Hispanics through her agency. Some interviewees appreciated the American world view, which rewards individualism, personal ambition, and achievement. Antonio Gil, a technology entrepreneur, comments: "It's the opportunity that this society offers. You can be what ever you want to be. . . . If you want to be good, you can be the best. That's what I did with my business, even though I have an accent." Mercedes Báez, who previously was a designer in the fashion industry, comments similarly about her acceptance in the field: "I was the only Latin in the design teams. I had to prove myself. I was the darkest on the floor. After your prove yourself, then it's wonderful. I was there for ten years."

A Need for Selected Fixity and Localization

Although numerous Dominican immigrants pride themselves on their flexibility and adaptability, I would argue that a boundedness and more static hybridity eventually supplant fluidity and continued transnational behavior, even within social groups who have more options to transcend such barriers. The only exceptions seem to be among those individuals whose professions are directly related to global and transnational commerce. This gradual tendency toward localized connections and a spatial reattachment has been discussed by numerous scholars, who comment on the apparently normative behavior of seeking fixity, order, stability, and consistency of identity, particularly as a response to flux, movement, and change (Massey 1994a,

1994b; Rapport 1995). Aihwa Ong's study of Chinese entrepreneurs indicated differential localization: they became locally bounded in terms of their extended families, somewhat localized to the larger community (on a rather strategic and superficial level), and not localized to the host country (1998, 137). Arjun Appadurai, while emphasizing the new deterritorialization of group identities, also describes transnational populations as regrouping in new locations and reconstructing their histories locally (1997, 48).

As middle-class Dominican immigrants in South Florida settle in, buy homes, and become successful at their careers, they too develop solid social ties and begin to restructure their lives locally. When Cándido Nadal first immigrated with his family to Brooklyn, his social life was totally circumscribed by his ethnic neighborhood, which shielded him from the dissonance of migrancy: "We didn't go outside of this protection. We didn't make friends outside of the community." Today, though Cándido travels frequently between the United States and the Dominican Republic, he now claims South Florida as his home: "This is the land of my children. It is where I work. It has given me opportunity. This is where professionally I am known. I have made my career here. I own a house. I have respect in the community." Order replaces the flux and dissonance of the initial years. New boundaries and relationships replace old ones. Identities are restructured to fit the time and situation. José Facundo, working in the education field, comments on his new identity: "I think that I was given the chance to live two lives in one. It is as if you believe in reincarnation and can remember past lives. Both identities are separate."

Localized Transnationalism and Bounded Cosmopolitanism

As the span of immigrant relocation lengthens, new homes and new spaces replace old ones. New networks are mapped through neighborhoods and cities. What was once transient and fluid now becomes more stabilized and rooted. I suggest that this juxtaposition of flux and fixity in the lives of middle-class immigrants positions them on a path leading away from transnationalism and toward a bounded multiculturalism, such as is described by Glick Schiller as a variant of the U.S. nationalist emphasis for immigrants (2000, 115). Cheah and Robbins, in their book *Cosmopolitics,* conceptualize this localization of mobile populations as a new type of "cosmopolitanism," which is characterized not only by a universality and partial independence from national boundaries, but also by an inevitable localization solidified through relationships, obligations, and fate (1998, 1). I propose that middle-class Dominican immigrants, who are at least symbolically transnational and also locally bound on many levels, are good examples of this new urban cosmopolitanism. Studies of other ethnic groups in South Florida would no doubt show similar patterns of increasing boundedness balanced by continuing biculturality and transnational identification, particularly among ethnic groups who have facilitated access to their homelands: Jamaicans, Puerto Ricans, and other Caribbean islanders. The Puerto Rican communities in the Orlando and Tampa areas of Florida are also burgeoning and purchasing homes in middle-class neighborhoods (2000 census); comparative studies of Hispanic transnationalism in South and Central Florida should be undertaken soon.

The concept of "cosmopolitanism" has recently undergone some retooling, as social scientists put a new twist on a word that formerly connoted not only worldly sophistication, but perhaps a certain decadent dilettantism. Hannerz redefined "cosmopolitanism" as an interplay between the mastery of and surrender to alien cultures (1996, 103).[8] Numerous writers have also emphasized the "non-elite," vernacular, or "from below" aspect of both cosmopolitanism and transnationalism, which has essentially been overlooked in the "from above" approaches to globalization (Smith and Guarnizo 1998; Appadurai 1997, 64–65; Sassen 1998, xxx–xxxi). Ong uses the word "flexible cosmopolitans" to describe the Chinese transnational executives who negotiate their political and cultural positions in different countries, selectively participate in various local discourses, and strategically alter their cultural values and class attachments (1998, 156–57). The experiences of South Florida's Dominicans mirror these various descriptions of localized cosmopolitans, including Clifford's description of immigrants who demonstrate a resilience in migrancy, a personal autonomy, and a redefining of assimilation (1998, 367–69; 1997, 252).

As I mentioned in my introduction, I believe that transnational activity today should be viewed as part of a flowing continuum, moving from emigration to resettlement and transnational activities to a more localized cosmopolitanism. This continuum spans both time and space, varies among individuals and groups, and plays out uniquely in different local contexts where immigrants must negotiate appropriate compromises that rarely lead to total assimilation, but instead to many hybridizations or multiculturalisms. I suggest that the use of the word "cosmopolitanism" (unless someone coins a better one) could help resolve the conflict regarding the degree of mobility necessary for ascribing the term "transnational" to an individual. While "transnational" implies movement and connection between two nations, a term such as "urban cosmopolitanism" embodies the uniqueness that technology, knowledge, and communication have bestowed on this new era of transnational migration.

On Christmas Eve, 2000, I visited the home of Gerardo and his wife Viviana, who had recently relocated from Hialeah into a secure, tranquil, gated community in western Broward County. Gerardo, who comes from an extended family of Dominican professionals, brought his family to Miami in the 1960s after years of higher education in New York City. He and his wife rarely travel back to the Dominican Republic, except for funerals, but still they are Dominican—the food, the music, the family. Their main contact today with family over *there* is by phone and e-mail. The couple goes on American cruises, delights in Disney World, and shops in Americanized malls. Their more assimilated adult children grew up locally, have graduate degrees, married non-Dominicans (one an American minority, the other from South America), and their networks are decidedly multicultural American.

Both Gerardo and Viviana are American citizens, but they are not totally assimilated Americans. Spanish is spoken almost exclusively in the home. The extended family has become a hybridized mix of many cultures—Dominican, American, Middle Eastern, rural American, and Floridian with Hispanic influences, including Cuban—just like most of their neighbors in this gated community.

Late in the night on Christmas Eve, which is the primary celebration day for Caribbeans, a *rondalla* or group of wandering singers came strolling through the streets, visiting the homes of their neighbors. The doors and garages of the $200,000-plus homes were flung open street-side, as residents signaled their welcome to the singers and their *aguinaldos* (a special Christmas music). The visible customs are a blend of Caribbean Hispanic and urban American. Adults sat outside on lawn chairs, teenagers leaned against expensive cars, and children played with their new and latest toys. Food and drinks from many different cultures were shared all around. The sounds and smells and traditions were largely Caribbean, but the homes were ultramodern California or Arizona or Texas, with tiled roofs, swimming pools, and twinkling holiday icicle lights from Walgreen's. Gerardo and Viviana don't need to return to the Dominican Republic—the best and most cosmopolitan of Caribbean life is available right here in South Florida.

Future Study

The South Florida Dominican study presents only a small portion of the middle-class immigrant experience in the United States today. To document further the relationship between the middle class, immigration, and transnational behavior, there must be more longitudinal studies of all classes of immigrants, both within one ethnic group and cross-culturally. Such studies should map this behavior geographically, ethnically, and from the time of initial migration through the present day. Additional studies need to done on the specific benefits and disadvantages of being a middle- or higher-class immigrant. Studies should also compare and contrast the degree of cultural retention and transnational behavior among different classes of immigrants, particularly over the extended period of migration and resettlement in the host nation. Such studies should also contrast middle-class immigrant experiences in different groups, cities, and in urban versus suburban contexts. A more extensive study of immigrant class could make a detailed comparison of both pre- and post-immigration middle classes to determine their differences and similarities in transnational and acculturation activities.

This new non-elite cosmopolitanism of immigrants suggests a related trend that also warrants further documentation and mapping—the relocation of immigrants in suburbs throughout the American landscape (see Engebretson 2000, 15–16; Viglucci, Driscoll, and Henderson 2001). The 2000 census has been a useful tool in locating these new transnationalized, cosmopolitan suburbanites, whose homes, communities, and identities are transcending many borders. The 2000 Miami-Dade County PUMS report will no doubt give added insight into the backgrounds, assets, and incomes of these new Americans.

Notes

1. All interviewees or respondents are given pseudonyms for reasons of confidentiality and privacy. Real names are used when a statement is nonpersonal from a community leader. These names will be so indicated.

2. South Florida includes two counties on the southeast coast, Miami-Dade and Broward.

3. The Miami-Dade PUMS data represents approximately 1.7 percent of the total 23,475 Dominicans in Miami-Dade County. The Miami-Dade PUMS data given in this chapter was selected for individuals between sixteen and ninety-nine years old, with a wage/salary income greater than $5,000.

4. Percentages vary according to how one defines these suburban areas, either by census "place" or "tract."

5. Based on Mahler's observation of Salvadoran refugees in the United States (primarily in the New York City area), she invites a more systematic inventorying of the various practices of different immigrants as a means of indicating the extent and persistence of transnational behavior cross-culturally (1998, 81–87).

6. The Miami figures are from the 1990 PUMS Census; the New York City figures are 1996 figures in a table in Hernández and Rivera-Batiz 1997, 50.

7. See Portes and Zhou's "segmented assimilation" theory, 1993.

8. See also Hannerz 1990; Wilson and Dissanayake 1996.

References

Alvarez, Julia. 1999. Interview by Marcia Facundo. *El Nuevo Herald,* May 2.

Appadurai, Arjun. 1997. *Modernity at Large: Cultural Dimensions of Globalization.* Minneapolis: University of Minnesota Press.

Cheah, Pheng, and Bruce Robbins, eds. 1998. *Cosmopolitics: Thinking and Feeling Beyond the Nation.* Minneapolis: University of Minnesota Press.

Clifford, James. 1997. *Routes: Travel and Translation in the Late Twentieth Century.* Cambridge, Mass.: Harvard University Press.

———. 1998. "Mixed Feelings." In *Cosmopolitics: Thinking and Feeling Beyond the Nation,* ed. Pheng Cheah and Bruce Robbins. Minneapolis: University of Minnesota Press.

Driscoll, Amy. 2001a. "S. Florida Hispanics Seek out Diversity." *Miami Herald,* July 30, 1B–2B.

———. 2001b. "Go West? In Dade, They Sure Did." *Miami Herald,* March 28, 25A.

Driscoll, Amy, and Tim Henderson. 2001. "Many Lands Give Florida Its Latin Flavor." *Miami Herald,* July 25, 17A.

Duany, Jorge. 1997. "The Creation of a Transnational Caribbean Identity: Dominican Immigrants in San Juan and New York City." In *Ethnicity, Race, and Nationality in the Caribbean,* ed. Juan Manuel Carrion. San Juan, P.R.: Institute of Caribbean Studies, University of Puerto Rico.

Elliott, Andrea. 2001. "A Quantum Leap: Census Survey Finds S. Florida's Caribbean Population Has Almost Doubled in the Last 10 Years." *Miami Herald,* August 6, 1A, 10A–11A.

Engebretson, Mark. 2000. "Suburbia Goes Global." *Utne Reader,* no. 100 (July–August): 15–16.

Foner, Nancy. 1987. "The Jamaicans: Race and Ethnicity among Migrants in New York City." In *New Immigrants in New York,* ed. Nancy Foner. New York: Columbia University Press.

Glick Schiller, Nina. 2000. "Transmigrants and Nation-States: Something Old and Something New in the U.S. Immigrant Experience." In *Handbook of International Migration: The American Experience,* ed. Charles Hirschman, Philip Kasinitz, and Josh DeWind. New York: Russell Sage Foundation.

Goldring, Luin. 1998. "The Power of Status in Transnational Social Fields." In *Transnationalism from Below,* ed. Michael Peter Smith and Luis Eduardo Guarnizo. New Brunswick, N.J.: Transaction Publishers.

Granovetter, Mark. 1973. "The Strength of Weak Ties." *American Journal of Sociology* 78(6): 1360–80.

Guarnizo, Luis Eduardo. 1997. "The Emergence of a Transnational Social Formation and the Mirage of Return Migration among Dominican Transmigrants." *Identities: Global Studies in Culture and Power* 4(2): 281–322.

Hannerz, Ulf. 1990. "Cosmopolitans and Locals in World Culture." In *Global Culture: Nationalism, Globalization, and Modernity,* ed. Michael Featherstone. London: Sage.

———. 1996. *Transnational Connections: Culture, People, Places*. London: Routledge.

Hernández, Ramona, and Francisco Rivera-Batiz. 1997. *Dominican New Yorkers: A Socioeconomic Profile, 1997*. New York: Dominican Studies Institute, City University of New York.

Itzigsohn, José, Carlos Dore Cabral, Esther Hernández Medina, and Obed Vásquez. 1999. "Mapping Dominican Transnationalism: Narrow and Broad Transnational Practices." *Ethnic and Racial Studies* 22(2): 316–39.

Kerner, Donna. 1992. "Dominican Emigration to Miami: The Impact on Households and Gender Ideology." Unpublished paper, Florida International University, Miami.

Lewis Mumford Center. 2001. "Hispanic Population Data for the Metropolitan Statistical Areas." University at Albany, http://www.albany.edu/mumford/census/, December 27.

Mahler, Sarah J. 1998. "Theoretical and Empirical Contributions Toward a Research Agenda for Transnationalism." In *Transnationalism from Below*, ed. Michael Peter Smith and Luis Eduardo Guarnizo. New Brunswick, N.J.: Transaction Publishers.

Massey, Doreen. 1994a. "Double Articulation: A Place in the World." In *Displacements: Cultural Identities in Question*, ed. Angelika Bammer. Bloomington: Indiana University Press.

———. 1994b. *Space, Place, and Gender*. Minneapolis: University of Minnesota Press.

Mintz, Sidney W. 1974. *Caribbean Transformations*. New York: Columbia University Press.

Mintz, Sidney W., and Sally Price, eds. 1985. *Caribbean Contours*. Baltimore: Johns Hopkins University Press.

Ong, Aihwa. 1998. "Flexible Citizenship among Chinese Cosmopolitans." In *Cosmopolitics: Thinking and Feeling Beyond the Nation*, ed. Pheng Cheah and Bruce Robbins. Minneapolis: University of Minnesota Press.

Peters, John Durham. 1997. "Seeing Bifocally: Media, Place, Culture." In *Culture, Power, and Place: Explorations in Critical Anthropology*, ed. Akhil Gupta and James Ferguson. Durham, N.C.: Duke University Press.

Portes, Alejandro, and Luis E. Guarnizo. 1990. "Tropical Capitalists: U.S.-Bound Immigration and Small-Enterprise Development in the Dominican Republic." Report submitted to the Commission for the Study of International Migration and Cooperative Economic Development, Congress of the United States. Baltimore: John Hopkins University.

Portes, Alejandro, Luis E. Guarnizo, and Patricia Landolt. 1999. "The Study of Transnationalism: Pitfalls and Promise of an Emergent Research Field." *Ethnic and Racial Studies* 22(2): 217–237.

Portes, Alejandro, and Alex Stepick. 1993. *City on the Edge*. Berkeley: University of California Press.

Portes, Alejandro, and Min Zhou. 1993. "The New Second Generation: Segmented

Assimilation and Its Variants." *The Annals of the American Academy of Political and Social Science* 530: 74–96.

Rapport, Nigel. 1995. "Migrant Selves and Stereotypes: Personal Context in a Postmodern World." In *Mapping the Subject: Geographies of Cultural Transformation,* ed. Steve Pile and Nigel Thrift. London: Routledge.

Sassen, Saskia. 1998. *Globalization and Its Discontents.* New York: New Press.

Smart, Alan, and Josephine Smart. 1998. "Transnational Social Networks and Negotiated Identities in Interactions between Hong Kong and China." In *Transnationalism from Below,* ed. Michael Peter Smith and Luis Eduardo Guarnizo. New Brunswick, N.J.: Transaction Publishers.

Smith, Michael Peter, and Luis Eduardo Guarnizo. 1998. *Transnationalism from Below.* New Brunswick, N.J.: Transaction Publishers.

Sørensen, Ninna Nyberg. 1997. "There Are No Indians in the Dominican Republic: The Cultural Construction of Dominican Identities." In *Siting Culture: The Shifting Anthropological Object,* ed. Karen Fog Olwig and Kirsten Hastrup. London: Routledge.

Stafford, Susan Buchanan. 1987. "The Haitian: The Cultural Meaning of Race and Ethnicity." In *New Immigrants in New York,* ed. Nancy Foner. New York: Columbia University Press.

Strauss, Anselm, and Juliet Corbin. 1990. *Basics of Qualitative Research: Grounded Theory Procedures and Techniques.* Newbury Park, Calif.: Sage Publications.

Viglucci, Andrés, Amy Driscoll, and Tim Henderson. 2001. "How We've Changed." *Miami Herald,* March 28, 1A, 22–26A.

Waters, Mary C. 1994. "Ethnic and Racial Identities of Second-Generation Black Immigrants in New York City." *International Migration Review* 28(4): 795–820.

———. 1999. *Black Identities.* New York: Russell Sage Foundation.

Wilson, Rob, and Wimal Dissanayake, eds. 1996. *Global/Local: Cultural Production and the Transnational Imaginary.* Durham, N.C.: Duke University Press.

Zukin, Sharon. 1992. "Postmodern Urban Landscapes: Mapping Culture and Power." In *Modernity and Identity,* ed. George Marcus. Oxford: Blackwell.

6

Dominican Transmigrants in Spain

Domingo Lilón with Juleyka J. Lantigua

For Latin Americans in general—and Dominicans are no exception—Spain has been *la Madre Patria* (the Motherland). Spain conquered, colonized, and settled the New World, which it controlled for more than three centuries. Even after independence, Latin American elites still considered Spain to be their cultural reference point. Moreover, for centuries Spaniards migrated to the New World, establishing a one-way migratory flow that lasted well into the twentieth century. Only rarely did Latin Americans settle in Spain—until recently. The economic crisis that affected Latin America in the 1980s, also known as "the lost decade," generated a massive outflow of migrants who often moved to Spain. Again, Dominicans were no exception.

Besides the traditional target destinations of Dominican migration during the 1980s—the continental United States, Puerto Rico, and Venezuela—Europe also became a target destination for Dominicans at this time. Within Europe, Spain became the country preferred by most potential Dominican migrants because of its linguistic commonality and its visa exemption for Dominicans.[1] In addition to the regional economic crisis of the 1980s, and the increasing difficulty of migrating to the United States, Puerto Rico, or Venezuela, there was another factor that had an effect on Dominican migration toward Europe: the rapid development of the tourist industry in the Dominican Republic during the 1980s and 1990s. The rapidly growing Dominican tourist industry, which mainly targeted the middle-class European market, sparked a major inflow of Spanish, German, Italian, Swiss, and French tourists, and led to a large number of marriages between (mainly female) Dominicans and Europeans. These unions then led to the establishment of the basic transnational social networks that other Dominican migrants would use in the future.[2] By the mid to late 1980s Spain had become a well-known destination for Dominican migrants, particularly for those whose lack of resources or family connections prevented them from reaching the United States.

This work examines Dominican transmigration to Spain throughout the last two decades. Its main argument is that the Spanish case presents particular characteristics not seen in other Dominican transmigratory communities. First, Dominican migration to Spain is a relatively recent phenomenon that developed under very specific conditions. Second, most Dominican transmigrants in Spain are females. Third, most of them are from small towns and villages in the Dominican Republic's remote southwestern region. Fourth, most tend to come from rural backgrounds and have little formal education.[3] And finally, as a result of their cultural isolation, Dominican transmigrants in Spain are actively involved in deeply rooted transnational practices, such as the sending of remittances to relatives back home, the maintenance of Dominican cultural practices, and the recreation of local social bonds.

This work will also analyze different aspects of the Dominican experience in Spain. The first section will examine the factors that led, and still lead, Dominicans to migrate to and settle in Spain. Some of these factors are inherent to Spain, to the Dominican Republic, and to the very particular nature of contemporary transnational migration, or transmigration. Next, we tackle the very difficult question of determining the size of Spain's Dominican community, a task rendered more difficult by imprecise, faulty data. The bulk of the work, including the next two sections, concentrates on the mostly female nature of this migration, the migrants' insertion into the Spanish labor force, and the development of a Dominican transnational community in Spain. Finally, and before concluding, we highlight the case of Lucrecia Pérez, a poor Dominican immigrant murdered by young, xenophobic Spaniards. Pérez's case is symptomatic of the problems immigrants face with European neo-racists, even in countries where there are long-standing historical, cultural, and linguistic links, as is the case of *la Madre Patria.*

Dominicans, Spain, and Transmigration

Dominican migration to Spain is a recent phenomenon, as is the case of immigration to the Iberian peninsula in general. Historically, it was Spain that exported its citizens. This phenomenon has been due to Spain's traditional isolation from Europe, and to the low economic development of Spain compared to other countries in western Europe; the latter has been attributed—among other factors—to the long dictatorship of General Francisco Franco (1939–1975). After the death of the dictator, the necessary steps for a political transition from dictatorship to democracy took place, which coincided with the economic crisis of the late 1970s. For all these reasons, and with some exceptions, Spain was not considered a target destination for immigrants.

The structural changes in Spain's economy in the second half of the 1980s, its admission into the European Economic Community (EEC) in 1986—today the European Union (EU)—and the inflow of foreign capital and investments conditioned the prospects of migration mainly from the countries of Latin America, though also from Maghreb (given the geographical vicinity), as well as from other countries, such as Equatorial Guinea and the Philippines, that have been historically linked to Spain. However, the admission of Spain into the European Union led to an adjustment of its legislation in agreement with EU legislation, which notably affected the relationship of Spain with Latin American countries. In the case of migration, the principal problems derive from the International Agreements of Schengen (1985, and the 1990 Agreement of Its Application) and of Dublin (1990), which established free movement, entrance, work, and residency for the citizens of the member countries of the European Union (Article 7A of the Agreement of the European Union), and resulted in the limitation and control of non-EU citizens. In other words, "The problem is how to allow Community (i.e., EU) citizens to move freely from place to place and at the same time impede non-Communitarians from doing it within a space without borders" (Oraá Oraá, Ruiz Vieytez, and Gil Bazo 1997, 287).[4]

Other factors that have led to the increase of migration toward the EU, and consequently to Spain as well, are the political and economic changes that took place at the end of the 1980s in the countries of central and eastern Europe, as well as in the former Soviet Union, whose citizens typically have more education and skills than Latin Americans and Maghrebis, although Spain does not represent for them, currently, a major target destination. But their preparation, often superior to that of the citizens of the EU country that they target, does not secure them better employment in the labor market. They often have to apply for and accept jobs very different from their professional preparation.

From being a sending country of migrants—both internal and external—Spanish society has witnessed an increase in foreign immigration during the last decade, although one cannot speak of a mass phenomenon, since the number of Spaniards who live abroad (1.6 million) far exceeds the number of foreigners residing legally in Spain (499,773), according to recent figures (Izquierdo 1996, 280). Furthermore, about 50 percent of these foreigners are British, German, and French, that is, EU citizens whose motives for migrating are not necessarily economic ones, but rather of another nature (e.g., retirement, seeking a warmer climate). That number, including the so-called *ilegales* (illegal or undocumented migrants),[5] would not exceed 1 percent of the

Spanish population (a total of 38,872,268 inhabitants according to the 1991 census), a small percentage of foreigners compared to other European countries, such as Luxemburg (32 percent), Switzerland (17.5 percent), Belgium (9 percent), Germany (8 percent), Austria (6.5 percent), France (7 percent), Sweden (5.7 percent), Holland (4.8 percent), and the United Kingdom (7 percent) (Achotegui 1997, 40; Salt 1994).

The issue of migration to Europe is a phenomenon that is also related to the low indices of population growth in many European countries, with Spain being one of the most affected. According to Sánchez Cano,

> The question of immigration in the European Union is a crossroads of diverse tensions, some of which are conflicting. The European Union has, on one hand, the real necessity of a demographic growth that would sustain the current rates of production and consumption. The low birth rates indicate that, in order to be able to count on a necessary labor force in the future, the European population—which is aging—will have to be complemented by foreign workers. A recent study made by the European Commission indicates that in order to palliate the effects of the decrease in birth rates in Europe the entry of foreign workers will be more and more indispensable. (1997, 21)

In the specific case of Spain, its population growth rate appears to be one of the lowest in the world: "Currently, the fecundity rate of Spanish women is 1.18 children per woman, and the annual rate of growth of the Spanish population is 0.3 per thousand. Particularly notable is the case of Catalonia, where these indices are even more negative, since the fecundity rate of women is 1.14 children and the demographic growth rate is zero" (Achotegui 1997, 36). Owing to low demographic growth, Spain and other EU countries need the labor force of foreign workers; Dominicans—as well as other Latin Americans—were certainly attracted by these prospects of easily available employment.

For 1998, a quota of 28,000 foreign workers who would receive residency and work permits was established, but a report of the Bilbao Vizcaya Bank "calculated at 90,000 the number of foreign workers that would have to be incorporated into the Spanish labor market every year from now until 2010 in order to maintain the actual rate of the economically active population" (*El País,* August 27, 1998, 8). This issue is directly related to the problem of an aging Spanish population.

Finally, migration and unemployment are the two fundamental issues that affect the majority of EU citizens, particularly in countries such as Spain, where unemployment is very high (18.55 percent according to 1998 estimates) (*El País Negocios,* January 10, 1999, 21). By observing the correlation between the rate of immigration and that of unemployment in Spain, table 6.1 shows that there should not exist a fear and rejection of immigrants as "competitors" for jobs or as "receivers" of benefits offered by the Spanish welfare state.

Clearly, the correlation between unemployment and immigration in the case of Spain does not constitute the "danger" that the latter is presumed to represent. Moreover, the Spanish public seems to believe that there is a real need for imported labor. More than 50 percent of the Spanish people agree with the introduction of visa requirements for immigrants from less developed countries to come to Spain (Izquierdo 1996, 46). The Spanish people are in favor of a regulated labor flow, with quotas established on a per-country basis, and with bilateral agreements detailing the type of workers who may immigrate. In December 2001, the governments of Spain and the Dominican Republic signed an agreement to regularize the flow of Dominican workers to Spain (López 2001).

From the perspective of the Dominican Republic, the factors that influence emigration are very clear. The Dominican economy suffered major transformations from the mid-1970s to the late 1980s. Low prices for sugar, its main export back then, and other agricultural commodities shifted the economy into mineral exports for a brief while, and then into a services economy, led by the assembly sector and tourism. As the country's economy was transformed from a rurally based agricultural model to an urban-based one, thousands of Dominicans migrated to cities and towns in search of the jobs created by these new economic sectors. Unfortunately, the Dominican economy has not been able to keep pace with its growing population, thus producing high levels of unemployment, underemployment, and a large "underground" informal economy. When the economic crisis of the 1980s hit an already troubled economy, creating a large—and unmanageable—external debt, high inflation rates, soaring consumer prices, power blackouts, currency devaluation problems, trade deficits, and finally food riots in 1984, thousands of Dominicans decided to seek better fortunes elsewhere. Particularly for those who could not meet the increasingly stringent requirements of the U.S. Consulate in Santo Domingo, or who did not have relatives in the United States, Spain looked like a viable, attainable alternative.

But Dominican transmigration to Spain is more than just the result of simple "push" and "pull" economic factors that broadly apply to most developing nations, particularly in Latin America. The Dominican case falls neatly within the realm of transnationalism theories, with their emphasis on the construction of social networks as the explanatory cause for migratory flows. The theory of transnationalism and the processes of transnationali-

Table 6.1. Immigration and Unemployment Rates in Spain, 1985–1992

Year	Immigration rate	Unemployment rate
1985	0.60%	21.0%
1986	0.63%	21.3%
1987	0.76%	20.6%
1988	0.86%	19.9%
1989	0.93%	17.3%
1990	1.02%	16.3%
1991	1.05%	15.9%
1992	0.92%	17.7%

Source: Santacoloma Sanz 1997, 206.

zation have been defined in several—and often overlapping—ways by numerous scholars (please see the introduction). For brevity and to avoid repetition, here we will simply mention Nina Glick Schiller's latest and most recent redefinition of transnational migration as "a pattern of migration in which persons, although they move across international borders and settle and establish social relations in a new state, maintain social connections within the polity from which they originated." This new phenomenon is described as "transmigration" and individuals as "transmigrants," that is, "people who claim and are claimed by two or more nation-states, into which they are incorporated as social actors, one of which is widely acknowledged to be their state of origin" (1999, 96).

Such is the case of Dominicans in Spain, as is clearly shown in this work. Dominican transmigrants in Spain exhibit numerous characteristics and practices that could be classified as "transnational." However, given the broad range of transnational practices and the very broad nature of the concept itself, some scholars have sought to classify them according to their prevalence and intensity. In this vein, José Itzigsohn et al. have developed the notion of "narrow" and "broad" transnational practices as two poles in a continuum: narrow practices require regular movement within the transnational social field, a high level of institutionalization, or constant personal involvement; broad practices represent the opposite, though always including two (or more) countries as reference points (1999, 323). Dominican transmigration to Spain, and the transnational practices of this community—or social field—are analyzed in this work using this theoretical framework so as to determine their degree of transnationalization, as well as the nature of their practices within the rather specific Spanish context.

A Question of Numbers

As with any migratory flow, the first task here is to determine how many Dominicans are in Spain. First of all, it is very difficult to establish the total number of Dominicans, legal or undocumented, residing in Spain. Given the lack of reliable official figures, there are only wildly ranging guess-estimates regarding the size of Spain's Dominican community. This problem is due not only to the difficulties in counting undocumented migrants, but also to deficiencies in data collection by Spanish state institutions. Antonio Izquierdo describes the problem in the following manner:

> In Spain the annual inflow of foreigners is not registered. We have data regarding how many applications are handed in annually for work and refugee grants, but we do not know the total flow of immigrants, nor the motive of their entrance. This is a serious hindrance to determine if the policies of control adjust to the real dimension of admittances and departures of migrants. In my opinion, this is the most important gap in the data and it alone would be enough to question official registrations. Until this requirement is covered in their categories (workers, relatives, refugees, pensioners, and students) one cannot speak of the statistics of migration to Spain. (1996, 241)

Furthermore, the problem is compounded due to the fact that many Dominicans go from being residents of general/regular status to that of EU status by means of marrying EU citizens as well as by nationalization, that is, adopting Spanish citizenship (or that of any other EU country). From that point on, many of them no longer figure in the Spanish national statistics as Dominicans. In 1993, the number of Dominicans with EU status, that is, those who had passed from the general status of resident to that of EU citizen, either by receiving Spanish nationality or by means of family ties, was 9,228, while for 1994 this number was 12,475 (Izquierdo 1996, 72). Among migrants from Latin American countries, Dominicans occupied the first place in naturalizations, followed by Colombians (6,247 in 1993; 6,614 in 1994), Brazilians (4,414 in 1993; 4,819 in 1994), and Cubans (3,539 in 1993; 4,642 in 1994) (Izquierdo 1996, 72).

According to official sources[6] from Spain's Ministry of Labor, some 12,000 Dominicans currently are legal residents, of whom around 9,000 are female. About 56 percent of Dominicans live in Madrid (5,200 women and 762 men in 1995), although there are estimates that the real number of Dominicans residing just in Madrid may reach 25,000 (Piña Contreras 1995, 8). Between May and December of 1991 the Process of Extraordinary Regularization of Foreign Workers took place, by means of which the regularization of the legal status of resident foreigners in Spain was achieved. According to

Table 6.2. Work Permits Issued to Dominicans in Spain, 1992–1994

Year	Work Permits (both sexes)	Work Permits (Dominican women)	Percentage female
1992	3,750	3,172	84.58
1993	3,769	3,150	83.55
1994	4,229	3,563	84.23

Sources: Ministerio de Trabajo y Seguridad Social 1992–1994.

its figures, the Dominican community comprised 5,547 persons, being the fourth largest, surpassed in number only by Moroccans (48,284), Argentineans (7,415), and Peruvians (5,677) (Gallardo Rivas 1996, 312).

In 1992, according to data from the Dominican Republic's embassy in Madrid, there were some 15,000 Dominicans in Spain: 11,000 of them had been legalized at the beginning of that year by the process of regularization, while the number of those who were in the process of legalization of their situation was estimated at between 2,500 and 3,000 (*El País,* November 15, 1992, 15). For no apparent reason, given the prevailing democratic climate in the Dominican Republic, 1,857 Dominicans applied for the status of refugees in Spain in 1993. All those applications were rejected (Izquierdo 1996, 104; Ruiz Olabuénaga, Arístegui Fradua, and Vicente Torrado 1997, 118), while in 1994 an additional 2,752 Dominicans regularized their situation through the quota of that year. According to the estimates from the General Directorate of the Ministry of the Interior and Police, the size of the Dominican population in Spain between 1990–1994 was the following: 1,500 in 1990, 6,640 in 1991, 6,766 in 1992, 9,228 in 1993, and 12,475 in 1994 (Izquierdo 1996, 109). Between 1992–1994 the number of Dominican workers (of both sexes) who did not obtain EU status was 5,481 (in 1992), 5,228 (in 1993), and 7,070 (in 1994). As seen, it is a very unclear picture and an almost impossible task to determine the number of Dominicans in Spain with any scientific precision.

Something that is very clear, however, even when working with these disparate figures, is the enormous gender difference among Dominican transmigrants in Spain, with women representing the immense majority of the migrant population. Table 6.2 presents statistical data based on work permits conceded to Dominicans of both sexes and permits specifically conceded to Dominican women between 1992–1994.

As seen, the numerical difference between men and women was of 578 in 1992, 619 in 1993, and 666 in 1994. This disproportion in work permits in favor of Dominican women is explained by the fact that the majority of them are employed in domestic services, mainly in big cities such as Madrid and tion in the migratory flows to the United States or to other European destinations" (Gallardo Rivas 1996, 314–15). According to her, some five thousand Dominican women have immigrated to Spain just from the town of Vicente Noble (they represented 40–50 percent of the town's female population). With their help, formal and informal networks have been created for the migration of Dominican women from the poverty-stricken southwest of the Dominican Republic to Spain (Gallardo Rivas 1996, 315).

Most Dominican women initially come to Spain attracted by job opportunities in the domestic service sector, where most of them are employed. According to a study by Colectivo Ioé, in Madrid and its surrounding suburbs there was a total of 81 Dominican women working in domestic services in 1986; 65 of them were in the city of Madrid proper, and 16 in the suburbs. Already by that early date, Dominicans represented a numerous group among Latin Americans employed in that sector, outnumbered only by Filipinos (353), Portuguese (210), and Moroccans (120) (Colectivo Ioé 1991, 19). This phenomenon had its origin in the growth of the Spanish upper classes, whose newly achieved economic well-being led to an increased demand for this type of service. Also, most Spanish women would not work in a job characterized as condescending and low-paying, instead seeking other labor alternatives and therefore abandoning this sector. Poor immigrants have come to fill this gap and replace them.

In Madrid, the Dominican community employed in domestic services is divided between "internal" and "external" workers, that is, those who live in the residence where they work and those who commute to work, with a preference (among workers) for the latter modality. The advantage of the internal service is not having to pay for lodging and meals, thus there are more possibilities of saving and sending money to relatives in the Dominican Republic. Its disadvantages are that by living with the family there are more "unofficial" working hours and the salary becomes diluted relative to the hours worked. Internal workers are found in upper middle-class homes in zones such as Pozuelo and Aravaca, in northern Madrid. In many cases, Dominican women accept internal domestic service until they are able to regularize their legal status. Women in the external domestic service receive a higher salary (usually on an hourly basis), depending on how well they do their work. However, external domestic service implies more expenses, since workers have to pay for rent, services, meals, and so forth. The zones of concentration of the external workers vary depending on the cost of rents; this is not a simple situation, however, since many Spanish landlords are not inclined to rent their properties to immigrants. This practice is illegal, but it is not commonly reported by undocumented Dominicans for fear of being turned over to Spanish immigration authorities.

Prostitution is generally not spoken of in public, although it is well known and commented upon among Dominican transmigrants. Euphemistically, prostitution is practiced in the so-called *bares de alterne* and in the services of *relax,* advertised every day in almost all the written media of Spain. The *bares de alterne* are bars where the sexual workers approach the clients. The client invites the worker to one or more drinks, for which the worker earns a determined percentage. If the deal becomes more intimate, then sexual intercourse takes place in the establishment itself. These bars are very popular alongside highways, where merchants and truck drivers constitute an important clientele. But these places are also very often frequented by the police in order to find and arrest the undocumented migrants. More sophisticated is the service of *relax,* which consists of the prostitute receiving the client in her apartment, offering her services in the house or apartment of the client, or in the hotel where he is staying. In this type of service the price is specified depending on the time and the service to be performed. Of the Dominican women who are involved in this type of work, some do it on a part-time basis, only when they have extra time for it (as in the case of some domestic servants) and as a secondary source of income. As expressed by some interviewees, perhaps back in the Dominican Republic relatives may suspect that the money they receive is earned through prostitution, although in this case "necessity knows no law," or, in the best of cases, they adjust to the popular expression that "what is not seen by the eyes cannot be felt by the heart."

The Transnational Community

The Dominican community in Madrid has created its own transnational social networks in that global city, which revolve around a whole range of services that help transmigrants stay in touch with the Dominican Republic and even feel like they are in their own land. These networks are the result, partly, not only of the desire and necessity of identifying and maintaining contacts with the Dominican Republic, but also of a certain rejection coming from the dominant Spanish society.

A place of central importance for Dominican transmigrants in Spain, and a major cause of friction with the Spanish, is the Plaza Aurora Boreal, a town square located in the center of Aravaca in Madrid, a zone where a large number of Dominican women, mostly workers in domestic services, congregate on Thursday and Sunday afternoons. Gatherings of Dominican transmigrants at this plaza are a classic example of narrow cultural transnationality, as migrants use the occasion to partake in and reaffirm their native culture in a foreign land. Every Thursday and Sunday—rest days—the square is full of Dominicans, and the atmosphere transforms into that of a plaza back in the Dominican Republic, with its bars, discos, hairdressers, money transfer agencies, and even *locutorios,* special agencies that offer long distance telephone service at a discount. There, in that square, Dominicans briefly exteriorize all their Dominican being, their *dominicanidad* (Dominicanness) mainly through the musical rhythm of *merengue,* which, because of the loud volume at which it is played, has given rise to protests from the Spanish residents of the zone, who do not always look favorably on this group of immigrants. Part of the problem for these transmigrants—many of whom are recent arrivals—lies in how to integrate into a society without losing their roots or identity to the dominant culture. Even in a Spanish-speaking country, the "cultural shock" trauma can be an effective, isolating barrier. The other part of the problem is the fact that Dominican migration is a relatively recent—and booming—phenomenon and thus Spanish society has not matured yet in the sense of being able to accept "others." The rather unsympathetic disposition of the authorities of the community of Madrid toward immigrants is another cause for the problems that affect both parties. Complaints of mistreatment of immigrants by police officers are commonplace.

Feeling Dominican in Madrid is not difficult at all: the city has several ethnic enclaves, and transnational goods and services ranging from beauty parlors with an entire Dominican staff to restaurants and bars where one may savor a *pica pollo, sancocho, longanizas,* and other typical Dominican dishes. Regarding entertainment, Madrid (mainly in the neighborhood of Orense) offers a whole range of discos where one can enjoy Dominican music. They even have Dominican names like the Guácara Latina, Puerto Plata, Club Bailódromo Latino, and Bar Tropicana. Even more, in Madrid one can acquire all sorts of Dominican goods: rum (Brugal, Barceló, Don Ron), beer (Presidente, Malta India), Santo Domingo coffee, Clamato, and even plantains, *guandules, yuca, ñame,* and *casabe.* Again, all these can be visualized as good examples of narrow cultural transnational practices.

Besides the Dominican embassy and the consulate, the thriving Dominican community in Madrid has several transnational organizations, such as the Association of Dominican Women in Spain (AMDE), the Voluntariado of Dominican Mothers (VOMADE), the Union of Dominican Immigrants in Spain (UIDE), the Juan Pablo Duarte Cultural Association, the House of Santo Domingo in Spain Association, the Association of Dominican Professionals, and also the local offices of Dominican political parties, such as the Partido de la Liberación Dominicana (PLD) and the Partido Revolucionario Dominicano (PRD). These organizations play a very important role in the transnational life of the community; not only are they involved in activities of aid for the new arrivals who are in need of help (as in the cases of VOMADE,

UIDE, and AMDE), and cultural activities (the Juan Pablo Duarte Cultural Association, for example), but they also defend the rights of the Dominican community in Spain (as do the Association of Dominican Professionals and the Dominican Association of Odontological Studies, or ADEO, which deals with the serious problem of the nonrecognition of Dominican university degrees by the Spanish authorities). The Dominican community also has its own publications: *Areíto* and *Información de Quisqueya,* which are delivered to almost all the places where there is a Dominican community in Spain. As we have seen, even though the Dominican transmigrant community in Spain (particularly in Madrid) is not as large as New York's or Miami's, it is a microcosm of what a transnational community should be, with its services, organizations, and networks that maintain economic, political, social, and cultural ties between the country of origin and the host country. The services provided by these organizations overlap both the narrow and broad transnational fields. Whether their activities fall into one category or the other is difficult to determine at times, as it usually boils down to the degree of involvement and recurrence of the individuals who partake in them. Plus, we must not forget that transnationality is a continuum where "narrow" and "broad" are just opposite poles (Itzigsohn et al. 1999, 323).

In spite of the cultural spaces described above, the life of the typical Dominican transmigrant in Spain is hard in general, particularly for those who have not regularized their status. These problems are manifested in the eternal fear of detention and deportation, low wages, long working days, lack of labor security, and lack of medical assistance, all related to their undocumented status. Currently, for the majority of Dominican transmigrants, Spain represents a temporary solution to their economic problems. Proof of it lies in the constant sending of remittances to the Dominican Republic, the exchange of *pesetas* (and now euros) into dollars (owing to the transmigrants' view of the U.S. dollar as the global currency standard), and the little inclination of Dominicans to integrate into Spanish society, although in this latter aspect not much cooperation is evidenced by the Spanish, either.

The constant flow of remittances to the Dominican Republic is a major factor in the transnationalization of Dominicans in Spain and an example of a broad economic transnational practice. Remittances from overseas Dominicans are a major source of revenue for the Dominican Republic (second only to tourism in the amount of hard currency that they contribute), but in the case of Dominican transmigrants in Spain their impact is particularly noticeable because they flow to mostly poor, rural communities located far away from Santo Domingo and Santiago (the country's major urban centers). Thus, it can be argued that for small villages like Vicente Noble and Tamayo (in the Dominican Republic's deep southwestern region) remittances represent their mainstay, while for major urban centers like Santo Domingo they are just another source of revenue among other economic activities. For example, 74.4 percent of Madrid's Dominican population is from the Southwest, and it is estimated that Spain's Dominican transmigrants remit an average of U.S.$728.88 per person per year, a substantial amount for small towns like Vicente Noble (18,152 inhabitants) and Tamayo (19,080 inhabitants). Local authorities from Vicente Noble estimate that slightly more than one million U.S. dollars are received by the town's population in total on a monthly basis, which makes remittances the town's main source of income, with agriculture a distant second. Not surprisingly given the preponderance of females among Dominican transmigrants in Spain, 78 percent of remittances from Spain were sent by females (Soldevila 2001). These remittances have sparked a perceivable construction boom in what used to be traditional, laid-back villages. Now, in towns like Vicente Noble (popularly known as the "Gateway to Heaven") brand-new palatial cement homes coexist uneasily with the wooden shacks of families who are still hoping to build theirs—and it could be just a matter of time since 95 percent of the townspeople have relatives in Spain (*El Siglo,* March 28, 2001).

We have previously referred to the fact that one of the main causes of Dominican migration to Spain is the linguistic commonality. However, it is a simplistic assumption to believe that shared cultural traits facilitate the integration of Dominican migrants in Spain. That is not usually the case. As we have seen, Dominican transmigrants constantly engage in narrow cultural transnational practices that they use to reaffirm their identity or *dominicanidad* in a foreign country. That daily reaffirmation of their "otherness" by Dominican transmigrants—and by the dominant Spanish society—acts in a reinforcing manner to develop further in them a transnational existence. Moreover, mostly because the Dominican transnational community under study is made of individuals with a low educational and cultural level, lexical differences can become a barrier even in a Spanish-speaking host country such as Spain. For example, in Spain *ají* (pepper) is known as *pimiento,* the *petit pois* is *guisante,* the *guineo* is *plátano,* and so on. Furthermore, in the case of the Dominican women working in domestic services, their lack of knowledge of Spanish cuisine, as well as the long duration of the Spanish "lunch" (which, in some cases, can last from 2:00 P.M. until 5:00 P.M.) are noticeable cultural adjustments. Finally, the skin color and lower-class status of most Dominicans makes them the object of discrimination, jokes, humiliations, and detention by the Spanish police. Although not as intense as in other countries in Europe (e.g., France or Germany), racism is also present in Spanish society.

Racism in Spain: The Case of Lucrecia Pérez

The case of Lucrecia Pérez is symptomatic of the neo-racist, xenophobic wave of intolerance developing throughout Europe in response to the perceived "threat" that foreigners represent. According to a survey carried out in December of 1997 on racism and immigration among the fifteen countries of the European Union, 49 percent of the Spanish people did not consider themselves to be racist at all, 31 percent thought they were racist to some extent, 16 percent thought they were somewhat racist, and 4 percent considered themselves to be very racist. In the category of "very racist" individuals, Spain was preceded only by Luxemburg (2 percent), Sweden (2 percent), and Portugal (3 percent); while the greatest indices of racism were detected in Belgium (22 percent), France (16 percent), Austria (14 percent), and Denmark (12 percent) (*El País*, December 20, 1997, 30). If we compare the percentages in those countries to Spain's, we may conclude that generalized racism in Spain is very low. But it must be emphasized again that until recently Spain was a country from which people emigrated, and only in the last decade and a half or so has it become a country receiving immigrant flows.

It may also seem paradoxical that precisely Spain has been the former metropolis of groups toward which racism is now expressed: Gypsies, "blacks" (not only Africans, but nowadays also Dominicans), Maghrebis (demeaningly called *moros*), Asians, Jews, and Latin Americans (demeaningly called *sudacas*). The Gypsies have lived for centuries in Spain, representing today one of the country's typical tourist attractions: the flamenco. Regarding "blacks," until not that long ago Spain maintained a colony in Africa, today's Equatorial Guinea. For Maghrebis and other Africans, Spain is the first stop in their journey into Europe, owing to its geographical vicinity. With the Maghrebis there has also been a long historical relationship because of the Spanish Sahara. Moreover, Spain still retains two towns there: Ceuta and Melilla. Regarding Asians, mainly Chinese and Filipinos, until 1898 the Philippine Islands were Spanish overseas' territories. In the case of the Jews, not only did they live together with the Spanish for centuries, but they also made great contributions to the sciences and Iberian culture. For many Jews dispersed in Israel, the Balkans, and North Africa, Spain continues to be *Sefarad.* These examples allow us to grasp the paradox of this "new" racism, since these groups have always been intimately bound to the history and the culture of Spain. In spite of that, racism exists in Spain and it is quite obvious.

On November 13, 1992, four Dominicans, among them Lucrecia Pérez, an unfortunate thirty-three-year-old Dominican woman from Vicente Noble who had lived hardly more than one month in Madrid after paying forty thousand Dominican *pesos* for her journey to Spain, were finishing dinner by the light of a candle in the abandoned disco called Four Roses in Aravaca (Madrid) when they suddenly heard blows at the door. Four Spaniards, Carlos Felipe Brave Martin, seventeen, Javier Quílez Martínez and Víctor Julián Reviejo Flowers, both eighteen, and twenty-six-year-old Luis Merino, who was a member of the law-enforcement arm known as the Guardia Civil, had been consuming alcoholic drinks and smoking marijuana hours before the crime. The idea of "giving them [foreigners] a punishment," a scare, or what eventually happened, came from Quílez Martínez, who chose the abandoned disco in Aravaca. After arriving there, the police officer Luis Merino used his regulation weapon and fired four times, killing Lucrecia Pérez (one of the bullets also injured another Dominican). According to court testimony, Lucrecia had spoken about her intention of returning to the Dominican Republic since she could not find work in Madrid; according to Enrique Grass, one of the Dominicans at Four Roses, Lucrecia had found work and planned to stay in Madrid.

On July 7, 1994, more than one and a half years later, the courts of Madrid doled out heavy sentences against the authors of the crime, amounting to 126 years of jail time in total: police officer Merino was condemned to 54 years in jail, while his three companions were condemned to 24 years in jail each. The sentence also specified the payment of a compensation of twenty million Spanish *pesetas* to Lucrecia's daughter Kenya, who was then six years old, and declared the Spanish state liable for the incident (*El País,* July 7, 1994, 13).

The murder of Lucrecia Pérez gave rise to an outcry of Spanish public opinion, which qualified it as the first xenophobic crime in Madrid. The press, particularly the daily *El País,* published detailed information about the crime.[7] On November 21, 1992, there was a march against racism in Madrid. According to the national police, some twelve thousand people, including Spaniards, immigrants (both legal and undocumented), and political leaders from several parties, rallied to protest racism. Slogans such as "Spanish friends, don't leave us alone with the racist minority and the discriminating immigration law," "Immigration law, cradle of racism," "Spanish or foreigner, it is the same labor class," and "If there is racism there will be Fascism" spoke for themselves regarding the views of the demonstrators. The murder of Lucrecia Pérez served, unfortunately, as a wake-up call so that public opinion, Spanish society, and its politicians became aware of the ramifications of an issue that affects and will continue to affect Spain: foreign immigration.

Conclusion

Compared to other cases (e.g., New York and Puerto Rico), Dominican transmigration to Spain is a relatively recent phenomenon. The majority of Dominican immigrants there initially consider Spain as just a short-term solution to their current economic situation, whose improvement is not visualized in the Dominican Republic's immediate future. That is why the intentions and goals of these migrants seem temporary at best and their cultural transnational practices are "narrower." Dominican transmigration to Spain is also characterized, on the average, by individuals with a low educational level, which limits their opportunities in finding employment in the Spanish labor market. Therefore, the majority of them, mainly women, are employed in the domestic service, where work loads are long and salaries are low. At the same time, the cultural, social, and even racial alienation of Dominicans in Spain promotes the maintenance and development of narrow transnational cultural practices, and a constant flow of remittances and communications with relatives back in the Dominican Republic. These social and economic exchanges have brought about profound transformations to small, laid-back villages that, until recently, mostly lived off agriculture. It is clear that we are facing a new phenomenon in the case of the Dominican diaspora, with Spain now representing a new alternative to potential migrants from regions and classes without the contacts or resources to migrate to the traditionally favored destinations of the United States and Puerto Rico.

It is still too early to determine how this transnational community will develop, or whether the majority of Dominican transmigrants even desire to reunite their families in Spain, something that is already occurring, although to a minor extent, and which would add a new dimension to Dominican transmigration to Spain. The latter would lead, as in other cases, to the rise of a new generation of children of Dominican transmigrants (the Dominican Spanish), either born in Spain or who arrived there at an early age, who would then possibly enjoy the benefits of the Spanish welfare state (e.g., education, health, leisure, sports, and so on), and who, in spite of possibly identifying themselves with the country and customs of their parents, would become more integrated into Spanish society, provided that they succeed in being accepted and are not marginalized in immigrants' ghettos. In this potential outcome, the migration policies of the Spanish state will play an important role, as well as the capacity of tolerance and acceptance of others by Spanish society. So far, Dominican transmigration to Spain still looks like a two-way street: Dominican transmigrants, cultural patterns, goods, and remittances constantly come and go. It certainly is an atypical case, but one that seems to be repeating itself—on a minor scale—in other European nations.

Notes

1. Currently, a Spanish visa is required only—of Latin Americans—for the citizens of Peru, Cuba, and the Dominican Republic (since 1993). Colombia was also added recently to this list.

2. For example, there are now social networks connecting mostly female migrants from Higüey—in the eastern Dominican Republic—to Switzerland. These women are popularly known as *las suizanas* (the Swiss ones) (Soldevila 2001).

3. There are more than seven hundred Dominican dentists working in Spain as well.

4. All translations are by the authors.

5. Data on undocumented migrants in Spain are not available except as rough estimates and figures tend to diverge wildly. The total number of undocumented immigrants is estimated at 800,000 by Unión General de Trabajadores, at 300,000 by Caritas, at 150,000 by Antonio Izquierdo (1996, 280), at 50,000 by Comisiones Obreras (*El País,* June 21, 1998, 12), and at 100,000 by José Ramón Ónega López, the general director of the Interior Police (*El País,* August 9, 1998, 14).

6. These sources are questioned by some scholars.

7. See the various articles in *El País,* on November 15, 16, 20, 21, and 22, 1992.

References

Achotegui, José. 1997. "Planteamientos políticos básicos para la integración de los inmigrantes." In *Año europeo contra el racismo: Un enfoque progresista,* ed. José Achotegui and Javier Sánchez. Barcelona: Grupo Parlamentario del Partido de los Socialistas Europeos.

Colectivo Ioé. 1990. *El servicio doméstico en España entre trabajo invisible y la economía sumergida: Informe de investigación.* Madrid: J.O.C.E.

———. 1991. *Trabajadoras extranjeras del servicio doméstico en Madrid, España.* Geneva: O.I.T.

Gallardo Rivas, Gina. 1996. "La inmigrante dominicana en España." *Homines* 19(2)/20(1): 311–21.

Glick Schiller, Nina. 1999. "Transmigrants and Nation-States: Something Old and Something New in the U.S. Immigrant Experience." In *The Handbook of International Migration: The American Experience,* ed. Charles Hirschman, Philip Kasinitz, and Josh DeWind. New York: Russell Sage Foundation.

Itzigsohn, José, Carlos Dore Cabral, Esther Hernández Medina, and Obed Vázquez. 1999. "Mapping Dominican Transnationalism: Narrow and Broad Transnational Practices." *Ethnic and Racial Studies* 22(2): 316–39.

Izquierdo, Antonio. 1996. *La inmigración inesperada: La población extranjera en España, 1991–1995.* Madrid: Editorial Trotta.

Lantigua, Juleyka. 1996. "Nosotras vinimos a España para quedarnos." *Listín Diario,* December 1, 3.

López, Kleiner. 2001. "Acuerdo protegerá a inmigrantes laborales dominicanos y españoles." *Listín Diario,* December 18.

Ministerio de Trabajo y Seguridad Social. 1992–1993. *Estadística de permisos de trabajo a extranjeros.* Madrid: Ministerio de Trabajo y Seguridad Social.

———. 1993–1994. *Anuario de estadísticas laborales y de asuntos sociales.* Madrid: Ministerio de Trabajo y Seguridad Social.

Oraá Oraá, Jaime, Eduardo Ruiz Vieytez, and María Teresa Gil Bazo. 1997. "El extranjero ante el Derecho." In *El extranjero en la cultura europea de nuestros días,* ed. José Ignacio Ruiz Olabuénaga et al. Bilbao, Spain: Universidad de Deusto.

Piña Contreras, Guillermo. 1995. "Dominicanos en España: La tragedia de una migración." *Rumbo,* November 20, 8–22.

Ruiz Olabuénaga, José I., Iratxe E. Arístegui Fradua, and Trinidad L. Vicente Torrado. 1997. "La sociedad migrante." In *El extranjero en la cultura europea de nuestros días,* ed. José Ignacio Ruiz Olabuénaga et al. Bilbao, Spain: Universidad de Deusto.

Salt, John. 1994. *Evolution actuelle et future des migrations internationales en Europe.* Brussels: Conseil de l'Europe.

Sánchez Cano, Javier. 1997. "Migraciones, racismo, y políticas comunitarias." In *Año europeo contra el racismo: Un enfoque progresista,* ed. José Achotegui and Javier Sánchez. Barcelona: Grupo Parlamentario del Partido de los Socialistas Europeos.

Santacoloma Sanz, Juan F. 1997. "El problema de la emigración: Aspectos económicos." In *El extranjero en la cultura europea de nuestros días,* ed. José Ignacio Ruiz Olabuénaga et al. Bilbao, Spain: Universidad de Deusto.

Soldevila, María I. 2001. "El país que vive de las mujeres." *Rumbo,* January 29, 40–44.

7

Dominican Women *"Con un Pie Aquí y Otro Allá"*

Transnational Practices at the Crossroads of Local/Global Agendas

Karin Weyland

This chapter will explore the formation of emerging transnational identities in the context of women's migrant worlds and an increased economic and social globalization.[1] A genderized global approach to migration should include a historical analysis of the relationship between transnational capital and national development projects affecting women's work and home cultures (Weyland 1999a). However, owing to space constraints, I will focus on women's transnational practices that develop between the Dominican Republic and the United States in the context of neoliberal policies. Since the 1970s, U.S. factories have increased in Free Trade Export Zones located in Dominican cities, and New York City has increased its demand for women to work in garment sweatshops. Both events led to the increment of migrant flows to the United States, and the settlement of thousands of Dominicans in Washington Heights, the home of the largest Dominican community in the United States. My research spans two and one-half years between 1993 and 1996 when I worked directly with Dominican families and various organizations both in New York City and the Dominican Republic. Before traveling to the Dominican Republic with a fellowship from the Organization of American States, I lived in Washington Heights and became a daily observer of the local culture and community dynamics. I became a volunteer at the Dominican Women's Center and I had access to all the programs organized by this and other community centers. From the summer of 1994 on I conducted interviews with a small number of women I had met in the field. In the Dominican Republic, I contacted some of the relatives of the families I had met in New York and interviewed them as well. In both places, I participated in political and cultural parades, social gatherings, church festivities, and other social events, which gave me the opportunity to use street photography to record the idiosyncrasies of Dominican culture and the hybrid forms that originate as a result of existing transnational practices.

In this chapter I will analyze the effects of transnationalism on migrant families and their changing definition of "community" from national views to more liberating forms of individual and group identification that transcend national borders. My data point to a greater acceptance of transnationalism and border identities in the face of dual citizenship and globalization, and I argue that, to a degree, the effect of corporate economic policy can liberate women by taking them out of traditional settings, increasing the value of their labor, and enabling them to "break out" of traditional roles and statuses. Furthermore, women's economic liberation in the United States helps low-income families back home to achieve upper mobility by democratizing cultural practices previously restricted to Dominican upper classes, and making these accessible to them. While the goal of this chapter is to analyze the emancipatory aspects of transnationalism for women and to bring visibility to the globalization of women's labor, I do not intend to undermine the fact that corporative representatives and owners of small firms continue to see high profits in the flexibility offered by women's vulnerability, wage differentials, and absence of unions in predominantly female work forces (Fernández-Kelly 1983). On the contrary, my data support the belief that women's work in today's global economy is characterized by poor working conditions, such as long hours of strenuous work in front of a machine with hardly any benefits, being subject to pregnancy tests, and the inability to exercise the right to unionization owing to external pressures (Pessar 1987; Pineda 1991). I also emphasize that women have to overcome a good number of obstacles in the United States before engaging in transnational practices and becoming part of more liberating "transnational social fields" (Basch, Glick Schiller, and Szanton Blanc 1994).

For example, my study shows that becoming part of a transnational cheap labor force implies some sacrifices on the part of women, such as being separated from their families, especially their children, for indeterminate periods of time (five to ten years) and assuming individual responsibility for the well-being of entire families that are spread between two separate nations. Once they assume this new form of responsibility, however, they become part of a transnational system of stratification that enhances cross-border solidarity between Latinos in the United States and Latin Americans, contributing to the formation of a "trans-Latino identity" (Flores 2000). Based on this individual/family experience that has now become a common practice in many Latino communities in the United States,[2] a transnational perspective on migration may encourage the spread of transnational labor and community-based organizing. However, I also recognize that there are still many challenges ahead in order to influence the decision-making process so that corporate and government policies achieve a more balanced development between the First and Third Worlds. Until social responsibility becomes a main priority in corporate and government agendas, I argue that women's participation in today's global economy may continue to inform global/local trends "from below" and at an individual family level (Guarnizo and Smith 1998). I also argue that women are contributing to a new way in which culture and power are represented, and I raise the question whether these changes, step by step, may contribute to the building of political unity that functions at the crossroads of a local/global vision of place, culture, and identity.

Transnational Gender Identities in an Increasingly Global Economy

The inclusion of gender in the discussion of global/local trends is crucial if we approach transnationalism as a global process, that is, if we recognize that women are largely participating in the development of capitalism as a global mode of production and consumption. Today, women's transnational labor and consumption contribute to the merging of local/global values, providing researchers with new layers of interpretation, and pointing to political and social changes in those communities where people are now adhering to "hybrid" or mixed identities. For example, just to mention the transcendence of national music forms, *merengue* and *bachata,* which have been strongly identified with a Dominican national identity, are today contributing to the "Latinization" of New York City (Laó Montes and Dávila 2001). Dominican migrants have played an important role in the "transculturation" of such music and other practices in the fields of business, religion, and social customs (Ortiz 1947). Conversely, as migrants communicate with their families back home and travel back and forth on a regular basis, they play a crucial role in the Dominican Republic, being identified there as the carriers of U.S. brand names and other U.S. contemporary icons. Tommy Hilfiger, Nike, Coca-Cola, and others permeate local cultures in the most remote areas of the Dominican Republic, thus localizing global hegemonic culture, which is modeled after a U.S. middle-class life-style. As my data will show, women are the principal carriers of this U.S. global consumption ideology, and following Fernando Ortiz's concept of transculturation, cultural hybridity is a strong element in their emancipation.

The predominance of women in the global economy and international migrant flows has brought attention to their form of participation not only as consumers but also as producers in "global factories" and "neo-sweatshops." For the most part, however, women's contributions have remained invisible, even as they form part of dramatic changes in the labor markets of both core and peripheral countries. As capital undergoes global restructuring, the number of Dominican women has increased drastically in export-processing industries. Conversely, the number of Dominican workers in New

York City sweatshops has also increased, pointing to the intimate connection between the "global assembly line" and the reemergence of sweatshops in U.S. metropolitan centers where Latinos agglomerate (Fernández-Kelly 1983). In order for smaller firms to compete with multinationals, and owing to the way corporate representatives undermine political and economic risks through geographical dispersion and the fragmentation of production, the clothing-manufacturing industry has depended more and more on subcontracting and sweatshop workers to lower its production costs and keep up with rapidly changing fashion markets.[3]

The New York City service economy has also been expanded as a result of global restructuring, incorporating thousands of undocumented and unskilled workers who cater to the needs of the FIRE (finance, insurance, and real state) sector, and therefore are indirectly catering to the global economy (Sassen 1991, 1998). As Sassen's work illustrates, the high demand for these workers, in turn, encourages many more to migrate to the United States, despite serious structural changes reducing the industrial working class in entire sectors of the city. This relationship explains why at the same time that New York City was undergoing a process of de-industrialization, losing half a million jobs by 1990, Dominican migration was at its height, averaging 100,000 Dominicans entering the United States per year. Furthermore, as Sassen's work points out, the increasing gap between those working at the bottom and those at the top is mainly ignored because most discussions of globalization focus on the restructuring of capital and undermine the place of women and others who play a crucial role, although at the bottom, and on whose work also depends the functioning of the global economy.

My study, in contrast, emphasizes the position of individuals within labor markets, communities, and households because it is the only way of understanding the valuable contributions of women, and bringing new valorization to their work. Without due regard to the contributions and needs of people at the local level, consolidation of cross-border solidarity would not materialize, thus ignoring shared objective economic and social experiences as the basis for transnational organizing.

Focusing my attention on the individual families who participate today in transnational practices is also an attempt to acknowledge the expansion of an "international civil society" governed by notions of membership that grow outside the narrative of the state. For example, the emergence of an international human rights regime and of a large variety of nonstate actors in the international arena signals the expansion of a new normative space for political and social action, which originated in their claims to the state to act globally. Thus, multinational corporations are mainly responsible for this change and the creation of these new forms of legalities (Sassen 1998). This is a contested space, however, given that the goal of multinational corporations is the maximization of profits, and that of workers is the maximization of social benefits. Sassen argues, nonetheless, that it represents "a space where women can gain visibility as individuals and as collective actors, and come out of the invisibility of aggregate membership in a nation- state exclusively represented by the sovereign. . . . The needs and agendas of women are not necessarily defined exclusively by state borders. We are seeing the formation of cross-border solidarities and notions of membership rooted in gender, sexuality and feminism, as well as in questions of class and country status, i.e. First versus Third World, which cut across all of these membership notions" (Sassen 1998, 99–100). The following narratives, I hope, will illuminate the way to acknowledge and strengthen the benefits of transnationalism in the struggle for a more equally balanced development.

Under a broader vision of place, culture, and identity, Dominican women are engaging in transnational practices and contributing to new notions of membership that are grounded on transnational social fields, that is, in the re-valorization of one place based on the value and economic system of the other. For example, despite doing jobs similar to those they did in the Dominican Republic, in retrospective, women experience the decision to move to the United States and their new position here as a liberating step forward toward gaining visibility and inclusion in larger global processes:

> I really came to venture *(a aventurarme)*. My parents thought that I would not be able to work and get ahead if I moved to the United States. And when I arrived at the airport, I stood still without knowing what to do, as if I had arrived at a different planet. I always think that it was destined for me to come here or that they [Immigration] didn't care; the picture in the passport didn't even look like me and they still let me in. Other times I think I arrived here based on my ignorance because after you pay for the trip, you are not thinking about anything else but just getting there. I had with me a small bag, which I still keep as a souvenir, with a skirt, a blouse, and a pair of underwear. My sister lived in New York but I had no papers or any money, just myself. It was like saying to the world, "Here I am." (Paulina)

As in the Dominican Republic, women also experience gender discrimination in New York City as they see a gender division in the kinds of jobs that they are able to get, in contrast to their male counterparts. However, in New York, gender discrimination is much mitigated as most women balance their gender status with the benefits the new market offers them. The new transnational position they come to occupy, either by taking advantage of higher wages in one place to sustain their families back home, or by selling products from one place to the other, is another cause for mitigating poor working conditions and minimum pay. As expressed by María and Milagros:

> No man is going to work for the minimum wage while he can earn more money setting up his own business. We work in the garment industry for five dollars an hour because we are women, doing some of the most painstaking jobs such as sewing leather, cleaning threads, and sewing labels onto clothing. Every time I could, however, I would double my pay so that I could earn still more money and send my kid back in the Dominican Republic to one of the best private schools in the capital city. I would have never been able to do so with my previous job [office maintenance] in the Dominican Republic where I earned in one month half of the costs of my child's schooling. (María)

> In New York I always find ways to earn money, which makes me feel more independent than my sisters back in the Dominican Republic. For eight years I have worked in the garment industry, either sewing or cleaning threads, and earned an average of two hundred dollars a week, as opposed to two hundred dollars a month if I had stayed in the Dominican Republic. On top of this, I am always looking for something extra to do, like making food at my house and selling it outside, bringing things from the Dominican Republic to sell here, or managing a *sociedad* [rotating credit associations]. In New York money seems to move faster, and there are more chances to make money for women and men alike. (Milagros)

During the early 1970s, when migration was at its height despite the emergence of the "global assembly line," which was supposed to reduce migration by creating jobs in the Dominican Republic, many women came to depend on the New York City garment industry's demand for cheap labor. This market change attracted women for their manual dexterity and contributed to labor segregation by gender, increasing women's vulnerability to corporate manipulation and market fluctuations both in the United States and in the Dominican Republic. At the same time, however, it provided women with expanded job opportunities and the possibility of establishing transnational networks with the money earned. For the first time, women gained a much higher social and economic standing, which opened new opportunities previously granted only to the men. "What a woman earns now is enough to put food on the table and more," is a common phrase depicting the new valorization of women's work among their families and communities.

As the Dominican community of Washington Heights grew larger, women also found forms of self-employment. Many became street vendors and sold ethnic food or cooked at home and sold homemade products to small businesses, restaurants, and individuals working in the community, making the home a center for generating income (see Figure 7.1). Women also penetrated the service sector, becoming domestic servants and baby-sitters as well as home attendants, maintenance workers, beauticians, and restaurant helpers. Most women who work and sew at home when hired by smaller sweatshops have the advantage that they can look after their children while they work; however, most work "under the table" and receive much less pay and no benefits. Thus, many women prefer unskilled and semiskilled jobs as laborers and operators in factories over the informal economy, but in most cases, women combine both types of work in order to meet household needs. If to this we add the sustenance of their families back home, women's liberation in the United States entails much work and sacrifice.

For black women, especially those who had come at an earlier age and obtained an education in the United States as well as learned the English language, their immersion into U.S. society was also liberating, as expressed by the founder and director of a women's center in Washington Heights:

> Since we founded the center I have had great personal satisfaction not only because I could see the effects this process had on myself and my own family, but also on other women and their families. Women are great sources of power, but many times this is dormant due to the socialization most of us have received. For example, my childhood in the Dominican Republic was very limiting because I had to take care of my younger brothers and sisters, and could not advance in my own studies. Here I have learned to negotiate my own time with my husband and my own children, as well as to claim my own space to study and go out to enjoy life. Above all, I feel now I can talk and express myself without fear. I am not afraid to say what I need and to claim my own rights as a woman. Furthermore, if it were not for the women's organization I created, today I would not be in the position of a business executive. In Santo Domingo as well as in New York there are very few opportunities for black Dominican women to excel in their own professions due to racial, status, and gender discrimination. (Teresita)

While the proportion of Dominican migrants twenty-five years of age or older with college degrees more than doubled between 1980 and 1990 from 3.5 to 7.5 percent respectively, the proportion of U.S.-born Dominicans, twenty-five years of age or older with college degrees actually dropped from 16.7 percent in 1980 to 12.2 percent in 1990 (Hernández, Rivera-Batiz, and Agodini 1995). These data indicate that Dominicans who came to the United States at a young age finished college in larger numbers than their parents and

Figure 7.1. Ramona (1994). Some of the economic strategies women use to support themselves and their families resemble traditional gender roles. For example, they often resort to providing child care or cooking *empanadillas, chicharrones de pollo,* and *bizcochos* in the informal economy. Ramona has been selling ethnic foods on this busy street corner for a few months. She serves passerby clients as well as a regular clientele, consisting of restaurants and other members in the community. Used by permission of Karin Weyland.

U.S.-born Dominicans. Discouraged by the dearth of entry-level jobs and pervasive underemployment in New York City, fewer U.S.-born Dominicans finish high school and/or continue university studies. In contrast to their parent's generation, factory, maintenance, or other service jobs are not a suitable option for many Dominican youth today. In the face of declining U.S. educational opportunities and stable, unionized jobs, Teresita's philosophy, "to educate ourselves in order to empower women and their children in Washington Heights," seems to be an appropriate message for U.S. community organizing. Needless to say that a low overall educational level and fewer local jobs require more immediate attention than the transnational community organizing necessary to incorporate existing forms of cross-border solidarity into a well-organized massive movement.

Furthermore, even for those women who came with professional degrees and legal papers, achieving upper mobility, which would lead to a more mobile transnational life, is also somewhat difficult, especially if family reunification becomes the main priority in women's lives and if family sustenance depends only on women, which is quite often the case:

> In Santo Domingo our economic situation was pretty stable. My kids were going to school and I worked as a kindergarten teacher. My husband would send me money from New York to support the kids so I could afford to pay someone to look after them while I worked. However, I wanted for all of us to be together, so I quit my job and moved out of my father's house where we lived in Santiago. I tried to teach in New York but they told me that I had to learn English first and then get a teacher's certification. So instead I got a job in a toy factory and earned four times as much what I earned in Santiago. While I worked I was enrolled in an English class once a week, but I learned very little English. I came home very tired from work and it was difficult to study. At that time I couldn't afford to stop working because my earnings contributed to those of my husband. I would have preferred to continue studying but I had to get a job first to have money to bring my kids and show Immigration I had an income. They had asked me for a letter from my job in order to process their residence. On top of this, my husband had not been doing well in the construction business, so I kept my factory job all these years, even after I was able to reunify my family in New York. (María)

The many strategies women choose to follow in order to sustain two homes, one in New York, where it is assumed they live with all the comforts of a First World nation, and one in Santo Domingo, indicate that while they become part of a transnational support network that maximizes their material resources, transnationalism has hardly changed the ideological basis guiding women's behavior and expectations.[4] At the same time, transnationalism has helped women to increase the status of their labor, bringing visibility to their steady family and community contributions.

The Historical Roots of Women's Transnational Identities

Throughout the first half of the twentieth century, aided by U.S. transnational state and private capital, Dominican schools taught women activities that required manual dexterity, such as cooking, ironing, cleaning, and especially sewing.[5] These were established under the name of "Vocational Schools for Young Women," *Escuelas vocacionales para señoritas* (Guerrero 1991, 76).[6] The belief that women have greater manual dexterity than men, as best represented by needlework, household chores, and agricultural work for family subsistence, has been used to subjugate a large number of them to these types of jobs. Nowadays, women continue to occupy such positions back home as well as in the newly formed Dominican community in the United States.

In both places, these tasks are thought of as an extension of household work and thus are badly remunerated, increasing the demand for women's work, even if they had never worked in the industrial sector. For example, in 1981, the largest sector employing women was the domestic one, with a labor force of 205,727, while only 57,689 women were employed in the industrial sector. In 1990, this number increased to 127,991 owing to the expansion of Free Trade Export Zones (FTEZ), while the domestic sector continued to employ the largest number of women, reaching a total of 331,369 workers (Báez 1992, 104). These data show that women's employment in global factories represented a major shift in the labor market composition since such employment attracted a large number of women who entered the labor market for the first time. It also downgraded men's jobs because their previous experience in the industrial sector and union participation made them less "suitable" for export manufacturing. It is important to clarify here that while FTEZ were approved in 1968 under Balaguer's government, it was only between 1980 and 1990, when pressured by the IMF and the World Bank's structural adjustment policies, that the Dominican Republic experienced an expansive boom in "global factories," reaching 325 operating businesses in 1990 (Báez 1992,105). This is another example indicating how transnational capital orients local industries toward the export market, impeding the development of labor organizing locally and transnationally as production and thus labor are geographically dispersed. As other theorists have pointed out (Fernández-Kelly 1983; Arraigada 1992) transnational capital attracts women's labor for its low cost, uprooting women from their traditional modes of existence, and incrementing their number in the search for employment in specific industrial sectors. Concomitant economic stagnation in specific labor sectors leads to women's increased participation in migration flows (Fernández-Kelly and Sassen 1995).

Once women establish themselves in the most profitable U.S. economic niches and labor markets accessible to them, they begin to create transnational networks around family subsistence and reunification as well as individual family gains, thus reversing traditional gender roles and family dynamics (Grasmuck and Pessar 1991; Georges 1990, 1992). While it is difficult to estimate the number of women involved in transnational practices today, the Dominican Chamber of Commerce in New York City estimated that by 1993 3.5 million Dominican families received some kind of help in order to gain access to basic housing and health and educational services.

Figure 7.2. Carmen and her mother (1994) at the *colmadito,* a grocery store her mother built with the money Carmen had sent her from abroad. The last time I saw Carmen, she had decided to return for good and expand her business in San Cristóbal, where her mother and her children lived. After Carmen migrated, Carmen's mother took care of Carmen's five children. In a few years, Carmen was able to bring her two oldest children to live with her and her husband in Washington Heights, New York City. Working as a baby-sitter from within her home, and with the help of her husband, Carmen sustained her two homes. I met Carmen at the community-based organization where we both volunteered to educate other women and their families. Carmen was involved in an educational health program and she visited many schools and women's centers to promote women's health habits. After fifteen years of living in New York City, she moved back to San Cristóbal to the same house she had lived in with her husband, and which she helped remodel throughout the years. Her husband, however, was not yet ready to move back, and Carmen was hoping that he would join her in the near future. Used by permission of Karin Weyland.

These families also profit from the large amount of residential and business investments, which became immediate sources of employment for nonmigrants.[7] My study shows that both women and men play an important role in transnationalism, and it is fair to estimate that women play a larger role than men since they continue to see themselves as the pillars of "social life and family stability"—a nineteenth-century view imposed by a strong Catholic and capitalist ideology (Guerrero 1991). This perspective adds new information to previous studies of gender and migration that interpreted women's gains in the United States as a desire, from the part of women, to settle down in the "host" society, as opposed to men, who were more willing to return to the "home country." Therefore, despite transnationalism hardly changing the general beliefs guiding women's behavior and expectations, women have been able to expand their terms of membership based on their transnational networks, creating a more inclusive relationship between work, gender, and family *aquí y allá* (here and there). The formation of these transnational identities was aided mainly by structural factors pointing to the interconnectedness of our economic histories as the basis of our identities and collective memories, and to the potentiality of transnationalism in bringing about change to such institutions as the family and the workplace.

Transnationalism as the Basis for New Contested Narratives

In the Dominican Republic transnational experiences have proved to be very fruitful and empowering for women and their status continues to increase as their remittances help to pay for their children's tuition, basic living, medical expenses, and home improvements. Many times electronic money transfers help to create new sources of jobs for family members left behind. For example, opening a *colmadito* (small grocery store) or buying a car for public transportation are common practices among migrant families as well as helping to build and taking care of other residential and business investments (see Figure 7.2). In the beginning, however, most women could only enjoy their increased status from a distance because, quite often, their illegal resident status did not permit them to travel back and forth. It takes an average of eight years for someone who crossed the Atlantic border with illegal papers or who has overstayed her tourist visa to legalize her status. For those who leave children behind, family separation is most difficult, as stated by Paulina and many more Dominican mothers throughout my research (also see Figure 7.3):

> When I came to New York I left my two-year-old daughter in the care of her grandmother from her father's side. My oldest son, who was seven, stayed with my mother. It was so difficult to leave my children so far away. I saw them again when they were five and ten. As soon as I got my papers I went to visit them but three years had passed. Life was difficult then. (Paulina)

> When I left the Dominican Republic my son was two years old, and I saw him again when he was ten. It was so sad. He didn't recognize me. Can you imagine a child who doesn't recognize his own mother? As

soon as I saw him, I told him, "I am your mother," and he said, "But I don't know you." So I asked him to give me a kiss and he walked toward me and hugged me really hard. We both started to cry. It was very difficult to be away from him, and I still blame myself for anything bad that happens to him. Only if I had obtained my residence card sooner, I would have visited him earlier, but I didn't want to leave without my residence because I would have never been able to come back to New York. I also had to think about my two other children born in New York. (María)

Figure 7.3. Altagracia (1994). It took Altagracia some ten years to unite her family in New York City. During this time, her sister and her mother raised her four daughters, whom she saw only on occasional visits to Santo Domingo. After working as a domestic at a tourist resort in Curaçao for eight years, she entered the United States with Dutch papers and a tourist visa. She continued to work as a domestic, commuting from Washington Heights to Brooklyn and into New Jersey, and two years later she obtained her green card by marrying a Puerto Rican/U.S. citizen. During the past five years, she has been building a house near her mother's house. With the money she makes in New York she is able to employ her own brothers, who work in the construction industry in the Dominican Republic. On her last visit, Altagracia sent furniture and a refrigerator she had bought in Washington Heights. Her dream is to move to the Dominican Republic for good, near her mother, and have her daughters send them remittances to sustain themselves. Used by permission of Karin Weyland.

These examples point to the hardships many women face after migrating and leaving their children behind. And even after establishing some form of transnational connection, for example by sending money to support their children, the impossibility of traveling back and forth makes transnationalism a harsh reality. Until traveling is accomplished,[8] women feel they are trapped in the United States, and this feeling is augmented by the experiences of living in the inner city, such as cramping two families in one apartment, not having adequate building maintenance and regular garbage pick-ups, and sounds of gunfire being a constant reminder of criminal life in the city. Once women can resume their travel back and forth, they are able to enjoy the improved conditions that transnationalism can offer. The ability to purchase consumer goods in the United States and send them back to the extended families left behind plays a crucial role in marking a more affluent mobile transnational life-style. This new position, in contrast to the marginal life of many migrant families, transforms women into carriers of the "American way of life" in a transnational system of stratification.

Transnationalism, in turn, advances the interests of the lower classes in the Dominican Republic by providing access to and democratizing the symbolic markers of social prestige and economic success. While migrant women are able to alter the relationship between cultural gains and class power back home, their unlimited access to U.S. consumption goods such as brand name clothing, electronics, and household appliances, contributes to the perception that they have achieved a middle-class living standard, and by transnational terms, this is the case (see Figures 7.4 and 7.5). In the history of U.S. immigration, such a high standard of living was seldom achieved by the first generation of migrant groups. New forms of transnationalism have put it within the reach of the newest migrant groups.

Keeping close ties with the Dominican Republic has also helped women to replicate many of their cultural practices in New York. The community of Washington Heights has been transformed into a vibrant "border cultural zone," soothing earlier feelings of alienation and displacement (see Figures 7.6, 7.7, and 7.8). My data show that these new forms of transnationalism refute the idea that while Dominicans invest their time and material resources back home, they lose the possibility of setting a strong foothold in U.S. institutions. On the contrary, community leaders and politicians I interviewed saw transnational investments as a more effective way of laying out claims on state and corporate organizations and of establishing policies that safeguard the interests of transnational individual and collective actors.

Unfortunately, quite often women are excluded from this public political process, thus neither group can benefit from each other's ideas and strategies. Finding a way to bridge this gap is crucial in order to value women's family

Figure 7.4. Young men in front of a *colmado* (1994). Young men standing in the *colmado* exhibit imported American goods, such as FILA sneakers, baseball caps, loose pants, and T-shirts, all brought back by circulating migrants. Prototypical icons of U.S. culture, mass consumption articles reach even the poorest neighborhoods of the Dominican Republic, merging local values with global cultural practices. The ideas of independence and material comfort embedded in these products contrast sharply with the gender ideology depicted on the walls of this *colmado,* where women are portrayed as homemakers and sex objects. Used by permission of Karin Weyland.

and community organizing and translate this organizing into broader efforts. Focusing on the globalization of labor and the manner in which today's fluctuating markets affect women's movements is a first step toward making women's cultures more visible, which could lead to a more inclusive vision of Latina/Latin American political unity.

For example, during the Eighth Latin American and Caribbean Feminist Encounter, which was celebrated in the Dominican Republic in November 1998, a group of Dominican women, who lived and worked in Washington Heights, openly identified themselves as Latinas because they felt that it would enhance their political struggle to obtain more community resources in New York City. Similarly, they chose to support the European platform, as expressed by feminists from Holland and Germany, that favored the elimina-

Figure 7.5. Barber shop (1994). Migrants' access to U.S. consumer goods sends a much clearer message about status and prestige to Dominicans on the island than Hollywood movies and TV series do. Despite the negative image of Dominican-Yorks among Dominican upper classes for wearing too many gold chains and exhibiting their newly achieved wealth, Dominican lower classes look up to migrant families for having achieved a middle-class life-style. The owner of this barber shop, Jhova, shows his success abroad by installing a business and creating his self-portrait in a wall graffiti that shows him wearing a baseball cap and a gold chain with his name. Used by permission of Karin Weyland.

tion of national borders. They argued that nationalism promotes a patriarchal system of oppression that favors big business against the rights of women and lower-class segments of society.

Adopting a cultural identity in a "multicultural" era remains a "natural process" of U.S. ethnic and national identification. For Dominicans, "being at the crossroads" provides new ways of positioning themselves through self-definitions of a transnational identity that is no longer attached to a specific national geography. With their own identity on solid ground, their participation in hybrid/border cultures has elevated their sense of personal self-worth. Dominican women can now find a great source of power in those spaces referred to as being "in-between" or as "border cultural zones" that are not mediated by the nation-state. Transnational practices have already provided

Figure 7.6. First communion (1994). Dominican transnational practices have contributed to the prosperity of many ethnic stores in Washington Heights, especially travel agencies, multiple service agencies, and photographic studios. Wedding, baptism, first communion, and graduation albums are in great demand among migrants because they are confirmations of a newly acquired life-style. Celebrations of religious occasions commonly symbolize success and social status. Through such events, many of the cultural elements that underlie the participants' class and gender identities in the United States and abroad are transformed. Used by permission of Karin Weyland.

women with the experience necessary for cross-border solidarity. It is only a matter of time before these spaces begin to create more narratives of contestation. The gap between local needs and global profits, the rich and the poor may stretch only that far.

Conclusion

During Christmas of 1995, at a time when official counts estimated that the Dominican community in New York City had reached 300,000, in contrast to community leaders whose numbers were close to 800,000 (more than 10 percent of the Dominican population in the island), I witnessed a neighborhood contest that helped me to understand the way Dominicans saw themselves as part of a transnational political, cultural, and social field. This

Figures 7.7 and 7.8. Dominican political activism (1994). By living abroad, Dominicans have gained leverage in the political struggle over national resources in the home country. Even after taking steps to obtain political representation in the United States by electing one of their own to the New York City Council, they maintain their allegiances to political parties on the island. Unified by the diaspora experience, they are becoming a transnational interest group. On the basis of their ethnicity and upper mobility, they have gained access to economic resources and political representation in U.S. and Dominican politics. Used by permission of Karin Weyland.

"imaginary" space, which I titled "Las Américas-J. F. Kennedy round-trip," has the potential for new contested narratives regarding Dominicans' accessibility to resources and labor markets. Residents of Guachupita, an inner city neighborhood in the capital of Santo Domingo, decided to create their own airport for a Christmas neighborhood contest. Decorated with lights and flowers, "Guachupita Airport" stood as a symbol of power with respect to the free movement of individuals, labor, resources, and prestige. If read in the context of transnational social fields, this make-believe airport symbolized many of Guachupita's community claims in favor of the eradication of national borders and more tolerance toward broader notions of membership rooted simply in basic local needs and a more inclusive vision of identity and place. The U.S. corporate message, "Think Globally," used in many commercial campaigns in recent years, resonated in my mind as I watched the entrance to the "Guachupita Airport" and questioned whether we are ready to open this door all the way, or just the corporate way.

My data show that bringing visibility to women in the study of globalization provides a new understanding of transnationalism, seen here as a contested space with potential for future labor and social organizing across national borders. In the case of women, I pointed to the origins and formation of these new transnational identities in the context of transnational capital and labor. Working within the parameters of a global economy unfit to protect labor rights, migrant women lead a transnational life in search of a broader American identity, reversing the gender and class identities that national projects for development had circumscribed for them. This new world view has become increasingly influential in defining the interplay between culture and power in local as well as global manifestations. No longer is the nation a reference to shape cultural identity, but on the contrary, now these parameters need to be reworked and rewritten in the actions of transnational social actors. Seeking a transnational life by embracing a "border identity" forces migrants to find new spaces of empowerment. My description of transnationalism, I hope, has shed new light on the understanding of this space's potentiality and challenges. National governments, multinational corporations, and migrant communities should all lead the way toward the formation of transnational organizations that, if rooted in local labor markets and communities, would acknowledge and comprehensively delineate the benefits of transnationalism. A transnational perspective on migration should begin with the recognition that transnational capital can no longer survive without those at the bottom, and that a more balanced development is necessary for both transnational labor and capital to merge and benefit equally from each other.

Notes

1. By "globalization" I mean the integration of economic and value systems that otherwise would be limited by national policies and narratives for group and individual identification.

2. See Davis 2000, 77–89.

3. The global restructuring of capital and labor in New York City has also affected other ethnic groups; for the study of Chinese sweatshop organizing by women in Chinatown and the reorganization of the garment industry in light of global/local changes, see Lin 1998.

4. This is not to ignore existing women's struggles and movements, but quite the opposite, to acknowledge that much remains to be done in order for women to overcome the challenges to equal power. The feminist movement in the Dominican Republic has been very strong, especially throughout the 1980s and 1990s, as have women's individual struggles throughout different historical periods (e.g., the Mirabal sisters during the Trujillo dictatorship and many other women who fought against the 1965 U.S. invasion). Nonetheless, here as well as in the rest of Latin America and the United States, in lesser or higher degree, feminism has been criticized for being a middle-class movement with limited reach into working-class and migrant families (Safa 1995b).

5. For an analysis of the historical roots of Dominican women's migration to the United States in relation to their early socialization and education toward export manufacturing, in particular sewing, see Weyland 1999a, chapter 1. As early as the 1900s, textile manufacturing was the most important economic sector for Dominican women, who dominated its labor force (Guerrero 1991). In a total labor force of 202,807, there were 5,332 women textile workers. They worked in needlework workshops and small-scale commerce and in state-owned workshops producing for the army. Many more worked from within the home. However, U.S. control over tax policies during the eight-year occupation (1916–1924) truncated the development of the textile trades into a full-grown industry. After the Tariff Act of 1919, which enabled the United States to become the leading importer of industrial and food products, local forms of production declined, displacing many needleworkers. Subcontracting women, who worked in the home, became the dominant form of female labor in the textile industry. As national production was pushed further into the domestic sphere, the home continued to be the site of marginal production, minimizing the importance of national goals. This further contributed to the low remuneration and general instability of women's work. Therefore, the decline in the national textile sector, caused by U.S. policies, not only curtailed women's labor organization but also contributed to a crisis in production at the initial stage of the textile-manufacturing industry. (For an account of women's failed efforts to form unions during this period, see Cassá 1990.) The organization of a female labor force, organized around local production and not foreign capital, was blocked. And the U.S. occupation government restructured the Dominican educational system by absorbing needlework workshops, known as *talleres de labores y costura,* into vocational schools for women.

6. The range of U.S. globalization practices transcended the Dominican Republic to incorporate other nations in the Caribbean. For example, during this time, working women in Puerto Rico experienced a similar interventionist process as the United States converted the island into a "sweatshop" with the approval of the governor of Puerto Rico, who officially incorporated sewing into public schools' curricula (González García 1990 and 1993).

7. We also know that remittances reached U.S.$330 million per year in the late 1980s, and then almost doubled in less than seven years, reaching U.S.$571 million in 1994 (Báez Evertsz 1995). By 1995, the Dominican Senate estimated that remittances reached U.S.$700 million yearly. In 1993, the Central Bank estimated that remittances constituted 25.7 percent of all Dominican imports, and 5.3 percent of the gross national income. In their study of emigration from the Cibao, a major source of migrants, Sherri Grasmuck and Patricia Pessar (1991) note that one-third of all families in Santiago de los Caballeros receive remittances from overseas, and nearly one-fifth obtain steady incomes from this source.

8. According to Dominican officials, and contrary to earlier years, the average number of Dominicans residing abroad and returning yearly to the Dominican Republic reached 335,376 in the early 1990s. In 1992 tourist expenditures by Dominicans, calculated on an average of U.S.$25 a day for an average stay of nineteen days per year, added U.S.$169.7 million to the economy; this sum equals 16 percent of the total income from the tourist sector and 30 percent of all exports (Báez Evertsz 1995).

References

Aihwa, Ong. 1999. *Flexible Citizenship: The Cultural Logics of Transnationality.* Durham, N.C.: Duke University Press.

Anderson, Benedict. 1983. *Imagined Communities: Reflections on the Origin and Spread of Nationalism.* New York: Verso.

Arraigada, Irma. 1992. "Mujeres rurales de América Latina y el Caribe: Resultados de programas y projectos." In *Una nueva lectura: Género en el desarrollo,* ed. Virginia Guzmán, Patricia Portocarrero, and Virginia Vargas. Santo Domingo: Ediciones Populares Feministas.

Báez, Clara. 1992. "Mujeres: Fuerza laboral y sector informal." *Estudios Sociales* 25(88): 99– 116.

Báez Evertsz, Franc. 1995. "Emigración al exterior: Migración de retorno." Paper presented at Seminario Problemas de Población en República Dominicana, Santo Domingo.

Barnet, Richard, and R. Muller. 1974. *Global Reach: The Power of the Multinational Corporations.* New York: Simon and Schuster.

Basch, Linda, Nina Glick Schiller, and Cristina Szanton Blanc. 1994. *Nations Unbound: Transnational Projects, Postcolonial Predicaments, and Deterritorialized Nation-States.* Langhorne, Pa.: Gordon and Breach.

Cassá, Roberto. 1990. *Movimiento obrero y lucha socialista en la República Dominicana (desde sus orígenes hasta el 1960).* Santo Domingo: Fundación Cultural Dominicana.

Davis, Mike. 2000. *Magical Urbanism: Latinos Reinvent the U.S. Big City.* New York: Verso.

Fernández-Kelly, Patricia. 1983. *For We Are Sold, I and My People: Women and Industry in Mexico's Frontier.* Albany: State University of New York Press.

Fernández-Kelly, Patricia, and Saskia Sassen. 1995. "Recasting Women in the Global Economy: Internationalization and Changing Definitions of Gender." In *Women in the Latin American Development Process,* ed. Christine E. Bose and Edna Acosta-Belén. Philadelphia: Temple University Press.

FLACSO. 1993. *Mujeres latinoamericanas en cifras: República Dominicana.* Madrid: Instituto de la Mujer, FLACSO.

Flores, Juan. 2000. *From Bomba to Hip-Hop: Puerto Rican Culture and Latino Identity.* New York: Columbia University Press.

Georges, Eugenia. 1990. *The Making of a Transnational Community: Migration, Development, and Cultural Change in the Dominican Republic.* New York: Columbia University Press.

———. 1992. "Gender, Class, and Migration in the Dominican Republic." In *Towards a Transnational Perspective on Migration: Race, Class, Ethnicity, and Nationalism Reconsidered,* ed. Nina Glick Schiller, Linda Basch, and Cristina Blanc-Szanton. New York: New York Academy of Sciences.

González García, Lydia Milagros. 1990. *Una puntada en el tiempo: La industria de la aguja en Puerto Rico (1900–1929).* Santo Domingo: CIPAF.

———. 1993. "La industria de la aguja en Puerto Rico y sus orígenes en los Estados Unidos." In *Género y trabajo: La industria de la aguja en Puerto Rico y el Caribe Hispánico,* ed. María del Carmen Baerga. San Juan: Editorial de la Universidad de Puerto Rico.

Grasmuck, Sherri, and Patricia Pessar. 1991. *Between Two Islands: Dominican International Migration.* Berkeley: University of California Press.

Guarnizo, Luis, and Michael Peter Smith. 1998. *Transnationalism from Below.* New Brunswick, N.J.: Transaction Publishers.

Guerrero, María Angustias. 1991. *Tras las huellas: La mujer dominicana en el mundo del trabajo 1900–1950.* Santo Domingo: CIPAF.

———. 1993. "Tras las huellas . . . La mujer dominicana en la industria de la confección de ropa (1900–1950)." In *Género y trabajo: La industria de la aguja en Puerto Rico y el Caribe Hispánico,* ed. María del Carmen Baerga. San Juan: Editorial de la Universidad de Puerto Rico.

Hernández, Ramona, Francisco Rivera-Batiz, and Roberto Agodini. 1995. *Dominican New Yorkers: A Socioeconomic Profile.* New York: CUNY Dominican Studies Institute.

Laó-Montes, Agustín, and Arlene Dávila. 2001. *Mambo Montage: The Latinization of New York.* New York: Columbia University Press.

Lin, Jan. 1998. *Reconstructing Chinatown: Ethnic Enclave, Global Change.* Minneapolis: University of Minnesota Press.

Mitchell, Christopher. 1990. "Import-Substitution Industrialization in the Dominican Republic, 1925–61." *Hispanic American Historical Review* 70:539–77.

———. 1992. "U.S. Foreign Policy and Dominican Migration to the United States."

In *Western Hemisphere Immigration and United States Foreign Policy,* ed. Christopher Mitchell. University Park, Pa.: Pennsylvania State University Press.
Ortiz, Fernando. 1947. *Cuban Counterpoint: Tobacco and Sugar.* Trans. Harriet de Onís. New York: Knopf.
Pessar, Patricia. 1987. "The Dominicans: Women in the Household and the Garment Industry." In *New Immigrants in New York,* ed. Nancy Foner. New York: Columbia University Press.
Pineda, Magaly. 1991. ". . . *La vida mía no es fácil: La otra cara de la zona franca.*" Santo Domingo: CIPAF.
Safa, Helen. 1995a. *The Myth of the Male Breadwinner: Women and Industrialization in the Caribbean.* Boulder, Colo.: Westview Press.
———. 1995b. "Women's Social Movements in Latin America." In *Women in the Latin American Development Process,* ed. Christine E. Bose and Edna Acosta-Belén. Philadelphia: Temple University Press.
Sassen, Saskia. 1991. *The Global City: New York, London, Tokyo.* Princeton, N.J.: Princeton University Press.
———. 1998. *Globalization and Its Discontents: Essays on the New Mobility of People and Money.* New York: The New Press.
Weyland, Karin. 1999a. "Dominican Women *'Con un Pie Aquí y el Otro Allá':* International Migration, Class, Gender, and Cultural Change." Ph.D. diss., New School for Social Research, New York.
———. 1999b. "Dominicanness at the Crossroads: Surviving the Translocal-Global Village." *Hopscotch: A Cultural Review* 1(3): 64–95.
Wilson, Rob, and Wimal Dissanayake. 1996. *Global/Local: Cultural Production and the Transnational Imaginary.* Durham, N.C.: Duke University Press.

8

Transnational Changing Gender Roles

Second-Generation Dominicans in New York City

Nancy López

> If you are a guy you need money to go out. You want to go out with a girl, you need money because you got to buy her stuff. So, it puts an extra burden if you study. You want to work because you want to go out and you want things.
>
> **—Andrés, 24, a second-generation Dominican man who grew up in Corona, Queens**

> I see my mother. She always wanted to get a better job, but she didn't speak English. She couldn't read. She couldn't write. So, to me, that was a push for me. I have to do better than that. It's not that I didn't want to become my mother, because to me my mother is the most wonderful person. But, I didn't want to go through all the obstacles she went through. Right now, I am definitely planning to go back for my master's degree.
>
> **—Cassandra, 27, a second-generation Dominican woman who grew up in Washington Heights, Manhattan**

Andrés and Cassandra, quoted above, point to one piece of the puzzle of why second-generation Dominican women attain higher levels of education than men. In this chapter I explore how changing gender roles in family life among second-generation Dominican young adults who grew up in New York City is a transnational phenomenon that affects their outlooks toward education.[1]

The data for this study are qualitative and are part of a larger study on second-generation youth in metropolitan New York (1996–1998).[2] The second generation was defined as the U.S.-born children of immigrants or children who had been primarily schooled in the United States.[3] The primary data were face-to-face life history surveys with eighteen to thirty-year-old second-generation Dominicans who grew up in New York City. These data were part of a larger study on second-generation youth living in metropolitan New York, where I, a New York City-born and raised Dominican woman in my late twenties, conducted the interviews.[4] The sampling approach was door-to-door solicitation in 1990 block-level census tracts with high and low concentrations of Dominicans in the boroughs of Manhattan, Brooklyn, the Bronx, and Queens. In total twenty-seven Dominican youth were interviewed: twelve men and fifteen women.[5] Participants were from low-income and working-class backgrounds. None of the participants had two parents with college degrees. Only three women in the sample had earned four-year college degrees. I also conducted follow-up life history interviews with twenty-one of the twenty-seven young adults surveyed.[6] Respondents included ten Dominican men and eleven Dominican women. The quotes included in the analysis come from the in-depth interviews. Participants were selected with a view to striking a balance between age, gender, and varied educational attainment.[7]

I found that whereas women maintain transnational social relations and articulate optimistic outlooks about the role of education in their lives, men lack these transnational relationships and express ambivalence about their prospects for social mobility. As we will see in the life narratives of second-generation Dominican men and women, changing gender roles are being fashioned and reshaped in a transnational space that is part and parcel of restructured global economies, both in the Dominican Republic and the Dominican diaspora in the United States.

The first part of the chapter creates a dialogue between the literature on transnationalism and the second generation. Methodologically, I focus on transnationalism as lived experience. Next, women's experiences in family life as a transnational social space are analyzed. The third section unravels men's lived experiences in transnational social spaces against the backdrop of changing gender roles. I end with a discussion of the implications of these findings for the study of transnationalism, gender, and the second generation.

On Transnationalism and the Second Generation

Transnationalism, or "the processes by which immigrants forge and sustain multi-stranded social relations that link together their societies of origin and settlement,"[8] must be examined as a byproduct of global capitalism with consequences in both the First and Third World (Basch, Glick Schiller, and Szanton Blanc 1994, 22; Smith and Guarnizo 1998). Furthermore, the literature on transnational global processes has featured the significant impact of changing gender roles on family life (Georges 1990; Weyland 2000; Ho 1999; Charles 1995; Safa 1995; Hernández and López 1997; Levitt 1998; Hondagneu-Sotelo 1994; Foner 1999, Pessar 1999). Accordingly, gender is a central organizing principle of transnational processes, social relations, identities, and practices (Pessar 1999; Foner 1999; Weyland 2000; Ho 1999;

Charles 1995; Hernández and López 1997; Levitt 1998; Hondagneu-Sotelo 1994, Weyland, this volume).[9] Perhaps the most important of these changes involves the feminization of the work force (Hartmann 1987). In addition, family life, as a social space traversed by structural changes, cultural transitions, and human agency, is a dynamic site in which to unravel transnational processes (Foner 1999; Pessar 1999). In other words, the gendered social relations that are created in family life provide snapshots of transnationalism as lived experience (Foner 1999, 257; Pessar 1999; Hondagneu-Sotelo 1994; Sierra 1986; Wing 1997; Baca-Zinn and Thorton-Dill 1994; Hill-Collins 1996; Frankenberg 1993). In this light, transnational processes occur not only at the macro-level of economic and political institutions, but also at the micro-level of social remittances, where human agency and social relations are key processes (Levitt 1998).

One limitation of the growing literature on transnationalism is that it tends to focus exclusively on first-generation immigrants, thereby neglecting the burgeoning second generation—the children of immigrants (Glick Schiler 1999; Hirschman, Kasinitz, and DeWind, 1999; Mollenkopf et al. 1998; Grasmuck and Pessar 1996; Valverde, 2002; Portes and Schauffler 1996; Gibson 1988; Rumbaut 1998; Zhou and Bankston 1998; Matute-Bianchi 1991; Grasmuck and Pessar 1996; López 1998, 1999, 2000). Yet there is growing evidence that the lives of the second generation are deeply affected by transnational processes. In a study of second-generation Vietnamese young adults in California, Valverde (2002) finds that transnational practices and consciousness are a part of the lived experiences of these youth. In a study of second-generation Asian Indian youth in New York City, Maira (2001) also finds that gender ideologies are shifting against the backdrop of local and global conditions.

Women's Gender(ing): Transnational Dual Frame of Reference

The globalization of the economy has brought about striking changes in gender roles and family structures that can be viewed as transnational processes that transcend national boundaries (Milkman 1987; Hondagneu-Sotelo 1994; Espiritu 1997; Mahler 1997; López Springfield 1997; Baca-Zinn and Thorton-Dill 1994; Rubin 1997). In *The Myth of the Male Breadwinner: Women and Industrialization in the Caribbean,* Safa (1995) posits that as Dominican women enter the paid work force, men are no longer the breadwinners in their households. As wage earners, women living in the Dominican Republic (as well as in the United States) have a weapon with which to negotiate more egalitarian relationships in the household (Safa 1995; Hernández and López 1997). To be sure, as more and more Dominican women are entering the labor force, marriage rates have been declining, and divorce rates are rising.[10] In 1950 there were 5.6 divorces for every 100 marriages, but by 1985 there were 40 divorces for the same number of marriages (FLACSO 1993, 31). Given these trends it is not surprising that Dominican women on the island head about a third of households (CESDEM 1996, 25).

More than fifteen million immigrants have entered the United States since 1965. After Mexico, the Caribbean produced the most immigrants during the 1980s.[11] New York City, as a main entry point, has attracted about one-fifth of all immigrant arrivals in recent decades. It is significant that women are important social actors in the globalization of the economy. For instance, Dominican women dominate migration flows to the United States, Spain, Puerto Rico, and the rest of the Caribbean Basin (Weyland, this volume; Hernández et al. 1995; Pessar and Grasmuck 1991). Since women are often the first to migrate, Dominican immigrant mothers are often the sole economic providers for their families, with more than half of Dominican households in New York headed by women.[12] A combination of immigration and changing labor market structures have contributed to Dominican women heading their families both in the island and in the diaspora.

The first waves of immigrant Dominican women in New York City were concentrated into the lowest echelons of the declining sectors of manufacturing, especially in the garment industry, and since the 1980s they predominate in low-level service sector jobs, such as home attendant and nurse's aide (Pessar and Grasmuck 1991). Consequently, Dominicans have the highest rate of poverty of any ethnic group or immigrant group in New York City (33 percent) (Grasmuck and Grosfoguel 1997; Hernández et al. 1995).

The entry of Dominican immigrant mothers into the paid labor force has had a palpable effect on the lives of their U.S.-born daughters. Consequently, women narrated life histories that depicted their mothers as one of the most important figures in their lives. Yvonne, a twenty-two-year-old woman who grew up in Williamsburg, Brooklyn, recalled how her outlooks on education crystallized when reflecting on her mother's past hardships: "What really influenced me was my mother. She was the oldest of the eight children who came to the United States. She was sixteen and all the other ones were much younger, so they went through elementary school and high school here; so they basically grew up knowing more English than Spanish. Then my grandmother and grandfather were working, so it was basically upon my mother to come home, cook, clean, and help with the raising of the children."

As members of the working class, Dominican women clearly differentiate their home experiences from those of middle-class European-Americans. Katia, a nineteen-year-old woman who grew up in Inwood, Manhattan, giggled when discussing the differences she noticed between Dominican families in the United States and other American families: "For Dominican girls, by the age of twelve, you know how to cook, clean, and wash by hand. We had no washing machine, back then. It seems to me that in a [white] American home, a typical one, the mother does everything, while the daughter is out shopping at the mall after school. And, she has her own car and everything."

Historically, staying at home has never been an option for low-income women, particularly those who are racial minorities. As Katia pointed out, while their mothers work, daughters growing up in these households are charged with responsibilities at an early age, such as serving as surrogate mothers to their siblings—engaging in a new form of "transnational mothering" (Pessar 1999). These sets of race, class, and gender-differentiated experiences provide women with a backdrop from which to evaluate their options regarding work, education, and family roles.

Women spoke about their views on education in terms of a transnational dual frame of reference, whereby they consistently assessed their educational and employment opportunities against the backdrop of their mothers' experiences as low-income women who did not have educational opportunities (Ogbu and Simons 1998). Cassandra and Yvonne, previously quoted, indicated that they were interested in pursuing their education in order to achieve financial independence from men.

The transnational dual frame of reference echoed by women in their life narratives resembled that unearthed by Suárez-Orozco among Salvadoran youth in California. Suárez-Orozco (1987) posits that these youths maintained a dual frame of reference in which they compared and contrasted their present situation with that which their parents had left in the home country. Accordingly, an intense feeling of guilt and obligation toward a sacrificing mother, along with the dream of ending family hardship, led them to emphasize academic success as a means of bringing honor to their families, and their mother in particular.[13]

Transnational Social Relations

Familism, a sense of affinity, obligation, and closeness to the family, permeated the narratives of the women. For women, "home" was a place where women felt the strong hand of social control and bore the brunt of a gender-biased division of labor, but it was also a "safe space" where they sought support through woman-centered social relations that were transnational spaces (Pastor, McCormick, and Fine 1996; Zhou and Bankston 1998). Janet, a twenty-six-year-old woman who grew up in Washington Heights, Manhattan, reminisced:

> In some ways, I think, Hispanics, in general, tend to be a little bit more on top of their children than white Americans. White Americans tend to be more individualistic. I don't see them having the heart-to-heart talks. In Hispanic families and in my family, if one of us did something, immediately someone would be calling an aunt to tell her. It didn't matter if it was just a bad report card; everybody knew your business. Whereas, I find that in white American families it was a little different. I think there was probably a little bit more affection in Dominican families. We were more touchy, feely—you get hugged a lot more. But I think you also get a lot more sheltering sometimes and you feel caught between two worlds. You have that very strong Dominican heritage and that family influence, but then there was also this very independent, be-on-your-own mentality.

Women's narratives were peppered with stories like Janet's, about extended family members, such as aunts, godmothers, grandmothers, and adoptive mothers, residing both in the United States and in the Dominican Republic, as central figures in their lives. These social relationships formed the nodes in the woman-centered webs of emotional support that women were able to draw upon during difficult times (see Pérez 1996; Suárez-Orozco and Suárez-Orozco 1995). Pastor, McCormick, and Fine (1996) posit that "homespaces" that provide emotional support are not limited to relatives and home life, but may include other social spaces found in schools and spiritual communities.[14] Significantly, these "homespaces" need not exist in one bounded nation, but are part of gendered transnational webs of social relations that are diasporic.

The fact that second-generation women were more likely to be bilingual than their male counterparts facilitates their ability to maintain transnational social relationships with relatives back on the island (Portes and Schauffler 1996). Against the backdrop of transnational social relations, women mature more quickly than their male counterparts and consequently they cultivate a sense of responsibility for their families. Cassandra remembers nostalgically how much she enjoyed translating for her family: "Translating for my parents made me feel like an English-speaking brain. It felt good to know that I knew a lot of English." Through engaging in these "feminine" adult obligations, women not only felt proud of themselves, but at an early age they learned how to navigate through a maze of institutions that were unfamiliar to their parents (Valenzuela 1999; hooks 1981; Pastor, McCormick, and Fine 1996; Stanton-Salazar 1997). These types of experiences were significant because they helped women foster a sense of competence and efficacy in their journey of becoming women. Given these gendered responsibilities, it is not surprising that research has found that women are more likely to retain the mother language than their male counterparts (Portes and Schauffler 1996).[15]

Women were also subjected to strict social control and sexual policing. When asked to describe their childhood activities in the street, women responded with bewilderment that they usually tried to stay off of the streets.[16] Cassandra explained that while her brothers were allowed to go to baseball games, she was not given the same liberties: "I had to come home straight from school. Some of my friends were in young adults clubs, but my mother didn't believe in that. Oh, no!"

Women spoke about how parents "protected" them from "the street" by limiting the amount of time they could spend socializing outside the home in the company of young men. The gender(ed) social control of women in second-generation Dominican households resulted in the cloistering of women in their homes, thereby reinforcing their connection to their families.[17]

Transnational Feminism

Complicating the dynamic of shifting gender roles is the larger issue of the traditional role of men as economic providers and women as homemakers. As a break from conventional gender roles, women's narratives were pierced by the assumption that they would assume full responsibility for the well-being of their families. When asked about her marriage and child-bearing plans, Lidia, a twenty-year-old college student who grew up in Inwood, Manhattan, asserted: "I don't think I'm ready to have kids. I don't think it's the time for me to have kids. I think I'm too young. I should wait until I graduate from college and have a degree because my child will depend on me. I want to have something to give my child while it is growing up."

Implicit in Lidia's comments was an acknowledgment that women can no longer depend on men for the economic stability of the family. Some women even said that they did not want to have any children, and a few admitted that they had never thought about raising children until I posed the question to them.

Two explanations prevail for the development of feminist practices among Third World immigrant women living in the United States. The hegemonic explanation posits that the development of feminist practices among immigrant women is a by-product of their assimilation into mainstream U.S. society (Pessar and Grasmuck 1991; Georges 1990; Gil and Inoa Vasquez 1996). In this equation, changing gender roles among Dominican women in the United States is seen as a direct result of their exposure to U.S. feminism—a product of assimilation or "Americanization" (Georges 1990; Pessar and

Grasmuck 1991; Pessar 1999; Levitt 1998). It has even been suggested that first-generation Dominican women fear returning to the Dominican Republic because they may have to revert to traditional gender roles (Pessar and Grasmuck 1991).

A counter-hegemonic vein of research argues that the development of feminist practices among Third World women living in the United States is a complex phenomenon involving the cultural legacies of the sending societies. In this context, feminist practices among Dominican women, as well as other Third World women, must be seen as part of a continuum that has its historical roots in their home countries and can be examined as a transnational phenomenon (Mahler 1997; Molina 1998; Paravisini-Gebert 1997; Safa 1995; Moraga and Anzaldúa 1983). As argued by Foner (1999, 258) "immigrants continue to draw on pre-migration family experiences, norms, and cultural frameworks as they carve out new lives for themselves in the U.S."

Women articulated a "homegrown" feminist standpoint that was anchored in the formal and informal lessons they had gleaned from their mother's agency in the face of daunting obstacles (Shepherd, Brereton, and Bailey 1995; Alvarez 1991, 1994, 1997). When asked about her views on family, marriage, and gender roles, Janet boasted: "I just have no desire to be married. I think I have a lot more to accomplish and kind of follow through on before I commit myself to somebody." When I asked her if her ideas were somewhat different from those of her sister or her mother, Janet replied: "No, my sister is very career oriented and actually we get that from my mother. My mother married in part to get out of the house and kind of gave up her dream career to be married. . . . If a woman comes from a strong Dominican family and her family was a big influence on her, she has two choices: either get married, or go to college and get a degree and become something. Guys come in and out whenever they want, they can do whatever they want. You'll find that women want to get as independent as they possibly can, otherwise you will have to stay in the house for the rest of your life!" Previous research has found that minority and immigrant women have remained optimistic about the future, and they have actively pursued education as a way of rebuilding their families (Anzaldúa 1987; De León 1996).[18]

Women remembered that their parents, mothers and fathers alike, exhorted them to obtain an education because of their subordinate gender position. Mothers, in particular, warned their daughters about the perils of depending upon a man for economic support (Washington and Newman 1991). Diana, an eighteen-year-old woman who grew up in Washington Heights, Manhattan, and who was attending a neighborhood high school, reflects on some of the lessons she learned from her mother: "We're in the

1990s, you know; it's equal rights. We have the same rights as men. My mother would have wanted it to be that way for her, but now she can't do anything about it because she already has kids. She can't work now. She doesn't know English. She didn't have a chance to go to school. But she tells me that equality is the way it's got to be—that it's got to be fifty-fifty—that I cannot be the way that she is now. Because the way she's living now is not the way that she wanted it to be. She's depending on my father and she doesn't like that." Diana's remarks indicate that she learned about male domination by witnessing the gender dynamics in her home. Dominican mothers' life choices and experiences and their ability to communicate their feelings about those choices to their daughters have an important impact on the kinds of decisions their daughters eventually make for themselves.

The emergence of feminist practices has already been documented among Dominican women on the island who have never migrated (Levitt 1998; Charles 1995; Safa 1995). Dominican women have a long history of engaging in feminist practices through insubordination. As explained by Foner (1999, 258) the cultures that immigrants come from are constantly changing so it would be misleading to think that dramatic transitions in family patterns have not occurred in the sending societies. Indeed, the act of migrating may be interpreted as a prime example of feminist agency (Hernández and López 1997).

A similar pattern of transnational feminist agency is already discernible in the United States. Cassandra, who was divorced, explains why she is in no rush to find a husband: "I'm just waiting for the right thing to happen. Because I'm not just going to pick any guy from the street just to know that I have a man. No. I can take care of my child. My child and I, we're doing fine. It's rough being a single parent, but especially since I grew up with my Mom and my Dad; they [were] married for so many years that for me it is very hard to put myself in this situation. But, I'm not just going to take anybody. No way . . ." Second-generation Dominican women's feminist agency and outlooks regarding traditional gender roles and independence are not merely adopted once they come to the United States, but rather reflect a transnational phenomenon that can be observed both in the sending and the receiving societies.

I also queried Jahaira, a thirty-year-old woman who lives in a civil union in Flushing, Queens, about whether or not she wanted to change her marital status: "You mean like get married? *No*. I'm not rushing to do it . . . because a lot of marriages are failing. And I don't see these children's father and me being the perfect, ideal couple that will last untold years. So, if we get married that's okay. But, it's not something I have to do. I am self-sufficient. A lot of people get married and it is out of love and stuff, but sometimes it is convenient and it is economically sane to do. I take care of myself." Women's strong insistence that they can take care of themselves resonates with the marital patterns that predominate in the Dominican Republic, where the percentage of women who are married is smaller than those who choose to remain in a civil union *(unión libre)*. In the Dominican Republic only half of women are in civil unions or married, and among these women, *unión libre* is more prevalent than marriage (125 civil unions for every 100 marriages) (PROFAMILIA 1991, 10). In 1996 only 22.8 percent of women ages fifteen to forty-nine were married, compared to 36.4 percent who were in a civil union.[19]

The development of feminist practices among Dominican women in the United States is a "messy" and complex process that can trace its origins to the legacy of resistance to male domination that is rooted in the Dominican Republic (Hernández and López 1997; Safa 1995). Janet, a thirty-year-old Dominican woman who grew up in Bushwick, Brooklyn, but spent the better part of her adolescence in the Dominican Republic, remarked that the women in her family, both in the Dominican Republic and in the United States, have historically exercised their agency: "We didn't grow up with that big a male dominance. My Mom was the person that you asked permission to, and the person who said whether you can go or not. Or you can have this or not. Even though my father was there at times, she was always the steady person there, so she was the one who said what to do and when to go. In my family we're strange because we tend, now in our relationships, to be dominant." Changes in gender relations result from experiences in the home rather than from a "modernizing" Anglo influence or the acculturation process (Hondagneu-Sotelo 1994, 195; Safa 1995). Although Cassandra resented her father's behavior in the home as a *caudillo* (the strongman of the household), she also noted that her mother, despite her wifely submissiveness, asserted her agency and was not completely dependent on him for financial support: "My mother always used to put in an equal share of the household money because even though she was at home raising us, she never sat down in the house. She was never home waiting for my father to bring the check. My mother was making more money than my Dad. We used to go out and clean apartments together and we used to baby-sit. I used to go and help her out. She was always doing something. She used to bring in more money than he did. My father never even knew how much."

Although Cassandra's mother probably did not view herself as a feminist (Hondagneu-Sotelo 1994, 196), her behavior can be described as feminist because she actively sought self-determination. Most importantly, because these changing gender roles are occurring both in the Dominican Republic and in the diaspora, they can be viewed as transnational processes that defy national boundaries and mutually affect one another.

Men's Gender(ing): The Absence of a Dual Frame

The men in this study were absolved from the adult-like responsibilities imposed on their female siblings. Men were not expected to perform domestic duties or serve as surrogate parents to younger siblings. When asked about his household responsibilities while growing up, Andrés, a twenty-four-year-old man who grew up in Corona, Queens, chuckled: "We were boys. We didn't have to do [many] chores around the house. My mother used to take care of the house and do the cooking. When my mother was working she used to have a neighbor come over and stay with us until she returned."

As Andrés explained, even in households where there were no girls, another woman, usually a relative or friend, was assigned the domestic chores in the mother's absence. This pattern differs from the conclusions in Valenzuela's (1999) study of the role children played in the settlement process of Mexican immigrants living in California. Valenzuela found that while daughters were often expected to play a more active role in helping the family, the eldest child regardless of sex had to assume these chores.

Men did not personally identify with their mothers' positions as women who are simultaneously mothers, homemakers, and low-wage laborers. José, a twenty-five-year-old man who grew up in Inwood, Manhattan, smiled when he explained that his mother never expected him to perform household duties, but she did teach his sisters: "I never washed dishes. I was never expected to wash dishes. But my sisters, my mother showed them how to cook. She showed them how to clean the house." Absolved from the adult-like responsibilities imposed on their sisters, men did not compare their present situation with that of their parents, even when their fathers were present.

The gender(ing) that took place within family life reinforced men's traditional views on gender roles and family ideologies. When asked about the differences between how boys and girls were raised, Rodrigo, a nineteen-year-old man who grew up in the Lower East Side of Manhattan, remembers with a smirk: "My sisters had to clean the house and stuff like that. Me, I just had to stay and watch TV. I didn't really have that much responsibility. I'm not good at housework." While Rodrigo believed that in a marriage both the husband and wife should work and contribute to the household expenses, he still felt that child-care responsibilities were primarily the responsibility of the wife. Not surprisingly, twice as many men as women in the study indicated that they felt that in a marriage, housework and child care were primarily the responsibilities of women.[20]

Men also did not speak about serving as institutional brokers for their families. Indeed, several men mentioned that during the few times they did serve as translators for their parents, they felt somewhat embarrassed. According to Rodrigo, "Well, when I was growing up that [translating] was usually done by my sisters. That was usually their forte. Now, that I'm the only one at home, if they have a phone call or anything that they need me to help them out with, then I do it." When I asked him how he felt about that, Rodrigo replied, "It feels okay. But, I mean, they've been here for so many years, I wish they would have learned English by now." The ambivalent feelings men associated with the task of translating for their families contrasted sharply with women's affirmation that they felt "smart" and proud that they were able to help their parents.

Men also did not talk about having close relationships with family members and lacked many of the emotional supports readily available to their female kin. In other words, while women thrived on transnational family networks, men seldom mentioned having close relationships with their families. As argued by Hondagneu-Sotelo (1994) men and women often have very different social networks. While men's exemption from the adult responsibilities imposed on their female counterparts left them more free time than their female counterparts, it also deprived them of some of the emotional supports readily available to women.

In spite of the greater freedom men enjoyed, young men occupied marginal spaces within family life. Severe overcrowding in many low-income and poor Dominican homes was often resolved by making the living room into a substitute bedroom. In accordance with the principle of maintaining the privacy of women in the home, the sole bedroom in the apartment was often treated as a woman's space, while the more public living room quarters were designated a male space. This was the case in the homes of Peter, a twenty-three-year-old who grew up in Washington Heights, Rodrigo, and Joaquín. Joaquín, a nineteen-year-old man who grew up in Inwood, Manhattan, and his brother shared a sofa bed in the living room, while his mother and two sisters shared the only bedroom in the apartment. Perhaps young men growing up in these overcrowded homes do not want to stay home all day because their bedrooms are public spaces during the daytime.

A number of the interviews with men took place in parks, on the street, or literally on the run in a car. Rodrigo, who at one time shared a one-bedroom dilapidated tenement apartment with his mother, father, and sister in the Lower East Side of Manhattan, insisted that we conduct the interview outside, saying, "I hate being upstairs cramped up with my parents. I'd rather do the interview downstairs in the park." In spite of the brisk early March weather, Rodrigo's interview was conducted on a park bench, while he greeted his neighborhood friends and kept an eye on his motorcycle.

Becoming a Man

Freed from the onerous domestic tasks required of their sisters, men had much more leisure time on their hands. Despite parental efforts to protect both daughters and sons from the vices of the street, in practice men were given more liberties. Not surprisingly, one unifying thread in the narratives of men was their fixation on sports (O'Donnell and Sharpe 2000; Gilbert and Gilbert 1998). The makeshift basketball courts, which lined the streets of the neighborhoods I visited, attested to the fact that sports have become a metaphor for masculinity and independence. Men's stories about their childhoods were peppered with episodes of spending time "in the streets," playing basketball and hanging out with other young men (Díaz 1997; O'Donnell and Sharpe 2000; Gilbert and Gilbert 1998). In their quest to cultivate a sense of masculinity, the street for men becomes a social space were they can display their sense of what it means to be a man. In part because of the displacement of men as the breadwinners in the home, at the dawn of the twenty-first century masculinities are in flux across the globe (O'Donnell and Sharpe 2000). Consequently, the quest to establish a firm sense of gender identity—a deep-seated sense of self as "masculine" or "feminine"—became a project that occupied much of men's free time. Young men had a more formidable task before them than their female counterparts, regardless of whether or not their fathers were present. Another aspect of men's efforts to fashion a gender identity was the active distancing of themselves from their mothers. Many of the young men viewed being at home with their mothers as problematic. Men had to create spaces outside the home to establish their sense of manhood.

A second space in which men sought to assert their masculinity was through work. The time-honored bastion of maleness—the military—was Reynaldo's hope for establishing his sense of manhood: "I'm going to the military to see if I can make a man of myself because I like to chill too much. I don't like school that much. I barely made it through high school because I like chilling too much. You know, like hanging out with your friends playing basketball and stuff." At the age of nineteen, Reynaldo thought that joining the military was the first step in becoming a man and feeling like an adult. While men struggled to achieve a secure sense of gender identity, their female counterparts had long achieved their sense of womanhood. In contrast, at a very early age, women already felt like adult women.

Andrés, a twenty-four-year-old Dominican man, also remarked that becoming a police officer was part of his quest to become a man. As explained by Andrés in one of the epigraphs at the beginning of this chapter, young men feel a need to establish their manhood by fulfilling the traditional "masculine" role of provider by working. This finding differs from studies that suggest that men may not want to pursue academic success because they may be accused of being feminine (Bourgois 1995; Fordham 1996; Willis 1981). In a study of African-Americans enrolled in a public high school in Washington, D.C., Fordham (1996) found that low achieving men were also preoccupied with their masculinity. These young men measured their manhood in terms of having sexual freedom and not committing themselves to any particular women. In contrast, the high-achieving men tended to have only one serious girlfriend. Fordham (1996) also argued that some of the high-achieving men faced more pressure to reject school achievement because they feared that their peers would accuse them of losing their identity or being homosexual.

The men in this study did not define academic success as a feminine trait. However, they did attempt to establish their masculinity through pursuing romantic relationships with women. Men made reference to many episodes of being preoccupied with having girlfriends throughout their adolescence (Fordham 1996). When asked about the most important aspect of high school, many of the men, especially those who had not done well in school, typically responded: "Chilling, talking to the girls." Some of the men indicated that they sometimes skipped out of classes during high school in order to follow girls. Twenty-five-year-old José, who grew up in Washington Heights, remarked: "We are *tígueres*.[21] We are chilling in the street all the time. You won't see girls in the corner, especially in Dominican families. They lock down. Then, the only thing the girls can do is open a book and read." While men in this study did report that their parents warned them about "getting a girl pregnant," they did not share any of these worries themselves (Vera et al. 1996). Since men did not see themselves as responsible for child care, they expressed little concern about becoming parents at an early age. Men even defended the double standard and boasted that they took an active role in keeping their sisters away from the *tígueres*. Whereas women talked about not letting men "screw up" their lives, men did not express such concerns.

Conclusion

This study began with the question of why second-generation Dominican women attain higher levels of education than men. Drawing on the life histories of second-generation Dominican men and women who grew up in New York City, I examined changing gender roles in family life as a transnational phenomenon that affected their outlooks toward education. In examining family life as a dynamic and gendered social space where we can examine the lived experiences of second-generation Dominican men and women, I hope to contribute to the budding literature on transnational processes among the second generation.

Second-generation Dominican women's narratives revealed that transnational mothering plays an important role in how they view their prospects for the future. At a young age, women assume adult responsibilities and in some cases become surrogate mothers to their younger siblings. They also become institutional brokers for their families and feel pride about being able to assist their parents in this capacity. This lived experience led women to have closer ties to the family and to develop transnational networks, as well as strong gender identities as women. In due course, women developed a transnational dual frame of reference in which they compared and contrasted their own situations with those of their mothers. Influenced by the feminist practices of Dominican women on the island and in the diaspora, second-generation Dominican women in New York City are carving feminist identities and practices whereby they look toward schooling as a means of not depending on men.

For several reasons, men did not articulate a transnational dual frame of reference. First, gender-biased child-rearing practices generally absolved men from many of the adult responsibilities imposed on their sisters. Men also spent many of their adolescent years outside their homes, usually playing sports. Moreover, men occupied rather marginal spaces in family life and they had very weak ties to transnational social relations and social spaces through their extended kin. At the same time, achieving gender identity was fraught with problems for men. Men established their sense of manhood by becoming preoccupied with asserting their masculinity through distancing themselves from home life. Whereas women's narratives of womanhood and independence were linked to the importance of receiving an education, men discursively linked their feelings of independence and masculinity to work and establishing romantic relationships with women. Moreover, while women expressed deep concern about the consequences of premature childbearing, men did not articulate any of these worries. Seemingly, qualitative differences in the lived experiences of men and women in family life, accompanied by shifting transnational gender roles, are an important part of the reason why second-generation Dominican women attain higher levels of education than their male counterparts.[22]

What are the implications of these findings for the study of the second generation and transnational social fields in the Dominican diaspora? In exploring the education of second-generation Dominicans in the United States, first we must play close attention to how family life is a transnational social space that is gendered. Second, we must always be cognizant of how gender roles are fluid and constantly changing in social spaces that defy national boundaries. In this light, before assuming that the second generation is only affected by the acculturation process in the United States, we will also scrutinize how the "cultural legacies" immigrant families bring with them from the sending society are rearticulated as social remittances to the receiving society. As such, transnational processes include not only the movement of people, goods, and remittances, but also social and cultural ideas that flow from the sending society to the receiving society and vice versa as a two-way street.

Future studies on transnationalism could benefit from an examination of the Dominican community, which must be seen as a diasporic community comprised of the first and second generations, where new gender identities and life perspectives are continually being fashioned and rearticulated in transnational social spaces.

Several questions remain. How can we re-create family life? How can we work toward the elimination of gender-based oppression? How can we refashion gender roles so that the members of a two-gendered community are not defined in opposition to one another, but rather speak to a collaborative effort to build community? The answers to these questions will have important repercussions for the Dominican diaspora, as well as other transnational communities. More importantly, perhaps the answers to these questions will lead to high school graduation ceremonies where all Dominican young men and women will have an opportunity to complete their education successfully and pursue their dreams.

Notes

1. The gender gap in educational attainment is already visible in the Dominican Republic, where 57 percent of women of high school age were enrolled in school compared to only 44 percent of their male counterparts (FLACSO 1993, 59). Moreover, 28 percent of women in the Dominican Republic have completed high school or college, compared to only 23 percent of men (CESDEM 1996, 18–19). Indeed, in the Dominican Republic women represent 52 percent of enrolled students at the university level (FLACSO 1993, 63).

2. For a detailed discussion of the research design, see López 1999.

3. Among participants who were born abroad, the average age upon entering the United States was seven.

4. The focus groups and in-depth interviews are part of an on-going study of second-generation Caribbean youth in New York City at the Center for Urban Research at the Graduate School and University Center, City University of New York. As

a research assistant for the Second-Generation Project, I worked with principal investigators John Mollenkopf, Philip Kasinitz, and Mary Waters.

5. The following is a gender breakdown of the young adults surveyed: for Dominicans there were twelve men and fifteen women; for West Indians there were fifteen men and seven women; and for Haitians there were eight men and nine women.

6. I conducted all but three of the follow-up in-depth interviews.

7. As a qualitative study, this chapter is not intended to be a representative sample of Dominican youth. Rather, its goal is a thick description of the lived experiences of second-generation Dominican youth who grew up in New York City during the 1970–1990s.

8. Basch, Glick Schiller, and Szanton Blanc (1994, 7); quoted in Pessar 1999.

9. A guiding premise of the study is that gender is a socially constructed and historically variable process through which biological differences between males and females are assigned social significance and used as means of social classification (Lorber 1994). Contrary to the popular perception that only women possess an essential "gender," at any historical point both men and women are gender(ed) in relationship to one another (Hondagneu-Sotelo 1994, 1999). In other words, gender is not interchangeable with sex.

10. For instance, the decrease in marriage rates in the Dominican Republic has been a growing trend over the past fifty years. The marriage rate in 1950 was 6.2 percent for every one thousand people. Then in the 1970s it declined to 3.8 percent and it was 2.3 percent for every one thousand people in 1980. See FLACSO 1993, 31.

11. The Dominican Republic yielded more than half a million immigrants (580,225), followed by Cuba (456,997), Jamaica (417,652), Haiti (275,581), Guyana (179,627), and Trinidad and Tobago (129,618). See Parillo 1999, 426; Hernández et al. 1995.

12. It is important to note that female-headed households are not the cause of high poverty rates in the Dominican community. Even households with two or more workers are often below the poverty rates (Candelario and López 1995).

13. Suárez-Orozco (1987) did not discuss gender differences, if any, between men's and women's dual frame of reference (Suárez-Orozco and Suárez-Orozco 1995).

14. Growing evidence suggests that another space in which women cultivate webs of social support is the sphere of spirituality. Through religious connections to a higher power, women draw the strength to overcome great obstacles (Hurtado 1996; Fine and Weis 1998; Pastor, McCormick, and Fine 1996).

15. It is important to note that Portes and Schauffler (1996) have found that second-generation women are more likely to speak the parental language than their male counterparts. This may be explained in part because women have closer ties to their families and, unlike their male counterparts, they interact regularly with their first-generation relatives.

16. Eighteen-year-old Diana lived a couple of blocks from the researcher's home. However, Diana insisted that the interview take place in my office because her mother was working during the daytime and she did not allow strangers in her home. In contrast, many of the young men interviewed expressed shock and concern that I, a woman in her mid-twenties, would enter a stranger's home, especially a man's home,

unaccompanied. One young man even warned me about calling from my home phone number when scheduling appointments because caller identification devices identify my home number.

17. Research posits that the cloistering of young women may actually propel them to achieve academically (Waters 1996). In a study of second-generation Vietnamese students' social adaptation to the United States, Zhou and Bankston (1998) found that young women, unlike young men, were subjected to strict social control and were responsible for more household work than their male counterparts. They conclude that the strict social control of young women had a positive influence on their education, whereby it encouraged them to pursue academic achievement. In effect, the strict social control of second-generation Vietnamese young women inadvertently subverts traditional gender roles.

18. In a study of poor and working-class young adults in the Northeast, Fine and Weis (1998) found that Latina and African-American women were engaged in a quiet revolution, whereby they pursued education even more vehemently than men.

19. The rest were single (25.6 percent), separated (12.5 percent), divorced (2.1 percent), or widowed (.75 percent). See CESDEM 1996, 82.

20. In the larger survey, 44 percent of the men compared to 21 percent of the women felt that in a marriage the wife should be primarily responsible for housework (See López 1999).

21. In Dominican culture, a *tíguere* is a male cultural form. The literal English translation of *tíguere* is tiger. A *tíguere* is a man who is quick on his feet, witty, and can fend for himself against insurmountable odds. He is deemed to be a maverick in the art of persuasion and sexual prowess.

22. For a more detailed look at how racialization processes differ for men and women, in public spaces, schools, and the workplace see López 1999, 2000, 2003a, 2003b.

References

Alvarez, Julia. 1991. *How the García Girls Lost Their Accents.* Chapel Hill, N.C.: Algonquin Books.

———. 1994. *In the Time of Butterflies.* Chapel Hill, N.C.: Algonquin Books.

———. 1997. *Yo!* Chapel Hill, N.C.: Algonquin Books.

Anzaldúa, Gloria. 1987. *Borderlands: La Frontera, the New Mestiza.* San Francisco: Aunt Lute.

Baca-Zinn, Maxine, and Bonnie Thorton-Dill. 1994. "Difference and Domination." In *Women of Color in United States Society,* ed. Maxine Baca-Zinn and Bonnie Thorton-Dill. Philadelphia: Temple University Press.

Basch, Linda, Nina Glick Schiller, and Christina Szanton Blanc. 1994. *Nations Unbound: Transnational Projects, Postcolonial Predicaments, and Deterritorialized Nation-States.* Langhorne, Pa.: Gordon and Breach.

Bourgois, Philippe. 1995. *In Search of Respect: Selling Crack in El Barrio.* Cambridge: Cambridge University Press.

Candelario, Ginetta, and Nancy López. 1995. "The Latest Edition of the Welfare

Queen Story: Dominicans in New York City." *Phoebe: Journal of Feminist Scholarship Theory and Aesthetics* 7(1–2): 7–22.

CESDEM. 1996. *República Dominicana: Encuesta demográfica y de salud.* Santo Domingo: Centro de Estudios Sociales y Demográficos.

Charles, Carole. 1995. "Gender and Politics in Contemporary Haiti: The Duvalierist State, Transnationalism, and the Emergence of a New Feminism (1980–1990)." *Feminist Studies* 21(1): 135–64.

City University of New York. 1995. "Immigration and the CUNY Student of the Year 2000." New York: CUNY.

———. 1996. "CUNY Student Data Book: Fall 1996." Vol. 1. New York: CUNY.

College Board. 1999. "Reaching the Top: A Report on the National Task Force on Minority High Achievement." New York: College Board Publications.

De León, Brunilda. 1996. " Career Development of Hispanic Adolescent Girls." In *Urban Girls: Resisting Stereotypes, Creating Identities,* ed. Bonnie Leadbeater and Niobe Way. New York: New York University Press.

Díaz, Junot. 1997. *Drown.* New York: Riverhead Books.

Espiritu, Yen Le. 1997. *Asian American Men and Women: Labor, Law, and Love.* Thousand Oaks, Calif.: Sage Publications.

Fine, Michelle, and Lois Weis. 1998. *The Unknown City: Lives of Poor and Working-Class Young Adults.* Boston: Beacon Press.

FLACSO. 1993. *Mujeres latinoamericanas en cifras: República Dominicana.* Santiago, Chile: FLACSO.

Foner, Nancy. 1999. "The Immigrant Family: Cultural Legacies and Cultural Changes." In *The Handbook of International Migration: The American Experience,* ed. Charles Hirschman, Philip Kasinitz, and Josh DeWind. New York: Russell Sage Foundation.

———, ed. 1987. *New Immigrants in New York.* New York: Columbia University Press.

Fordham, Signithia. 1996. *Blacked Out: Dilemmas of Race, Identity, and Success at Capital High.* Chicago: University of Chicago Press.

Frankenberg, Ruth. 1993. *White Women, Race Matters: The Social Construction of Whiteness.* Minneapolis: University of Minnesota Press.

Georges, Eugenia. 1990. *The Making of a Transnational Community: Migration, Development, and Cultural Change in the Dominican Republic.* New York: Columbia University Press.

Gibson, Margaret A. 1988. *Accommodation Without Assimilation: Sikh Immigrants in an American High School.* Ithaca, N.Y.: Cornell University Press.

Gil, Rosa María, and Carmen Inoa Vázquez. 1996. *La paradoja de María.* New York. Putnam.

Gilbert, Rob, and Pam Gilbert. 1998. *Masculinity Goes to School.* New York: Routledge.

Glick Schiller, Nina. 1999. "Transmigrants and Nation-States: Something Old and Something New in the U.S. Experience." In *The Handbook of International Migration: The American Experience,* ed. Charles Hirschman, Philip Kasinitz, and Josh DeWind. New York: Russell Sage Foundation.

Glick Schiller, Nina, Linda Basch, and Christina Blanc-Szanton. 1992. "Transnationalism: A New Framework for Understanding Migration." In *Towards a Transnational Perspective on Migration: Race, Class, Ethnicity, and Nationalism Reconsidered,* ed. Nina Glick Schiller, Linda Basch, and Cristina Blanc-Szanton. New York: The New York Academy of Sciences.

Grasmuck, Sherri, and Ramón Grosfoguel. 1997. "Geopolitics, Economic Niches, and Social Capital among Recent Caribbean Immigrants." Paper presented at conference, Transnational Communities and the Political Economy of New York City in the 1990s. Robert J. Milano Graduate School of Management and Urban Policy, New School for Social Research, New York.

Grasmuck, Sherri, and Patricia Pessar. 1996. "Dominicans in the United States: First and Second Generation Settlement, 1960–1990." In *Origins and Destinies: Immigration, Race, and Ethnicity in America,* ed. Silvia Pedraza and Rubén G. Rumbaut. Belmont, Calif.: Wadsworth Publishing Company.

Hartman, Heidi. 1987. "Changes in Women's Economic and Family Roles in Post-World War II United States." In *Women, Households, and the Economy,* ed. Lourdes Benería and Catherine Stimpson. New Brunswick, N.J.: Rutgers University Press.

Hawkins, Denise. 1996. "Gender Gap: Black Females Outpace Male Counterparts at Three Degree Levels." *Black Issues in Higher Education* 13(10): 20–22.

Hernández, Ramona, Francisco Rivera-Batiz, and Roberto Agodini. 1995. *Dominican New Yorkers: A Socioeconomic Profile, 1990.* New York: City University of New York, Dominican Studies Institute.

Hernández, Ramona, and Nancy López. 1997. "Yola and Gender: Dominican Women's Unregulated Migration." *Dominican Studies: Resources and Research Questions.* Dominican Research Monographs. New York: The City University of New York, Dominican Studies Institute.

Hill-Collins, Patricia. 1996. "Toward a New Vision: Race, Class, and Gender as Categories of Analysis and Connection." In *The Meaning of Difference: American Constructions of Race, Sex and Gender, Social Class, and Sexual Orientation,* ed. Karen Rosenblum and Toni-Michelle Travis. New York: McGraw-Hill.

Hirschman, Charles, Philip Kasinitz, and Josh DeWind, eds. 1999. *The Handbook of International Migration: The American Experience.* New York: Russell Sage Foundation.

Ho, Christine. 1999. "Caribbean Transnationalism as a Gendered Process." *Latin American Perspectives* 26(5): 34–54.

Hondagneu-Sotelo, Pierrette. 1994. *Gendered Transitions: Mexican Experiences of Migration.* Berkeley: University of California.

———. 1999. "Gender and Contemporary U.S. Immigration." *American Behavioral Scientist* 42(4): 565–76.

hooks, bell. 1981. *Ain't I a Woman? Black Women and Feminism.* Boston: South End Press.

Hurtado, Aida. 1996. *The Color of Privilege: Three Blasphemies on Race and Feminism.* Ann Arbor: University of Michigan Press.

Kasinitz, Philip. 1992. *Caribbean New York: Black Immigrants and the Politics of Race.* Ithaca, N.Y.: Cornell University Press.

Levitt, Peggy. 1998. "Social Remittances: Migration Driven Local-Level Forms of Cultural Diffusion." *International Migration Review* 32(4): 926–48.

Lewin, Tamar. 1998. "American Colleges Begin to Ask, Where Have All the Men Gone?" *New York Times,* December 6, A1.

López, Nancy. 1998. "The Structural Origins of High School Dropout among Second Generation Dominicans in New York City." *Latino Studies Journal* 9(3): 85–105.

———. 1999. "Race-Gender Matters: Schooling among Second-Generation Dominicans, West Indians, and Haitians in New York City." Ph.D. diss., Graduate School and University Center, City University of New York.

———. 2000. "The Missing Link: Latinos and Educational Opportunity Programs." *Equity and Excellence* 33(3): 48–53.

———. 2003a. "Disentangling Race-Gender Experiences at Work: Second-Generation Caribbean Young Adults in New York City." In *Gender and U.S. Immigration: Contemporary Trends,* ed. Pierrette Hondagneu-Sotelo. Berkeley: University of California Press.

———. 2003b. *Hopeful Girls, Troubled Boys: Race and Gender Disparity in Urban Education.* New York: Routledge.

López Springfield, Consuelo. 1997. *Daughters of Caliban: Caribbean Women in the Twentieth Century.* Bloomington: Indiana University Press.

Lorber, Judith. 1994. *Paradoxes of Gender.* New Haven, Conn.: Yale University Press.

Mahler, Sarah. 1997. "Bringing Gender to a Transnational Focus: Theoretical and Empirical Ideas." Presentation at the Latin American Studies Association Annual Meeting. Guadalajara, Mexico.

Maira, Sunaina. 2001. *Mixed Desires: Indian American Youth Culture in New York.* Philadelphia: Temple University Press.

Matute-Bianchi, Maria Eugenia. 1991. "Situational Identity and Patterns of School Performance among Immigrant and Non-Immigrant Mexican Descent Students." In *Minority Status and Schooling: A Comparative Study of Immigrant and Involuntary Minorities,* ed. John Ogbu and Margaret Gibson. New York: Garland Publishers.

Milkman, Ruth. 1987. *Gender at Work.* Chicago: University of Illinois Press.

Molina, Sintia. 1998. "La mujer dominicana en ambos lados: La mujer dominicana y la educación." *Estudios Sociales* 113:81–99.

Mollenkopf, John, Philip Kasinitz, Mary Waters, Nancy López, and Dae Young Kim. 1998. "The School to Work Transition of Second Generation Immigrants in Metropolitan New York: Some Preliminary Findings." The Jerome Levy Economics Institute of Bard College. Working Paper 214.

Moraga, Cherrie, and Gloria Anzaldúa, eds. 1983. *This Bridge Called My Back: Writings by Radical Women of Color.* New York: Kitchen Table Press.

O'Donnell, Mike, and Sue Sharpe. 2000. *Uncertain Masculinities: Youth, Ethnicity, and Class in Contemporary Britain.* London: Routledge.

Ogbu, John, and Herbert Simons. 1998. "Voluntary and Involuntary Minorities: A Cultural- Ecological Theory of School Performance with Some Implications for Education." *Anthropology and Education Quarterly* 29(2): 155–88.

Paravisini-Gebert, Lizabeth. 1997. "Decolonizing Feminism: The Home-Grown Roots of Caribbean Women's Movement." In *Daughters of Caliban: Caribbean Women in the Twentieth Century,* ed. Consuelo López Springfield. Bloomington: Indiana University Press.

Parillo, Vincent. 1999. *Strangers to These Shores: Race and Ethnic Relations in the United States.* Boston: Allyn and Bacon.

Pastor, Jennifer, Jennifer McCormick, and Michelle Fine. 1996. "Making Homes: An Urban Girl Thing." In *Urban Girls: Resisting Stereotypes, Creating Identities,* ed. Bonnie Leadbeater and Niobe Way. New York: New York University Press.

Pérez, Lisandro. 1996. "The Households of Children of Immigrants in South Florida: An Exploratory Study of Extended Family Arrangements." In *The New Second Generation,* ed. Alejandro Portes. New York: Russell Sage Foundation.

Pessar, Patricia. 1999. "The Role of Gender, Households, and Social Networks in the Migration Process: A Review and Appraisal." In *The Handbook of International Migration: The American Experience,* ed. Charles Hirschman, Philip Kasinitz, and Josh DeWind. New York: Russell Sage Foundation.

Pessar, Patricia, and Sherri Grasmuck. 1991. *Between Two Islands: Dominican International Migration.* Berkeley: University of California Press.

Portes, Alejandro, and Richard Schauffler. 1996. "Language and the Second Generation: Bilingualism Today and Yesterday." In *The New Second Generation,* ed. Alejandro Portes. New York: Russell Sage Foundation.

PROFAMILIA. 1991. *Resultados generales cuestionario hogar ampliado: Encuesta demográfica y de salud 1991.* Santo Domingo: PROFAMILIA.

Rubin, Lillian. 1997. "The Transformation of Family Life." In *Reconstructing Gender: A Multicultural Anthology,* ed. Estelle Disch. Mountain View, Calif.: Mayfield Publishing.

Rumbaut, Rubén. 1998. "Transformations: The Post-Immigrant Generation in an Age of Diversity." Paper presented at the Annual Meeting of the Eastern Sociological Society. Philadelphia, Pa.

Safa, Helen. 1995. *The Myth of the Male Breadwinner: Women and Industrialization in the Caribbean.* Boulder, Colo.: Westview.

Shepherd, Verene, Bridget Brereton, and Barbara Bailey. 1995. *Engender(ing) History: Caribbean Women in Historical Perspective.* New York: St. Martin's Press.

Sierra, Christine Marie. 1986. "The University Setting Reinforces Inequality." In *Chicana Voices: Intersections of Class, Race, and Gender,* ed. Center for Mexican Studies. Austin: University of Texas Press.

Smith, Michael, and Luis Guarnizo. 1998. *Transnationalism from Below.* New Brunswick, N.J.: Transaction Publications.

Stanton-Salazar, Ricardo. 1997. "A Social Capital Framework for Understanding the Socialization of Racial Minority Children and Youths." *Harvard Educational Review* 67(1): 1–40.

Suárez-Orozco, Marcelo. 1987. "'Becoming Somebody': Central American Immigrants in U.S. Inner-City Schools." *Anthropology and Education Quarterly* 18(4): 287–99.

Suárez-Orozco, Marcelo, and Carola Suárez-Orozco. 1995. *Transformations: Immigration, Family Life, and Achievement Motivation among Latino Adolescents.* Stanford, Calif.: Stanford University Press.

Valenzuela, Abel. 1999. "Gender Roles and Settlement Activities among Children and Their Immigrant Families." *American Behavioral Scientist* 42(4): 720–42.

Valverde, Caroline Keieu Linh. 2002. "Making Transnational Viet Nam: Vietnamese American Community-Viet Nam through Money, Music, and Modems." Ph.D. diss., University of California, Berkeley.

Vera, Elizabeth M., Le'Roy E. Reese, Roberta L. Paikoff, and Robin L. Jarett. 1996. "Contextual Factor of Sexual Risk-Taking in Urban African American Preadolescent Children." In *Urban Girls: Resisting Stereotypes, Creating Identities,* ed. Bonnie J. Ross Leadbeater and Niobe Way. New York: New York University Press.

Washington, Valora, and Joanna Newman. 1991. "Setting Our Own Agenda: Exploring the Meaning of Gender Disparities among Blacks in Higher Education" *Journal of Negro Education* 60(1): 19–35.

Waters, Mary. 1996. "The Intersections of Gender, Race, and Ethnicity in Identity Development of Caribbean American Teens." In *Urban Girls: Resisting Stereotypes, Creating Identities,* ed. Bonnie Leadbeater and Niobe Way. New York: New York University Press.

Weyland, Karin. 2000. "Dominican Women *'Con un Pie Aquí y el Otro Allá':* International Migration, Class, Gender, and Cultural Change." Ph.D. diss., New School for Social Research, New York.

Willis, Paul. 1981. *Learning to Labor: How Working Class Kids Get Working Class Jobs.* New York: Columbia University Press.

Wing, Adrien Katherine, ed. 1997. *Critical Race Feminism: A Reader.* New York: New York University Press.

Zhou, Min, and Carl L. Bankston. 1998. *Growing Up American: How Vietnamese Children Adapt to Life in the United States.* New York: Russell Sage Foundation.

9

Transnational Consciousness

Negotiating Identity in the Works of Julia Alvarez and Junot Díaz

Janira Bonilla

> Like her mother's and father's too, her soul had transformed into a complex and resilient thing able to accommodate the best and worst. Everything she had experienced; everything she continued to feel for those whose lives would be inextricably bound with hers; everything she had inherited from her parents and had gleaned from her siblings would aid her in her passage through the world. She would leave no memories behind. All of them were her self. All of them were home.
>
> —**Loida Maritza Pérez, *Geographies of Home***

The word *home* often conjures up the idea of a safe and stable haven embodied by kinship ties, a native language, and culturally specific practices. The idea of a familiar fixed home is a pivotal component in identity formation. Thus, a geographical point of origin such as one's hometown or country becomes a key marker of identity. For many Dominicans, home is synonymous with political and/or economic repression and it is all too often a point of departure on a journey of survival. The majority of Dominicans who emigrate to the United States do so in hopes of better economic opportunities that will enable them to achieve some level of material comfort for their families in the United States and those left behind on the island. Although the process of immigration is usually facilitated through kinship ties and/or social networks, it is usually an alienating and marginalizing experience. As they negotiate their place in the United States, Dominicans confront ethnic and racial prejudices, labor exploitation, and a seemingly insurmountable language barrier. Despite the harsh welcome and the assumption by many that they are a transitory immigrant group, Dominicans have established firm roots in the United States, particularly in New York City, where they are now the fastest growing immigrant group. With a foot in two or more cultures, Dominican identity takes on new dimensions. The life-style of many

Dominicans who remain connected to the island via cash remittances, letters, phone calls, e-mails, and regular visits constitutes what many refer to as a transnational existence. Even for those Dominicans who lack the means to maintain these connections to the island, the island remains with them through cultural practices. Under either of these circumstances, "home" is no longer a fixed geographical point but multiple spaces that take root in a transnational consciousness.

Dominican-American authors have begun to embrace the experiences of Dominican immigration through their narratives. Coming of age narratives set against the historical background of forced immigration via political or economic exile have emerged as a site for the formation of a transnational consciousness that disrupts existing models of Dominican identity. In particular, Julia Alvarez and Junot Díaz present distinct experiences that are marked by differences in race, class, and gender. As Dominican-Americans, Alvarez and Díaz question the construction of race, class, and gender both on the island and in the United States from the perspective of an outsider/insider. Their works are an interrogation and reflection on the historical erasure of the African diaspora within the Dominican Republic that informs Dominican notions of racial identity, the lasting legacy of colonialism, as well as the detrimental effects of imperialism in its various manifestations on the island and its diaspora. In this chapter, I will explore assimilation and identity formation as experienced by Dominicans in the United States through Julia Alvarez's *How the García Girls Lost Their Accents* and Junot Díaz's *Drown.* I also argue that both Alvarez and Díaz put forth alternative identity models that articulate a transnational consciousness developed vis-à-vis the United States as both the receiving country and the imperial Other that is in large part responsible for creating the conditions that force Dominicans to leave the island in the first place.

With the exception of the work of Alvarez and Díaz, historically Dominican literature has received marginal attention in the United States because most of the literary production by diasporic Dominicans is in Spanish and therefore has had little access to the mainstream markets. However, during the last ten years, with the introduction of Alvarez and Díaz, the growth of the Dominican community within the United States, and increased scholarship on Dominican studies, Dominican literature has begun to emerge from the margins. More recently, Loida Maritza Pérez, another Dominican author, has joined the U.S. literary scene. At the center of Pérez's novel, *Geographies of Home,* is an Afro-Dominican woman's struggle to come to terms with her identity and dysfunctional, poor, working-class family in Brooklyn, New York. Pérez problematizes Dominican identity by bringing to the forefront the cultural, racial, and gender tensions that exist within a racially diverse patriarchal family of immigrants. Contrary to the stereotypes of Dominicans promoted by the media, there are no welfare recipients, nor are there any drug dealers in the family. Instead, Pérez presents a hard-working family and although they struggle to make ends meet, they are religious, law-abiding people who own a very modest home. The parents are strict Seventh-Day Adventists and therefore do not dance or listen to *merengue* and *bachata,* considered by many to be staples of Dominican identity. Pérez's depiction of a working-class Dominican family is an interesting contrast to the works of Alvarez and Díaz because it expands upon the diversity of the Dominican experience in the United States. Yet for the purposes of this discussion, I will limit myself to the works of Alvarez and Díaz.

Redefining Transnationalism: A Survival Strategy

In order to explore the notion of a transnational consciousness and identity in the works of Alvarez and Díaz, a redefinition of transnationalism and what it means to live as a Dominican outside of the island context are needed. The question of identity looms large for Dominicans as they carve out their niche in the United States. Alvarez and Díaz in part use their narratives to ask: Where exactly do Dominicans fit in and who are they? Where do second- and third-generation Dominicans fit in? In their comprehensive profile of the Dominican community in New York City, entitled *The Dominican Americans,* Silvio Torres-Saillant and Ramona Hernández (1998) attempt to address these questions. It is important to note that the largest community of Dominicans outside of the island live in New York City. The majority of New York Dominicans are characterized by Torres-Saillant and Hernández as a hard-working community, striving to attain political and social equity in a receiving society that often views them as a source of cheap labor to be exploited, considers them to be a racialized Other within the dominant culture of the "heteromasculinized" white Anglo-Saxon model of citizenship in the United States, and/or stereotypes them as negative elements, such as drug dealers and welfare queens.

Torres-Saillant and Hernández acknowledge that the ethnic label Dominican-Americans, which is also the title of their work, is problematic on multiple levels. First, the Dominican Republic is part of the Americas and as such Dominicans have every right to call themselves Americans, thus making the term Dominican-American redundant. Furthermore, the term Dominican-American places Dominicans in the role of ethnics instead of a racialized minority and belies the inherent racism that comes along with being a racialized body in the United States. Torres-Saillant and Hernández justify the use of the term because "negotiating nomenclature is part of the predicament of the immigrant" (Torres-Saillant and Hernández 1998, xxi). Therefore, they choose to work with the label instead of rejecting it because on some levels it becomes a useful and empowering term.

Nonetheless, Torres-Saillant and Hernández also recognize that many scholars and mainstream media tend to characterize the Dominican community in New York as a transnational and/or transient community. Indeed, the social networks established by many Dominicans who live outside of the Dominican Republic seem to bear out this view since they remain connected to family and social institutions on the island through cash remittances and social obligations. For example, in *Quisqueya on the Hudson,* Jorge Duany makes the following observation about the Dominican community in New York City: "Due to the proximity of the island, the ability to travel back and forth with ease and the connections to family and friends on the island, Dominicans defy the melting pot assimilation patterns of earlier European immigrants. In fact 'most Dominicans view migration as a temporary stage in the life cycle, not as an irreversible decision leading to complete absorption into the American melting pot'" (Duany 1994, 44).

The fact that Dominicans are discriminated against as a racialized Other in the United States is a key factor that prevents them from following previously established "melting pot" assimilation patterns. In negotiating their identity, Dominicans maintain strong ties to their national culture, specifically through language, food, and music, but not all of them have the ability to travel back and forth nor do they have the resources to maintain links, such as cash remittances. Although some Dominicans may arrive in the United States with the dream of returning to the island, there are many, including second- and third-generation Dominicans, who remain rooted in the United States who are still culturally Dominican as well as North American. With their ethnic and racial identity under constant assault from the dominant culture, Dominicans may cling to their culture, yet they incorporate many aspects of U.S. culture into it.

Rather than limiting transnationalism to a traditional definition based on geographical and economic ties, Torres-Saillant and Hernández view transnationalism as a "cultural state of mind that permits them to remain actively linked to life in the native land while becoming acclimated to the values and norms of the receiving society" (Torres-Saillant and Hernández 1998, 156). Choosing to define the parameters of transnationalism as a form of consciousness, Torres-Saillant and Hernández emphasize that this "state of mind" is an important factor in establishing a cultural identity for Dominicans living in the United States. This consciousness reflects the ability to negotiate multiple spaces at once and develop new models of Dominicanness that are more inclusive: "One of the most obvious results of the immigrant experience for Dominicans is that the space of their physical and existential mobility increases tremendously. Their living space after migration encompasses both the native country and the North American mainland. [Dominicans] now can access a larger mental habitat within which to configure their human identity. Their ampler sphere of experience entails an ability to harmonize English with Spanish, snowstorms with tropical rains and merengue with rock, or rap . . . it also entails the possibility of creating alternative models by rearranging existing ones" (Torres-Saillant and Hernández 1998, 146). Clearly, for Torres-Saillant and Hernández the formation of Dominican identity within the United States is a process that transcends economic and kinship ties as well as fixed geographical points. Regardless of where they find themselves in the world, Dominicans are surviving, adapting, making connections, and establishing roots that have the ability to be transplanted without damage so that they remain in large part Dominican roots; rooted in new soil they develop new characteristics that allow them to adapt and survive. Torres-Saillant and Hernández emphasize that Dominican identity formation remains a process of mediation and harmonizing to produce a multifaceted and resilient identity that challenges notions of identity in the native culture and the new culture as well.

The ability to harmonize between cultures is precisely what Alvarez and Díaz illustrate when they write in English *con un poco de español,* Spanish woven into their narratives. It is important to note that they are not only labeled as Dominican writers and Latinos but they are also recognized as part of the U.S. literary landscape. As writers and intellectuals, they simultaneously negotiate multiple cultural spaces informed by their experiences on the island and in the United States, yet their work attests to the fact that the negotiation between cultures is not an easy process for most Dominican immigrants. Both Alvarez and Díaz make their readers aware of this crucial point in their narratives from the very beginning. Alvarez's first chapter, "Antojos," has the narrator, Yolanda, going through the process of identity negotiation as a result of a transnational existence in the traditional sense as well as in her state of mind.: "In halting Spanish, Yolanda reports on her sisters. When she reverts to English, she is scolded, '¡En Español!' The more she practices, the sooner she'll have her native tongue, the aunts insist. Yes, and when she returns to the States, she'll find herself suddenly going blank over some word in English or, like her mother, mixing up some common phrase" (Alvarez 1991, 7). The give and take between English and *español* produces the struggle for identity in Yolanda, who is attempting to harmonize between two worlds, although with much difficulty.

Díaz, in contrast, chooses to express the same dilemma by citing the verse of Gustavo Pérez Firmat as the preface to his collection of stories.

The fact that I
am writing to you

in English
already falsifies what I
wanted to tell you.
My subject:
How to explain to you that I
don't belong to English
though I belong nowhere else.

Díaz's choice of lines expresses the cultural displacement as a result of attempting to express two distinct cultures that are part of his experience in only one language. English as the imposed language removes Díaz from his native language and yet his experiences are still rooted in that language. In an essay entitled "Duality and Displacement in Dominican Literature," Sintia Molina observes, "For a large population of Dominicans who were raised and others who were born in the United States to mediate between two cultures is to feel 50–50, not totally of one or the other" (Molina 1998, 66). Alvarez and Díaz use language to express the duality and displacement that Molina refers to. The use of Spanish and Dominicanisms in their narratives reveals their constant struggle to be a part of two cultures that is inextricably bound in their stories.

For Alvarez and Díaz, some things transcend language while others do not. Culturally specific experiences such as childhood memories on the island are infused, enhanced, and best articulated with the use of their native vernacular. These experiences do not translate for Alvarez and Díaz, nor do they translate for the reader, which creates the disorienting effect for non-Spanish readers that Spanish speakers feel when they encounter incomprehensible words in English. However, the irony of these two authors lies in the fact that they have to express themselves in English because it is the language in which they were educated and it is also the language imposed through education and the pressures of assimilation. The use of Spanish and particularly Dominicanisms illustrates Alvarez's and Díaz's resistance to the dominant culture and the ever present assimilationist rhetoric of the United States as well as their attempts to reconcile multiple and diverse identities within the pages of their texts.

A Privileged but Painful Political Exile: Alvarez's *How the García Girls Lost Their Accents*

Even under the best circumstances, immigration is a difficult and often disorienting process. Whether an immigrant leaves his or her home by choice or by force, inevitably something or someone is left behind. Learning a new language and negotiating a new culture is a painful and alienating experience for many. The history of immigration in the United States clearly illustrates that immigration narratives differ greatly and are often determined by an individual's point of origin as well as race, class, and gender. The very personal experiences of immigrants are frequently dictated by political machinations that have very little to do with human rights but very much to do with political and economic expediency for the imperial Other. A case in point is the history of immigration from the Dominican Republic to the United States throughout the last century, which is inextricably woven with U.S. imperialism in the Caribbean and Latin America, as Alvarez's work illustrates.

The U.S. military occupation of the Dominican Republic from 1916 to 1924 set the stage for the rise of the totalitarian regime of Rafael Leónidas Trujillo Molina, who controlled the island from 1930 until his assassination in 1961. Fearful of another Cuban Revolution in the Caribbean, the United States opened its doors to Dominican immigration in hopes that it would destabilize any opposition and eliminate the threat of revolution. As a result, Dominicans immigrated to the United States in large numbers to escape political persecution and turmoil. Although many Dominicans fled the island in fear of political repression and human rights violations, the United States did not receive them with the same generosity and financial assistance it gave to the Cuban refugees. The majority of these Dominicans settled in New York City and had to fend for themselves.

Alvarez's novel *How the García Girls Lost Their Accents* is an autobiographical novel set against the background of Trujillo's dictatorship and its sociopolitical aftermath. Alvarez looks at Dominican society through the lens of four Dominican-born sisters, Yolanda, Sandi, Fifi, and Carla, who leave their homeland as children in the middle of the night with their parents to escape the political persecution of Trujillo's regime. The novel, structured as a series of related stories, begins in the present in 1989, when the García girls are adults in the United States, and moves in retrospective episodes back to 1960 and their childhood in the Dominican Republic shortly before the family flees into exile.

In Alvarez's novel, each sister tells her piece of the puzzle, revealing not only the family drama but also the political drama that informs their decisions as adults. Their distinctive voices provide a window into how the sisters are affected by exile and assimilation. The sisters each give their unique account from their childhood recollections and the painful ghosts of displacement and assimilation that haunt them as adults. Alvarez's fiction recreates the past through a narrative that focuses on the Garcías' painful struggle to harmonize more than one culture while exposing the repression of Trujillo's regime and the political involvement of the United States in the events that lead to their political exile.

Themes that resonate clearly in Alvarez's novel are the search for identity, assimilation, displacement, racism, and gender roles, all mitigated by the Garcías' class status. On the island, the Garcías are a wealthy, elite Dominican family with powerful connections. The family proudly traces its roots back to the Spanish conquistadores and a Swedish grandmother. Prior to exile, Laura, the mother of the García girls, contemplates her ancestors as "those fair-skinned Conquistadores arriving in this new world" (Alvarez 1991, 212). Despite the fact that some of the García girls have thick, dark, curly hair and that some of the sisters are darker, their class status allows them to enjoy a life of privilege that keeps them segregated from the majority of poor working classes, who are overwhelmingly darker skinned, mulattos, and blacks. Members of the García family, like many Dominican elites, identify with the colonizers and not with the "noble" extinct Taínos, the island's indigenous population, or the African ancestry that is visible throughout the island. The family's wealth and connections allow them to travel out of the country at a time when Trujillo's restrictive immigration policies keep everyone else island bound.

In many ways, the Garcías have a transnational life-style even before they leave the island since their material conditions permit them to have a privileged foot in more than one culture. For example, many of the girl's relatives, including Carlos and Laura, their parents, attend or attended elite colleges and universities in Canada and the United States. The leather chairs in Tío Mundín's office display the emblem of Yale University, not only Mundín's alma mater, but a clear marker of elite values and privilege. Members of the family make regular shopping trips to New York City, where the grandfather holds a diplomatic post. The girls play with toys from F.A.O. Schwartz, a high-end New York City toy store. Laura raises her girls "American style, reading all the new literature" (202). The Garcías culturally adhere to Dominican upper-class values as well as U.S. cultural practices that they associate with progress.

The Garcías' class-biased beliefs in the cultural superiority and the progress of the imperial Other against the backwardness of the Dominican lower classes is present in the Dominican Republic. For example, while still on the island, Carlos displays a paternalistic attitude toward the servants; he infantilizes them, much like the master of the plantation toward his slaves. Carla, the eldest daughter, recalls her father commenting to his wife Laura on servants, "They're like children" (266). Carlos and Laura establish relationships with their servants that echo a master/slave paradigm. Carlos identifies as a white Dominican of European ancestry while the servants are identified as Dominican mulattos and blacks or Haitians.

On the island, the Garcías live under a hierarchy that is shaped by race, class, and gender divisions. Laura's attitude toward Trujillo's SIM guards is yet another example that mirrors her husband's attitude toward the servants. When the SIM arrive to question Carlos, Laura contemplates them in the following manner: "The grand manner will usually disarm these poor lackeys from the countryside, who have joined the SIM, most of them, in order to put money in their pockets, food, and rum in their stomachs, and guns at their hips. But deep down, they are still boys in rags bringing down coconuts for el patrón when he visits his fincas with his family on Sundays" (202). Laura's response to the guards reveals her class bias toward the lower classes as well as the inherent racism that is a part of her class consciousness. Laura, like her husband, infantilizes the men by referring to them as boys with an attitude, which is very much a throwback to the island's colonial power structure. Alvarez's use of the words "el patrón" and "fincas" emphasizes Laura's colonial mentality, which smacks of privilege. As Yolanda observes, the guards are "café con leche or khaki," revealing not only that they are mulattos but that they are different from the Garcías, who consider themselves "blancos." Yolanda goes on to reveal "that no one would ever pick as a favorite color" the khaki color of their skin and their uniforms (197). Alvarez illustrates that class and race intersect. The girls are socialized to value white above café con leche or black. When Laura implies that the guards will always be coconut pickers for their masters, she essentially believes that race dictates their class status and therefore they cannot rise above the level of domestics or subordinate roles.

And yet despite all these advantages on the island, the Garcías still have to negotiate the difficulties of adjusting to a "socially unprivileged" life in the United States. Initially the family falls on hard times financially. Carlos García is unable to practice medicine without obtaining certifications and Laura is forced to sell her valuables, including a much-valued fur coat. The Garcías survive their initial poverty in the United States through social networks from the island. Laura reminds her daughters, "Without papito we would have to go on welfare." The girls are already aware that "Welfare . . . was what people in this country got so they wouldn't turn into beggars like those outside La Catedral back home" (174). The family survives on monthly remittances from Laura's father that allow them to pay for rent, clothing, and an occasional trip to the ballet. Thus, the Garcías have access to social capital that enables them to survive their initial economic hardships and helps them improve their material conditions in the United States much faster than a garment worker or a mechanic, for example, who most likely has to send remittances to his or her family on the island and forgo the ballet in favor of basic living necessities.

The process of negotiating a new space as the racialized Other is a rude awakening for the family. Thus their exile and subsequent settlement in the United States is a difficult and sometimes anguished experience. The young García girls are confronted by racial discrimination and loss of social status. In the United States, they find themselves at the bottom of the social ladder as racialized subjects instead of the privileged position they maintained on the island.

The four frightened little girls are forced to confront the demons that most immigrants have to deal with, such as language, racial and ethnic discrimination, assimilation, and loss of identity. Sandi, one of the sisters, vividly recalls the family's reception in the United States by a neighbor: "The old woman in the apartment below, who had a helmet of beauty parlor blue hair, had been complaining to the super since the day the family moved in a few months ago. The Garcías should be evicted. Their food smelled. They spoke too loudly and not in English. The kids sounded like a herd of wild burros" (170). In a complete reversal, whites in the United States of all classes view the girls much the same way that the Garcías view the Dominican lower classes, as inferior racialized subjects. The intolerant blue-haired neighbor only sees a stereotype in the García family and cannot acknowledge them as equal human beings. The García girls no longer represent an elite Dominican society but an inferior, filthy, dark, and exotic element that has to be tolerated but not mingled with because the García girls are now the coconut pickers too.

The turbulence of assimilation is most strongly felt by the four impressionable girls as they make their way through the education system, both public and private. First the girls are all left back a year, which was standard procedure for immigrant children at the time despite their academic abilities. Then the girls are subjected to the psychological violence of racism on the playground when ethnic Anglo-American children taunt them with racial slurs. The oldest, Carla, who not only has to contend with a new language and a new school but also the changes brought on by puberty, is haunted by these initial experiences for many years. In "Trespass," Carla's painful experiences haunt her. Alvarez writes, "Out of sight of the nuns, the boys pelted Carla with stones, aiming them at her feet so there would be no bruises. Go back to where you came from, you dirty spic!" (153). The stones thrown at Carla do not leave visible bruises, nonetheless she is psychologically scarred by these events since she cannot forget the faces of boys who harassed her as a child. Carla felt unwelcome and unwanted in her new home. All four of the García girls will experience similar discrimination and alienation as they navigate their way through the school system. As a result of their initial encounters on the playground, the girls plead to return home. In "Daughter of Invention" Yolanda tells her parents, "We're not going to school anymore, Mami! . . . You want us to get killed" (135). Yolanda articulates the feelings of fear, rejection, displacement, and alienation felt by the girls on the playground and throughout their education. Yolanda recalls that in high school she was the only immigrant in her class.

In hopes of placing her daughters with a better class of Anglo-Americans, a class-conscious Laura sends her daughters to an elite school. Laura erroneously believes middle- and upper-class white Anglo-Saxon Protestant types will accept her girls because they belong to the same class. However, unbeknownst to their mother, the girls do not escape racist stereotypes: "We had our own kind of fame, based mostly on the rich girls' supposition and our own silence. García de la Torre didn't mean a thing to them, but those brand-named beauties simply assumed that, like all third world foreign students in boarding schools, we were filthy rich and related to some dictator or other. Our privilege smacked of evil and mystery whereas as theirs came in recognizable pantyhose packages and candy wrappers and vacuum cleaner bags" (108).

Although the Garcías have the means to remove their daughters from a public school in an attempt to shelter the girls, it does not protect them from racism. In the United States, the illustrious family name the Garcías are so proud of no longer carries any prestige vis-à-vis the names of elite Anglo-American families. Their Anglo-American classmates are ignorant of how their privilege feeds off the Third World dictators they ridicule. The imperialist policies that the United States imposed throughout the world, particularly in Latin America and the Caribbean, sustain the racial and economic privilege of these families while they remain in denial about their complicity within that system.

For the Garcías, a privileged education assures that the girls move in circles that remove them from the other minorities as well as significant historical events such as the Civil Rights movement. It is telling that Alvarez does not delve very much into this area. For the García girls, the sixties are about rebelling against the rigid gender norms and old-world traditions represented by the patriarchal ideas of their father: "His daughters had had to put up with this kind of attitude in an unsympathetic era. They grew up in the late sixties. Those were the days when wearing jeans and hoop earrings, smoking a little dope, and sleeping with their classmates were considered political acts against the military-industrial complex" (28). For the girls, sex, drugs, and a pair of funky jeans constitute political acts against the repression they see around them. The García girls subscribe to white middle-class feminist values that focus on gender equality and do not seem to take into account Third-World women and women of color in general. Nor do they appear to identify with the social inequalities brought about by racist institutionalized practices in the United States.

Nonetheless, Alvarez does explore the practice of "blanqueamiento," whitening as a mechanism to "mejorar la raza," which translates to "improve the race" by marriage to a white or lighter-skinned person. The ideology of "blanqueamiento" is internalized by the García family and is reflected in the manner in which lighter members of the family are viewed. Laura clearly thinks her daughter Sandi is the prettiest of her daughters because she inherits her Swedish grandmother's "blue eyes and peaches and ice cream skin," which makes her better than her sisters. Yet Sandi feels displaced within the family. Laura comments, "The others aren't bad looking, don't get me wrong. But Sandi, Sandi got her fine looks, blue eyes, peaches and ice cream skin, everything going for her . . . So the family has light-colored blood, and that Sandi got it all. But imagine spirit of contradiction, she wanted to be darker complected like her sisters" (52). The García girls come in all colors owing to the mixture of African, European, and indigenous origins that make up Dominicans. Although Laura loves all her daughters, she thinks that Sandi's Nordic looks are more desirable and give her an advantage over the others. So when Fifi, the youngest daughter, marries a German man, Laura is absolutely thrilled because her granddaughter will be "pink and blond."

The father, Carlos, also shares his wife's view. When he views Fifi's newborn son, Carlos is overwhelmed by pride at his daughter's accomplishment as well as relieved. "All the grandfather's Caribbean fondness for a male heir and for fair Nordic looks had surfaced. There was now good blood in the family against a future bad choice by one of its women" (27). The father's thoughts indicate that he believes that his daughters are responsible for "whitening" the family or at least maintaining a light complexion in their children. The implication is that if any of the García girls marries a darker man, then the family would be infused with bad dark blood as opposed to good light blood. Carlos and Laura are socialized to believe that "blanqueamiento" is acceptable and do not recognize it as a racist practice that privileges whiteness and attempts to eradicate blackness from Dominican society.

Alvarez most definitely addresses race as it manifests itself in the Dominican Republic, with Haitians as the racialized Other against which Dominicans define their identity. The García family categorizes their domestic staff with clear socially constructed racial distinctions. Chucha, the cook, is "Haitian blue-black, not Dominican *café con leche*" (218). Another maid, Nivea, is regarded as black-black: "Nivea, the latest of our laundry maids, was 'black-black': my mother said it twice to darken the color to full, matching strength. She'd been nicknamed Nivea after an American face cream her mother used to rub on her, hoping the milky white applications would lighten the baby's black skin" (260). Although Nivea and Chucha are both black, the mother uses that expression "black-black" to emphasize Nivea's skin color and to differentiate her from Chucha, who is Haitian-black. Nivea's name and the reasoning behind it indicate the value placed on lighter skin in the Dominican Republic. Since Nivea's mother is unable to lighten her baby by picking a lighter partner, she attempts to do so cosmetically perhaps in an attempt to shield her from racial prejudices. However, the actions of Nivea's mother also reflect internalized prejudices across class lines and emphasize that she considers a dark complexion unattractive.

Even though there is no difference in phenotype between Nivea and Chucha, in a Dominican context Nivea is socially lighter and more acceptable than Chucha. Regardless of the fact that Chucha has lived in the Dominican Republic more years than she lived in Haiti, and speaks Spanish, and is essentially culturally Dominican, Nivea and the other Dominican servants fear her because she is Haitian born. In *Race and Politics in the Dominican Republic,* Ernesto Sagás posits that the racist ideology of *antihaitianismo* advances the idea that Dominicans and Haitians belong to different races. In general, Dominicans tend to define themselves as a Catholic nation of mixed Spanish and Taíno ancestry, *indios* in opposition to Haitians, who are viewed as black descendants of African slaves who practice vodou. "From its origins as Hispanic racism, to its transformation into anti-Haitian nationalism, to its culmination as Trujillo's state ideology, antihaitianismo has had one main objective: the protection of powerful and personal elite interests through the subjugation of the lower (and darker) of the Dominican population" (Sagás 2000, 119). Sagás further argues that a small group of Dominican elites, most of whom are light skinned, controls the Dominican Republic both politically and economically by promoting *antihaitianismo* sentiments that are now ingrained in the Dominican psyche.

Alvarez effectively uses characters like Chucha and Pilar, a Dominican of Haitian descent, to illustrate how Haitians have been historically exploited, mistrusted, and discriminated against by Trujillo's policies as well as elites such as the García family. The other Dominican servants gossip about Pilar and suspect her of stealing even before there is any proof. Both Pilar and Chucha are feared by the other domestics because they are associated with vodou, an Afro-Haitian religion that is often misunderstood and stereotyped by many, especially Dominicans. In Chucha's case, the fear is so extreme that other servants refuse to share a room with her. Despite the fact that Haitians are often vilified in Dominican society, Alvarez alludes to the fact that Dominicans rely heavily on and often exploit Haitian labor. However, it must be noted that in exposing the stereotypes, Alvarez falls into the same trap since she only presents a few Haitian characters as vodou-practicing domestics who are shrouded in mystery and mysticism. Alvarez fails to juxtapose these images with other types of Haitian characters.

Notwithstanding, Alvarez does utilize Chucha on multiple levels, providing the character with a strong voice of resistance and love. On a symbolic level, Chucha represents the atrocities and oppression of the Trujillo regime because she arrives at Papito's door and begs for asylum as a survivor of the Haitian massacres ordered by the dictator in 1937. Chucha remains devoted to the García family for the rest of her life out of gratitude and perhaps because she has no other place to go. Chucha is a powerful maternal figure for the García girls and caretaker of family secrets. Although she recognizes that the family exploits her, she also feels as if they are her family too and therefore has a right to speak whenever she chooses" "Chucha's [complaints] were a daily litany, sometimes cried out at the dog, sometimes scolded at the rice kettle she had to scrub, sometimes mumbled under her breath at Doña Laura, whose diapers she changed and whose actions, therefore, she had a right to criticize" (Alvarez 1991, 262). Chucha is highly aware that her saviors are also her subjugators, who are part of the system that oppresses her. The elite life-style of the García family is supported by the exploitation.

Chucha also remains a constant central figure in the memories of the adult García girls as they recall their flight from the island. As an exile herself, Chucha represents the finality of being uprooted from home and settling in a foreign and hostile environment. Once the Garcías leave, they can never return to the moment and place they left behind, but the events remain like ghostly images to haunt them. The life the girls know is about to end with the finality of death. The experience is embodied in Chucha's symbolic death. As the girls leave for the United States, Chucha anticipates the troubles the girls will face in the future as they try to assimilate in their new home as she remembers her own experience as an immigrant in the Dominican Republic. When the family leaves, Chucha contemplates their future exile as she climbs into a coffin for a long sleep. "I feel their losses pile up like dirt thrown on a box after it has been lowered into the earth. I see their future, the troublesome life ahead" (22). Chucha knows from personal experience that there is no going back to this home ever again. They are going to a new place where they have to contend with the loss of the past and the violent imposition of a new present as racialized subjects.

Although the García girls are never the same again, they survive the painful assimilation process by developing a consciousness that allows them to piece together bits of old memories and old ghosts with new realities that transcend geographies. Chucha notes that her girls "will be haunted by what they do and don't remember. But they have the spirit in them. They will invent what they need to survive" (22). Perhaps the one García who is most haunted by the ghosts of memories is Yolanda, the writer.

The last chapter, entitled "The Drum," symbolically foreshadows the problems the girls will face in the future and also represents the guilt and loss of the past as well as Yolanda's struggle to master English. Yolanda receives a red, white, and blue drum trimmed in gold from F.A.O. Schwarz, an upscale New York City toy store. The drum becomes symbolic of the García family's problematic relationship with the United States as the catalyst of their exile, their savior, and the hostile receiving country that will shake up the family as they struggle to assimilate. Like the drum, the United States represents an exciting, bright, and shiny paradigm of hopeful progress. Yet as Yolanda beats the drum with exuberance, making loud rhythmic sounds, her mother, who originally encourages her to play, tries to restrict Yolanda's revelry since it is too loud and jarring. After Yolanda loses one drumstick and the other is broken by her aunt, the drum never sounds the same again; it is as if the spell is broken.

Yolanda's subsequent encounter with an American hunter is equally significant. Like the drum, the hunter comes across as a handsome, kind, and wise character who advises Yolanda not to take a kitten away from its mother too soon because it will die and then proceeds to hunt a bird. Outraged by the hypocrisy of the American, who tells the island natives to behave one way and shoots a defenseless bird who Yolanda imagines is carrying worms to its offspring, she ignores him and throws the kitten whom she names Schwarz into the drum. Yolanda then plays a terrible game with the kitten's black mother, who stalks her as she tries to escape with the kitten, trying to drown out the meows by pounding on the drum, "BARRA BOOM! (Meow! Meow!) BOOM." After she escapes inside the house Yolanda is tormented by the mother cat's meows, the "THUNDER, THUNDER!" of the American hunter's gun, and the kitten's cries from within the belly of the drum. Frustrated and angry, Yolanda takes the kitten, with "its little human face" and "accusing sound of meow," and throws it out of the window in a fit of violence. That morning, Yolanda watches the "wounded kitten make a broken progress across the lawn" (288). The next day the cat, the crazy American hunter shooting in the orange grove, and the kitten disappear.

This powerful symbolism is revealing. The kitten with its human face is young, scared, and defenseless, like Yolanda. Alvarez describes it as having "four little white paws, and a white spot between its ears." Alvarez purposefully describes a mixed black and white cat, but her focus on its white spots mirrors Dominican racial attitudes. The kitten is helplessly caught up in the drum that represents the United States and its BARRA BOOM, the English language. The ordeal in the drum will be Yolanda's struggle to learn a new language and survive the violent barrage of assimilating a new culture. Somehow, the kitten manages to raise a meow above the drum, much the same way Yolanda and Alvarez will tell their stories despite the marginalization of Latina and Dominican writers in the mainstream literary scene. The hunter represents U.S. imperialism and foreign policy. The bird and the orange groves, which the hunter feels free to trespass upon, represent the island's resources. And the black mother cat is the island that Yolanda and her sisters are about to leave behind, but it also the ghost that will haunt Yolanda even as an adult, "a black furred thing lurking in the corners of my life, her magenta mouth opening, wailing over some violation that lies at the center of my art" (290). The violation Yolanda and Alvarez refer to is that of another language. Both the fictional Yolanda and the author Alvarez write Dominican narratives in English, the imposed language they have mastery over instead of their native *español,* which trips clumsily over their tongues.

Alvarez's indictment of U.S. involvement in Dominican affairs is most evident in her portrayal of U.S. Anglo-Americans on the island. The hunter is a crazy hypocrite. A crazy aunt is married to an American and is always on the verge of divorce. And then there is Tío Vic, the family friend and schoolmate of Tío Mundín and friendly CIA agent posing as a diplomatic consul. "Vic is, in fact, a CIA agent whose orders changed midstream from organize the underground and get that SOB out to hold your horses, let's take a second look around to see what's best for us" (217). The relationship of U.S. Anglo-Americans to the island is one based on consumption and political expediency. As long as Trujillo's regime works for U.S. interests, the United States is content to leave the status quo intact. Perhaps the most telling sign of U.S. relations with the island is how Vic looks at the women on the island, "Fellas got him fixed up with Tatica, who has kept him in the little girls he likes, hot little numbers, dark and sweet like the little cups of sugar so full of goddam caffeine and Island sugar you're shaking half the day" (206). For Vic and the United States, the island and its women seem available for consumption. Vic likes very young girls who are prostitutes, which he compares to coffee and sugar, commodities on the island. Of course, not only is Vic instrumental in getting Carlos exposed to arrest for participating in a coup, he also gets to play the savior by arranging for the García family to escape the regime within the so-called welcoming safety of the United States.

Yet when the García girls arrive in the United States their reception is less than hospitable. As four frightened little girls, they are forced as Chucha predicts to confront the demons that most immigrants have to deal with, such as language, discrimination, assimilation, and loss of identity. Their mother has to contend with turning four girls into proper Dominican *señoritas* in the midst of the sexual revolution and the feminist movement of the 1960s and 70s. The culture clash becomes evident as the girls start assimilating new values and want to leave the "old-world" behind them as their mother struggles to instill those very values in her girls. The sisters also have to deal with assimilation into a new and unfriendly culture by attempting to shed their island identities and immerse themselves in so-called normative models of identity. However, the island does not let go of the girls so easily and what ensues is an alienating and painful internal tug of war between cultures.

As teenagers the girls develop an ambivalent relation with the island as they become accustomed to living in the United States, saturated in U.S. culture. The girls are acknowledged by the family as the wild American cousins whose Spanish is constantly threatening to abandon them because their tongues are too crowded with English. On their annual trips to visit family, they have a difficult time adjusting to traditional gender roles. Once again, their reactions to the expectations placed on women are class specific because poor working-class women have always had unchaperoned access outside the homes because they often have to work. The sisters disapprove of Fifi's conversion to a traditional island girl, complete with hair, nails, and Dominican boyfriend, Manuel, who exudes machismo. They are outraged by his demands on their sister and fearful that if he gets Fifi pregnant she will be forced to marry him and remain on the island. In order to thwart Manuel's plans, they leave Fifi unchaperoned with him in order to gain their mother's intervention. However, the plan backfires because Laura's reaction is to pack up the girls and take them all back to the United States immediately with a promise never to send them back. Fifi must return home with her sisters, and Carlos, their father, must never find out, or it would be a disgrace to the family. The girls realize that perhaps they are not ready to leave: "We look at each other, and drop our gaze to hide our confusion. We are free at last, but here, just at that moment the gate swings open, and we can fly the coop, Tía Carmen's love revives our old homesickness" (131). The homesickness keeps the girls rooted in the island even from the states. Yet this episode also illustrates that middle-class women's virginity is very much tied to notions of family honor among Dominicans.

The girls become independent women who subscribe to white middle-class feminist values and do not quite fit in with the island society, where they feel the pressure to become proper and obedient wives. The García girls struggle with their identity and have to find a way to bridge both worlds within themselves. The clash of white middle-class feminism and Dominican women's views of gender is evident in how the García sisters judge their island relatives through their U.S. feminist perspective. The behavior of the García sisters implies that they believe women are conditioned to accept their subservient role by the patriarchal system of power. The independent sisters who embrace the freedom of the United States are disgusted with the situation and voice it, "For the benefit of an invisible sisterhood, since our aunts and girl cousins consider it very unfeminine for a woman to go around demonstrating for her rights, Yoyo sighs and all of us roll our eyes. We don't even try anymore to raise consciousness here" (121).

In the United States, the García girls feel that they have tasted freedom from the ever watchful and repressive eyes of island society, and they are no longer willing to accept what they perceive to be a submissive role. Interestingly, Tía Flor does not feel subjugated in the least, "Look at me, I'm a queen," she argued. "My husband has to go to work everyday. I can sleep until noon, if I want, I'm going to protest for my rights?" (121). Flor views her privileged middle-class life-style as a blessing since she has servants to tend to the house, nannies for the children, and her husband to provide her with a comfortable life-style that allows her to run a household with very little stress and gives her time for herself. The liberal ideas and attitudes the García girls have taken as their own are barely tolerated on the island. It is the common assumption by their Dominican relatives that years of living in the United States have corrupted the girls with U.S. culture and loose moral values, the effects of which may be countered by yearly visits to the island and possible marriage to a Dominican man.

The assumption by their Dominican relatives is that the García girls have been transformed from proper Dominican *señoritas* to dreaded American teenagers after living in the United States. For the García girls, it seems as if living in the United States forces them to undergo a metamorphosis called "Americanization," which causes them to lost part of their "Dominicanness." On the island, many Dominicans tend to view Dominicans who live in the United States as foreigners or gringos. This is the subject in Alvarez's essay, "La Gringuita." Alvarez writes about a time she went back to the island for the summer and how she did not quite fit. Her family dismisses her differences by labeling her "American" and tries to eradicate her "Americanness" by means of language. Alvarez recalls the experience: "My aunts and uncles tried unsuccessfully to stem this tide of our Americanization, whose main expression was, of course, our use of the English language. . . . By now, we couldn't go back as easily as that. Our Spanish was full of English" (64). For Alvarez, her native language is synonymous with her native culture. It becomes a major factor in forming identity because it is the tool by which she expresses who she is.

The García girls eventually conquer the English language, or rather it conquers them, and they "develop a taste for the American teenage good life, and soon, island life was old hat" (109). The girls embrace their liberation from strict island customs. In the United States, they become opinionated, independent teenagers who think they know better than their traditional, old-world parents. They try new things like hair removal creams, tampons, cigarettes, drugs, birth control, and sex, most of the vices from which their mother is trying to protect them. This is where the "revolution" heats up, "the problem boiled down to the fact that they wanted to become Americans and their father—and their mother, too, at first—would have none of it"

(135). In their struggle to fit in their new home, the girls feel like they can blend in easier if they attempt to forget the old customs and adopt new ones.

All of a sudden, they feel free to express themselves in any way without fear of political repercussions. Laura García reflects this issue, "In the old country, any whisper of a challenge to authority could bring the secret police in their black V.W.'s. But this was America. People could say what they thought" (145). Alvarez expresses this newly found freedom of expression through the character of Yolanda, the writer, but she complicates it by utilizing it as a defense strategy for racist anti-ethnic sentiments that constantly make her feel like an outsider in her new home. Yolanda comments, "[I]n New York, she needed to settle somewhere, and since the natives where unfriendly, and the country inhospitable, she took root in the language" (141). Through her writing, Yolanda could distinguish herself from the other children and her siblings as well as find a place for herself in a place where she frequently feels marginalized as "the only immigrant in her class" (166).

On one occasion, when Yolanda writes a speech for Teacher Appreciation Day that criticizes the teachers, her father, who represents the old country, is enraged that his daughter would dare write down such insubordinate and subversive thoughts, instead of being complimentary and gracious. Laura, a character in transition between the old world and the new, is very proud of Yolanda's eloquent effort. What follows is a battle between old Dominican traditional values versus North American values of modernity. Laura fiercely defends the speech, and Yolanda expresses her frustration and rejection of the old world by yelling at her father, "This is America, Papi, America! You are not in a savage country anymore!" (146). Carlos is baffled by the way his wife and daughter are expressing themselves: "It was bad enough that his daughter was rebelling, but here was his own wife joining forces with her. Soon he would be surrounded by a household of independent American women" (146). The García family's response to their new surroundings is a direct result of their class status. Yolanda's reference to the island as a savage country reflects how she has internalized her parent's ideas on class and the lines that are drawn across race and gender.

Alvarez illustrates that even under the best circumstances, immigration is a difficult and often a disorienting process. Whether an immigrant leaves his or her home by choice or by force, inevitably something or someone is left behind. Regardless of how Americanized the Garcías become they never quite leave the island. And yet when they go to the island, they never quite leave the United States. Although learning a new language and negotiating a new culture in a wholly racialized and genderized environment is a painful and alienating experience for the García girls in particular, they gain from a sense of survival and adaptability and they are always involved in a process of negotiation to find a place for themselves within themselves.

The history of immigration in the United States clearly illustrates that immigration narratives differ greatly and are often determined by an individual's point of origin as well as race, class, and gender. Certainly, *How the García Girls Lost Their Accents* reflects a privileged immigration narrative that does not represent the reality of the immigration saga for many Dominicans. Nonetheless, Alvarez touches upon many themes and issues that are faced by many Dominicans living in the United States and that resonate strongly with women.

Struggling to Stay Afloat in Díaz's *Drown*

Drown is a collection of interrelated short stories that portray a Dominican experience very different from that of Alvarez's narrative. The main character, Yunior, narrates the stories as a child and later as an adult trying to find his place in the world. Díaz effectively uses Dominican and American vernacular to express the changes in Yunior's point of view that transports us from a poor town in the Dominican Republic to the streets of Edison, New Jersey, and then Washington Heights, in New York City. The characters who make up his family evolve through the realities they face in leaving their poverty-stricken country and adjusting to the United States, where life is supposed to be better. Unlike the middle-class characters in Alvarez's novel who immigrate to get away from the political turmoil and persecution, Díaz's characters are economic exiles. They represent the new wave of economic refugees from the Dominican Republic in the late 1970s and 1980s who were affected by harsh economic conditions brought about by poor and frequently corrupt economic policies that favored elites and foreign investors. Yunior's family is severely affected by the father's abuse and absence. For Díaz, the family conflicts, extreme poverty, and the search for identity that are part of Yunior's immigration story take root in language, race, class, and gender. In the process, Díaz too exposes how U.S. imperialism is inextricably linked in this very personal family drama that reflects the nation.

Díaz takes us on a tour of despair, poverty, survival, and hope. The family unit is dysfunctional, scarred by the father's abuse, infidelity, and abandonment. His stories are dark and gritty because they express the reality of second-generation Dominican immigrants who arrived in the late 1970s and 1980s to escape desperate economic conditions. Díaz's characters reflect the loneliness and alienation that result from the everyday struggle of survival in a harsh and foreign environment. These are disillusioned people who have been battered by the hardships of poverty and the immigrant experience. And yet through it all, Díaz's characters adapt, survive, and move forward.

Throughout the stories, the narrator is trying to reconstruct a sketch of his parents, his home, his experiences, and his history through memories and photographs and in turn sketch out his own identity. Díaz introduces some pivotal moments in Yunior's parents' lives and Dominican history through snapshots of the past as if they were small pieces of the puzzle that serve as background information for his characters. He repeatedly uses retrospection to present these elements of historical facts in his stories. Díaz is sketching Yunior's parents, unraveling their stories and retelling history through their personal narratives. For example, in the story "Fiesta, 1980," Yunior remembers a photo of his mother before she was married that shows she was a vibrant woman: "The only photograph our family had of Mami as a young woman, before she married Papi, was one that somebody took of her at an election party . . . In the photo, she's surrounded by laughing cousins I will never meet . . . she sits straight and even in a crowd she stands out, smiling quietly like maybe she's the one everybody's celebrating" (Díaz 1996, 41). The image of Virta in the photo is a far cry from the woman that Yunior knows to be his mother. Years of spousal neglect, verbal abuse, and quiet suffering and struggle as a single mother have emotionally shut her down and have taken away her vitality and verve to live. The images of the cousins Yunior will never meet is a sad commentary on how many Dominicans living outside of the island are irrevocably disconnected from their family by lack of resources and/or an inability to travel back and forth to the island. Díaz also indirectly captures the essence of this historical time in the snapshot. After Trujillo's death, free elections were held on December 20, 1962. Juan Bosch, a former exile who was a social democrat, won in an overwhelming show of popular support.

Yunior desperately wants to understand his parent's history and the history of his island so that he can find his place within that history and understand why his life has been disrupted and uprooted permanently to the United States. In "Aguantando" we get another piece of this personal and historical puzzle when Yunior remembers a photograph of his father: "When I thought of Papi I thought of one shot specifically. Taken days before the U.S. invasion: 1965. I wasn't even alive then; Mami had been pregnant with my first never-born brother. . . . He was dressed in his Guardia uniform, his tan cap at an angle on his shaved head, an unlit Constitución squeezed between his lips" (69–70). The photo reveals the calm before the violent and political storm erupts on the island when Yunior's parents are still full of hopes and expectations for themselves and their country. Yunior's father is in the army at the time of the 1965 invasion by the United States, which means he most likely is forced into battle. Yunior later reveals that his mother bears "across her stomach and back the scars from the rocket attack she'd survived in 1965" (71). These scars are not just physical but psychological as well since Virta apparently has a miscarriage as a result of the attack. In another story,

"How to Date a Browngirl, Blackgirl, Whitegirl or Halfie," we find out that years after the invasion, while they are living in New Jersey, Yunior's mother can still recognize the smell of tear gas because it was used against them in the invasion. Although official accounts from the United States view the invasion as a peace-keeping mission to restore order, Díaz clearly indicates that Yunior's mother is victim and survivor of a violent conflict, if not war fueled by imperialism.

Unfortunately, what follows the 1965 invasion by the United States is the appearance of democracy with corrupt policies and a great deal of foreign aid that leave the island and its people facing severe economic conditions. In "Aguantando," Yunior and his family face severe poverty. The economic conditions are so bad that although she is employed and working long hours, Virta, her two sons, and her father are almost starving. As Yunior describes it, "We were poor. The only way we could have been poorer was to have lived in the *campo* or to have been Haitian immigrants, Mami regularly offered these to us as brutal consolation" (70). They barely have food; they live in a wood-framed house with a leaky roof. If they have to buy medicine to cure Yunior and his brother Rafa of worms, their mother has to hold back on food. They barely eat meat; it is a treat if they even get fried cheese. The children don't have schoolbooks or uniforms. Their mother has to borrow pencils and sew a notebook together for them out of scraps she finds or people give her. When Virta is unable to put food on the table, she frequently ships the children off to different relatives who are well off to keep them from starving. However, it is important to note that even in their poverty-stricken state, they still consider themselves better than Haitians. In other words, it is fine for the Haitians to be dirt poor and eat rocks because they are black.

Díaz illustrates yet another example of how deeply embedded anti-Haitian sentiments are in Dominican society while simultaneously fleshing out the commonalities between the Dominicans and Haitians. Yunior recalls how his brother Rafa teases him about his own appearance: "Unless, of course, he was mad and then he had about five hundred routines he liked to lay on me. Most of them had to do with my complexion, my hair, the size of my lips. It's the Haitian, he'd say to his buddies. Hey Señor Haitian, Mami found you on the border and only took you in because she felt sorry for you" (5). Rafa teases Yunior by accusing him of being Haitian. The label Haitian takes on negative and derogatory connotations in a Dominican context. At the same time, Díaz rejects the belief that Dominicans and Haitians are different by citing Yunior's complexion, lips, and hair, which link the two nations with their African ancestry. Instead, Díaz's description of Yunior's African features contests Dominican notions of a racial identity based primarily or exclusively on indigenist and European roots.

In "The Tribulations of Blackness: Stages in Dominican Racial Identity," Silvio Torres-Saillant (2000) asserts that there is a growing awareness of blackness by Dominicans, particularly those who immigrate to the United States, where they are faced with two choices: black or white, neither of which fit in with how Dominicans view themselves. It is significant that within this context, some Dominicans (particularly those educated in the United States) achieve a certain consciousness about their African roots and may embrace or acknowledge Dominican blackness. Díaz's narrative reflects this consciousness through Yunior's experiences as a black-identified Dominican man who is born on the island but raised in the United States.

This consciousness takes form in a struggle for economic survival across the Caribbean sea in the land of opportunity. Yunior's father, Ramón, is the first in the family to leave the island and encounter racial and ethnic prejudices as well as economic exploitation. Driven by desperation, the family pins all their hopes on Ramón. Yunior's grandfather gives Ramón the last of his savings for the plane ticket even though his son-in-law breaks his daughter's heart with his infidelities. All he asks of him is to take care of his family, who needs him. In "Aguantando"—a word with multiple meanings, which for Virta and her children translates into bearing with poverty, loneliness, hunger, humiliation, depression, perseverance, abandonment, infidelities, lies, hustles, broken promises, disillusionment, and heartbreak—the family holds on to the promise that Ramón will take care of them. Virta and the children hold on for dear life until he finally remembers them in a bout of guilt and brings them to the United States.

For many years after his departure from the island, Ramón abandons his family so that he not only becomes an absentee father but a mysterious and sporadically disruptive phantom in their lives. Yunior recalls his childhood without his father: "On the days I tried to imagine him—not often, since Mami didn't much speak of him anymore—he was the soldier in the photo. He was a cloud of cigar smoke, the traces of which could still be found on the uniforms he'd left behind. He was pieces of my friends' fathers, of the domino players on the corner, pieces of Mami and Abuelo, I didn't know him at all. I didn't know why he abandoned us. That this waiting for him was all a sham" (Díaz 1996, 70). Yunior's comments illustrate the sadness and pain of abandonment. Although Yunior's mother remains faithful to Ramón and continues to write to him pleading for him to help his children, she is essentially a widow in mourning. Yunior's recollections do in fact reflect the heartache and abandonment that those left behind feel. Unlike Alvarez's narrative, Díaz's narrative resonates closer to reality for the multitudes of Dominicans who left their homes and for those relatives left behind.

In "Negocios," which translates into hustling and/or business, we see the business of immigration and the hustle to survive through Ramón's experience in the United States. Ramón gets lost in his struggle to achieve material comfort based on a model of capitalism and modernity where the individual comes first and the family is sacrificed for the dollar. "Negocios" is also the same story that Yunior narrates in "Aguantando" from another point of view. It is Yunior's version of his father's story and also that of Nilda, Ramón's other wife in the United States. In order to survive in the states, Ramón literally banishes his family to the recesses of his mind. Yunior describes Ramón's mental state: "He was twenty-four. He didn't dream about his familia and wouldn't for many years. He dreamed instead of gold coins, like the ones that had been salvaged from the many wrecks about our island, stacked as high as sugar cane" (169). Díaz's imagery suggests that Ramón is a product of colonial indoctrination because his voyage to the United States mirrors that of the colonizer arriving to plunder the new world's riches. Yet the reference to sugarcane reminds us that the prosperity that Ramón desires is built on racist exploitation. Yunior points out that his father is too busy looking for "negocios" that will make him a success in the United States to think about his family. When he first arrives in Miami, he works long hours and he is willing to do any job no matter how menial. After a few months, he hitchhikes all the way to New York, looking for an opportunity to swing its doors wide open for him. Like so many immigrants, he is hopeful and optimistic since he believes that "Nueva York was the city of jobs, the city that had first called the Cubanos and their cigar industry, then the Bootstrap Puerto Ricans and now him" (167). Unfortunately, those doors have as many locks as any apartment in Washington Heights, and you need all the keys to get in.

The most important key that one needs is a residency card, and those do not come easily. Until he gets one, Ramón's life as an undocumented immigrant is perilous. In "Negocios," Ramón ponders this when he sees federal marshals pulling up to him: "His visa had expired five weeks earlier and if caught, he'd go home in chains. He'd heard plenty of tales about the North American police from the other illegals, how they liked to beat you before they turned you over to la migra and how sometimes they just take your money and tossed you out toothless on an abandoned road" (175). Ramón is well versed on how he might be treated as a man of color and a foreigner by the immigration officials in the United States. Getting caught, imprisoned, and subsequently sent back is every illegal immigrant's worst nightmare, but they live with it because going home is not a viable option. Often immigrants prefer to risk living as fugitives from "la migra" than to go back and face unsafe and/or unlivable conditions back home. Many immigrants like Ramón scheme any way they can to get their papers. In Ramón's case, he has to find a woman to marry, get his papers, and then divorce her after he is legal.

It's a business deal, nothing more. One person gets paid and the other gets papers. "He was sick often but was able to work through it and succeeded in saving up enough money to start looking for a wife to marry. It was the old routine, the oldest routine, the oldest of postwar maromas. Find a citizen, get married, wait and then divorce her. The routine was well practiced and expensive and riddled with swindlers" (178).

Ramón's initial intention is to bring Virta and the children to Nueva York once he gets his papers, but he gets hustled in the process and becomes hardened and bitter. His first attempt at marriage fails miserably after he is robbed of his hard-earned money and he plunges into an angry and frustrated existence. "He often drank too much and went home to his room, and there he'd fume, spinning, angry at the stupidity that had brought him to this freezing hell of a country, angry that a man his age had to masturbate when he had a wife, and angry at the blinkered existence his jobs and the city imposed on him" (179). Ramón's life as an immigrant in New York City is difficult and hard; he is beaten, robbed, hustled, underpaid and overworked, and cold. The separation from his family and his homeland is painful. The loneliness, the back-breaking work, the long hours, the weather, the squalor of his temporary home are frustrating and hard to take. Out of desperation, anger, and even loneliness, Ramón then makes a decision to hustle Nilda into marrying him for love while all the while he is thinking of his needs. In the process, Ramón makes two families: women and children dependent on him and victimized by his abandonment.

Throughout Díaz's stories, Yunior's father emerges as an abusive, violent patriarch who asserts his dominance on all his family members, especially the women. His infidelities are commonplace, and he does not show any remorse for them. Ramón behaves as if women are there to serve his needs, and he does not have to account to any of them for his deeds. "I know it wasn't a smart thing to do, but I didn't know the woman would lie like she did" (165). In "Fiestas, 1980," he takes his sons to his mistress's house without giving it a second thought. He is not concerned that his sons might tell their mother because he does not feel accountable to her. The fact that he abandons his family for five years and marries another woman in the United States with whom he has a child does not seem to disturb him until things start going badly with his second wife, Nilda.

Only when things become uncomfortable does Ramón return to the island and reclaim his role as the family patriarch. Ramón's word is law at home and his wrath is to be feared. Ramón is a tyrant in his home, and his wife is forced to bend to his iron will because she has been socialized to accept her submissive role. Yunior is very aware of their roles: "Papi's voice was loud and argumentative; you didn't have to be anywhere near him to catch his drift. And Mami, you had to put cups to your ears to hear hers" (33). The father smothers the mother's voice and personality. She is not an individual, only his wife and the mother of his children. To assert his role of patriarch in the family, he controls his children with violent authority. Virta's silence is a form of self-imposed exile. She becomes a phantom in her son's life.

Despite Ramón's reprehensible behavior toward the family, Yunior attempts to gain acceptance and love from his father. Sadly, Ramón is neglectful, abusive, and distant from his sons, whom he missed raising for nine years. Madai, Yunior's sister who was born in the United States and has been around Ramón all her life, is a scared little girl, frightened at the mere sound of her father's booming voice. Yunior describes his sister, "Being around Papi all her life had turned her into a major league wuss. Anytime Papi raised his voice her lip would start trembling, like some specialized tuning fork" (26). Despite Yunior's efforts, his relationship with his father is damaged beyond repair by Ramón's harsh authoritative demeanor. In a school essay, Yunior describes his father as an inventive torturer who devises different ways of physically disciplining his son. Yunior feels unloved by his father as a result of abuse and abandonment. Yunior confides, "I still wanted him to love me, something that never seemed strange or contradictory until years later, when he was out of our lives" (27). Although Yunior desperately wants to forge a connection with his father, Ramón remains an elusive enigma, hardened by a lifetime of hustling.

Against this bitter family drama, Yunior has to find himself while learning a new language and dealing with a new culture that does not necessarily accept him because he is considered an ethnic minority. In *Drown,* Yunior sums up his education, "One teacher, whose family had two grammar schools named after it, compared us to shuttles. A few of you are going to make it. Those are the orbiters. But the majority of you are just going to burn out. Going nowhere. He dropped his hands onto his desk. I could already see myself losing altitude, fading, the earth spread out beneath me, hard and bright" (106). The teacher is obviously white and represents not only the educational system for Yunior but also another male authority figure who gives up on him and abandons him. Subjected to institutionalized racism, Yunior is taught from an early age that he is going to fail not because of his lack of ability but because of his ethnicity and skin color.

As a means of survival against the pervasive racism they encounter, Dominicans, like many other ethnic groups, take root in their cultural traditions that reinforce pride and a sense of security. In "Fiesta, 1980," Yunior observes a family gathering: "It must be some Dominican tradition or something. There was everything I liked—chicharrones, fried chicken, tostones, sancocho, rice, fried cheese, yucca, avocado, potato salad, a meteor-sized hunk of pernil, even a tossed salad" (36). The feast Yunior describes represents the island palate. Food can be a powerful tool in maintaining cultural identity. The expression "we are what we eat" comes to mind. In this case, the food is Dominican regardless of what country it is served in. The aroma and flavors of island cooking become a connection to home for Dominicans in the United States as well as an integral part of maintaining their identity. Yet along with these goodies, Dominicans also develop a taste for burgers, hotdogs, Chinese and Mexican cuisine, and a host of other tastes when they arrive in the United States so that it is not unusual to find Yunior's feast served alongside lasagna and Chinese fried rice.

Along with the food, music and dancing are strong parts of Dominican culture that serve to keep Dominicans in touch with the island. *Merengue* and *bachata,* popular Dominican music, seem to be synonymous with identity. As a reporter from the *New York Times* states, "It is the record buying fever of these homesick émigrés that provides the cash that pumps the hit factories of Santo Domingo" (McLane 1991, 28). Dominicans in the United States in large part support the music industry on the island and yet they also listen to salsa, reggae, R&B, and more. Yunior recalls, "Whenever I peered into the main room I saw about twenty moms and dads dancing and drinking beers. Every now and then somebody yelled, Quisqueya! And then everybody would yell and stomp their feet" (Díaz 1996, 40). Music and dance transport Yunior's relatives back to the warmth and exuberance of the island. Dancing becomes a joyous and carefree event that temporarily helps them forget the long hours of work, the cold weather, the bills, the pursuit of green cards, and the families left behind.

Dominicans in the United States seem to have embraced the American way of life with a twist. They have carved out their own communities and established firm roots in the United States. For example, in New York City there is a large thriving community of Dominicans in the neighborhood known as Washington Heights. Areas such as this, which are "populated by significant numbers of Dominicans[,] normally exhibit the cultural accent of the community in a visually striking way" (Torres-Saillant and Hernández 1998, 138). As Yunior observes, "Everything in Washington Heights is Dominican. You can't go a block without passing a Quisqueya Bakery or a Quisqueya supermercado or a Hotel Quisqueya. If I were to park the truck and get out nobody would take me for a delivery man; I could be the guy who's on the street corner selling Dominican flags. I could be on my way home to my girl. Everybody's on the street and the merengue's falling out the windows like TVs" (Díaz 1996, 137). Although the Washington Heights community in New York City is a large and established Dominican community, it is also an ethnic enclave formed as a defense mechanism as well as a resistance to the dominant culture. Yunior feels right at home in this community because he feels a sense of belonging. He knows who he is in this place. However, once he steps out of this environment he becomes an outsider, an immigrant. Indeed, this community has become a home for many Dominican immigrants. As noted in a *New York Times* article, "Their entrepreneurial zeal has apparently bought them most of the city's bodegas and many of its livery cabs, and, to an exuberant merengue beat, they have revived a decaying Washington Heights" (Rimer 1991). They have transformed this community into a vibrant extension of the island. It is a place where they feel at home, a place where they are free to be themselves. However, there are many Dominicans in the United States who are not part of the picture of prosperity and are suffering at the lowest levels of economic indicators.

Searching for an Identity: Transnational Consciousness

The problem faced by many Dominicans living in the United States, but especially by Dominicans born and/or raised in the United States, is the issue of identity. It is a complicated issue that touches upon immigration and culture but also race, class, and gender. W.E.B. DuBois uses the term "double consciousness" when he writes about the experiences of African-Americans and how they perceive themselves and are perceived by others. DuBois writes: "In this merging he wishes neither of the older selves to be lost. He would not Africanize America, for America has too much to teach the world and Africa. He would not bleach his Negro soul in a flood of white Americanism, for he knows that Negro blood has a message for the world" (Farganis 1996, 188). The merging of souls that DuBois refers to goes to the heart of this discussion of a transnational consciousness. Dominicans in the United States do not see themselves as part of just one race, one culture, or one geographical space. Instead, they seem to have their consciousness planted in multiple spaces whether or not they have the means to travel. Who they were there very much informs who they are here.

Dominicans develop a consciousness that allows them to retain their native culture while assimilating to the new without sacrificing what is most important in each cultural space and without forgetting the pain involved in the process. While the idea of inventing one's self anew as a member of the national imaginary seems to be the foundation on which mainstream American culture is built, this does not seem to apply to racialized minorities, particularly those of the African diaspora. With every new ethnic group that is introduced to the United States, there is a give and take or infusion of culture that changes both groups. For Dominicans, it is not as exciting as Alvarez implies because it involves a clash of cultures and a negotiation process that often produces a transnational consciousness as a means of survival.

Gaining acceptance is an elusive proposition for Dominicans in the United

States because it is based on the perception of others. In an interview, Junot Díaz expresses his thoughts on belonging: "When I go back to the island, I am an immigrant . . . and in here . . . it has been 20 years, I am living here and I still consider myself an immigrant" (quoted in Molina 1998, 67). Díaz's comment implies that regardless of how much you immerse yourself into the culture, as a racialized ethnic you are still considered a foreigner and you may never feel fully accepted by the dominant culture. Alvarez captures this attitude perfectly in her essay "A Vermont Writer from the Dominican Republic." She writes about an old Vermonter who says the following: "Just because your cat went and had kittens in the oven, you wouldn't call them biscuits, now would you?" (Alvarez 1998, 188). The Vermonter's comment is a strong sentiment that sums up the perception many have about the Dominicans as transitory foreigners instead of a permanent fixture with long-established roots in the cultural landscape of the United States.

Alvarez, who refers to herself as a Dominican-American, explains that the duality she feels in language also expresses itself as an essential part of her identity, Dominican and American. Once removed from the native culture and assimilated into another, a new entity has been created: a hybrid of two cultures. Both cultures shape the identity and mold the individual so that they belong to both worlds. Alvarez comments on this hybridism in "Doña Aída, with Your Permission": "It's a world formed of contradictions, clashes, commingling—the gringa and the Dominican, it is precisely that tension and richness that interests me. Being in and out of both worlds, looking at one side from the other side. . . . These unusual perspectives are often what I write about. A duality that I hope in the writing transcends itself and becomes a new consciousness, a new place on the map, a synthesizing way of looking at the world" (Alvarez 1998, 173). Alvarez and Díaz have forged links across cultures and closed the gap between the two worlds through language. They are "a new generation of Dominican writers [that] has found the ground to mediate between two languages, two cultures" (Molina 1998, 66).

By looking at the experience of Dominicans in the United States through literature their story unfolds with familiar voices. The characters in the works of Alvarez and Díaz are representative of a small segment of a diverse Dominican community. Some of these characters can be found living in Washington Heights, for example. A conversation with an old-timer would produce countless tales about Trujillo's regime that are similar to Alvarez's. The local *bodega* could produce a steady stream of Dominicans who have come to the United States, looking for economic opportunities like those in Díaz's stories. Their stories would be about survival in the United States and the struggle to provide their children with a better future. Any one of them would proudly proclaim that they are Dominican even though they have been living in the United States for twenty-five years or were born in Washington Heights. They might even comment on how one day they hope to build a house and retire or start a business back home on the island. Yet these same Dominicans have established firm roots in the United States. They have raised their families despite the inherent racism in being cast as racialized minorities and all that it entails. Dominicans in the United States have adjusted their values to include U.S. cultural values and practices as means of adaptation and survival. Dominicans have learned to harmonize, producing a transnational consciousness that allows them to integrate and inhabit multiple spaces at once.

References

Alvarez, Julia. 1991. *How the García Girls Lost Their Accents.* New York: Plume.

———. 1998. *Something to Declare.* Chapel Hill, N.C.: Algonquin.

Díaz, Junot. 1996. *Drown.* New York: Riverhead.

Duany, Jorge. 1994. *Quisqueya on the Hudson: The Transnational Identity of Dominicans in Washington Heights.* New York: CUNY Dominican Studies Institute.

Farganis, James. 1996. *Readings in Social Theory: The Classic Tradition to Post-Modernism.* Boston: McGraw-Hill.

McLane, Daisann. 1991. "Dance-Till-You-Drop Merengue." *New York Times,* January 4, 28.

Molina, Sintia E. 1998. "Duality and Displacement in the Dominican Literature in the United States." *Latino Studies Journal* 9(3):65–84.

Pérez, Loida Maritza. 1999. *Geographies of Home.* New York: Viking.

Rimer, Sara. 1991. "Between 2 Worlds: Dominicans in New York." *New York Times,* September 16, A1.

Sagás, Ernesto. 2000. *Race and Politics in the Dominican Republic.* Gainesville, Fla.: University of Florida Press.

Torres-Saillant, Silvio. 2000. "The Tribulations of Blackness: Stages in Dominican Racial Identity." *Callaloo* 23(3): 1086–1111.

Torres-Saillant, Silvio, and Ramona Hernández. 1998. *The Dominican Americans.* Westport, Conn.: Greenwood.

10

Writing New York City

A Study on Transnational Dominican-American Literature

Sintia E. Molina

The urban space of New York has been habited, desolated, and relived by many artists and writers of the modern world. Its crowded but lively and decadent streets, its glamorous and productive ambience, its creativity and destruction have made of New York City an inspiration, a place where the best and the worst of the world meet. But one of the main characteristics that make New York City what it is today is its diversity: In the last two centuries the city has become an immigrant-populated metropolis.

In this chapter I will analyze how New York City is portrayed in Dominican and Dominican-American literature. I will discuss briefly the immigrants' literary history and how this literature has contributed to the transnationalization of Dominican culture. I will use the term transnational as a way of exploring how the immigrant subject carries nationality as it carries culture, as a form of baggage, and how that is in turn transformed and reproduced in literature. I will also explore the transition of Dominican transnational literature and how that literature contributes to a dual perception of a city that is at the same time great and painful, lively and decadent, loved and rejected.

Transnationalism and Identity

Néstor García Canclini (1990, 83) analyzes the notion of transnationalism as a process that combines the social and cultural values of one or more national local traditions with new ones, creating then something that seems different, yet familiar. For immigrants, this process occurs through the actual experience of migration, through the physical act of moving, of leaving a place that they recognize as their own, as home, crossing a physical border, and settling in a new geographical space. The experience of dislocation caused by the actual movement, by the need to establish new social relations and the pressure of maintaining the old ones, forces them to re-create themselves and construct a new identity, one that goes beyond borders and that encloses the past, the present, and the future status of an immigrant.

Traditionally, Dominican immigrants who settle in the United States, specifically in the New York City area, keep in contact with family and friends from their native homeland and develop a new relationship based upon an exchange of cultural, social, and economic activities. This relation is made possible mainly because of the closeness of New York City to the island, which permits frequent visits to the country, and the effective means of communications, which allow this relationship to stay strong. At the same time, it results in the construction of overseas communities that re-create the cultural traits of the native country.

These factors have brought into existence a new identity for Dominicans, one that exceeds the borders of nationality and cultural identification: a transnational identity. The study of social relationships among Dominicans reveals an interesting and, I would even say, unique paradigm, an intensive communication that seems to overcome all odds, including distance. These individuals experience a "crossover" into new values without jeopardizing the existence of the traditional ones. The result is, then, a hybrid identity that encompasses the "old" national values and those of the host "new" society (Duany, 1997). Nina Glick Schiller argues that immigrants who maintain connection with their nation by participating in social, political, cultural, and economic relations with the home society while living abroad become "transmigrants" (1999, 96). I will have to add that the prefix "trans," as I use it, goes beyond its semantic meanings. I intend to embrace a group of common experiences as well as a state, that of transition, of movement from one society to another. This is in two senses: the original migration of Dominicans to New York City, and the coming and going between identities and identification that the Dominican-American experiences while living in the United States.

The Role of the Transmigrant

The transmigrant, according to Glick Schiller (1999, 99), has a function in the modern city, that is to reconstruct the nation and the state. Dominican immigrants have contributed to changing the dynamics in the New York City area. Their mere presence as a community has redesigned the structure of the *barrio:* from the establishment of different businesses to the way in which the Spanish language is spoken to the reconstruction of the Latino image. However, their condition of "transnational" beings is completed because of their importance in the structure of the state back home, in the island. It is the strong economic influence of the Dominican-Americans as well as the constant communication, the flow of Dominicans that visit the island, that have also changed the dynamics of the city. The language itself is charged with *niuyorquismos*, slangs and resonances of the popular New York culture. The exchange is still ongoing and changing, and the process is alive and ever growing.

The Dominican literature of the last few decades has served as a perfect example of these transnational communities. Dominicans tied by transnational networks "were influenced by the development and dissemination of narratives of national identities in both localities" (Glick Schiller 1999, 110). Both the Dominican Republic and New York City have witnessed the development of a literature that deals with the reality of Dominicans in the island and overseas. For Dominicans in the island, migration is the ideal solution to their social and economic problems, an idea supported by the—sometimes false—image of the returning immigrant who possesses the "American dream." Meanwhile, in New York there is no solution: either to die there after years of hard work or to return to the native country.

Dominican Literature in the United States

Dominican literature, particularly that written in New York City, presents the awkward and dismal picture of the immigrant as an isolated and displaced being, but also as a transnational individual from two worlds. The character is an individual struggling in a hostile environment, in a crowded and yet empty, cold city, albeit becoming part of it. The city becomes, with all its problems, the emotional and social support of the individual. This vibrant city, crowded and inhumane, is the modern city of the twentieth century.

Metropolises have long been the subjects for writers from Baudelaire (1986) and Federico García Lorca (1980) to Piri Thomas (1997). Paris and New York, two important centers of culture, technology, and industrial revolution, have served as the intertext of many novels, poems, and other forms of artistic manifestations. Writing the city is writing the life of the immigrant, she or he who could only "belong" in a place where no one really belongs, a place that no one can posses entirely or partially: the modern metropolitan city. It is this space that allows the enunciation of the hybrid, the juxtaposition of the new and the old, the palimpsest of the histories. No matter how the times may have changed, the city stays the same. What matters is not who reads it, but who writes about it. At the beginning of the twentieth century, Latin American immigrants wrote of Paris as the space of both escape and imprisonment, yet in the 1960s Latino writers did the same with New York

City. In *Down These Mean Streets,* Piri Thomas describes how ungenerous New York City's streets are for poor, uneducated immigrants. New York City is "scary, specially that dirty stone trestle of New York Central that ran right down the middle of the avenue making long, gloomy tunnels at each corner. I watched the moving shadows in the street . . . , 'Ohhhh, no, please don't.' I wondered if it hurt all that much" (1997, 4). Piri Thomas's struggle reflects the pain suffered by the Puerto Ricans who first settled in New York City, something that will be shared later by Dominican immigrants. Thomas struggles to define himself, to search for his Puertoricanness and his race in a mean city. The city is portrayed as a character parallel to the human/fictional character.

Decades later we see that the contemporary Dominican-American literature embraces the same preoccupation that other immigrant writers have had: the desolation, the poverty, the lack of power, the climate of the city, the language barrier, the nostalgia for that nation left behind. Their writings show a migratory fact: the immigrant, no matter where she or he is from, belongs to the city. Her or his condition of exile, of not belonging, makes her or him part of the disfunctionality and foreignness of the city. In some instances, the literature also expresses in native languages the ambiguity of being from both worlds and becoming global.

Mirroring the Immigrant, Doubling the City

Since the 1960s, New York City has housed hundreds of thousands of Dominican immigrants. For many of them, writers and workers, the city is a place to work, to save money to later enjoy life in the Dominican Republic. New York City is never home (Molina 1998, 77) even though a lot of Dominicans end up staying there. New York is both the dream destination and the cause of desperation, unhappiness, and marginality. This ambiguity is sustained by the Dominican-American dream: a few years of hard work in the city and a lifetime of happiness in the island. So there is always this play with the city as a desire. When in the island, the Dominican longs, dreams for a chance to live in New York City, but once in New York City, it is the return to the island that she or he longs for, being therefore trapped in the transit as a subject who belongs to two worlds and yet to neither one. And it is indeed this transnational subject that is reproduced in much of the Dominican and Dominican-American literature of today. Miriam Mejía in her short story "El viaje" depicts the experience of the poor, homeless, and powerless immigrant who lives in what seems to be a crude and cold New York City:

> A sus veinticinco años recién cumplidos, Alba se sentía vieja. . . . Acostada en posición fetal en un improvisado camastro de cartones y

> ropa vieja. . . . Recorrió con la vista el entorno. Por más de tres años, todo aquello había sido su hogar. Su mirada se entretuvo en una gota de agua que se filtraba del puente seco, el cual le servía de techo. (1997, 18)
>
> (She was just twenty-five years old, but Alba felt old . . . lying down in fetal position in an improvised bed made out of cardboard and old clothes, . . . she looked around her surroundings. For more than three years, all that had been her home. Her eyes were fixed on a drop of water falling from the bridge that served as her roof).

The city described in "El viaje" is one that is cruel. It is a geography of dryness, emptiness, and infertility. The subject is a young woman who has been deprived of her youth by the vicissitudes experienced through migration. The pain shown in this story recreates a universal theme in urban writing, that of poverty in the city. The city appears indeed as a cruel place where the immigrant, the poor are obvious (that is, visible in the streets), yet forgotten.

In contrast, writers such as Julia Alvarez and Loida Pérez document contrasting images of the actual experience of transnationalization. They write about the initial migration to New York City, the trauma of language acquisition, and the dilemma of cultural assimilation versus cultural preservation. Their depiction, like Dominican identity itself, which is transnational, travels between the island and the city, reproducing the imaginary of the Dominican-American world. In the novels *Yo!* (1997) and *How the García Girls Lost Their Accents* (1992) by Julia Alvarez, the preservation of the culture is depicted by the name of the main character, Yolanda García, the use of the Spanish language as the main instrument of culture and identity preservation, respect and obedience to her father, eating habits and some others, while she adopts those from the new country. One of the voices from *Yo!*'s narration describes Yolanda's behavior as that of the foreigner who has preserved her traditional values and has adopted new ones: "Only when she signs the lease do I finally get that her name is Yolanda García. . . . One thing I appreciate about these foreigners . . . is how willing they are to go along with the way we do things in this country" (1997, 156).

Yolanda officializes her name in a legal document. The preservation of her name—Yolanda García—symbolizes her identity consciousness in a new space (nation-state) outside her native country. She knows that in this space she is not well accepted, so that she has to become like someone from this space by practicing her new values and learning the English language. However, her consciousness makes her willing to accept her dual identity: Dominican and American. Yolanda's preservation of traditional values as well as the adoption of new ones is shown in her role as a crusader, a defender of human and women's rights in both the Dominican Republic and the United States, creating an image of a woman from two worlds: one traditional and the other modern, hence a transnational woman.

New York City provides Dominican writers with elements that enable them to create and to experiment with a new literature within the American mainstream. This literature expresses the experience and the reality of immigrants, as well as the writers' themselves, who also live "in the borders," in the "trans," and write the city as they view it, in a historical moment, a moment of transnationalization and transculturalization.

By exposing life in New York, Dominican writers make the Dominican government responsible for the immigrants' suffering and their despair, showing the reality, the demagogic propaganda, and the ultimate deception that is New York City. These writers feel spiritually and psychologically exiled in New York. The writers' feelings of displacement—by being away from home—and the fact that New York City is far from their expectations are very significant elements in their writings. To come to New York is to look for freedom and self-realization in spite of the fact that sometimes this is not accomplished. By transcribing their feelings and the life of the city's people, Dominican writers transport the image of New York City to those in the Dominican Republic, sharing with them their condition as immigrants in a dual city: one that is both heaven and hell, one that in the same terms makes you succeed or succumb. Meanwhile, in this exchange of communication, of writing, they are transnationalizing a new culture developed and adopted by Dominican-Americans.

For example, the language spoken by Dominican-Americans is, for the most part, a combination of Spanish and English, while other customs and patterns go through the same acculturation process. This cultural transformation results from the interaction of Dominicans with the city and its different ethnic groups, literary creations, and cultures that help with the conceptualization of a transnational Dominicanness.

Dominican authors in the island use these experiences in their writings to represent how the culture and the language is being constantly changed by the returning immigrants. Aurora Arias, a young Dominican writer from the Dominican Republic, in her short story collection *Invi's Paradise y otros relatos* (1998), combines the language of Dominicans in New York with the popular speech of the Dominican Republic. Nowadays, Dominican popular language has adopted lexical terms and idiomatic expressions similar to those from New York City's Dominican *barrio*. Words such as "men," "parking," "slow," "friquees" (from freak out) are frequently used by the characters in the story who have come into contact with New York Spanglish. Interestingly, in many cases, these individuals have not necessarily visited or lived in the metropolis. But, the contact with one another has allowed both groups (those in the Dominican Republic and those in New York City) to acquire the common speech style needed for communication. Such interaction and word choice reinforce the transnationality of Dominican literature and its lexical forms. The adoption of this language causes a feeling of despair and vagueness in some Dominican writers who believe that this literature lacks originality, creativity, and seriousness. Thus in *Invi's Paradise* Arias presents the reality of Dominican society nowadays where North American values have been assimilated. The title itself—*Invi's Paradise*—exemplifies the transnationalism of the language style. The short stories show the adaptation of *niuyorquismos* in the speech of most ordinary Dominicans. It is mainly observed in the characters' language. In the story, Irena and López, after their intoxication with drugs, sustained this dialogue:

> —Siento que pronto voy a sentir miedo—dijo Irena a López momentos antes de la aparición.
> —¿Por qué?—le susurra él muy quieto y hondo. . . .—Relájate, no te friquees, lo importante en estos casos es no dejarse dominar. (1998, 21)
>
> ("I feel that I'm going to be afraid soon," Irena told López minutes before the hallucination. "Why?" he whispers to her. . . . "Relax, don't freak out, it is important in these cases not to allow anything to dominate you").

The characters are not afraid of the drug's effect but of the new elements and values that are becoming part of Dominican culture and life-style, which are transforming the reality of Dominican society.

English or Spanish?

The Dominican-American literature written in English is highly politicized. It is a literature that denounces the life of the Dominican in the city, its hardships and struggles. It is a literature aimed for mainstream Americans, and not necessarily for Dominicans. In contrast, the literature written in Spanish seems to focus on the Dominican Republic and its people as the main audience. However, in both genres—Spanish and English—New York City is described as a snapshot of broken dreams. As a character, New York destroys people's lives and dreams because both the city and the individual are in rapid transformation (Augustine 1991, 76). Thus the individual is forced to become a citizen of this dual city. In her novel, *Geographies of Home,* Loida Pérez shows the despair caused by the broken dreams of immigrants in the big city: "Everything had seemed grim and violent; the faces encountered on New York streets, the dirty snow hardened into ice stained with blood where someone had been wounded; the news read in El Diario and heard on channel 47 . . ." (1999, 23). The autobiographical narrator expresses her decision: "She chose the university because of its location five hours from New York City—a distance too great for her parents to visit her" (1). However, away from New York Iliana felt lost, like she did not belong. She returned to New York City where she found herself and those of her own. New York City is for Iliana where life and memories reside, memory as the root of the past and the identity of the present.

New York is a monster as well as a savior, the place where high expectations are put forward. In the novel *Marina de la Cruz* by Félix Mendoza (1994), the main character migrates to New York City after experiencing economic hardships and personal abuses in her own country, the Dominican Republic, and in Puerto Rico, where she first settled as an immigrant. For the protagonist, Marina, and her companions, New York is their final destination, the realization of dreams and their salvation. This expectation about New York is expressed by the narrator in these terms: "No veían llegar el momento de la salida hacia el norte en donde esperaban encontrar dicha, dinero y progreso" (They were anxious to see the day of their departure for the North where they expected to find happiness, money and progress) (22). The North, which represents the United States, is salvation. It is the climax of their lives, their last hope for success.

The importance of Puerto Rico in this experience is very significant in the transnational literature. Puerto Rico is the bridge to New York City. Once there, success is only a step away. In some instances, the trip is made first to Miami, Florida; the last stop, the final destination, is always New York City, such as is expressed in Junot Díaz's short story "Negocios." The main character's father arrived in Miami because "the ticket to Miami had saved him money, but he intended to continue on to Nueva York as soon as he could. Nueva York was the city of jobs, the city that had first called the Cubanos and their cigar industry, then the Bootstrap Puerto Ricans and now him" (1996, 167). This multiple-stop migratory voyage transforms these immigrants into dual immigrants who are forced to relocate themselves, therefore prolonging their condition as foreigners. In many cases they are forced to stay for months or even years in these "stops," be it Miami or Puerto Rico, becoming part of those cities' dynamics and changing, at the same time, their identity.

Literature and the City as a Transnational Place

Writers of urban literature denounce the brutal daily reality of metropolitan life, focusing on the conditions of the ghettos and the problems of the individuals who live there. By documenting the pain and suffering of people in the city, urban literature intends to escape the desperation that the city produces because the city has become a referent and a motive. The city offers writers a reality of their own, with which they identify. Urban literary characters live in constant friction, interacting with the many other diverse elements within the city: dilapidated buildings, strange places and customs, the ideologies and life-styles of their neighbors, and violence and crime. In fact, the difficulties and extremes of modern urban life are expressed in literature as an inherent flux of the city dwellers, and the city presents itself as a central, omnipotent character that dominates people's lives and choices.

For Dominicans, the living experience of immigrants in an industrialized city—the daily reality and their interaction with thousands of other immigrants—is the main referent of their literature. By expressing their urban immigrant experience, Dominican-American writers have placed their literature in a specific historical moment that has allowed them to achieve a state of self-awareness. The country of origin is remembered and re-created as a nostalgic place, and as such is described in this sentence: "El olor a lluvia, hierba y salitre forzaba a muchos a pensar en las comarcas que habían dejado atrás" (The smell of rain, grass and seawater forced many of them to think about the territories they had left behind) (Mendoza 1994, 24). The New York City experience allows these writers to face the new reality by exposing the chaos of the city without forgetting their native country. The Dominican Republic, as a space longed for, is re-created in the memory of many of the characters who find the identity they have been deprived of. For instance, this place of origin is recreated in the memory of Iliana in *Geographies of Home*, but it is combined with the memory of New York City as the second alternative home. The narrator describes the state of being of the character: "While she'd been away, her memory had consisted of images imbued with the warmth of a Caribbean sun magically transported to New York and of a house furnished with objects lovingly carved by the inhabitants of an island she had dreamed of" (Pérez 1999, 30). For immigrants dreams come true in memories. Dreams symbolize freedom and in order for the character to realize them she or he must become aware of her or his identity. For Pérez freedom is found in the re-creation of memories and the reconstruction of the Dominican places she loves in her writing. Thus, it is expressed in the saga the main character endures in New York City. She leaves New York City to go to college. Away from home and her family, she thinks she will find the desired freedom and self confidence needed to succeed in the United States. Instead she encounters isolation and loneliness, and returns to New York City to the patriarchal environment of her family.

It is, indeed, in the postmodern age that writers portray urban life with all its consequences, its ugliness and its beauty, in a similar way to what the naturalists and realists did in the nineteenth century. Dominican writers find describing New York's life as another motivation for their writings, although they expose city life as detrimental too. For them, life in the adopted home—New York—is a continuation of suffering, isolation, and, in some instances, the Americanization of the values and norms they have experienced in their native country. Dominican writers on the island consider the interchange and adaptation to other norms as being due to the transnationalization process, a cultural clash as seen in Aurora Arias's *Invi's Paradise y otros relatos* (1998).

Dominican writers also describe life in New York City as apocalyptical, the result of broken and unrealized dreams. For some of the writers, dreams only come true in the memory by re-creating what they have left behind. Commonly, the re-creation of the native place in the memory is the realization of the dream. A strong and destructive image of the city is expressed in this verse of the poem "Son del vacilador" by Alexis Gómez Rosa (1998): "Ojerosa la calle, en el crudo meridiano al sur del Bronx/ le salen como ganglios y cerosas membranas" (The street having black circles under its eyes, in the raw meridian of the South Bronx/ coming out from the street like lymph nodes and wax membranes). This verse is a prelude to the destruction and ignominious perception of the city life described in the poem. In Dominican literature, the image of the city is decadent and pernicious. The life of Dominican dwellers in New York City is affected by drugs, unemployment, homelessness, and family disintegration. Such destruction and dysfunction of the Dominican family as a consequence of migration are well expressed in Julia Alvarez's *How the García Girls Lost Their Accents* (1992). She describes the chaotic family life in the city once the girls have assimilated and adopted American norms and values. In *Por nada del mundo* by José Carvajal, the narrator blames New York City's living conditions for family destruction: "Desde que llegaron a New York perdieron el sentido de la unión familiar, el respeto" (since they arrived in New York City they lost the sense of family unity and respect) (1991, 48). The city appears as a place where values are destroyed and families become dysfunctional. This idea is recurrent in many Dominican-American texts as a way of depicting the daily life of families that deal with assimilation and acculturation of American values.

Likewise, this literature intends to represent the hope, the safety, and the transnational network connection experience within the Dominican Republic itself. In the drama *Temor rojizo,* New York City transforms itself into the refuge and sole salvation for the women who escape the misery, pain, and patriarchal oppression characteristic of Dominican culture (Madera 1999). However, women find in New York City the continuation of their existential oppression, the victimization and isolation the metropolitan city causes. The existential oppression and the victimization of the individual by the environment is well described in Junot Díaz's short story "Nilda" (1999, 89): Nilda "was Dominican from here." As a first- or second-generation immigrant, she has been isolated and victimized by both societies. In the Dominican Republic, poverty and hunger dominated her existence until her mother immigrated to the United States looking for a better life. In New York, poverty, prostitution, drugs, and the *barrio* culture constitute her life. Nilda also feels victim to the machismo that dominates Dominican culture, which is reflected in the literature of Díaz and his selection of female characters and the roles they play in the story.

In the Dominican literature written nowadays the transnational element is permanent as a style and theme, as well as the motivation and imagination. This does not mean that in previous literary works the transnational referent did not exist, but it is nowadays that it has been popularized because of the transglobal status of Dominican migrants. Even though the Dominican-American literature expresses the characteristics of the immigration literature, it is not a literature of exile. It is a literature looking for its own space to become independent and expand itself. Writers such as Alvarez, Díaz, and Pérez have constructed a cultural space because they have overcome and transported the linguistic, thematic, and cultural referent to other spaces. They have transnationalized Dominican literature by exchanging with others their cultural and personal motivations and concerns.

Viriato Sención, for example, who writes mainly in Spanish, and whose themes are solely about the Dominican Republic, but who lives in New York, has transnationalized his works through translations into English of his novel *They Forged the Signature of God* (1995). Some other writers have not been able to cross the language barrier because they write in Spanish only and their works have not been translated, but they have been able to transnationalize and to cross the frontier with their themes. Writers such as Miriam Mejía, Teonilda Madera, Juan Rivero, Alexis Gómez Rosa, José Carvajal, Franklyn Gutiérrez, and others, who are well known in the Dominican Republic as well as in New York, support their narration with themes and linguistic elements from New York City and the Dominican Republic. Linguistically, these writers use the language of the city with all its euphemisms and the graphicness unique to city street people. For instance, it is common to find the language of the Dominican-York from Washington Heights, Manhattan in their works. Dominican-York language is transported to the Dominican Republic and it is appropriated by the people. This vocabulary creates a language style that connects Dominicans at large—the ones from Washington Heights and the ones from Santo Domingo—and represents a reality that identifies both. Henry Rosa and Diego Rojas (1998) study the linguistic effects on the Spanish language of the Dominican Republic nowadays. They argue that the interpolation of the English language in the spoken Spanish of Dominican youths is caused by the U.S. cultural influence and its psycho-cultural effect on the individual and is responsible for the identity crisis suffered by the new generation. This condition is caused by contact with Dominicans who reside in the United States and visit their country often. Thus, the writers interconnect two languages—English and Spanish—and develop a literature from two worlds, expressing two realities: that from the Dominican Republic and this from New York.

Conclusion

Multi-ethnic and multinational cities such as New York tend to preserve and interrelate traditional values from diverse cultures. These cities are a "neutral grid in which cultural differences, historical memory and societal organization are inscribed" (Gupta and Ferguson 1997, 34). Dominican-American writers are in the process of constructing their historical memory and permanently inscribing it in New York City through literature. The current Dominican literature is becoming a biographical document, because it portrays the life of the immigrant and it is in constant transition from a first-person point of view. Therefore, one should ask: Does the process of transnationality carry some problems, when in reality transmigrants build cultural spaces in both places? Are those cultural spaces accepted by the nationals of the host country? The search for an answer is not complicated if one thinks about what types of spaces immigrants build, where these spaces are located, and whether the transmigrants can assimilate to the host country.

Therefore, the coming and going of immigrants from the Dominican Republic to New York City and vice versa has created the problem of the Americanization of Dominican culture, or the assimilation of American values. It seems as if the United States is the only place capable of solving the problems that affect Dominican immigrants, and New York City is the idealized space. Among other problems of transnationalization, there is the conception and interrelation between the immigrant and the city. According to Gupta and Ferguson (1997), the city is the "totality of many parts"; in Dominican literature, New York City is only one part and it is fragmented. This fragmentation makes difficult the integration of the individual to the total dynamic of the city. For the immigrant in New York City it is hard to become part of the whole because sometimes she or he can find nothing outside her or his *barrio* or environment to relate to. In spite of decades of Dominican migration to the United States, Dominican immigrants continue to be isolated and dependent on their own *barrio* in order to keep the authenticity of their values. They have not trespassed other spaces because it is difficult for them to overcome their own ambivalent spaces. This concentration and almost exclusive restriction to their specific environment is dangerous and not recommendable for socialization with other ethnic groups because it impedes social and cultural exchanges. These exchanges only occur between Dominican nationals from the Dominican Republic and from the United States: from "here" and from "there."

Transnationalization as a literary referent in Dominican literature in both places, even though it is still in the periphery and limited to its physical, linguistic, and cultural spaces, has been an effective means for the cultural, social, and economic exchange we experience today. It helps to establish the presence of Dominican literature in the United States and of Dominicans as dwellers of two cities: New York City and Santo Domingo. While both cities are depicted as monstrous and inhumane, they are also described as great, as the only possible places to inhabit.

References

Alvarez, Julia. 1992. *How the García Girls Lost Their Accents.* New York: Plume.

———. 1994. *In the Time of the Butterflies.* New York: Plume.

———. 1997. *Yo!* New York: Plume.

Arias, Aurora. 1998. *Invi's Paradise y otros relatos.* Santo Domingo: Búho.

Augustine, Jane. 1991. "From *Topos* to Anthropoid: The City as Character in Twentieth-Century Texts." In *City Images: Perspectives from Literature, Philosophy, and Film,* ed. Mary Ann Caws. New York: Gordon and Breach.

Baudelaire, Charles. 1986. *The Painter of Modern Life and Other Essays.* Ed. and trans. Jonathan Mayne. New York: Da Capo Press.

Carvajal, José. 1990. *Por nada del mundo.* New York: Mambrú.

Díaz, Junot. 1996. *Drown.* New York: Riverhead Books.

———. 1999. "Nilda." *New Yorker Magazine* 75(29): 89–97.

Duany, Jorge. 1997. "The Creation of a Transnational Caribbean Identity: Dominican Immigrants in San Juan and New York." In *Ethnicity, Race, and Nationality in the Caribbean,* ed. Juan Manuel Carrión. Río Piedras, P.R.: University Puerto Rico.

García Canclini, Néstor. 1990. *Culturas híbridas: Estrategias para entrar y salir de la modernidad.* Mexico City: Grijalbo.

García Lorca, Federico. 1980. "Poeta en Nueva York." In *Obras completas,* comp. Arturo de Hoyo. Madrid: Aguilar.

Glick Schiller, Nina. 1999. "Transmigrants and Nation-States: Something Old and Something New in the U.S. Immigrant Experience." In *The Handbook of International Migration: The American Experience,* ed. Charles Hirschman, Philip Kasinitz, and Josh DeWind. New York: Russell Sage Foundation.

Gómez Rosa, Alexis. 1998. "Son del vacilador." In *New York City en tránsito de pie quebrado.* 2d ed. Santo Domingo: Búho.

Gupta, Akhil, and James Ferguson. 1997. "Beyond 'Culture': Space, Identity, and the Politics of Difference." In *Culture, Power, Place: Explorations in Critical Anthropology,* ed. Akhil Gupta and James Ferguson. Durham, N.C.: Duke University Press.

Madera, Teonilda. [c. 1999]. *Temor rojizo.* Unpublished play. Santo Domingo.

Mejía, Miriam. 1997. *Crisálida.* [New York?]: n.p.

Mendoza, Félix. 1994. *Marina de la Cruz.* Santo Domingo: Taller.

Molina, Sintia. 1998. "Duality and Displacement in Dominican Literature in the United States." *Latino Studies Journal* 9(3): 65–84.

Pérez, Loida M. 1999. *Geographies of Home.* New York: Penguin.

Rosa, Henry, and Diego Rojas. 1998. "De bonche con la juventud actual." *Estudios Sociales* 113:5–18.

Sención, Viriato. 1995. *They Forged the Signature of God.* Trans. Asa Zats. New York: Curbstone.

Thomas, Piri. 1997. *Down These Mean Streets.* 4th ed. New York: Vintage Books.

11

Transnational Music and Dance in Dominican New York

Thomas van Buren and Leonardo Iván Domínguez

The Dominican community of New York is the largest outside of the Caribbean and for more than seventy years it has been an essential site in the development of Dominican transnational culture. Within the context of the Hispanic Caribbean community that comprises fully one quarter of the overall population of New York, Dominicans play an essential role in the "Caribbean crossroads" of cultural interaction there (see Allen and Wilcken 1998). Music has served as both a vehicle and a manifestation of the evolution and development of the Dominican presence in New York, long before the current large-scale community was established. Music has continued to thrive, both in performance and recorded media, as a virtual meeting ground of the transnational community, and also serves as a key element of the larger intercultural evolution in New York, with repercussions in the Caribbean, and throughout Latin America.

The development of immigration studies, from analyses of migration patterns and modes of assimilation to the notion of transnational cultural identity, is fully exemplified in the Dominican community, in which large numbers of people regularly travel between the Caribbean nation and the northeastern United States. This travel constitutes more than physical displacement as culture is transmitted in all directions, through recordings, the mass media, and the routine physical travel of musicians and bands. Beyond this development, the performance media of the culture itself travel from person to person, community to community, and nation to nation. These media include the symbolic role of *merengue* in Dominican identity and nationalism through the 1950s and the widespread promotion and popularity of the music in the 1970s, the sociocultural associations of the *bachata* music in the late 1980s and 1990s, the development of transnational hybrid forms, and the syncretic folk religious resonance of the Afro-Dominican religious music. Like other central expressions of the Dominican transnational culture, music invites us closer into the life of the community, and serves as the means by which a transnational cultural identity is expressed.

Since the late 1980s, there has been a growing awareness among scholars of international migration of a complex phenomenon in current migration, in which cultural practices and developments take place across the geographic boundaries that were formerly thought to distinguish between national identities. At the same time, recent studies and experience with transnational communities have spurred a reevaluation of long-held assumptions about the process of migration, nationalism, and cultural identity, both in the United States and on an international scale. Post-colonial and cold war ideology in the United States have tended to overlook the persistence of transnational immigrant communities, assuming that they were bound to lose their identity through the assumption of North American capitalist cultural values. Even as increased levels and diversity of migration since 1965 have wakened a movement of "multiculturalism," there has been little recognition that transnational migration has been a major factor in the development of many national identities since the nineteenth century. Coining the term "transmigration," Glick Schiller (1999) maintains that transnational communities in the United States have long played a key role in the formation of nationalist identities both in Europe and in Asia, while providing a flow of financial resources, an educated elite, and volunteers to nationalist causes. It is, in fact, only in the period of white hegemony of mid-twentieth-century North America that the true nature of the cross border, or "transmigrant," immigrant experience has been obscured. The experience of the Dominican community in New York, among others, has helped awaken transnational studies to the contemporary reality of the tremendous number of dual citizens whose allegiances and cultures flow between the poles of eastern Hispaniola and the largest urban center on the eastern seaboard of the United States in a mixture of economics, political ideas, and cultural expressions.

Often used to describe political and economic associations, these terms "transnational" and "transmigrant" may also be applied to families, regional associations, and networks of cultural practice that simultaneously maintain ties in two countries. In the statement of their research problem on the subject, sociologists Basch, Glick Schiller and Szanton Blanc note that "immigrants develop networks, activities, patterns of living, and ideologies that span their home and host society" (1994, 4). The practice of expressive culture in transmigratory settings is clearly an activity that expands networks and reinforces patterns of thinking and of living. Beyond the mere reinforcement of cultural patterns, transnationalism also entails the maintenance of national identity, either through the re-creation of a home culture, or by the expression of a variation of it within the construct of the new environment. This notion is expressed in the fourth theoretical premise of the same study: "By living their lives across borders, transmigrants find themselves confronted with and engaged in national building processes of two or more nation states. Their identities and practices are configured by hegemonic categories such as race and ethnicity that are deeply embedded in the nation building processes of these nation states" (1994, 34).

A central concern for the study of the Dominican transmigrant communities in New York and elsewhere is what role expressive culture such as music, dance, poetry, and folk religious practice has played in the formation of a transnational identity. Conversely, we may also ask what effect the transmigrational experience has had on the development of Dominican culture at home. Music, dance, and other performance genres may be viewed through a variety of analytical lenses, either as a process of the re-creation of a national cultural practice within a transplanted community, or as an active dynamic within the imagining of a national identity that for a vast number of people spans physical space, while often dividing families, generations, and home community associations between divergent physical and conceptual frames of reference. To study this dynamic as it is expressed through the practice and appreciation of the arts helps to clarify an understanding of this transnational community by offering a chance to listen to the Dominican voice within the transnational dialogue.

Ethnomusicologist Martha Ellen Davis frames the issues defining the environment for Dominican musical culture in New York according to the following points: (1) the boundaries and limitations of race and class in the Dominican Republic are reconfigured in the new setting, allowing for greater experimentation and dialogue within the community; (2) New York City is a site of encounter across communities of the Hispanic Caribbean, especially concerning the wider Afro-Caribbean cultures represented in the communities there;[1] (3) New York City is an artistic capital that has offered a more international and cosmopolitan environment in which transnational Dominican culture could develop; and (4) New York City has provided a setting for a Dominican encounter with African-American culture, and jazz in particular (1996, 4). Under these conditions, along with other socioeconomic and political circumstances, we see the possibility for a complex interplay of cultural developments and subtexts. Following a survey of the history and variety of Dominican music and dance in New York, we will revisit the issues of transnational cultural identity and development.

The Role of Music in Dominican Migration

During the late 1920s, Dominican musicians visited and began to settle in New York City. They were attracted by recording and performance opportunities in the Hispanic Caribbean community already established in New York City by Puerto Ricans since the turn of the twentieth century. These early

Dominican musicians began to integrate themselves with that community. Later, they were to join in the ultimately pan-Latino musical developments of the *mambo* and *salsa* that were spurred on by a wave of Cuban migration during the 1940s and 50s. Only since the 1960s, however, has a major resident Dominican population established itself in New York. The discussion of Dominican performance culture in New York proceeds along two paths. One traces the development of Dominican music within the larger Latin music industry. The other follows the development of a music and dance community within the immigration and settlement of a permanent Dominican community that was to reach a population of more than half a million persons by the end of the century.[2]

These two paths overlap. Early Dominican musicians in New York first incorporated themselves into the growing Cuban and Puerto Rican musical life, and introduced early versions of *merengue* classics to the New York Latin music repertoire. It was only in the late 1960s that Dominican music made a major impact in the life of the city and came to serve as a cultural focus for the growing Dominican community there. By the end of the twentieth century, it was impossible to think of New York's Latin American and Caribbean culture apart from its Dominican component. Through the interaction of cultures in New York, and within the music recording industry there, Dominican musical forms are heard everywhere. *Merengue, bachata,* and recent variants such as *bachata-rengue, merenson, meren-house,* and numerous varieties of Dominican rap have infused cultural practice throughout the Caribbean, and in both South and Central America. It was not uncommon in the 1980s, for example, to find Puerto Rican, Colombian, and Salvadoran bands performing *merengue* music. At the same time, the increasing permanence of the Dominican community in New York has led to an adoption of less commercial forms, such as ritual practice of Afro-Dominican religious songs, such as the folk-Catholic *salves,* or the spiritual practice of the *maní* trance possession ritual, and the Haitian-influenced *gagá* processional music and dance. This chapter will thus follow both of these paths—that of the professional music industry, and that of the growing community culture—to reveal a more accurate if somewhat complex portrait of this aspect of the multicultural dynamic in New York City.

The Early Years: The First Dominicans in New York

The earliest documented influence of Dominican culture in New York was through the recordings of Dominican musicians made in the late 1920s. Following a major projection of U.S. power into the Caribbean that included the occupation of the Dominican Republic and Haiti by the United States Marines from 1916 to 1924, even the emerging recorded music business took an interest in the region as well. The Columbia label and the Victor Talking Machine Company (the forerunner of RCA Victor), both based in New York, began to experiment with the Dominican market at that time. Victor made the first commercial recording in the Dominican Republic in 1928, which included *merengue* selections, *boleros* (ballads), and *criollas* (early dance music combining European dance music such as the *mazurka,* for example, with Afro-Caribbean and folk Spanish forms). Columbia had already recorded Dominican singer Antonio Mesa in New York, and began selling his and other recordings in the Dominican Republic. Because of the poor quality of the early recording media then available in the Dominican Republic, and because of the presence of numerous Dominican musicians in New York, most of the significant recordings of Dominican music were made there until the 1940s (Pacini Hernández 1995, 49).

The Dominican community in New York was small, and frequently the musicians among them blended into other Latin musical settings. Recalling the situation of Dominican music in New York during the 1930s, singer Dioris Valladares reported: "In 1936, we had barely one hundred Dominicans in New York City, including the personnel at the consulate. Our popular music was virtually unknown and the orchestras did not play Dominican *merengue.*" (Dioris Valladares, personal interview by Leonardo Iván Domínguez, 1996). Dominican artists who were active at that time were better known for their work in other musical genres. One example was the singer Luis Herrero, who made a popular *rumba* recording in 1936 with North American musicians for Victor entitled *Muchacha bonita.* Gradually, Dominican musicians began to meet with success performing their own dance music, such as *merengue, mangulina, pri-prí,* and *pambiche.* Among them were important artists of this period such as accordionist Angel Viloria, who led one of the most successful *merengue conjuntos* outside the Dominican Republic during the 1930s. Also prominent were various pianists who interpreted accordion-based *merengue* for that instrument. These included "Negrito" Chapuseaux and Rafael Damirón. Many of these artists played for Puerto Rican audiences, but through their recordings made in New York they were widely known in other countries, including Cuba, Haiti, and Venezuela, where both Dominican *merengue* and regional variants were becoming increasingly popular (Roberts 1979, 145).

The concentration of the Dominican musical influence in New York was affected by social and political developments in the Dominican Republic itself. Under the rule of Dominican dictator Rafael Leónidas Trujillo, emigration was severely curtailed. At the same time, the Trujillo family controlled the fledgling radio network in the country and prevented the importation of modern recording equipment to discourage competition from other producers who might have recorded local musicians. Trujillo actively elevated *merengue* above other genres as a national musical symbol and as a tool in his political organizing. *Merengue* ensembles were hired to accompany him on his many visits around the county. This use of music toward political ends culminated in one episode in which Trujillo himself contracted with Spanish band leader Xavier Cugat in New York to record an album of *merengue* songs as a promotion for his Feria de la Paz y la Confraternidad del Mundo Libre. This event was a public relations extravaganza that was held in Santo Domingo in 1955, and was modeled on the 1939 World's Fair in New York, which Trujillo had visited (Austerlitz 1997, 75–76). During the same period that the recording and dissemination of Dominican music was increasing in New York, the market for it was increasing in the Dominican Republic itself. Through international marketing, and official intervention, the transformation of *merengue* into a national music had repercussions for Dominicans everywhere.

Under the restrictive conditions at home during the 1940s and early 1950s, there was a strong incentive to leave the country, for those musicians who were able to do so. New York was firmly established as a center of Dominican culture abroad and this may have contributed, to some degree, to the scale of immigration there that was to follow. During the late 1950s, as Trujillo's policies of economic control began to fail, the presence of Dominican music in New York began to grow in proportion to the Trujillo monopoly of the music recording industry and broadcasting in the Dominican Republic. Effectively limited at home, musicians, composers, and bandleaders felt a strong incentive to emigrate.

These artists began to visit and settle in New York in larger numbers, blending into the fledgling Latin music scene there. Singer Alberto Beltrán arrived in New York in early 1949, remaining for only a few years before moving to Cuba to work with the Cuban group La Sonora Matancera.[3] In the early 1950s, he returned to New York to perform and went on to popularize there such well-known *merengue* songs as "El negrito del batey" and Luis Alberti's 1936 classic, "Compadre Pedro Juan."

Through the 1950s, *merengue* began to be heard more regularly in New York clubs, such as the Caborrojeño, located on Broadway at 145th Street, and cabarets such as Habana-Madrid, in downtown Manhattan, as well as annual Latin dance shows such as the Harvest Moon events that were held at Madison Square Garden under the sponsorship of the *Daily News*. In the same decade, Rafael Pérez, from Yauco, Puerto Rico, decided to experiment with recordings of *merengue*. Pérez was a music promoter who saw the success of the Orquesta Sanabria, and contracted with them for a recording project. Of the ensuing recordings, four arrangements met with commercial success, including "La amaneca" and "La moña."[4] Pérez later formed an ensemble named the Conjunto Típico Cibaeño, in reference to Cibao, the northern Dominican region widely identified as the birthplace of *merengue.* This *conjunto* included Dominican musicians Angel Viloria (accordion), Ramón García (saxophone), Luis Quintero (*tambora* drum), Dioris Valladares (vocals), and Jaime Richetti (backup vocals). The group also included Willie Socías (bass) and Yayo "El Indio" (backup singer), both also from Puerto Rico.

While various *merengue* groups had established themselves by 1952 and could be heard regularly in more clubs, this exposure did not carry over to the radio. Access to the radio waves was very limited for new immigrants compared to the 1980s or 1990s. Other than at the few clubs that featured Dominican groups on the weekends, Dominican people in New York did not often hear their music except when they came together for occasional political, social, or festive occasions. Very few recordings of Dominican music of this period were available in the Dominican community other than those then being recorded in the Dominican Republic, which were composed in praise of and under sponsorship of the dictator Trujillo.[5]

Nevertheless, a cultural movement was taking place that would lay the foundation for the later explosion of Dominican culture in New York. A number of musical ensembles and individuals began to visit or settle in New York to perform and to seek opportunities to record outside of the Trujillo-dominated recording industry on the island. The Ansonia record label, based in East Rutherford, New Jersey, which was founded in 1949, began to record numerous Dominican artists in the early 1950s. Accordionist Angel Viloria and his Conjunto Típico Cibaeño recorded several albums with singer Dioris Valladares in 1953 with Ansonia (ALP1206, ALP1207). *Tambora* drummer Luis Quintero, who also performed in New York with Viloria in 1952, went on to form his own band in 1954, the Conjunto Alma Cibaeña, which included Milito "Tutti Fruti" Pérez, Luis Vásquez, and the Puerto Rican singer Mon Rivera. Soon they also recorded with Ansonia (*Merengues* ALP1233). In addition El Típico Trío Reynoso recorded its own album of *merengue* pieces entitled *Cibao Adentro* on the Riney label (LP026). Another key figure during this period, the band leader and accordionist Luis Kalaff, emigrated to New York by way of Puerto Rico in 1958. His band, Luis Kalaff y sus Alegres Dominicanos, also performed *merengue típico* at hotel shows and dances. Incorporating English into the title of an album of varied styles of music, he recorded *La bosa y el "boss"* (Alma records LP100). This and other recordings had begun selling very well by the early 1960s.

The Fall of Trujillo and the New Wave of Immigration and Music in New York City

In the 1960s, major changes were occurring in the Dominican Republic itself that would have repercussions in New York. In 1961, the assassination of Trujillo led to a major increase in quantity and variety in the production of music, inversely proportional to the control he had exercised during the previous thirty years. Musicians and bands recorded and performed in an unrestricted and open manner, often traveling to perform and record in New York as well. These included Chorolo y su Combo, the trio Los Andariegos, the Orquesta Super San José de Papa Molina, and the singers Grecios Aquino, Vinicio Franco, Miguelito Mieses, and Alejandra Dandrades. In spite of the new opportunity to travel back and forth, some chose to settle more permanently. One noted example was singer Santiago Cerón, who arrived in New York in 1964 and began working in the *orquestas* of Dominican flutist Johnny Pacheco, among others. Later he formed his own group, with which he recorded twenty-seven albums.[6] Primitivo Santos emigrated to New York in the mid-1960s and remained for twenty years, performing 1950s style ballroom *merengue* in New York until his return to the Dominican Republic in 1985 (Austerlitz 1997, 125).

Coinciding with the end of the "April Revolution" (the political uprising of April 1965 that led to the second occupation of the Dominican Republic by the U.S. military), U.S. immigration rules were greatly relaxed under the Hart-Celler immigration act of the same year. The end of the quota system allowed for an increasing number of Dominicans to emigrate and settle in New York. This development led to a higher demand for Dominican music there as well. These new arrivals also soon began to establish social and political organizations based on models from home, including sports clubs, political parties, community and regional associations, and cultural centers. These organizations attempted, through an organizing effort, to maintain their music so that it might serve as a means of political cohesion in the face of developments in the Dominican Republic. These were necessarily the product of the conflict at home, and the ensuing repressive policies taken by the new government of Joaquín Balaguer, Trujillo's deputy, who was handpicked by the United States to succeed him, following the military occupation.

During this period, Dominican music and *merengue* in particular began to take their place in the international Latin music industry through the efforts of New York based Dominicans, as well as those in the Dominican Republic. In 1967, singers Joseíto Mateo, Alberto Beltrán, and Primitivo Santos performed at the first major concert of *merengue* to be held at Madison Square Garden. Other bands began to include more Dominican music in their performance repertoire. Dominican flutist Johnny Pacheco, who was originally from the northern region of Cibao, led influential Latin bands in the city beginning in the early 1960s. He specialized in the performance of Cuban music such as the *charanga,* but in the later 1960s he began to include *merengue* songs in his performance and recordings. One noted example was the song "Los diablitos" on his 1973 album *Tres de café y dos de azúcar.*

However, no musician had a larger impact at this time, both in New York and in the Dominican Republic itself, than Juan de Dios Ventura y Soriano. Known as Johnny Ventura, he changed the musical panorama of *merengue* both in the Dominican Republic and New York with hit recordings such as "El cuabero" (a gatherer of *piñón* wood used to heat up cooking fires—a metaphor for hotter music). Ventura used a larger ensemble to produce a faster, brassier style of *merengue* mixed with innovative experiments with *salsa* and Latin rock. His rise to fame coincided with the burgeoning growth of the Dominican community, where his music was in great demand. He began to perform in New York at major annual *merengue* events such as those at Madison Square Garden, and recorded numerous albums in New York as well as in Santo Domingo.

Through the developments in immigration and in the rise of a transnational music industry, a transformation occurred within the community as Dominican New Yorkers began to demand a wider representation of the diverse forms of Dominican music, and sought to delve deeper into the roots of their culture. As a result of these forces, important cultural associations were established in the Dominican community of New York during the late 1960s and early 1970s. These included new organizations established in Washington Heights, such as the Centro Cultural Quisqueya, which was founded by Normandía Maldonado, the Centro Cívico Dominicano, and the Club María Trinidad Sánchez,[7] as well as numerous Dominican student associations in various universities in the region. Many of these groups focused on the preservation and development of Dominican music, but for the most part they dedicated their time and efforts to the *música culta* or classically based Hispanic art forms favored by the Dominican elite. Others focused on models then in use in the Dominican Republic to present Dominican folklore, giving disproportionate weight to couple and group dances choreographed to acoustic *merengue típico* and to the *mangulina* rhythm. There was also a tendency to present these forms as patriotic symbols, with numerous community shows and expositions around the time of the Dominican independence holiday (February 27).

Nevertheless, other cultural projects made efforts to recognize a wider cultural focus. One notable example was a collaborative effort between a Dominican community cultural organization and the Dominican-based musical group Convite.[8] In 1979, this progressive musical ensemble based in the Dominican Republic began a joint project to engage in the study of Dominican folklore and popular culture and came to New York to present, in cooperation with the Club María Trinidad Sánchez, a series of public programs. The goals of this effort were to reintroduce the community to its music and cultural roots, to organize public programs of popular culture and folklore, to create teaching materials for children, and to encourage support for performance and teaching of Dominican folklore.

This effort was largely the work of a small group of people who did not receive the necessary economic support to succeed. Nevertheless, it did result in the artistic creation of music, choreography, and writing, which had an impact back in the Dominican Republic through continued work there of Convite. The band performed in New York at major venues such as Madison Square Garden, but also for the Dominican community at LaGuardia Community College in Queens, at the Club María Trinidad Sánchez itself, and later at Hostos Community College in the Bronx. During these concerts, Convite performed some of the first examples in New York of an emerging musical fusion of *bachata* and rock that Luis Días, in particular, had been exploring in the Dominican Republic, and that he would go on to develop in New York during the 1990s.

The Musical Practice of Popular Religion

Throughout the period of accelerating immigration and community development after 1965, folk traditions, customs, beliefs, and regional cultural forms were also finding their way into common practice among the newer Dominican migrants. While the majority of Dominicans are Roman Catholic, Afro-Dominican contributions have been increasingly felt in the spiritual life of the community since the 1980s. Until this time, these ritual forms were only practiced and maintained by a small group of people who had access to the traditional knowledge in the Dominican Republic, as well as the mastery and authority necessary to officiate at ceremonies and religious observances throughout the community.

Since the 1950s, Dominicans have run or patronized *botánicas,* the storefront distributors of supplies and paraphernalia of the syncretic Afro-Caribbean folk worship often identified with the Cuban-derived *santería*. Dominicans were also known to take part in the ritual ceremonies, consultations, and divinations by readings of *baraja* (fortunetellers' cards) and of *la taza* (patterns in the residue in coffee cups). However, Dominican folk religious music was not practiced in these settings as it is today. Until recently, the favored music was that of Cuban *santería,* such as the widely popular "Que viva Changó," a *santería* hymn first performed by Cuban singer Celina González and her husband Reutilio Domínguez in 1948, which was subsequently recorded and widely distributed in the Caribbean and New York.[9]

Beginning in the 1970s, Afro-Dominican ritual celebrations that had been kept secret began to be practiced more openly. These served to address spiritual, economic, and social problems facing the growing community of the faithful. These early practices included the *horas santas* (Catholic prayer sessions) with sung verses, call and response singing in commemoration of the dead, and celebrations of the saints. These were practiced in two forms: The first were *salves,* hand-drum-accompanied choral songs derived from European sacred devotional songs and performed on Catholic saints' days, including particularly the celebration of the Virgen de la Altagracia (Virgin of the Highest Grace) on January 21st. The other forms, including the *palos* and *congos,* are derived from African ritual drumming, devotional song, and sometimes trance, and are associated with other saints, such as San Miguel. These forms reveal a continuum of European and African folk ritual practices that share cultural roots and have led to a uniquely Dominican form of bicultural, or bi-musical practice (Davis 1987b, 40–41).

Of folk Catholic practices, *salves* singing is the most pronounced. Associated most strongly with the eastern end of the Dominican Republic in the province of Altagracia, and in the capital district, *salves* singing is practiced widely by immigrants from those regions in New York City. While sometimes linked with events in the Catholic churches of North Harlem and Washington Heights, *salves* singing is more associated with the extra-ecclesiastical practice of women's hand drumming and call and response singing during devotional processions, such as that associated with the day of the Virgen de la Altagracia. During the 1990s, a key singer from the town of Villa Mella outside Santo Domingo was in residence in New York. Andrea Nolasco, also known as Dona Chicha, taught younger women parts of her repertoire and the accompanying *pandereta* drumming. She participated in public festivals in 1996 and 1998.[10] Her influence is still felt in the work of younger performers, such as the singer Francia Reyes.

At the most African-influenced end of the spectrum of spiritual practice are the *manís,* more complex celebrations with a full ritual, an order of practice officiated by *caballos de misterios,* and musical accompaniment of *palos* long drums and the *güira* scraper. The songs sung at such events begin with the *salves* and progress to invocations to syncretic saints, the "*luases*" or *deidades* with both European and African identities, of which there are twenty-one in what is popularly known as the *panteón vuduísta dominicano* (Dominican vodou pantheon) or *La 21 División.* In the latter part of the celebrations, a song to a *luá* or divine being, accompanied by the rhythm of the *palos* and *güira,* induces a trance in the celebrant and the participants.

These events vary little in form and content from similar celebrations that are practiced widely in the Dominican Republic.

Of the *palos* ensembles that accompany the *manís,* Claudio Fortunato y su Guedeses[11] is the most knowledgeable of the repertoire. Fortunato is primarily a musician who began his professional career shortly after arriving in New York in 1986, playing the *tambora* drum with *merengue conjuntos.* However, he soon found a much higher demand for his skills playing the *palos* long drums for the *maní* ceremonies (personal interview by Rosaida Benítez, 1995). The principal repertoire of his ensemble features devotional songs to the various saints, including "Belié Belcán" (San Miguel), "Anaísa" (Santa Ana), "Candelo" (San Carlos), "Ferrayé" (Santiago), "Santa Marta la Dominadora," and "El Barón del Cementerio" (San Elías), as well as songs dedicated to the more overtly African deities, such as "Los Ogunes," "Balenyó," "Los Petroses," and "Canto a los Guedeses." They also perform songs to the deified Olivorio Mateo, the leader of a Dominican messianic movement at the beginning of the twentieth century (Lundius and Lundahl 1988, 4).

Claudio Fortunato y sus Guedeses also adapted the method of tuning the *palos* drums from the traditional use of wooden shims and rope, to metal brackets that can be tuned with keys or wrenches, as on contemporary *conga* drums. This innovation helped them to achieve a better sound and offered more versatility in adjusting to the effects of changes in humidity on the tension of the drumheads. With such practical innovations, the group has become well known in New York, and the most highly sought after, both for *manís* and *hora santas,* and for performances at public programs and festivals of folk culture. In the latter programs, they perform only the *palo arriba* (literally "high drum"), a celebratory genre for festive occasions, but not the *palo abajo* ("low drum"), which is a repertoire and style played mainly for deceased members of a *cofradía* (socioreligious brotherhood). The latter is a highly valued and more guarded part of the *palos* repertoire and practice (Lizardo 1974, 84). This choice of repertoire indicates a significant issue. Despite the quality of the interpretations by Claudio Fortunato y su Guedeses of the songs, drumming, and rituals that they enact in the *manís,* the group is also commercial and plays for these events and celebrations for pay, in what is perhaps less a true act of personal devotion or spiritual commitment.

In the Dominican Republic, such drummers and singers would be members of the *cofradías,* organizations derived from the colonial period that were founded in certain black enclaves in the cities and towns of the Dominican Republic. The *cofradías* originally served African slaves not only for physical survival but also to enhance their spiritual life, traditions, and culture. The principal function of the *cofradía* was—and still is—to provide for mutual aid among the members as a burial society. The society convenes for various rituals associated with the death of its members, employing the *palos* ensembles to accompany processions to the cemetery for burial, to perform the final *novenas* to the dead, and to preside at the observance of the anniversary of the death. The *palos* and the *atabales* (short double-headed drums) used at these ceremonies represent the identity of the *cofradía* and are said to convey the actual voice of its patron saint (Davis 1987a, 86).

There are many variations in musical practice across the different *cofradías* in the Dominican Republic: Some use two *palos* drums and a *güira*. Others use two *palos* drums and the *catá* (sticks played on the body of the drums or on a wooden box). Others use three drums without *güira* or *catá*. Yet others use the variant exemplified by the group of Claudio Fortunato—a hybrid often found during the past thirty years in the outlying areas of the capital city of Santo Domingo consisting of three *palos* or *tumbadores* (larger and wider drums than the *palos*), playing a three-part rhythm comprising the *palo mayor*, the *burlador* or the *chiva*, and the *alcahuete*, all accompanied by the *güira*.

Within the Dominican Republic, a group such as los Guedeses would necessarily be associated with a *cofradía*. To date, there are no formal associations in New York that match that definition. There are individual *cofradía* members present, such as Roberto Aybar, of the *cofradía* of San Juan Bautista from La Vereda in the southwestern area of the Dominican Republic, but his activity has been mainly with folkloric performances and in other kinds of purely musical ensembles.[12] The most comparable phenomena in the New York community are the regional associations, also known as *embajadas* (literally, "embassies") often representing hometown affiliations. Some examples include the Asociación de la Comunidad Mocana in the Bronx, or the Embajada Cibaeña on Audubon Avenue in Washington Heights. These associations serve both as mutual aid organizations for their members and as a means to channel financial aid back to the home communities in the Dominican Republic. While they will sometimes sponsor a *merengue conjunto* or public event, they are not spiritual brotherhoods in the fashion of the *cofradías*. Perhaps over time, and with the passing of more persons, we may see the evolution of a spiritually based association somewhere between the regional clubs, *maní* participants, and groups such as los Guedeses.

The Use of Musical Folklore for Reinterpretation and Creative Experimentation

From the 1930s to the 1960s, Dominican musicians and ensembles came to New York to integrate themselves within the larger Latino musical life of the city. From 1970 onward, newer arrivals were also active both in the folk and popular areas, bringing Dominican folklore to a wider Afro-Caribbean audience and fusing it with other styles of popular music, including rock, funk, and jazz. It is among these groups that we begin to find an active movement to redefine Dominican culture from the vantage of New York City. It was there that Afro-Dominican folk practice came to be viewed not as a marginalized subculture, but as a valued and deep tradition that deserved an honored place within the context of the larger Afro-Caribbean spectrum.[13]

Of the musical ensembles that re-create Dominican folklore, the most active in the 1990s was AsaDifé, an ensemble of dedicated drummers, singers, and dancers who performed various genres of Dominican percussion-based music. For the most part, these musicians have continued to study and teach both inside and outside of the community through school programs, community celebrations, and public festivals. Under the direction of leader Tony Vicioso, AsaDifé performed between 1991 and the end of the decade. In the beginning, members of the ensemble began studying and presenting various genres including *palos, salves, congos, sarandunga* (the music of the *cofradía* of San Juan Bautista), and *gagá*. They most actively performed the latter genre, a processional music and dance originating in the southwestern part of the Dominican Republic among migrants from Haiti and performed as a part of carnival celebrations.

One of the key elements of the practice is the whirling dance and mime of the colorful rag-clad, whistle-blowing *mayores*. Within this group, dancers Pedro Raposo and Genaro Ozuna led the group's interaction with audiences. The musical accompaniment comprises *palos* drumming, led by Osvaldo Sánchez, Boni Raposo, and Roberto Aybar, and the sounding of *fututus* (end-blown bamboo single-tone trumpets) in a low-pitched hocket style bass line played by up to five musicians. Many of the members of this group perform with other ensembles, including Ecocumbé (see below), but their association in AsaDifé has encouraged a focus on Afro-Dominican musical and ritual forms not otherwise available in the New York community.

This practice also offers a religious system and a social structure that establishes cohesive roles and activities for the members (Rosenberg 1979, 189). Although the group's leader is a firm believer in both the performance and the spirituality of *gagá,* and has actively promoted the various expressions of the form to both the Dominican and the North American public, before such audiences, AsaDifé did not always offer enough explanation of the *gagá* phenomenon, and thus may have engendered a certain confusion about the connection between the *gagá* and the wider Dominican culture. Thus, the message that AsaDifé conveyed, one of playful group ritual, which was quite accessible to young non-Dominican multicultural audiences, did not always get the intended reaction from the Dominican audiences because it did not address the prejudices held by Dominicans toward their own African roots. The group consciously tried to address this problem through written and oral explanations in both school programs and at public events,[14] but the problem speaks to a wider issue of the presentation of sacred folk forms as performance for entertainment. Where general audiences in New York may accept them as exotic entertainment, Dominicans often see in them the Haitian roots of an essential part of their culture, which they have not been able to accept. Nevertheless, AsaDifé was the most complete and significant ensemble performing this genre in New York during the 1990s and it provided an essential opportunity for Dominican musicians to explore a long-neglected component of their cultural foundation.

Many of the musicians involved with AsaDifé went on to form other ensembles. Among them were Pa'lo Monte, led by Osvaldo Sánchez, and La 21 División, led by drummer Boni Raposo. The "21" in the name refers to the number of syncretic deities identified in Afro-Dominican religious practice. In 2000, Vicioso moved out of New York, bringing AsaDifé's life to a close. However, the movement he helped pioneer is well established in New York and is likely to thrive in the future. Some of these efforts stay closer to the roots of Afro-Dominican drumming and song, while others link these traditions with contemporary genres and influences from popular music and jazz.

Among the latter is Ecocumbé, a twelve-piece ensemble that also has performed elements of Dominican folk music, such as the *gagá* and *palos,* but combines them with the full rhythm section and brass of a Latin dance band, as well as keyboard and electric guitar. Ecocumbé blends a hybrid or fusion music that draws upon other Caribbean and Latin American cultures, as well as rock, funk, and jazz elements that many of its members have also mastered. Under the direction of singer William Alemán and guitarist Rafael Fland—both of whom also played *fututus* with this group and with AsaDifé—the ensemble has broken new ground in its educational work in the New York City School District 6 in Washington Heights, teaching children the variety of music on which the ensemble has drawn.

Dance Groups

As with many ethnic communities of New York, cultural expression through participatory and performed dance is an important component of the Dominican transnational phenomenon. A number of projects have been mounted by schools and churches, whose mission it is to involve children and young adults in dance as a means of education about Dominican identity and cultural associations. Over the past thirty years, two variations of dance have developed: on the one hand, companies that stylistically reinterpret popular culture, or what is presented as national culture, through both ballet and folklore-inspired modern dance choreography, and on the other hand, folklore ensembles with educational missions.

Of the former variant, the most significant is the Ballet Quisqueya of the Centro Cultural Quisqueya, founded by dancer Normandía Maldonado in the late 1960s. For more than thirty years, she has taught dance, choreographed, and staged dance programs involving mostly children in Washington Heights. These programs tended to emphasize the Hispanic aspects of Dominican culture through stylized costume and choreography presented as a national dance form.[15] In addition, there is also the group Coral América of the church of Santa Rosa de Lima, which follows the model of stylized dance created by choreographers Frank Usero and Oscar Batista, and the short-lived Batecan company, which was active in the late 1980s but folded because of financial problems. Finally, the company Raíces Folklóricas Dominicanas (Dominican Folk Roots) is another important group, based on the diversity, talent, and experience of its participants, who are all veterans of major folk dance companies in the Dominican Republic, including the Ballet Folklórico of the Autonomous University of Santo Domingo, the Federación Dominicana de Arte y Cultura (FEDORACU), the Ballet Folklórico Dominicano, and the Ballet Nacional. Raíces Folklóricas Dominicanas, however, does not rehearse regularly, and performs only on special occasions.

Of the education-based folklore ensembles, a group that is actively teaching and performing in the Washington Heights community is the Conjunto Folklórico. Under the auspices of Alianza Dominicana, a social service agency in Washington Heights, the ensemble trains youth and young adults in the variety of Dominican folk dance and music performance styles. The company practices a form of folklore reinterpretation through choreography to study and teach Dominican social history through the cultural contributions of the various indigenous, European, and African sectors of the population.[16]

The group's repertoire includes the Afro-Dominican forms of *palos, congos, sarandunga, gagá,* and *pri-prí.* Conjunto Folklórico also studies and performs popular dances associated with the historical social dance forms, such as the European-derived *guayubín, polca, mazurca, valse,* and *brinco.* In addition, the group studies and performs other musical and vocal styles, such as the *tumba mimética del árbol, el paludismo, décimas* (a ten-line Spanish poetry form), *cantos de hacha* (work songs), *pregones* and *salves* (devotional songs), and Dominican popular carnival *estampas.* In addition, the group performs a special current presentation entitled "Origen y evolución del merengue" ("The Origin and Evolution of *Merengue*"), which is intended to present the historical dimensions of *merengue* and to counter the simplified perception of Dominican music and dance maintained by the popular music industry.

These educational and participatory dance initiatives have played a significant role in the establishment of the transmigrant character of the Dominican community in New York. These are the primary public vehicles of sociocultural reinforcement, through which an important aspect of Dominican identity is maintained. Likewise, the companies have also facilitated the travel of artists and teachers between the Dominican Republic and New York, offering an international opportunity to veterans of major cultural institutions in the home society. From the vantage point of community participants and audiences, the work of folkloric dance groups is pivotal in the assertion of Dominican identity at community celebrations and commemorations of such events as Dominican independence day, the celebration of La Altagracia, Carnival, Holy Week, and at summer festivals where the Dominican flag and colors are in abundant display.

Contemporary Fusion: Dominican Culture and Urban Popular Music

The emergence of Dominican popular music at the forefront of New York's Latin music scene led to its influence on other musical styles just as it was incorporating important elements from other Latin music and North American rock and commercial music as well. Beginning in the mid-1970s, Dominican popular music came into its own in New York City, challenging the primacy of the *salsa* influenced by Cubans and Puerto Ricans, and developing a hybrid identity with other non-Latin musics.

An important band of this period was Millie, Jocelyn, y los Vecinos, which was founded by sisters Millie and Jocelyn Quezada and their brother Rafael, who played trumpet and served as the band's musical director. The band made its first recording in 1973. By 1976, *merengue* had matched the popularity of *salsa* music according to record sales and the frequency of performances. At the same time, Dominicans began to identify their music with New York itself, so that bands founded and performing in New York had a special attraction even at home. Bands such as La Gran Manzana (The Big Apple) and the New York Band incorporated the New York identity into their own and became known in the Dominican Republic and throughout Latin America as New York Dominican bands. At this same time, many Latin music promoters actively worked against *merengue* and continued to favor *salsa,* which was losing popularity at the time. By 1978, the tide had turned as new immigrants from Central and South America looked primarily to *merengue* as an international Latin dance genre. At the same time, in a synchronicity of cultural expression, the heavy duple meter of commercial *merengue* matched that of disco, the then dominant popular dance music, which shared some of the same musical devises (see Austerlitz 1997, 127; 1998, 53).

The mid-1980s saw the consolidation of the *merengue*'s international popularity, with a number of new recording companies appearing on the market, including the Kubaney label of renowned producer Mateo San Martín, and the Juan y Nelson record label. In addition, Dominican-based labels expanded their reach into New York. Karen Records of Santo Domingo opened an office in Miami as well as the "4.40" Studio in New York, named for the band of Juan Luis Guerra, whose major recordings were produced there, under the guidance of Bienvenido Rodríguez. Karen and Rodríguez also brought other key artists to prominence, including Wilfredo Vargas, who recorded "El gringo y el cibaeño" in 1984 and "La medicina" in 1985, as well as Los Hermanos Rosario. In addition, Latin music promoter Ralph Mercado, who had been a prime mover of the *salsa* recording industry, began to back *merengue* productions, sometimes in partnership with Dominican producer Cherry Jiménez. During this period, *merengue* in particular developed its transnational sound through which productions from Santo Domingo and New York became largely indistinguishable in style. By the end of the decade, a fully transmigrant cultural infrastructure was established, coinciding with the boom in Dominican immigration that had pushed the community's population in New York to more than half a million.

In the 1990s, *merengue* and *bachata* continued to develop and evolve, leading to the newer creations of *meren-house,* a fusion with synthesized dance hall music, *meren-rap,* a form of Spanish rap expression of Dominican urban youth delivered over a *merengue*-based rhythmic background, and *bachata-rengue,* a fusion of *merengue* and *bachata,* often sounding like a fast contemporary *merengue* performed on guitars. As a sign of the Dominican cultural integration in New York City, there was an immediate interplay of Dominican and mainstream youth-oriented and commercial musical developments. *Meren-house* was a fusion of commercial, studio-produced *merengue* and the synthesized deejay driven dance club music popular with young people across cultures in New York. *Meren-house* was exemplified by recordings such as the album *Brinca* by the group Proyecto Uno in the early 1990s. Other key *meren-house* groups were Los Ilegales and Sandy y Papo.

Dominican rap, performed by groups such as the current Fulanito, is another youth-oriented style, inspired by the improvised vocal styles and demeanor pioneered by African-American rap artists in the early 1980s, but also inspired by improvised poetic practice within Dominican culture. Although never out of style, the *décima* and other forms such as the *poesía coreada* (choral poetry), have enjoyed a recent resurgence in the past decade, and are often practiced in the New York community. An important *decimero* in the literary scene is poet Dagoberto López, who has been in New York since the 1970s, organizing readings and other events. His style combines dramatic oratory with radical politics, originating from his days of organizing against the dictatorship before coming to New York. One key venue in the mid-1990s was the site of the *Taberna cultural,* at the Don Quixote restaurant in the Inwood neighborhood of upper Manhattan, which was closed by the city government for lack of a cabaret license in 1997. The *Taberna* reopened and has operated at other venues in Washington Heights, and it also inspired a street fair in the Inwood neighborhood on Labor Day weekends for several years in the late 1990s.

Bachata-rengue had already developed during the early 1990s in the Dominican Republic, but received major exposure in the Dominican community and wider Latin American communities of New York City originally through the work of contemporary New York Dominican singer/guitarist Willie Lapache, and more recently through ensemble teams such as Bachata Mix. The variations on *merengue* created and distributed in New York were the result of a generation of youth born and raised there who were exposed to many musical alternatives on radio and television. This exposure created a demand for new forms of Dominican music that reflected this experience.

Through the period of the last decade, we have seen the rise and fall of many musical groups, who have attempted to meet the demand for faster tempos and the powerful beat of the bass drum. This development matched an earlier development of *merengue* in the 1940s, when the *tumbador* (conga drum) was introduced from Cuba to the Dominican *merengue orquestas* by the Cuban maestro Julio Gutiérrez. Along with the pedal bass drum, the conga took over an important function of carrying the fundamental rhythm of the native *tambora,* which was reduced to providing accent and color. The characteristic rhythm that is the central element of this type of *merengue* has also served as the basis for contemporary forms of *merengue.* The new variants follow the rhythmic structure and the style and tone used by classic *merengue* singers and orchestras, but they are much faster and louder and have obliged the dancers to change the form of the dance and the level of skill required. Whereas traditional *merengue* was always a couples' dance, new forms are danced as much alone or apart, taking on the style of dance in rock music and disco.

Even traditional acoustic *merengue* has continued to change throughout the contemporary period. The more conventional *merengue típico* groups of the *perico ripiao*[17] tradition of the accordion, *tambora* (double-headed drum), and *güira* (metal scraper) have given way, both in New York and the Dominican Republic, to the *pericombo,* which has found a mode of expression in the use of technology, with the electric bass guitar, amplification of the accordion and the saxophone, tuned *tambora* drums, and the more recent use of electronic percussion. The *típico* music is still widely popular, but almost all groups have adopted the new instrumentation. Some of them in New York include José Quezada y los Cinco Diablos,[18] Querube Ortiz, María Díaz and Franklyn Hernández, and David-David.

A final development of note is the adoption of *merengue* through the 1980s and early 1990s by non-Dominicans who performed it not only for Dominican audiences, but as a music of choice across the Latin American social spectrum. Among the many refugees fleeing the U.S.-sponsored wars in El Salvador and Guatemala were many migrants to the New York City area, including musicians who adopted *merengue* as a medium of cultural integration. Many Puerto Rican bands had already included Dominican music in their repertoire throughout the period discussed in this chapter, but in 1992 the band Caña Brava became the first non-Dominican group to play *merengue* exclusively, and they were accepted by Dominicans (Austerlitz 1997, 127; 1998). More recently, the conjunto of Elvis Crespo has also been performing *merengue,* but instead of the breakneck saxophone *jaleos* (instrumental breaks set between verses and coros, or call and response vocal passages), he employs slower horn section lines that borrow from the phrasing of *clave*-centered *salsa* (*clave* being a five beat key rhythm in Cuban influenced music), but adapts them to a distinct 2/2 beat of the Dominican *merengue* style.

Bachata in the 1990s: A Musical Voice of the Era

During the period that *merengue* was becoming the music of choice across a wide spectrum of Latin American communities, both in New York City and worldwide, Dominicans were developing musically in other directions. As a result of the efforts by artists such as Luis Días, Sonia Silvestre, Víctor Víctor, and Juan Luis Guerra to bring *bachata* to both national and international attention, this guitar-based song genre, which was formerly identified with the streets and lower-class neighborhoods in the Dominican Republic, now rivals *merengue* in popularity (see Pacini Hernández 1995).

Originally named for the crude bars and brothels where guitarists and singers would perform, this music first came into prominence in the 1970s with the work of such singer/guitarists as Rafael Encarnación, Bernardo Ortiz, José Manuel Calderón, Luis Segura, Mélida "La Sufrida," Fabio "El Policía," and "El Tineyer de Ébano," among others, who recorded with the Empresas Guarachita record label of the radio station Radio Guarachita.[19] This became the music of choice for the proletariat in the burgeoning cities of the Dominican Republic, who found in it a means of expression for sentiments of anguish, anxiety, joy, and sadness. The plain-speaking lyrics expressed these matters clearly in a direct yet sensitive language without the use of obscure metaphors.

Through the course of economic immigration, the same sociocultural dynamic has been transmitted to New York. Dominicans find in this music a balm for emotional problems associated with urban life, homesickness, displacement, and stress. As the community has matured and developed, the more complex expression of *bachata* has infused cultural territory previously dominated by commercial *merengue.* In the late 1990s, major productions in New York have featured *bachateros* such as Anthony Santos, Joe Veras, Luis Vargas, El Primo, Raulín Rodríguez, Bachatín, Teodoro Reyes, Olga Tañón, Boquita, La Sexy de la Bachata, Bachata Mix, Christian de Jesús, and Danny García, "El mano suave."

Unlike *merengue,* which is also performed by women singers, accordionists, saxophonists, and entire *orquestas, bachata* was predominantly performed by men, often addressing themes bordering on misogyny. In her exhaustive study of the genre, Deborah Pacini Hernández addresses the issue of gender in *bachata,* noting the power and use of song in social relations: "The power of song is used to construct and deconstruct emotions and emotional states. Romantic music serves as a surrogate voice for people who feel incapable of articulating their emotions and publicly expressing private feelings, and it helps them to negotiate their relationships, whether in the early stages of courtship, in the fullness of a mutually satisfying relationship, or in the painful and bitter moments of solitude" (1995, 153). But unlike many forms of romantic popular song, *bachata* lyrics sung during the 1980s were concerned with "casual sex with no pretense to longevity or legitimacy" as the singers reflected the deteriorating social and economic conditions of the Balaguer period that were affecting them, their families, and their audiences (1995, 154). These conditions contributed greatly to the accelerating immigration to the United States. Just as the evolution of *bachata* reflected changes in social and economic conditions in the Dominican Republic, the experience of immigration will gradually be reflected in the development of this music. To date, most New York *bachata* singers continue the form as developed in the Dominican Republic, while reflecting a more complex scenario of social and cultural dislocation within the transnational context.

A fertile subject of future investigation focuses on the development of this genre in New York, where a majority of Dominican migrants are women, and where the traditional culture of machismo is challenged by the increasing economic independence and assertiveness of women. If *bachata* continues to thrive, it may ultimately develop a New York adaptation to reflect the new social reality, or it may continue to be a medium for male frustration masquerading as bravado.

Bachata in New York is also a medium for intercultural experimentation, partly because of the instrumentation, which invites cross experimentation with other guitar-dominated music, such as blues and rock. An important figure in this exploration is guitarist Luis Días, who left the group Convite following its New York tour in 1979 and remained in New York until 1982. During that time, he founded a folkloric group called La Cofradía, which performed during 1981–1982 before he returned to Santo Domingo to found a new *bachata* rock fusion band called Transporte Urbano. The group performed in a style that Días first dubbed *tecno bachata* in the 1970s, which combines *bachata* guitar styles and other Caribbean music, such as Jamaican reggae and Haitian *compas,* with North American blues, rock, and funk. This band performed extensively throughout the 1980s, including tours throughout the Caribbean, to the former Soviet Union, and France. Although Días has resided for long periods in New York, he maintains contact with the other band members in the Dominican Republic with whom he performs when he returns there.

During the past decade in New York, Días has assembled a band similar in composition and style to Transporte Urbano, drawing upon musicians with a compatible commitment to Dominican folk traditions. Among these is one of the leading *palos*-style drummers, Osvaldo Sánchez, who has also been a mainstay with AsaDifé and other Afro-Domincan ensembles. Días's Dominican influence has not been limited to *bachata,* but draws upon the range of Dominican music, including many of its folk forms and rhythms. In the spirit of the *nueva canción* movement in which he was active during the 1970s, he has sought to convey the social reality of the Dominican people, with songs often addressing political and social conditions. One song titled "Rudinique" recounts the tragic story of a street character in the a cappella folk style of the poetic *canto de toros.* In another song, titled "La ciudad nueva," he sang of political disenfranchisement in Santo Domingo at the end of Balaguer's reign. This song opens with the line: "El gobierno se robó las eleciones . . ." ("the government stole the election . . .").[20] Other songs address themes of resistance to international popular culture. An example from his 1998 album *El Accidente* is "La manguera," which is sung in a classic plaintive *bachata* style about the singer Madonna, as if she were his unfaithful girlfriend. Although Días is a leading figure in the experimental side of Dominican popular music, whose song-writing credits are extensive in both *bachata* and *merengue* recordings, he has only produced a small number of his own recordings.[21] Nevertheless, his influence has far exceeded these through his composition and his willingness to break conventions and draw together musical and social elements of the Dominican transnational experience.

Apart from Días's work, most *bachata* songs recorded and performed in New York, however, continue in the dominant vein of songs about love, lust, and disappointment. The medium offers more flexibility to incorporate other Dominican styles, such as with the *bachata-rengue,* and to draw from North American popular music as well. The next decade will reveal whether this becomes the medium of a true transnational Dominican sound, and a site for negotiation of the social forces and gender issues encountered in the community.

Lyrical Content and Themes

For a music so clearly centered on vocal performance, it is pertinent to ask how the emergence of the transnational Dominican culture is expressed through song lyrics, and how the New York sound may have affected the music and its audience at home in the Dominican Republic. This is a subject suited to a detailed analysis of the body of Dominican lyrics composed, recorded, and performed in New York (and elsewhere outside of the Dominican Republic itself). Individual voices have emerged that have expressed through song critical perspectives on the immigrant experience. However, the overwhelming trend favored an internationally marketable musical style and lyrical content whose commercial success was built on a medium for social dance rather than literary content.

Ethnomusicologist Peter Manuel notes several examples of *merengue* songs in the period of 1980–1995 that express key themes of ambition to emigrate to and succeed in New York, and praise the style and fast pace of the life there. Conversely, they also express disappointment at the cold weather, economic hardship, and crime experienced by many migrants. At the same time, the dominance of the frenetic *merengue* in this period as a vehicle for Dominican expression inherently limited the nuance of such expression. Los Hermanos Rosario's "Un día en Nueva York" (1995 Karen 10793–0169–4) compresses the stereotypes of urban hardship and exhilaration into a single dance number (Manuel 1998, 31–34).

Most of the Dominican music recorded in New York, as in other sites, including Miami and Santo Domingo, was produced for the wider Dominican market. Rather than expressing themes specifically about the transnational experience, this music in fact has had the opposite effect of repeating forms and themes that are well established in Dominican music and that seem to avoid overt social or political content. As with most popular music, the industry that produces it exercises considerable control in favor of marketable associations such as sex, glamour, and status. A review of album covers on display in current Dominican CD jukeboxes and in music stores will illustrate this point. The vast majority of *merengue* lyrics address themes of love, passion, and general festivity, as popular music often does.

Manuel argues that Dominican popular music has played a decisive role in the de-politicizing of Latin music in New York, as the class and cultural consciousness of the progressive *salsa* movement of the 1970s gave way to the cynicism and frivolity of the 1980s, just as the economic condition of Latino communities in New York worsened considerably. "[T]he fervent and sanguine idealism and social realism of the classic *salsa* has given way to the glib ribaldry of *merengue*. . . . References to New York City, or to lived social reality in general, find little place in modern Latin dance music, whose sole purpose seems to be to divert rather than to mobilize or to educate" (1984, 40). Within the interplay of popular, mass-mediated culture, politics, and economics, the trend seems to be toward a transnational marketing of the deliberately noncontroversial, which even removes most specific references to place in favor of abstract generalities.

One may well argue that in spite of the predominance of the Dominican popular music industry, the strongest expression of Dominican immigrant identity and experience will come from other forms. They may be subtle, as in the branding of identities within the commercial culture, such as in the choice of names for some recent Dominican bands, including Los Ilegales (The Illegals), Sin Fronteras (Without Borders), and El Gringo de la Bachata. More specific references may emerge in *bachata*, which generally offers more room for lyrics and expression of mixed feelings. Ultimately, we ought to look within the evolving life of the transnational community, through other media such as poetry, literature, and film,[22] as well as in the renewal and growth of popular traditions and folk religion. It is in these areas that community specific expression is most likely to develop.

Conclusions: Musical Culture in the Transnational Experience

This overview of the Dominican musical life in New York City of the last seventy years is meant to convey a sense of the complexity of forms that have been and continue to be practiced there. Of equal importance is the role of that practice in the ongoing formation of a transnational Dominican culture in an environment that promotes an interrelationship between Dominican and other cultures, particularly Puerto Rican and Latin American, as well as North American. The Dominican transnational musical evolution in New York began in conjunction with the early development of the recording industry and its growing interest in the Dominican market. This development was followed by the gradual settlement of musicians, singers, and bandleaders in the city. Perhaps more than many ethnic groups in New York, Dominicans have participated loudly and clearly in the urban cultural dialogue, and would have done so if only by means of the talented and prolific resident and visiting artists.

During the first fifty years of this development, Dominican music in New York City closely reflected the music made in the Dominican Republic itself. *Conjuntos* and *orquestas* were formed, following the models of such leading Dominican Republic-based bandleaders as Johnny Ventura, Wilfrido Vargas, and Félix del Rosario. Through the necessary fusion with *mambo, salsa,* and other Latin styles in vogue through the formative years of the 1950s and 1960s in New York, Dominican music gradually came into its own, as conceived at home and finally expressed in full on the New York stage.

The rapid expansion of the New York Dominican community following the death of Trujillo in 1961 and the intervention in the Dominican Republic by the United States in 1965 radically changed the nature of this cultural development. The numbers and diversity of musical practitioners increased rapidly as their markets, performance contexts, and support networks expanded. Meanwhile, the Afro-Dominican spiritual practices, whether through *botánicas,* private *maní* ceremonies, or in public manifestations of didactic revival performance ensembles, were all signs of a simultaneous, complex community development. This development is also seen in the field of popular music. Beginning in the late 1980s bands that were founded in New York began to develop their own style by exploring new musical forms with which to express the sensibility of modern *merengue* and Dominican culture in general. In the beginning of the 1990s, a younger generation created *meren-house,* and through a fusion with the deejay-driven dance club scene and rap made important changes in the prevalent style of Dominican social dance. The changes brought by contemporary (often second-generation) musicians to *merengue* in New York City will have an increasing impact on the future Dominican music and dance everywhere.

Through these developments, we have traced a series of parallel developments, including an evolution of popular styles, community-based educational projects, folk religious practice, Afro-Dominican revivalist performance, and nationalistic stylized dance. Each of these forms speaks to a different aspect of the Dominican transnational community, at once both factual and imagined in the fashion outlined by Benedict Anderson (1991). Martha Davis's environmental factors all seem to be at play in the developments traced above, and her observation of Dominican bi-musicality, or multi-musicality bears out the fact that the culture has adapted well in the face of the challenges of survival and growth in the cultural landscape of New York City. The musical developments described above also lead to another path of analysis, which has been discussed in the context of other cultures: the advent of the deterritorialized nation-state, built upon reconfigured constructs of cultural and racial identity that may develop in an environment such as that of New York. In a study of Haitian, West Indian, and Filipino communities, Basch, Glick Schiller, and Szanton Blanc observe that "building transnational social fields and imagining a deterritorialized nation state can be seen as a form a resistance on the part of Caribbean and Filipino immigrants," in which they "re-appropriate nation building processes even as they accommodate to situations of unequal power" (1994, 46). National culture can develop, evolve, or be reinvented both in a home context and in a transnational one.

Anderson elaborates on these notions and considers the implications of cultural politics to nationalist culture. Even as he agrees that national identity is to a large extent invented as a visceral experience, he notes that national culture rarely expresses the hatred and xenophobia that nationalist politics thrives upon (1991, 141–42). We observe from the history of Dominican culture in New York that the predominant expressions are often festive, artful, and internally self-reverent. Yet with the changes that occurred in the 1960s and 70s, in which social upheaval and political struggle led to the U.S. invasion, and the ensuing social and economic order under Balaguer led to further rural to urban migration, the culture of displacement began to rival the culture of celebration. The emergence of the *bachata* of the urban underclass and the *nueva canción* of the political opposition framed a musical dialogue that Luis Días called *"la lucha sonora"* ("the sonic struggle") (See Pacini Hernández 1995, 103). As the same forces spurred migration to New York, the variety and contradictions in the culture of Dominican music and dance may be defining the transnational identity of the community as a participatory and sometimes conflicting sonic space, ever shifting and expanding in an elastic and usually adaptable manner.

Through such transnational environments as the *meren-house* dance club, the public school auditorium, the apartment-based *maní* ritual, and the airwaves of Radio WADO or Mega 97, the transnational culture is being realized by a generation of Dominicans who reflect the truly complex nature of their originating society. At the same time, they also reveal a truly "transmigrant" community that has come into its own, in terms of its capacity for self-reflection and for the reinterpretation of its roots, its identity, and its mode of relating to the larger cultural complex of New York City.

Acknowledgments

This article is a collaborative effort that stems from work by the authors on a joint project of support and presentation of Dominican traditional music as well as contemporary music and dance. Van Buren served as project director of the Dominican Community Cultural Initiative from 1995 to 1998, which resulted in the production of the Quisqueya en el Hudson festival in Washington Heights each June in 1996, 1997, and 1998. Domínguez, a folklorist and teacher, was a founding member of the musical study and performance group Convite. He currently directs the Conjunto Folklórico of Alianza Dominicana. The authors also note the contribution of ethnomusicologist Dr. Martha Ellen Davis, who conducted preliminary research for the Quisqueya en el Hudson project, and whose focus on Afro-Dominican spiritual practice greatly informed the early stages of the project, as well as elements of this article.

Notes

1. This point should be mitigated by the fact of the considerable direct influence of Cuban music on the Dominican Republic before 1958, and of Dominican influence on music in Puerto Rico through immigration to Puerto Rico across the Mona Passage.

2. This figure is supported by studies conducted by the New York City Department of City Planning and published in two volumes entitled *The Newest New Yorkers* for the periods of 1980–1987 and 1990–1994. They were published in 1990 and 1996, respectively.

3. Singer Alberto Beltrán recorded with Mario Hernández in Puerto Rico during 1948–1949. He first came to New York in 1949 with Hernández, but soon returned to the Dominican Republic. From 1953 to 1954 he worked in Cuba with the Sonora Matancera. At the end of 1954, he decided to leave the Sonora Matancera to return to Santo Domingo. He also worked in Mexico during this period. In 1959, he came to New York to sing at the Caravana Club in the Bronx, then owned by Salvador Mercier.

4. Based on interviews with Frank Domínguez, the father of the co-author of this chapter. Domínguez emigrated to New York by way of Havana, Cuba in 1956. He had introduced Beltrán into Cuba's cabarets in 1953 and made arrangements for him to be contracted in New York as well. Beltrán and Domínguez were *compadres* for sixty-five years.

5. As reported by Frank Domínguez, father of the co-author.

6. Cerón was honored in a public program in the upper Manhattan neighborhood of Inwood on January 29, 1999, at an event organized by the Centro Cultural Orlando Martínez, a newer community-based cultural association named for a martyred opposition Dominican journalist who died at the hands of President Balaguer's death squads in 1975.

7. Club María Trinidad Sánchez is a social service activist organization named for the woman who sewed the first Dominican national flag at the time of the independence from Haiti in 1844. The use of her name was a symbol of nationalist feeling in the New York Dominican community.

8. Convite was founded in 1975 as a *nueva canción* group. Based on principles of collective organization and work, the group was devoted to a musical investigation of rural folklore, although one of its leading members, Luis Días, was also a leading proponent of the creative use of the urban *bachata* music, which had not yet shed its low status within Dominican popular music and official culture. The original members of Convite also included Dagoberto Tejeda, José Castillo, and Leonardo Iván Domínguez (all associates of the current Dominican Folklore Institute), as well as José Rodríguez, Miguel Mañaná, Ana Marina Guzmán, and José Enrique Trinidad. The group first performed in New York in 1976.

9. González and Domínguez were recorded by María Teresa Linares on the Cuban Egrem label (LD 4075). This material is currently available on a qbadisc label compact disc (1993, QB9004).

10. Nolasco's work was the focus of a theatrical event entitled "Ya llegó la Virgen," which was held at the repertory theater of Hostos Community College in the Bronx in January of 1996 and was produced by the then Ethnic Folk Arts Center. A workshop and rehearsals for this event served as a catalyst for Nolasco to teach the *salves* tradition to younger women who have since made extensive use of it in other performances. Among these is Nina Paulino, who has served as chair of the organizing committee for the Quisqueya en el Hudson festival for many of the productions from 1996 to 2001.

11. Guedeses comes from the Haitian vodou *gedé,* a term for the African syncretic deities associated with death.

12. Roberto Aybar arrived in New York in 1994 for a performance and has since been a regular member of such groups as AsaDifé (mentioned later in this chapter).

13. This has been the message of five annual Quisqueya en el Hudson festivals, as well as the work of this chapter's co-author Domínguez in his folklore teaching at Alianza Dominicana in Washington Heights.

14. Members of the ensemble have played a key role in the organization of the annual Quisqueya en el Hudson festival in Washington Heights and have performed either on stage or in procession at each event (1996–1998). In the opinion of the authors, the most successful performances, measured in terms of audience appreciation, have been when the *gagá* was performed in procession, a form closer to its original practice. The program notes of the event offer the following statement by the group: "*AsaDifé* is a musical group that specializes in African-derived traditions . . . to counterbalance the official Dominican policy that claims the country to be racially white and culturally Spanish" (Program notes of the Quisqueya en el Hudson festival, June 29, 1998).

15. The Centro Cultural Quisqueya is now based within Intermediate School 90, one of the newer schools in the southeast corner of Washington Heights, built in the wake of the community crisis of 1986 and organization efforts around education for Dominican youth in Washington Heights.

16. "The folk group of Alianza Dominicana is comprised of young people from the ages of nine to twenty-one, who are developed as human resources in the field of folklore and popular culture through a program to build their capabilities. This program includes the teaching of knowledge about our economic, political, and social

reality, as well as the entire process of the historical formation of our country" (from the mission statement of the Conjunto Folklórico, 1998).

17. Literally "deboned parrot," possibly a name of a brothel in the Cibao region where the music first became popular (Davis 1996).

18. José Quezada is an accordionist in New York who is one of the most knowledgeable about Dominican folklore. He performed for almost twenty years with the maestro René Carrasco, and was occasionally the accordionist for the Ballet Folklórico of the Autonomous University of Santo Domingo (UASD) when the group was formed in 1970.

19. Empresas Guarachita was founded by Radhamés Aracena, one of the most successful independent record producers in the Dominican Republic during the 1950s and 1960s. See Pacini Hernández (1995) for a thorough discussion of Empresas Guarachita (56–61) and Radio Guarachita (87–102).

20. These songs were performed at the Quisqueya en el Hudson festival, June 23, 1996.

21. *Luis Terror Días* (Pareja Records #PR2297 Santo Domingo) was produced by Cholo Brenes. His most recent work was recorded in 1998 in Toronto and is entitled *El Accidente* (Diasong Records, 1999).

22. Two films have been made about the immigrant experience whose music addresses issues of poverty and aspirations for success. Johnny Ventura composed the soundtrack to the film *Buscando un sueño: Desde las calles de Santo Domingo a Nueva York. La cruda realidad de nuestros barrios* (Searching for a Dream: From the Streets of Santo Domingo to New York. The Cruel Realities of Our Neighborhoods). The film *Nueba Yol* updates this story with a depiction of the life of the Dominican migrant in the 1990s.

References

Allen, Ray, and Lois Wilcken, eds. 1998. *Island Sounds in the Global City.* New York: New York Folklore Society and Institute for Studies in American Music, Brooklyn College.

Anderson, Benedict. 1991. *Imagined Communities.* London, New York: Verso.

Austerlitz, Paul. 1997. *Merengue: Dominican Music and Dominican Identity.* Philadelphia: Temple University Press.

———. 1998. "From Transplant to Transnational Circuit: Merengue in New York." In *Island Sounds in the Global City,* ed. Ray Allen and Lois Wilcken. New York: New York Folklore Society and Institute for Studies in American Music, Brooklyn College.

Basch, Linda, Nina Glick Schiller, and Cristina Szanton Blanc. 1994. *Nations Unbound: Transnational Projects, Postcolonial Predicaments, and Deterritorialized Nation States.* Langhorne, Pa.: Gordon and Breach.

Brito Ureña, Luis Manuel. 1987. *El merengue y la realidad existencial del hombre dominicano.* Santo Domingo: Universidad Autónoma de Santo Domingo.

Davis, Martha Ellen. 1987a. *La otra ciencia: El vodú dominicano como religión y medicina populares.* Santo Domingo: Universidad Autónoma de Santo Domingo.

———. 1987b. "'Native Bi-Musicality': Case Studies from the Caribbean." *Pacific Review of Ethnomusicology* 4:39–55.

———. 1996. "Dominican Republic: A Creole Culture." *New Routes: Traditional Music and Dance in America* Winter:1–9.

Glick Schiller, Nina. 1999. "Transmigrants and Nation-States: Something Old and Something New in the U.S. Immigration Experience." In *The Handbook of International Migration: The American Experience,* ed. Charles Hirschman, Philip Kasinitz, and Josh DeWind. New York: Russell Sage Foundation.

Lizardo, Fradique. 1974. *Danzas y bailes folklóricos dominicanos.* Santo Domingo: Fundación García Arévalo.

Lundius, Jan, and Mats Lundahl. 1988. "Olivorio Mateo: Vida y muerte de un dios campesino." *Estudios Sociales* 76:3–87.

Manuel, Peter. 1998. "Representations of New York City in Latin Music." In *Island Sounds in the Global City,* ed. Ray Allen and Lois Wilcken. New York: New York Folklore Society and Institute for Studies in American Music, Brooklyn College.

Pacini Hernández, Deborah. 1995. *Bachata: A Social History of a Dominican Popular Music.* Philadelphia: Temple University Press.

Roberts, John Storm. 1979. *The Latin Tinge.* New York: Oxford University Press.

Rosenberg, June C. 1979. *El Gagá: Religión y sociedad de un culto dominicano.* Santo Domingo: Universidad Autónoma de Santo Domingo.

Valladares, Dioris. 1996. "Pequeña historia del merengue dominicano en la ciudad de New York." *Revista Homenaje 30 Años del Centro Cultural Ballet Quisqueya* (New York).

Contributors

Janira Bonilla was an Ada Comstock Scholar at Smith College, where she received a B.A. in comparative literature (English and Spanish) with a minor in Latin American studies in 2002.

Leonardo Iván Domínguez is the technical director of the Casa de la Cultura Dominicana in New York City. He is one of the organizers of Quisqueya en el Hudson, an annual festival of Dominican music in northern Manhattan.

Jorge Duany is associate professor of sociology and anthropology at the University of Puerto Rico. He is the author of *The Puerto Rican Nation on the Move: Identities on the Island and in the United States* (2002), co-author (with José Cobas) of *Cubans in Puerto Rico: Ethnic Economy and Cultural Identity* (UPF, 1997), and editor of *Los dominicanos en Puerto Rico: Migración en la semi-periferia* (1990).

Carol Hoffman-Guzmán received a Ph.D. in sociology from Florida International University in 2002. She also has master's and doctoral degrees in divinity, and is an ordained minister in the United Methodist Church.

José Itzigsohn is associate professor of sociology at Brown University. He is the author of *Developing Poverty: The State, Labor Market Deregulation, and the Informal Economy in Costa Rica and the Dominican Republic* (2000).

Juleyka J. Lantigua earned an M.S. in journalism from Boston University and a B.A. in Spanish literature and government from Skidmore College. She researched immigration policy and helped launch a monthly newspaper (*Prensa del Caribe*) and a quarterly magazine (*En Dialógo*) while on a Fulbright Scholarship in Spain. She currently is a freelance journalist and a nationally syndicated columnist.

Domingo Lilón is assistant professor of history at the University of Pécs, Hungary. He is the author of *Armas y poder: Los húngaros y la Armería de San Cristóbal* (2000).

Nancy López is assistant professor of sociology at the University of New Mexico. She is the author of *Hopeful Girls, Troubled Boys: Race and Gender Disparity in Urban Education* (2002).

Sintia E. Molina is assistant professor of literature at Saint Francis College, in Brooklyn Heights, New York. She is the author of *El Naturalismo en la novela cubana* (2001).

Ernesto Sagás is assistant professor of political science at Southern New Hampshire University. He is the author of *Race and Politics in the Dominican Republic* (UPF, 2000), and co-editor (with Orlando Inoa) of *The Dominican People: A Documentary History* (2003).

Thomas van Buren is an ethnomusicologist and director of field research at the Center for Traditional Music and Dance in New York City. He received a Ph.D. from the University of Maryland-College Park in 2001.

Karin Weyland is president of Fundación Melassa, a nonprofit organization based in the Dominican Republic. She received a Ph.D. in sociology from the New School for Social Research in 1999. She is also an amateur photographer whose work has been published in scholarly journals.

Index